Portrait of an
English Migration

MCGILL-QUEEN'S TRANSATLANTIC STUDIES
Series editors: Alan Dobson, Robert Hendershot, and Steve Marsh

The McGill-Queen's Transatlantic Studies series, in partnership with the Transatlantic Studies Association, provides a focal point for scholarship examining and interrogating the rich cultural, political, social, and economic connections between nations, organizations, and networks that border the Atlantic Ocean. The series combines traditional disciplinary studies with innovative interdisciplinary work, stimulating debate about and engagement with a field of transatlantic studies broadly defined to capture a breadth and richness of scholarship. Books in the series focus on but are not limited to the twentieth and twenty-first centuries, normally falling within the subfields of history, economics, politics and international relations, literature, and cultural studies.

1 Not Like Home
American Visitors to Britain in the 1950s
Michael John Law

2 Transatlantic Upper Canada
Portraits in Literature, Land, and
British-Indigenous Relations
Kevin Hutchings

3 Greatness and Decline
National Identity and British
Foreign Policy
Srdjan Vucetic

4 Portrait of an English Migration
North Yorkshire People in
North America
William E. Van Vugt

Portrait of an
English Migration

North Yorkshire People
in North America

William E. Van Vugt

McGill-Queen's University Press
Montreal & Kingston • London • Chicago

© McGill-Queen's University Press 2021

ISBN 978-0-2280-0584-1 (cloth)
ISBN 978-0-2280-0585-8 (paper)
ISBN 978-0-2280-0686-2 (ePDF)
ISBN 978-0-2280-0687-9 (ePUB)

Legal deposit first quarter 2021
Bibliothèque nationale du Québec

Printed in Canada on acid-free paper that is 100% ancient forest free (100% post-consumer recycled), processed chlorine free

This book was published with the help of grants from the Calvin Center for Christian Scholarship and the John Van Engen Faculty Development Fund.

Library and Archives Canada Cataloguing in Publication

Title: Portrait of an English migration : North Yorkshire people in North America / William E. Van Vugt.

Names: Van Vugt, William E., 1957- author.

Series: McGill-Queen's transatlantic studies ; 4.

Description: Series statement: McGill-Queen's transatlantic studies ; 4 | Includes bibliographical references and index.

Identifiers: Canadiana (print) 2020035552X | Canadiana (ebook) 20200355872 | ISBN 9780228005841 (cloth) | ISBN 9780228005858 (paper) | ISBN 9780228006862 (ePDF) | ISBN 9780228006879 (ePUB)

Subjects: LCSH: English – United States – History. | LCSH: English – Canada – History. | LCSH: Immigrants – United States – History. | LCSH: Immigrants – Canada – History. | LCSH: North Yorkshire (England) – Emigration and immigration – History. | LCSH: United States – Emigration and immigration – History. | LCSH: Canada – Emigration and immigration – History. | LCSH: North Yorkshire (England) – Biography.

Classification: LCC E184.B7 V36 2021 | DDC 973/.0421 – dc23

This book was designed and typeset by Peggy & Co. Design in 11.5/14 Adobe Garamond Pro.

For Dudley Baines

Contents

Figures   ix

Acknowledgments   xi

Introduction   3

1 Origins   14

2 Beginnings   22

3 After the Revolution   29

4 Lead   41

5 Leaving   53

6 The Journey   68

7 The Upper Mississippi   88

8 Adjustment and Assimilation   101

9 Mining and Smelting   112

10 Upper Canada   129

11 Farming   147

12 Iowa   164

13 Native Americans   173

14 Religion   181

15 The Gold Rush   204

16 Politics, Reform, and War   212

17 The Steamship   224

18 The Post-War Economy   231

19 Farming after the War   243

20 The Great Plains   251

21 Texas   264

22 Canada   275

Conclusion and Epilogue   290

Notes   301

Bibliography   363

Index   379

Figures

1.1   Map of England and Yorkshire   15

1.2   Map of North Yorkshire   16

1.3   Map of the Yorkshire Dales   19

2.1   Map of Upper Canada   25

3.1   Map of the North York Moors   39

4.1   Old Gang and Mill Gill in Swaledale. Used with permission of NYCRO.   46

4.2   Gunnerside. Used with permission of NYCRO.   48

4.3   Swinner Gill. Used with permission of NYCRO.   50

4.4   Interior of Brandy Bottle Incline Mine. Used with permission of NYCRO.   51

5.1   Matthew Dinsdale. Used with permission of Wisconsin Historical Society.   56

5.2   Historic photo of Askrigg. Used with permission of NYCRO.   57

5.3   Matthew Willis   58

5.4   A shipwreck at the Port of Whitby. Used with permission of NYCRO.   65

5.5   Map of Swaledale and Wensleydale   67

6.1   "Rama," c. 1880s   77

6.2   Map of the Mississippi River region   84

7.1   Map of the Upper Mississippi   89

7.2   Bolton Castle. Used with permission of NYCRO.   98

9.1   Portrait of Robert Bonson, dated 1845. Used with permission of descendant Bob Bonson.   114

9.2   Portrait of Richard Bonson, dated 1850. Used with permission
       of descendant Bob Bonson.   115
9.3   Bonson/Waller Lead Furnace, 1835. Photo dated 1836
       on the reverse. Used with permission of descendant
       Bob Bonson.   116
9.4   Richard and Harriet Bonson. Used with permission
       of descendant Bob Bonson.   117
9.5   Lead mine. Used with permission of Wisconsin
       Historical Society.   125
10.1   Map of Upper and Lower Canada   131
10.2   Photograph of Danby. Used with permission
       of NYCRO.   137
12.1   Map of Iowa   166
14.1a Portrait of Stephen Longstroth   193
14.1b Portrait of Ann Longstroth   193
14.2   Portrait of Willard Richards   203
21.1   Map of Texas   267
21.2   Thomas Wilson family in Rosedale   271
21.3   The Wilson family home, "Primrose Villa," in Rosedale   272

Acknowledgments

It is a pleasure to acknowledge the people and institutions who made this book possible. I was fortunate to have four superb mentors over many years of studying British-American history: Ronald Wells, Robert Swierenga, Charlotte Erickson, and Dudley Baines. Erickson and Baines were especially helpful and generous during graduate school and the decades that followed. Their pioneering work on the study of migration and other aspects of economic history will always remain the standard in the field. I hope this book reflects that.

I am grateful to Calvin University for its support in the form of a sabbatical leave, several course reductions, and a McGregor fellowship for my student, Spencer Cone, to conduct early research with the passenger lists, census manuscripts, and local newspapers. I am also grateful to my History Department chairs Will Katerberg, Kristin Du Mez, and Kate van Liere for their encouragement and support. Jenna Hunt was especially helpful with preparing the footnotes and bibliography and reading the manuscript for technical errors and clarity. I am also grateful for financial support from the John Van Engen Faculty Development Fund and the Calvin Center for Christian Scholarship.

In England I have incurred many debts that are a pleasure to acknowledge. I owe special thanks to Tanja Bueltmann, Donald MacRaild, and David Gleeson, who hosted me several times at Northumbria University in Newcastle for conferences and invited lectures. These scholars have advanced the study of British and Irish migration with several important works. Tanja and Don's recent *The English Diaspora in North America: Migration, Ethnicity, and Association, 1730s–1950s,* has added much knowledge to that subject and has led me to revise my own understanding in important ways. This book reflects their contributions to the field, and I owe them much for their support, dedication, and exemplary scholarship.

I am especially indebted to Marion Moverley of the Upper Dales Family History Group. When I first asked her for advice on sources on North Yorkshire, she contacted local and family historians who generously provided me with many letters and journals and permission to use them. She also read an early version of the manuscript and spotted areas for improvement that only an expert historian from North Yorkshire could do. Her vast and intimate knowledge of the region – everything from local families and traditions, early memories to accents and dialects, places, and how to farm – was invaluable. Any remaining errors or shortcomings are mine alone.

Helen Bainbridge, curator of the Swaledale Museum in Reeth, gave me encouragement and advice, allowed me to use their archives, and invited me to present a public lecture on an earlier version of this work. I am also indebted to Glenys Marriott of the Upper Dales Family History Group and editor of *Those Who Left the Dales*, a wonderful collection of letters by emigrants in many parts of the world. Christine Howie provided letters of her ancestors, the Wilkinsons of Nebraska and Wyoming. Others who did the same include Ruth Simpson, Jacqueline Auclair, and Janet Westwell, who also assisted with obtaining photographs, as did Christine Amsden and Phyllis Ruth Edwards. I would also like to thank Roger Burt and Mike Gill for their encouragement and expertise on mining history.

I am grateful to many archives and museums in both England and the United States. In North Yorkshire, the Dales Countryside Museum in Hawes provided sources and research space and permission to cite excerpts from their collections. The same is true of the North Yorkshire County Record Office (NYCRO) in Northallerton, the Keld Resource Centre in Keld, the Richmondshire Museum, in Richmond, the Ryedale Folk Museum in Ryedale, the Rosedale History Society and Reading Room in Rosedale Abbey, the Fylingdales Local History Group in Robin Hood's Bay, the Whitby Museum, the Beck Isle Museum and Archives in Pickering, the Skipton Library, and the Rosedale History Society. In other parts of Yorkshire, I found materials in the East Riding of Yorkshire Archives and Local Studies Service in the Treasure House, in Beverley. I also studied sources in the West Yorkshire Archives in Leeds, Bradford, Kirklees and Wakefield, and in the Durham Archives Museum. In London I found materials in the British Library of Economic and Political Science, the National Archives in Kew, and the Freemason's Hall on Great Queen Street.

In the United States the staff of Calvin University's Hekman Library obtained a vast number of primary sources through its miraculous interlibrary loan system. In addition, the following libraries and institutions were helpful: the Wisconsin State Historical Society in Madison; Lorus College in Dubuque; the University of Wisconsin-Platteville; the Ohio Historical Society, Columbus. Bob Bonson kindly sent me copies of the Bonson Diaries and allowed me to use his family photos. At Calvin University Jill Herlinger produced the maps according to my precise specifications and Vicky Seaburg assisted with image preparations. At McGill-Queen's University Press, Kyla Madden, Elli Stylianou, Kathleen Fraser, and Gillian Scobie made suggestions as the book was brought to publication.

During my many research trips to England I have benefited from conversations with David Ash, Simone Barnard, Patricia Orme, and Robin and Gill Haines. Jane Ferentzi-Sheppard of the Somerset and Dorset Family History Society has been helpful over many years. Finally, and most important, I thank Lynn, who shared our many adventures and was most encouraging throughout the project.

Portrait of an
English Migration

Introduction

I smiled at him. America, I said quietly, just like that. What is it? The sweepings of every country including our own. Isn't that true? That's a fact.

JAMES JOYCE

The history of migration is the history of the world. The movement of peoples has shaped cultures, economies, politics, and empires from earliest human history to the present. Migration can make or break institutions, politicians, and governments. Today, migration to Europe and North America is especially significant, for its contributions as well as the backlash against it. Any understanding of our past and present requires attention to migration.

British Migration

The British are the most migratory people in history. Between 1600 and the 1950s over 20 million people left the British Isles, and their culture – especially their language, religion, and political and economic institutions – shaped much of the world. The "modern British dispersion" (British emigrants and their descendants: those who can claim descent from British and Irish emigrants) is estimated at about 200 million. From 1815 to 1930 at least 12 million Britons (the English, Scots, and Welsh) permanently settled in North America, Australasia, and South Africa. The English alone numbered close to 10 million. About 56 per cent of them came to the United States. The remainder was evenly divided between Canada and Australasia.[1]

British migration was thus directed primarily to North America, where it had its greatest impact. Contrary to common assumptions, the English outnumbered the Scots and Irish in Canada, a misperception resulting in part from the fact that the Scots and Irish were more "visible" or noticeable than the English because of their clannishness, more distinctive dress, customs, and linguistic and other cultural traits.[2]

What the English brought to North American culture was so basic that it is often overlooked or taken for granted. From earliest colonial times through the nineteenth century, English immigrants established and reinforced an Anglo-American culture that in ways became dominant. One can certainly exaggerate England's contributions to North America, but so too can one gloss over them. Perhaps Otto von Bismarck was not exaggerating when he claimed that the most important fact in the modern world is that the English went to North America – "that the North Americans speak English."[3]

Identity Issues

English migration to North America is also connected with issues of identity. How English immigrants planted and formed North American culture is inherently problematic, prone to exaggeration, glorification, and the marginalization of others. The topic may be unfashionable in an era that rightly celebrates American diversity. But while some modern writers may be skeptical of the English characteristics of American culture, nineteenth-century writers were not. As one observed in 1818, "Whoever has well observed America cannot doubt that she still remains essentially English, in language, habits, laws, customs, manners, morals, and religion … the great many of our people is of English origin."[4] Perhaps the most important early observer of American culture, Alexis de Tocqueville, considered Americans as "the portion of the English people charged with exploiting the forests of the new world."[5] Ralph Waldo Emerson agreed: "The American is only the continuation of the English genius into new conditions, more or less propitious."[6] Tocqueville, Emerson, and others took the English foundations of American culture for granted. This was understandable. Because of the long, virtually uninterrupted migration of English (and other British) people to America – and Britain's long rule of the American colonies – English culture ran deep in America. There were essential differences, of course, but similar cultural patterns remained.[7]

British immigrants made such a deep and lasting impact in North America in part because of their settlement patterns. They did not settle randomly, but generally left specific parts of Britain for specific parts of North America, where they planted their specific regional culture. That culture evolved over time and was enriched by the arrival of other peoples, but nonetheless it endured.[8] As we shall see, such settlement patterns characterize migration from North Yorkshire; many from the Yorkshire Dales settled in the Upper Mississippi region whereas most from the North York Moors settled in Upper Canada, with people from other parts of North Yorkshire settling in other areas.

The common cultural roots and features of many English immigrants and North Americans – especially their language and religion – have raised the question of whether English immigrants were "invisible." That is, the English were not as noticeable as other immigrants, that is, those who didn't speak English, and could therefore blend in and assimilate more quickly.[9] Historian Charlotte Erickson, in a book by that title, cautiously raised the question of whether the English in the United States were "invisible immigrants." Others have applied it more firmly to Canada. In the view of Lucille Campey, the English "simply merged into the background, adapted to new ways, and became Canadians," with the result that too many historians "have comprehensively ignored" the early English colonizers of the eighteenth century "and have paid even less attention to the waves of English who followed them. Thus, the English have become the invisible and unsung heroes of Canada's immigration story."[10] One might say that the English in Canada were distinctive for not being distinctive.

Campey goes on to say that the English in Canada "did not regard themselves as having an ethnic identity" because they were already of the "dominant culture" and "saw no reason to define their distinguishing features to anyone." Furthermore, they were associated with the elite, "since they were very well represented in business and in the upper echelons of government," and this was a more important form of categorization than any English "ethnic identity," which in any case was complicated by a more general identity of "British."[11] If this was true of the English in Canada then it was also true, though perhaps less so, of the English in the United States, especially early in the nineteenth century, before large numbers of immigrants from other countries diversified American culture. Some scholars have gone so far as to claim that, from the American perspective, "the English had no ethnicity at all."[12]

The most recent scholarship, however, challenges this view and asserts that the English were a distinct group like other immigrants, such as the Irish and Germans, and behaved "ethnically" in important ways – even while enjoying cultural advantages, especially a common language, that eased their transfer to North America.[13] Tanja Bueltmann and Donald MacRaild have carefully examined the "English Diaspora in North America" through the various English ethnic and charitable associations, most notably the Order of the Sons of St George, to offer an exciting revision of our understanding of English migration. Though the St George's societies were elite organizations, Bueltmann and MacRaild show that they were rooted in a "heightening ethnic consciousness," and thus they related to English immigrants from all backgrounds. In fact, because of the Orders' charitable assistance, English immigrants were more connected and relevant to their poor countrymen and women in North America than in England itself. Bueltmann and MacRaild also offer a new conceptualization of diaspora, from simply "the dispersion of people across space" to "a conscious international community of people with shared ethnic-national roots and a heightened, potentially politicized, sense of common identity." By this definition the English formed an "imperial diaspora" that gave them an identity existing at both the imperial and national levels – one that was bound and maintained by various societies and clubs, like the St George's societies, but also by the monarchy and, later, the First World War.[14] Our look at migration from North Yorkshire to North America builds on this exploration of ethnicity and assimilation by examining the lives of these diverse people on both sides of the Atlantic, their precise origins and their precise locations of settlement. It reveals how these remarkable people did exhibit their ethnicity in visible ways, while in other ways seeming somewhat "invisible."

Issues of Modernity

English immigrants also played an important role in North America's industrial and economic development. America's industrial revolution was "transatlantic" because immigrants from Great Britain, the world's first industrial nation, brought their skills, experience, and technology to help make the United States the second industrial nation. This was true of coal, iron, steel (including fine crucible steel), hard-rock mining and quarrying, cutlery, fine tools, pottery, the tin-plate industry – and virtually all sectors of the textiles industries, including cotton, woolens, and silk (both spinning and weaving), calico printing, and machine making. In some cases, industries were directly transplanted to the United States by English and other British immigrants, complete with all the necessary skills, experience, and sometimes even the machines themselves.[15] It was fitting that Andrew Jackson dubbed immigrant Samuel Slater (1768–1835) the "Father of the American Manufactures" for bringing England's revolutionary carding and spinning machines to the United States, not to mention England's family system of labour. But Slater is just one of many examples.[16] English immigrants were disproportionately skilled because they came from the most advanced industrialized economy.[17] These were skills that would benefit North America.

Push versus Pull

In yet another way the English appear distinctive. Research on passenger lists and British and American censuses, as pioneered by Charlotte Erickson,[18] offers a clearer view of them. Very broadly speaking – and with many exceptions – English migrants appear to have been moving for essentially positive reasons, especially when compared with other immigrants. They were seizing opportunities rather than escaping desperation. This pattern has many indicators. First, during the peaks of English migration to America, workers who were threatened by technological displacement, unemployment, and poverty were less likely to leave for America than those whose occupations were still in demand in England and who could expect a good livelihood there. Even during the depression of 1840–42, and the famine-stricken late-1840s, those most distressed were apparently not swelling the ranks of English immigrants: the handloom weavers and foundry workers, who were suffering technological displacement or unemployment at the time, were *not* leaving in significant proportions. Rather, it was the engineers, mechanics, skilled machinists, miners, professionals – and others generally *not* facing unemployment in England – who left in proportionately high numbers.[19] Peaks in British migration to the United States appear more linked with economic growth cycles in America than with economic depressions in Britain. And when Britain's economy boomed, as it did in the early 1850s, migration increased, suggesting that rising wages and earnings enabled more to make the move.

The relationship between migration and economic growth was explored with new depth and sophistication by Dudley Baines. By estimating migrants' county of birth from census data on births and deaths, and by comparing those who still lived in their county of birth and those living in other counties, Baines calculated reliable figures for those who went overseas. This provides new knowledge about rates of return migration, the relationship between local economic and social conditions and migration, return migration, and related topics.[20]

One of Baines's most important conclusions was that, "in the main, the emigrants were not fleeing from problems at home nor were they going blindly overseas."[21] Countless letters and biographies support this assertion, and even those who *were* facing unemployment or other hardships were often motivated primarily by American opportunity. Their letters suggest that America's higher wages, independence, brighter future, greater political and social equality, and lower taxes, were behind many decisions to migrate. Most important was the promise of land. Less often do we see desperation as the main reason to leave. More evidence for this generalization lies in the way the English travelled: of all immigrants, the English – including those with jobs threatened by modernization, such as handloom weavers – had the highest number who could afford to travel with family members. They had resources and a significant portion of them were ultimately pursuing land. They might work for years in their trade to accumulate enough capital or combine craftwork with farming. But surprisingly large numbers – from an astonishing array of occupations – eventually took up farming in America. Lawyers, doctors, soldiers, tradesmen of all kinds, left England and became American farmers – some in the early twentieth century.[22] Miners were especially able and likely to switch to farming in America, as illustrated by those who left the Yorkshire Dales for the Upper Mississippi. Many had some farm experience in the Dales, mined in the Upper Mississippi, and then used their earnings to purchase local farms.

This rather positive view seems to apply to Canada as well. Campey concludes that "English immigration was driven primarily by a desire for economic self-betterment. Its motivation was *never* solely a flight from poverty."[23] English migration to Canada was more about the pull, including the possibility of land ownership, and "the freedom and benefits of a more egalitarian society."[24]

Why North Yorkshire?

This book focuses on the migration of people from North Yorkshire to North America, both the United States and Canada, during the "long nineteenth century" from 1789 to 1914.[25] It also includes other parts of Yorkshire, the north of England generally, and other parts of England for comparisons. Focusing on North Yorkshire offers several advantages for exploring English migration in general. We can look at their precise origins and communities, dig deeply into their lives and examine their migration decisions, and explore the great variations in North Yorkshire. Important questions include ones raised by Baines: especially whether internal migration was linked to emigration, whether internal migration was a substitute for emigration, and how important local conditions were to migration decisions.[26] We can also look at why people from certain parts of Yorkshire went to specific parts of the United States and Canada, what kinds of lives they found there, and how they contributed to its development. Studies of migration from precise origins can provide a focus that illuminates the larger whole.[27] Indeed, there are excellent studies of individual English migrants that illuminate the history of English migration generally.[28]

North Yorkshire has certain qualities that make it ideal for insights on English migration. Although North Yorkshire is not a perfect representation of the rest of England – it has no large cities or heavy modernizing industries like the textile industries of the West Riding or Lancashire, or the large iron and steel industries of Sheffield or the West Midlands – it can serve as a lens through which to view English migration generally according to the questions outlined above. Immigrants from the North and other parts of Yorkshire are especially important for Canada because they initiated the vast English migration to its various regions.[29]

North Yorkshire has other features that invite careful study. Relative to other English counties, North Yorkshire had a high rate of natural population increase, and as a largely rural county with few alternative employment opportunities, migration to other counties or North America was "an important safety valve" during periods of economic change. Between 1781 and 1831 North Yorkshire's natural population increased by an estimated 125,823, yet the population in the county grew by only a little more than 35,000. So more than 90,000 left for other counties or America.

North Yorkshire's average annual emigration rates, then, were the highest of any English or Welsh county.[30] Without such proportions leaving North Yorkshire, would population pressures and poverty have been greater than they were? Did internal migration "substitute" for emigration? Knowing more about those who left for North America provides clues. Furthermore, as one expert has noted, one part of North Yorkshire – Swaledale – was probably "the most common model of population redistribution over the long run" in nineteenth-century England, allowing much of what we observe about North Yorkshire to be applied to England as a whole.[31] And finally, North Yorkshire has an extraordinary wealth of primary sources – many of them never used before – and local historians of great skill and generosity.

Using North Yorkshire as a lens to bring English migration into sharper focus can address some additional enduring questions. How do emigrants from North Yorkshire fit into the common model of relative "invisibility?" How do they compare with English immigrants in other essential characteristics – occupational backgrounds, motives for leaving England, strategies for successful settlement, attitudes about American culture, and so on? To what extent are Yorkshire Dales emigrants typical of English emigrants? How "English" were they, how did they assimilate, and how and to what extent did they display their ethnicity? Were there significant differences between those who went to Canada and those who went to the United States? Were there differences in the common "push" and "pull" forces that are featured in most studies of migration? What did they leave behind in Yorkshire, and what did they bring to North America? These are just some of the questions explored below.

Chapter Summaries

This book is composed of short, concise chapters. Chapter 1 looks at the migrants' origins in North Yorkshire and describes their environment and culture, including how their landscape shaped their culture and religion, and how their culture of farming and mining influenced migration decisions. Chapter 2 provides an overview of North Yorkshire migration to North America in the colonial period, from the earliest settlement to the American Revolution. It describes the large migration to Nova Scotia and other parts of Canada, and how the revolution affected the flow and nature of migration. Chapter 3 surveys the first half of the long nineteenth century to describe the general pattern of North Yorkshire migration to Canada and the United States within the larger English context. It provides an overview of migration patterns that have already been explored and provides the economic context for migration from 1815 to the American Civil War. Chapter 4 turns to the Yorkshire Dales and describes the life of the lead mining communities and the conditions that sparked their movement to the Upper Mississippi River region. It takes a close look at the working conditions, wages and earnings, and people. Special attention is given to how they blended farming with lead mining, and how this ultimately led them to specific places in the Upper Mississippi. Chapter 5 looks at leaving Yorkshire in the first half of the century – everything from making decisions and preparations to departing a local village. It presents newly discovered letters from the entire region, and other sources, to provide an unprecedented view of the difficult and highly emotional decision to leave one country for another. It also reveals details about the migrants' resources: what they could sell, and especially how chains of letters enabled people to make such a life-changing move. Chapter 6 is about the journey – getting to a port, sailing on the transatlantic voyage, and then travelling to the interior. Newly discovered letters and journals, and local sources in Yorkshire allow us a close, personal look at the journey, and challenge us to comprehend what the experience was like. Modes of transportation, costs, conditions in the steerage and cabins, the role of religion, and how the journey forever shaped these people are explored in fresh perspective and detail, with the help of passenger lists. Chapter 7 surveys the lead region of the Upper Mississippi River – southwest Wisconsin, eastern Iowa, and northwest Illinois – where most of the emigrants from the Yorkshire Dales settled. It gives a history of the region, especially the early lead industry, the relationship between Native Americans and white settlers, and the rough and violent nature of the region to which Yorkshire immigrants were going. The challenges and opportunities of this newly developed region, and how immigrants from North Yorkshire reshaped it, are presented through personal stories in letters and diaries. Chapter 8 looks at North Yorkshire immigrants' adjustment and assimilation in the Upper Mississippi. It uses census records to determine settlement patterns and to explore their interactions with Americans and other immigrants. This chapter takes a special look at the role of their language and cultural traits, their ethnicity, and how those factors affected their adjustment and assimilation. Chapter 9 continues with this theme by presenting what mining and smelting was like in the region, and the important roles played by North Yorkshire immigrants. Details from letters and diaries, and some other sources, take us deep into the mines, and into the new smelters that immigrants from Yorkshire could build because of their experience in England. This chapter uses the census, local business records, and old histories of the region to explore the remarkable success and significance of these immigrants. Chapter 10 shifts focus by looking at Upper Canada, where most of the immigrants from the North York Moors settled. It presents previously unused letters from about a dozen families and traces their settlement, mainly in Ontario. It shows how "chain migration" was important, but also how immigrants could improvise in their choice of settlement. This chapter also explores the importance of Canadian culture in the Yorkshire newcomers' experience of settling and assimilating. Chapter 11 is dedicated to the theme of farming in North America and the various challenges the immigrants faced and how they succeeded. It takes a close view of what was required to clear the land, begin farming, and engage in the local economy and society. The agrarian "myth" is explored along with the remarkable ability of the English to shift from craftwork to farming in America, as revealed by a recently published statistical analysis of English immigrants. Chapter 12 continues with that theme, but in Iowa, where several colonies of English people – including those from North Yorkshire – were attempted. The nature of these colonies, why they were attempted, the limitations they imposed, and how they all soon dissolved are featured in this chapter. The failure of these colonies demonstrates how immigrants from Yorkshire and other parts of England were unique in not having to depend on such communities. Chapter 13 looks at the immigrants' interactions with and perceptions of Native Americans, especially the Menominee between the time of the Treaty of the Cedars (1836), and the Treaty of Lake Poygan (1848). Chapter 14 explores the central role that religion played in the migrants' lives in both Yorkshire and America. The nature of Methodism, and the interaction between English and American Methodists, are explored in fresh ways, especially as the immigrants established churches in southwest Wisconsin. This chapter demonstrates how religion was both a strong link between the English and Americans, and a source of assimilation. Mormonism is also explored through previously unpublished letters that recount the settlement of North Yorkshire Mormons in America, and their challenges, including the assassination of Joseph Smith. Chapter 15 tells the story of the California Gold Rush, as experienced by North Yorkshire immigrants. Their success in lead mining gave them an advantage in turning to gold mining in California. Chapter 16 discusses how political issues, reform movements, and the Civil War dominated the middle part of the century, and how this was true of immigrants from North Yorkshire. Their participation in reform, their political views, their participation in the Civil War – and how this forged them into true Americans – are largely recounted through letters never before used in scholarship. Chapter 17 discusses the domination of steamships after the Civil War, and how they transformed transatlantic migration via Liverpool, as seen through the eyes of North Yorkshire migrants. Details from letters give us an unprecedented account of the journey by steam, and how getting into the American interior was changing during this time. Chapters 18 and 19 are devoted to the economy and agriculture of Yorkshire and North America after the Civil War, and how this affected the nature and magnitude of English migration. England's agricultural depression, America's Gilded Age, and new attitudes toward migration are the topics of these chapters. Letters from North Yorkshire people leaving comfortable lives for dugouts on the Great Plains are featured in chapter 20. The long relationship between the English and Texas, and new roles played by people from the eastern part of North Yorkshire are explored in chapter 21. Chapter 22 turns to Canada in the late nineteenth century and why North Yorkshire immigrants were choosing that destination over the United States. The chapter also explores the changing nature of English immigrants at the turn of the century, that some were confronting a Canada that was not as welcoming as it used to be. We end with our conclusions and the epilogue. Throughout these chapters the term "emigrant" will be used in the context of leaving, "immigrant" in the context of arriving, but also "migrant" in the fuller context of people completing the change from one identity to another, from being people of North Yorkshire to people of North America.

The original documents, replete with misspellings, are reproduced here as they were written.

Origins

All around us are beautiful landscapes accompanied by the music of
the Swale, and in a wonderful way, God seems more readily present
and more easily accessed here than in most other places.

KELD RESOURCE CENTRE DISPLAY,
KELD, YORKSHIRE, JULY 2014

Though small in comparison with the North American continent, North
Yorkshire is England's largest county, with about 5,000 square kilometres.
And it is truly immense in its diversity of geography and geology, types of
agriculture and mining, its villages and cities and coastal towns, its people
and local cultures, and its long, rich history. One of the most famous
parts of the county[1] is the Yorkshire Dales, which have been featured in
many books and films and are precious to many throughout the world for
their remarkable landscapes. The iconic drystone walls that divide up the
endless hills and valleys, enclose local breeds of sheep, and define ancient
villages cast a spell on many visitors. The Dales, which comprise over
1,000 square kilometres, are part of the Pennines – mountains and hills
of limestone – and are divided by rivers that have named their respective
dale, among them the Swale, the Wharfe, the Ribble, Aire, and Ure. The
Yorkshire Dales alone hold a great deal of interest. Just Swaledale and
Wensleydale alone offer surprising depth because, though contiguous
and similar in some ways, they responded differently to industrialization.[2]

To the east of the Yorkshire Dales lies the Vale of York, a broad, low-
lying fertile valley of nearly 1,600 kilometres that is ideal for diverse types
of agriculture and the home of cottage industries. Its significant towns
include Northallerton, Thirsk, Wetherby, Tadcaster, Harrogate, and most
famous of all, the ancient city of York, established by the Romans as
Eboracum in 79 AD. Thirsk is perhaps best known as the home of the
world's most famous veterinarian, James Herriot, whose practice was based
there. More recently the fictional *Downton Abbey* was set near Thirsk,
though it was filmed in Southern England. The Vale of Mowbray is also

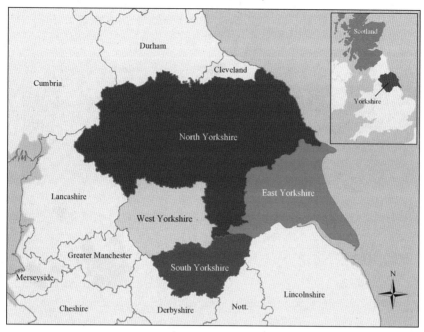

Figure 1.1   Map of England and Yorkshire, showing North, West, East, and South Yorkshire.

east of the Yorkshire Dales, north of and contiguous with the Vale of York. It has a more undulating landscape well suited for raising sheep, and on its northern edge lies the industrial town of Middlesbrough, located on the south bank of the River Tees.

To the east of the Vales of York and Mowbray lie the North York Moors, a region of roughly 800 square kilometres.[3] The Moors are similar in some ways to the Yorkshire Dales, especially in their elevation and striking grass-covered limestone landscapes that are perfect for grazing. In other ways the Moors are quite different. They did not have lead deposits but rather ironstone mines and quarries that peaked in production in the latter part of the nineteenth century. The Moors' main towns include Helmsley, Kirkbymoorside, and Pickering (with the Vale of Pickering lying to its south), and the dales of Ryedale and Rosedale, as well as Rievaulx Abbey, arguably England's finest monastic ruin. Charlotte Bronte set *Jane Eyre* in this region for good reason – the austere, beautiful landscapes and isolation were essential to her story. Finally, east of the Moors lies the North Yorkshire coast, dominated by the historic whaling port of Whitby, Scarborough, and to the south, in the East Riding, the emigration port

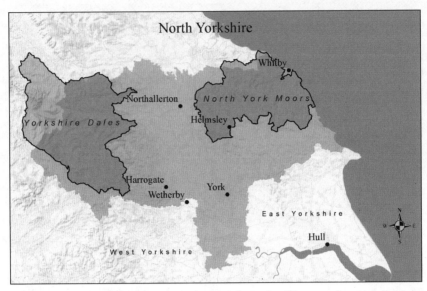

Figure 1.2   Map of North Yorkshire, showing the Dales, Moors, and major towns.

of Hull. Altogether, North Yorkshire and its surroundings comprise an astounding variety of landscapes, people, economies, and culture – all of which were reflected in its people who migrated to North America.

Religion

North Yorkshire's geography and landscape shaped its culture, including people's attitudes and belief systems – religion especially. Religious non-conformity thrived in North Yorkshire, where remoteness and isolation allowed relative independence from religious authority emanating from London. The simple austerity of nonconformist theology and liturgy suited the austerity of the landscape, the villages, and the practicality of the people. In the wake of the English Civil Wars and the temporary abolition of the Church of England under Oliver Cromwell, nonconformity became the norm and thrived in North Yorkshire. It started early in Swaledale, around 1650, when a group of people called the "Swaledale Seekers" pooled 20 pounds to pay for their own preacher, Thomas Taylor. Within a few years, after George Fox had spread his influence there, the group was absorbed into the Quakers, whose theology was similar. In the following century the clear, practical theology of John and Charles Wesley and their Methodist followers suited the local rural folk particularly well. Both North Yorkshire and North America were perfect places for Methodism to flourish.[4]

Along with other Protestant denominations, Methodism was planted in America by John and Charles Wesley themselves, who arrived in Georgia in 1736, and Francis Asbury, in 1771. Asbury paved the way for later Yorkshire immigrants through his continuous circuit riding, preaching, and organizing of communal services. In both England and America Methodists often held "camp meetings" and annual "love feasts," which became forums for church members to express their deep religious and social culture. Camp meetings provided opportunities to confirm one's faith, to have influence in the community, and for younger members to proclaim their maturity and perhaps eligibility for a spouse. Though there were differences in style and meeting places, Yorkshire and America had common religious traditions forged by migration – traditions that channelled later immigrants to specific places and helped them assimilate to American life.[5]

Yorkshire Culture

Along with these religious characteristics, North Yorkshire culture was highly traditional and linked with ancient folkways, rural traditions, and beliefs. One observer in Danby in 1847 found that most people in the area still believed in fairies, ghosts, and other superstitions rooted in old customs. Some feared being bewitched. Ancient rural festivals, parish feasts, and traditions defined much of what it meant to be a North Yorkshire person. Some alleged characteristics were negative, such as being obstinate and deceptive. But more often observers focused on their "peculiarity of manners and dress, … decided provincial character," and especially their distinctive speech and dialect.[6] The people of both the North and East Ridings of Yorkshire were known for having their own words and dialects, an identity that, as we shall see, stood out in North America.

North Yorkshire culture was also highly localized. People identified with their parish, dale, and the nearby surrounding "country" – the neighbourhood of the nearest market town where they likely had relatives and friends. This localism can be seen in their relative lack of internal migration within

Yorkshire or England, as revealed by the geographically tight distribution of Yorkshire surnames. It was not until the very late nineteenth and early twentieth centuries that a more general Yorkshire identity developed. Yorkshire branches of The Royal Society of St George, for example, were not established until the turn of the century, and even then, membership and leadership were dominated by the middle and upper classes.[7] Years later, when sport, especially cricket, was organized, local Yorkshire people developed a stronger sense of loyalty to and identity with their county.[8]

The localism of North Yorkshire culture – particularly its lack of internal migration – is especially interesting and important. Dudley Baines painstakingly examined English and Welsh migrants from 1861–1900 and found that, contrary to earlier assumptions, there was no significant correlation between internal migration from one county to another and emigration to America. This and other findings led him to conclude that local economic conditions were not the main cause of differences in emigration rates. Information through people already in America was a more important force and predictor of emigration.[9] North Yorkshire migration to North America appears to fit this model. According to a database that includes sixty-nine who left North Yorkshire for the United States in the nineteenth century, only one was born outside of North Yorkshire (in Durham). Nor were they going, as has been suspected, first to the more industrial West Yorkshire before proceeding overseas. Of 147 people who left West Yorkshire for the United States in the same period, only five had been born in North Yorkshire.[10] Information networks and chain migration do seem to explain much of the story of North Yorkshire migration. But so do some local conditions and traits in its mining culture.

Mining Culture

Whereas North Yorkshire's environment and landscapes shaped its people, the people shaped the landscapes. This was especially true of the miners, not only the lead miners of the Dales but also other types of miners in the Moors and elsewhere. Lead mining, especially, affected the people of Yorkshire deeply, not only their occupations and physical condition but also their attitudes and personalities. Observers often noted that those with "mining in their blood" were naturally enthusiastic and optimistic explorers with a sense of adventure – in a sense, gamblers looking for the

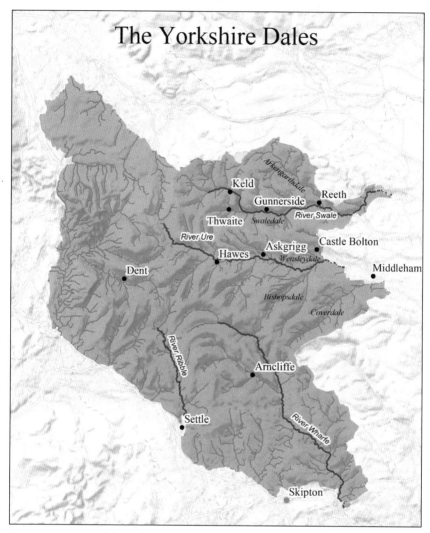

Figure 1.3   Map of the Yorkshire Dales, showing the main villages and rivers.

occasional big payoff with a "lucky strike." A good strike at a rich vein could bring sudden improvement in their lot, so to persist they had to believe in better times ahead. They had a tradition of search and discover that eventually led many to North America.[11]

Miners were known for their mobility. In mining regions like the Dales, mobility and migration, as one economic historian observed, were "generally regarded as normal."[12] In comparison with the rest of England, people of the Yorkshire Dales and North Yorkshire generally were less likely to leave their parish for another in England. The census of 1851 reveals that over 80 per cent of the population of Wensleydale and Swaledale had been born within their parish. In that sense this part of the Dales was "relatively closed." People moved out while few moved in.[13] However, if internal migration within England was relatively uncommon for Dales men and women, external migration to North America was relatively common. Lead miners and farmers responded to the decline of the local lead industry, and to its rise in the Upper Mississippi region. And with their characteristic optimism, mobility, and sense of adventure, it is not surprising that many sought their biggest payoff in America.

Lead mining in Yorkshire was often combined with a craft. Hand-knitting woolen stockings, caps, and other clothing was an important alternative form of work in the Dales, and Reeth was a centre for that trade. Both men and women knitted during what little spare time they had. Some miners, according to tradition, actually knitted as they walked to and from the mine, their needles clicking away furiously to produce woolen goods for a little extra cash.[14] Yorkshire miners also worked as the "wallers" who built and repaired the remarkable limestone walls that define the region, or they turned to roadbuilding.[15] Making hay and cheese also provided convenient alternative work. But miners turned most of all to farming, a combination that provided the inspiration, incentive, and means for going to North America.

Farming and Mining

Mining and farming were often inseparable in the Yorkshire Dales and left a deep imprint on the people and landscape. Over the centuries the large common pastures became divided by the stone walls that eventually made the Dales famous. Each householder was granted the right to graze a limited number of cattle – a right known as a "gait," or, less commonly, a "stint" – which was supposed to prevent overgrazing in the spring and summer.[16] Gaits were attached to the property; the number of gaits was based on custom and altered occasionally by agreement among the tenants. During the fall and winter the cattle could graze indiscriminately. In this way each tenant had rights to pasture their livestock and some time to work in the mines as well.[17] This blending of agriculture and mining defined many of the North Yorkshire migrants to America. They had the skills and experience necessary to adjust to a new land.

Miner-farmers often started with farming and then mined during the less busy days of the farm year. In the mid-1600s Swaledale farmers were already turning to part-time mining to supplement their incomes. By the late 1700s many were primarily miners engaged in part-time farming. Farming offered relief from the mines' poisonous air and dangerous conditions.[18]

In both Swaledale and Wensleydale, farming and mining were interdependent in several ways. When mining prospered, local farmers bred the horses needed to haul ore, pigs of lead, fuels, and other supplies. When farming prospered, farmers had money to invest in mining.[19] The close, symbiotic relationship between lead mining and farming was especially apparent in Gunnerside, the most significant mining township in Swaledale, where farming was often paramount. Here miners adapted their work to meet the farm schedule. Mine work was more flexible than farming, and farming was ultimately more desirable. Combining farming and mining in this way allowed the communities of the Northern Pennines to weather fluctuating lead prices.[20]

Altogether, the diverse nature of North Yorkshire's economy made the region generally more prosperous than most other parts of England. Its farm labourers benefited from increasing demands for labour in West Yorkshire, and they enjoyed better living standards, including better diets. Women and children often earned more than their counterparts in southern and eastern England, and the widespread "provision of allotments and cottage gardens" helped alleviate poverty. Rural crime was also relatively low in North Yorkshire.[21]

Of course, there were problems as well. In the eighteenth century, economic change and development harmed many, who then turned to emigration. Most significant was the enclosure movement, which combined small farm fields into large ones for pasturage, often displacing small farmers and creating landless and unemployed workers. This problem was especially acute in the Vale of York, the North York Moors, and the coastal regions. It was enclosure and rising land costs that undermined formerly prosperous farmers, tenants, and labourers and led many to consider moving to Canada. They formed the first large wave of Yorkshire immigrants to North America. But North Yorkshire people were settling in America even earlier, at the dawn of permanent English settlement.

2

Beginnings

Keld truly is what Celtic spirituality calls "a thin place," where the dividing
line between the holy and the ordinary seems exceptionally narrow.

KELD RESOURCE CENTRE DISPLAY,
KELD, YORKSHIRE, JULY 2014

During the seventeenth century some 400,000 English people crossed
the Atlantic to start new lives, and about half of them went to North
America.[1] From the beginning people from North Yorkshire were among
them. The Jamestown settlers of 1607 included 18-year-old John Dods
(later Dodson), who had hailed from Great Heck, just south of Selby,
in North Yorkshire. He was the brother-in-law of Captain John Smith
and sailed with him on 18 December 1606 aboard the *Susan Constant*,
under the command of Captain Christopher Newport, accompanied by
two other ships, the *Godspeed* and the *Discovery*. Dods was described as
a common labourer on the passenger list, but he was assigned the crucial
task of feeding his fellow voyagers.[2]

After a long, harrowing sailing – an ordeal that would continue to challenge future immigrants for centuries – Virginia was sighted on 26 April,
and the group of 105 men landed on 6 May. In the face of sickness and
starvation, Dods helped build the settlement and served as a soldier in
expeditions against Native Americans. He married Jane Dier, one of
fifty-seven women who landed in 1621 to become the wives of the men.
Jane was only about fifteen or sixteen when she arrived.[3] The young couple
nearly perished during the desperate "starving times," almost froze to death
during the extremely bitter winters, and narrowly escaped an attack by the
Powhatan Indian Confederacy in 1622. But survive they did. They appear
in the Virginia Company census of 1624–25 as John and Jane Dods in the
village of "Land of Neck" along with forty others.

John Dods was only the first of many North Yorkshire immigrants
to North America, and though he stands out as one of the original

founders of England's first North American colony, other settlers from that part of Yorkshire soon followed. Anthony Harker, for example, emigrated in 1633 from Swaledale, a place very different from John Dods's village of Great Heck, and other members of the Harker clan followed.[4] But the early Harkers were just a hint of the large migration from Swaledale that occurred two centuries later. From its earliest years, then, North Yorkshire's people were at the centre of the development of North America. They would continue that role throughout the following three centuries.

Transportation of Felons

In the early eighteenth century, after the starving times and wars with Native Americans, English migration to America increased. Some of the new arrivals came against their will as felons under the government policy of transporting convicted criminals out of English jails and into the American wilderness where they could be more useful. Altogether, about 20,000 convicts were settled in North America, most of them on Maryland's or Virginia's tobacco plantations. Some were from North Yorkshire. Three cases from what became the North Riding appear in the registers from 1720 to the 1730s. And in 1766 others arrived. They included a woman named Mary Rawlington who was convicted of stealing five meters of linen cloth from a person in Bedale, and another woman, Ann Richmond, who was convicted of setting fire to a barn and hay and corn crops. There was also a horse thief from the area of Thirsk. In the 1770s additional felons from Whitby and Hutton Moor arrived, all thieves of one kind or another. The available records reveal that between 1760 and 1773 a total of seventy felons from the North Riding were transported to America – thirty-five of them for seven years, twenty-three of them for fourteen years, and three for life. Eight of them were women.[5] Far outnumbering the felons were the many indentured servants who arrived from England during the seventeenth and eighteenth centuries – an indeterminable number of them having left North Yorkshire. Their terms of contract varied from harsh to reasonable, but ultimately they were remembered for their agency and fierce determination to succeed, many becoming landowners and prominent citizens.[6]

Canada

Whereas Yorkshire people continued to settle in the colonies that eventually became the United States, a major program of assisted migration from North Yorkshire to Canada was underway. The plan was designed to counter the French population that still dominated Acadia and much of Nova Scotia, even though France had ceded the region to Britain in 1713 as part of the settlement of Queen Anne's War (1702–13). Deeming the French-speaking, Catholic population that remained as a potential threat, the British government decided to offset them by promoting the settlement of English Protestants to secure the region. Thus, in 1749, Parliament issued a grant of £40,000 to pay for passages, land, and a full year of subsistence – including tools, arms, and ammunition – to bring English immigrants to Nova Scotia. Most were from London, but many were from North Yorkshire. A total of some 4,000 persons arrived in July of 1749 and were eventually joined by more.[7]

Immigration to Nova Scotia slowed in the 1760s, after the Seven Years War effectively eliminated French power in North America and English settlement became less urgent. But then, in the tumultuous decade of the 1770s, a large wave of Yorkshire people arrived as part of another program to increase settlement in Canada. It began in 1772 when a group of sixty-two persons from the area around Scarborough, Hull, Stockton-on-Tees, and Newcastle sailed from Liverpool. Between March and May of 1774, another group of 700 followed on three ships sailing from Hull: The *Two Friends* departing in March 1774; the *Albion* in April 1774, and the *Jenny* in April 1775 – all bound for Nova Scotia. Many had been recruited by Halifax's lieutenant-governor Michael Franklin, who was also a prominent merchant and land speculator. He targeted people from North Yorkshire because they had the kind of farming and craft skills he was looking for, as well as a desire to leave. Enclosure, rising costs, land rents, and other hardships were hitting Yorkshire at the time. Some people had been prosperous farmers but were now relying on parish relief.[8] Franklin also used special advertisements to appeal to Methodists who yearned for the complete religious freedom some still lacked in England. By 1775 a total of about 900 people from what are now the North and East Ridings of Yorkshire had arrived in Nova Scotia.[9]

This movement from Yorkshire to North America was part of a larger surge from various parts of England to various parts of North America,

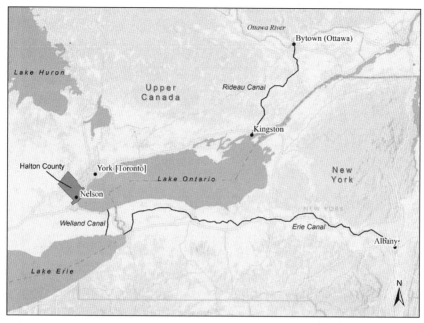

Figure 2.1   Map of Upper Canada, showing Halton County, where the Knaggses (discussed in chapter 10) and others from the North York Moors settled.

numbering 5,196 between late 1773 and early 1776. Fortunately, government officials recorded details about these migrants on passenger lists, out of concern that too many might leave and deplete the local workforce.[10] Nearly half (45.1 per cent) of the English had left the London region, but Yorkshire was the next most common origin, with a recorded 938 persons (over 18 per cent of the English). The precise Yorkshire origins are not indicated; however, information on their port of embarkation gives us some clues. Of the 5,181 English whose port is recorded, over 70 per cent left London. But the next most common port was Hull, with 424 of the 5,181 (8.2 per cent). Another 193 (3.7 per cent) left from Scarborough, whereas only 180 (3.5 per cent) had left from Liverpool.[11] The prominence of Hull and Scarborough may suggest that people from North and East Yorkshire dominated. The choice of eastern or western ports cannot be taken as proof of what part of Yorkshire they came from, and Hull would have also been a favourite port for people leaving Lincolnshire. But the fact that North Yorkshire already had a tradition of migration to Canada supports the notion that it was also an important source of all Yorkshire emigrants on the eve of the American Revolution.[12]

The 1770s immigrants' destinations are more certain: fully 60 per cent of those from Yorkshire were going to Nova Scotia.[13] They were less interested in Virginia or New York than those from other parts of England, and the reason has much to do with a longer tradition of Yorkshire people leaving for that part of North America that had begun in 1749. In some ways the Yorkshire immigrants of the 1770s were like those who had recently made their way to Nova Scotia and the Maritimes. They were composed mostly of families with children: in fact, they had by far the highest percentage (67.2) travelling in family groups, as opposed to a mere 7.5 per cent of those leaving from London.[14] Yorkshire families were also the largest on average, with 4.7 members, compared with 2.8 for London families.[15]

As for their occupations, the adult males were dominated by farmers. Nearly half (47 per cent) of those with known occupations were in agriculture. Most were described as "husbandman" or "farmer" and were tenant farmers, though some owned small parcels of land. It is possible that some described as "farmers" were more accurately farm workers with aspirations to own farms. But the average "quality" of these new North Americans seems to have been rather high: Over a third (36.3 per cent) of the males with occupations were skilled in various pre-industrial crafts or trades, including carpenters, masons, blacksmiths, tailors, millers, tanners, and joiners, and one linen draper. Most surprisingly, servants and unskilled labourers were notably underrepresented.[16] A mere 12 per cent were designated as "labourers," presumably unskilled, whereas the figure for all the English was 20 per cent. Those from Yorkshire, then, were on average more engaged in agriculture and more likely to be skilled than the English as a whole.[17]

Remarkably, the passenger lists also recorded the emigrants' "reason for leaving." Fully 78 per cent from Yorkshire gave reasons that seem "positive": "to settle," "to better self," to "follow occupation." "To seek a better Livelihood" was especially common.[18] The less common "negative" reasons include "bad economic conditions," "unemployment," "poverty," "high rents," or "on account of their rents being raised." "Provisions, Rents and every necessary being so very high they cannot support" was another, as was "Their rents being raised by his landlord," with the name of the offending landlord sometimes recorded as well.[19] Though these are rather vague impressions, the more numerous "positive" motives are supported by other indications that most of these people were not merely escaping poverty and misery. For example, evidence suggests that the late-colonial immigrants from England were more literate than those who stayed behind, and data on a specific group who left Hull for America in 1774–75 show that they were relatively prosperous.[20] To be sure, rising land rents were a common cause for this movement, but so too was hope for better circumstances and a determination to "settle," and "seek a better livelihood."[21] It was a classic case of both "push" and "pull" working together to precipitate a significant flow of people. It was not the poorest and least skilled who dominated, but rather those with skills, probably some resources, who had perhaps a mix of apprehension about Yorkshire's future and ambition to have greater rewards for their work, especially farming their own land.[22] As we shall see, this early characterization of Yorkshire's immigrants to North America had remarkable staying power for the following century.

A closer look at these Yorkshire immigrants in Nova Scotia reveals more evidence of skills. Some had experience draining Yorkshire's wet fen lands and now did the same in Nova Scotia and other areas. Charles Dixon was an expert in drainage. He arrived from Yorkshire in 1772 and immediately began to build dikes to drain his land. Within only six years he had surrounded 104 acres of marshland with dikes and had cleared thirty additional acres on his massive 2,500-acre estate near Sackville, New Brunswick. Other Yorkshire immigrants did the same, though on a smaller scale.[23] The early surge of Yorkshire people to Nova Scotia and New Brunswick in the 1770s, then, brought skills and energy to Canada and helped secure Britain's hold on it.[24]

Adjustment

Early Yorkshire immigrants to Nova Scotia and other parts of North America had advantages: they lived under British protection, had a common language and culture, and easy access to land. Nevertheless, it could still be hard to adjust. Some struggled to cope with their new environment and at first regretted their move, determined to reverse it. One of them, Luke Harrison, from Rillington, near Malton in North Yorkshire, who came to Nova Scotia, wrote back to a cousin saying that they "and a great many besides us" did not like their new home and were "coming back to England." Harrison eventually adjusted, and indeed a quarter-century later was heaping praise on Nova Scotia, but he was still thinking a lot about his Yorkshire village.[25] Others struggled with the vast scale of the wilderness, the undeveloped land and coastlines, which "appeared very discouraging and disagreeable – nothing but barren rocks and hills ... [which] greatly dampened the spirits," as some recorded. There were others who, like Luke Harrison, just wanted to get back to Yorkshire: "most of the passengers and several of them began to wish themselves in Old England."[26] Gradually, though, at least for those who stayed, the superabundance of land overcame the initial shock and adjustment, especially as the economy developed. As we shall see, this struggle to adjust to the wilderness was common among Yorkshire immigrants in the following century as well.

One unforeseen adjustment for many Yorkshire immigrants came in the form of the American Revolution. Inevitably, some supported the revolution, others remained loyal to the Crown, and a majority were probably neutral or indifferent.[27] But for many of those who remained loyal, leaving for Canada was the only option. The Loyalist Parkway in Ontario is testament to the large influx of people who left the rebellious colonies for freedom there under the Crown. The impact on Nova Scotia was also great: about 35,000 American Loyalists sought sanctuary there and became important contributors to Canada's development. Though most of the best lands of Nova Scotia were already taken, life was better there than in the American colonies, where Loyalists were threatened by violence and the loss of their property.[28] But it did not take long for Yorkshire people to resume migration to both Canada and the new United States of America.

After the Revolution

No evil is more to be deplored ... than Emigration.

JOHN WATKINS,
THE EMIGRANTS

Given the violence of the Revolution and high per capita American death toll,[1] the quick resumption of relations between the former colonies and mother country may seem surprising. But it was in both nations' interests to do so. Trade resumed the same year the war ended, in 1783, and by the late 1780s four-fifths of Philadelphia's imports and nearly all of New York's were from Britain. By 1790 about half of America's exports were bound for Britain and more than half of the US bonds sold abroad were held by British investors. The two economies were again as closely intertwined as their cultures.[2] King George's famous statement of friendship to the new American ambassador John Adams in 1785 could be taken seriously:

I wish you Sir, to believe, and that it may be understood in America, that I have done nothing in the late Contest, but what I thought myself indispensably bound to do, by the Duty which I owed to my People. I will be very frank with you. I was the last to consent to the Separation, but the Separation having been made and having become inevitable, I have always said, as I say now, that I would be the first to meet the Friendship of the United States as an independent Power ... let the Circumstances of Language; Religion and Blood have their natural and full Effect.[3]

Tensions soon flared again, however, when the young republic got tangled in Britain's struggle against Napoleonic France. Between 1803 and 1807 Britain seized over 500 American ships and the French nearly 400.[4] Britain's seizure of the USS *Chesapeake* in international waters in 1807 precipitated a crisis that resulted in Jefferson's ill-fated embargo on all trade with Britain and France, which only served to depress American ports. More significant was the War of 1812 – what some Americans called the "second war for independence." In reality it was an unnecessary sideshow of the Napoleonic Wars, involving disputed borders, lands, and posts like Fort Mackinac in Lake Huron. The naive assumption on the part of some Americans that merely marching into Canada and burning down York (now Toronto) would result in Canadians rebelling against Britain and joining the United States perhaps best illustrates how ill-conceived and unnecessary "Mr Madison's War" was.[5]

Even during these years of conflict, English migration to the United States resumed. It was a trickle at first, but that trickle included people from Yorkshire. John Ewbank seems typical, leaving an unspecified part of Yorkshire in 1805. He had married Ann Chapman, "a young woman of great force of character and a strict follower of Wesley" who converted Ewbank to Methodism. His religion was an important reason for his migration: his ninety-nine-year farm lease had expired, and his land-lord refused to renew it on account of his non-conformity. Thus, at age fifty-three he left his wife and ten children in Yorkshire, worked as a farm labourer and then farm manager in New York, and within two years was able to send for his wife and children to join him – an expensive journey involving eleven passage tickets. After renting land in New Jersey for four years, Ewbank sold his stock and tools, crossed the mountains, built a flatboat near Pittsburgh, floated down to Cincinnati, and soon bought land on Tanners Creek in Dearborn County, Indiana. He also served as leader of the local Methodist church.[6] Ewbank was the first English settler in the area, but soon others joined him, some from Yorkshire.

John Ewbank likely knew Richard Sedgwick, another early Yorkshire immigrant, who left in 1806 at age thirty-two and arrived in the same corner of Indiana in 1808. A shepherd and farmer in Yorkshire, Sedgwick used his farm experience wisely and flourished in his new Indiana home as a farmer and stock raiser. He imported the first short-horn bulls from England. But he also had mechanical experience and used his skills to build the area's first fanning-mill, a forerunner of the threshing machine. Richard Sedgwick was clearly an intelligent and resourceful person who seems to have reached his limit in Yorkshire but could use his multi-faceted skills and drive to rise higher in America as new lands like his in Indiana were opened to settlement. His contributions to that frontier region were invaluable for early development and created opportunities for more settlers like him.[7] The same was true of Robert Hargitt, another Yorkshire immigrant of the area, who arrived in 1814, and served as the first merchant.[8]

Other early North Yorkshire immigrants on the frontier include John Harrison, who left Otley, just south of the Yorkshire Dales, in 1814, came to Pittsburgh, and then two years later, after a return trip to Yorkshire, settled in Harrison County, Ohio. Harrison was by no means poor when he left: he owned an "excellent farm of 114 acres" near Otley, and like other Yorkshire immigrants in southern Indiana, was a person of some means. Harrison seemed somewhat restless and hard to please; he returned yet again to England in 1823 and died there ten years later.[9] What Ewbank, Sedgwick, Hargitt, Harrison, and other Yorkshire immigrants of the early nineteenth century saw in these freshly opened areas of the American frontier were rich opportunities for themselves and their fellow compatriots. But they could hardly have imagined the scale of immigration that was to follow, much less the economic and political forces that prompted it, or the diverse roles played by North Yorkshire people.

The fall of Napoleonic France and the 1815 Congress of Vienna marked a new era. Great Britain was the biggest winner, for with its main historic rival no longer a threat, it had little competition and was poised to become the world's dominant imperial and economic power. Its navy was supreme, it continued to expand its empire in British North America and India, and its trading relations with the young United States were back on track – despite the temporary blip of the War of 1812. But Britain was entering a conservative, reactionary phase, a wrongheaded response to the French Revolution that was defined by the new Corn Laws (tariffs on imported foods to protect prices and profits for landlords) and Manchester's infamous Peterloo Massacre of 1819. It was a time of great change and growing industrialization, and North Yorkshire had some adjustments to make. Because of its diverse economy and landscape North Yorkshire could respond in a variety of ways, and migration to North America was among them. Throughout England, emigration to America was becoming more common, regarded as normal, and was losing its social stigma of failure.[10] It was during the early part of the century that "settlerism" emerged in England, a new attitude that migration was not a result of failure, but more a hopeful act of raising one's status and attaining one's full potential.[11] People from North Yorkshire embraced this new attitude with gusto.

To Canada

In the wake of the Napoleonic Wars, as military contracts and mobilization dried up, much of England was hit by an economic recession sparking new interest in emigration. Farm workers in North and East Yorkshire's agricultural community, as well as Lincolnshire, were especially hard-hit and many looked to Canada for a new life. In 1816 the *Hull Advertiser* reported that "such are the distresses and difficulties in the agricultural districts as to induce numbers to emigration to America: In Marshland (near Howden) thirty-five individuals embarked last week for the island of St John, New Brunswick."[12]

A significant surge of Yorkshire migration to Canada began in 1817. This was a response to the post-war recession but also a new burst of transatlantic crossings that served the growing timber trade and made migration more affordable and available. The sea lanes became better connected when the new Black Ball Line of packet ships was established between New York and Liverpool in 1817 by Yorkshire immigrant Jeremiah Thompson. Now there were regularly scheduled transatlantic voyages that brought the two nations closer together while reducing the guesswork and some anxiety for passengers. The larger ships were reassuring as was the fact that the booming timber trade reduced prices and multiplied sailings for Canada.[13] As a result, between 1815 and 1830, whereas 40 per cent of the immigrant traffic came directly to the United States, 55 per cent arrived in Canada. During the decade after the Napoleonic Wars, about 10,000 arrived in Quebec alone.[14] Many who landed in Canada, however, soon crossed the border south, as did some from North Yorkshire.

At this time Yorkshire immigrants were also shifting their interest from Nova Scotia to New Brunswick and Prince Edward Island, where more good land was readily available.[15] Observers of those arriving in Prince Edward Island in 1817 described them as "very cautious" in their land choices and settlement, even though the country was ideal for farmers from the north of England. They chose the middle part of the island and founded Little York. Just nine years later another observer described their farms as "under excellent cultivation ... the neatness and cleanliness of everything about them reminded me of England." Other Yorkshire immigrants of 1817 settled in New Brunswick, in the Sackville area, across the Northumberland Straits, opposite Nova Scotia. Among them were John Towse and three of his brothers, who cleared their land, built their homes and a sawmill, established their gardens, and then sent for their families still in Yorkshire. More Yorkshire settlers arrived, forming a close and thriving Yorkshire community.[16]

Lower Canada was also attracting Yorkshire immigrants to new opportunities with the timber trade in the Richelieu Valley, in southwestern Quebec, which had been established through land grants following the Seven Years' War. Soon after the Napoleonic Wars, now that voyages were safe from French attack, tradesmen and farmers from East and North Yorkshire began arriving in greater numbers – at least eighty-one families – and they established a prosperous timber trade for both the British and American markets.[17] Soon, communities of Yorkshire immigrants were also established to the south, closer to the United States, in various townships.[18] But in the 1820s, new English arrivals, mainly farming families with resources, were already choosing Upper Canada over the Maritimes.[19] The rich open lands of Ontario especially were attracting attention.

Though the exact numbers of Yorkshire immigrants to Canada are impossible to determine – due to inadequate records and the fact that many arrivals were in transit to the United States – the numbers were significant. Between 1817 and 1830, some 18,000 English people arrived at Quebec. Of these, about three-fourths had left from northern ports; and of these, about a third had left from Hull.[20] Hull was the port of choice for many because it tapped into the widespread interest in eastern Yorkshire to emigrate, and because the costs of getting there and then sailing to America were usually lower. Hull became an early port for the timber trade after Napoleon had cut off supplies from the Baltic Sea, and now after the war it was an ideal port to take people to America and return with more timber. Two ships, the *Fame* and the *Nancy*, left Hull for Quebec in 1816 with emigrants, and their numbers grew. In 1819 alone, about 900 people left on Hull ships for Quebec.[21] These were largely Yorkshire immigrants, many from what was later defined as North Yorkshire. They often found the adjustment to a remote and unpopulated corner of Canada less difficult than people from the south of England because they had also left areas that were remote and underpopulated.[22]

People from all parts of Yorkshire, and northern England generally, dominated a significant flow of people to both Upper and Lower Canada in the 1820s and 1830s.[23] They were described as "chiefly farmers from Yorkshire" but there were also textile workers, especially handloom weavers who had been displaced by the new power looms in West Yorkshire.[24]

Though the emigration of textile workers is commonly associated with West Yorkshire, North Yorkshire did see some of their textile workers leave for America as well. Significant numbers of linen weavers and their families left from Brompton, near Northallerton, which was a linen production centre, as well as from Appleton Wiske, Hutton Rudby, and Swainby.[25] Between 1831 and 1851 Great Ayton, Whorlton, and Guisborough saw an exodus of its poor linen weavers, though they did not necessarily leave England.[26]

The number of people who left the North York Moors for Canada and the United States in the early part of the century was significant enough for the 1831 census to conclude that emigration was the main cause for population declines in Pickering, Lastingham, Loftus, Westerdale, and Glaisdale.[27] And in 1833 the Select Committee on Agriculture reported that virtually all townships and most families "had some of the inhabitants and some of their relations gone to America, both labourers and farmers."[28]

Some of the movement to Canada was triggered by new combine harvesters that displaced farm workers.[29] But even during these difficult years, emigration was not necessarily an escape. Most going to Canada were self-financing, and many of those who left Yorkshire for the region north of Lake Ontario in the 1830s and 1840s had extensive farming experience. Those sailing from Hull included some described as "very affluent,"[30] and people emigrating from the Malton area in 1830 were described as "persons of good property."[31] To be sure, there were some poor emigrants: the same Select Committee on Agriculture reported that those emigrating from Lockton, near Pickering, were small freeholders who had to sell out because of debt and that some farmers' costs were higher than their profits. Yet, others were labourers with savings of 20 to 30 pounds – a considerable sum.[32] Clearly the emigrant population was mixed. Some were poor, but others were not.

At the same time Canada's appeal was growing. Compared with its southern neighbour, Canada was more distinctly English in culture and institutions, and it offered greater equality. The United States was known for these characteristics as well, but Canada was special. It was still politically tied to Britain so that those moving to Canada were not compelled to forfeit their loyalty or identity. The same was true of the other settler colonies – Australia, New Zealand, or even South Africa, but their bad press reports and greater distances enhanced Canada's appeal. Even in 1851, during the Australian Gold Rush, people leaving the Driffield area of East Yorkshire were still choosing Canada because of "the very unsatisfactory accounts received from Australia and Port Natal."[33]

Canada's greater egalitarianism was another draw. More so than the United States, Canada offered a comparatively classless society in which immigrants could sell their labour freely to the highest bidder.[34] But changes were underway. Some observed that Canada was beginning to experience "a constant struggle between the aristocratic principle and the spirit of freedom and equality characteristic of the Americans." There was growing tension between those who had risen from poverty and those with affluent backgrounds and education.[35] As early as 1837–38 this social tension erupted in the Rebellions of 1837–38 in both Upper and Lower Canada, though they were occurring south of the border too. Upper Canada's labour costs were also rising, which benefited wage labourers but not so much farmers.[36]

To the United States

Although Yorkshire and other English immigrants filtered into Canada during the 1820s through the 1840s, greater numbers were going to the United States where the economy was more developed. Passenger lists for ships leaving England provide context for the people from North Yorkshire. By comparing the occupational profile of the emigrants with that of the whole English population, as recorded in the census, we can identify the kinds of workers who were more likely to emigrate. In 1831 and 1841 workers in modernizing industries, such as textiles and iron, were over-represented, though less so than the traditional craft workers. In 1841, industrial workers and craft workers together comprised more than half of adult male emigrants, whereas they formed little more than a third of the English and Welsh work force in 1831. In 1841 they were also over-represented, comprising nearly 55 per cent of the immigrants and 45 per cent of the adult population. But by mid-century the proportions of industrial workers among the emigrants had fallen so significantly that they were under-represented, whereas craftsmen were only marginally over-represented.[37]

Thus, during the 1830s and 1840s skilled pre-industrial workers – like miners, woodworkers, building trades workers, and so on – were proportionately more numerous than either farmers or industrial workers as immigrants to the United States. This is significant because generally pre-industrial workers were still in demand in England during these years, and their future there would seem comparatively bright. This occupational pattern casts doubt on the assumption that the increased immigration of the time was caused mainly by poverty. More evidence that the emigrants were not desperately poor is found in the way they travelled. In 1831 more than three-fourths of the English and Welsh examined on the passenger lists travelled as families and so could afford multiple passage tickets. No other immigrant group came close to this high percentage.[38] Additionally, with surprising frequency the available written sources observed Yorkshire immigrants to the United States or Canada who were clearly not poor, and were perhaps better described as affluent. In 1840, for example, an immigration agent in Quebec reported that Yorkshire families who had settled in York County were sailing back to England not only to bring along other family members, but to take "some very fine sheep" and a Yorkshire colt. He also observed that some of the new immigrant families were quite rich, some with about £1,500.[39]

This is not to say that there weren't many poor and unskilled English immigrants; we can certainly agree with the understatement by Bueltmann and MacRaild that "not all English workers were sought-after skilled craftsmen operating in particular elevated niches."[40] But it does appear that English immigrants included *relatively* high proportions of people with skills and resources. And many if not most of those from North Yorkshire appear to have had resources and cannot be assumed to have been desperately poor. This impression is supported by new data indicating that most of the immigrants from North Yorkshire to the United States had at least some degree of education, more so than the general English home population.[41] Poverty, in short, seems not to characterize or explain the sustained first noticeable wave of British migration to North America that occurred during the middle of the century. Nor does it explain the two later waves: the one following the Civil War, and the other from the 1880s to the Panic of 1893. Dudley Baines has shown that these post-war surges of migration were due not so much to agricultural depression in Britain, or to swings in Britain's building cycle, but more to the growing attractiveness of the United States, as conveyed by networks of information.[42]

Certainly the "quality" of Canada's Yorkshire immigrants – as measured by their levels of wealth, skill, and education – varied greatly. Some newspapers reported that those leaving Yorkshire for Canada were more suitable and successful than those leaving other parts of England.[43] Those from North Yorkshire were sometimes described as "the best of the laborers," or the "best" in terms of work ethic and competence. Some claimed that Yorkshire migration to the United States was of such good "quality" that for Yorkshire it was "a curse ... we lose the producers but keep the consumers."[44] On the other hand, in 1830 Yorkshire newspapers published complaints that impoverished English paupers had "inundated" an area 300 kilometres from New York City, and some observers saw Canada as "a dumping ground" of England's worst sort of people.[45] It is uncertain how many of these were from North Yorkshire, but it is certain that the flow of people from England, including Yorkshire, included some poor enough to need assistance.

Assisted Emigration

Soon after the Napoleonic Wars the British government introduced a £10 emigration scheme to assist poor families to Canada. A significant number used that assistance to leave the lead mining area of Alston, in Cumberland, for Smith Township, Peterborough County, Ontario. And in the 1830s more "Cumberland miners" were assisted to the area, along with some from Yorkshire, where they established a thriving farming community.[46] The new Poor Law Amendment Act of 1834 contributed to the rising migration tide to Canada by allowing parishes to borrow money from wealthy local people to finance the emigration of poor parishioners, to reduce continuing relief costs and help their poor get a better life. The Poor Law records indicate that most of North Yorkshire's assisted migrants had come from the Moors or Dales and went to Upper Canada, though some eventually crossed over to the United States.[47]

During the 1830s the English had higher proportions relying on assistance than even the Irish, in large part because England had the Poor Law to help them leave, whereas the Irish, until 1838, did not.[48] Because government assistance to the United States generally did not exist, assistance helped differentiate the two streams to North America: those assisted to Canada left poorer circumstances on average, whereas those to the United States did not qualify for government assistance, and so tended to be better off or had help from relatives.[49]

The cost of assisted emigration to North America could vary considerably from parish to parish. In 1819 the overseers of Guisborough paid £24 to sent Margaret Chipchase, but the same year it spent £15 to send off the entire Robert Ord family. In 1820 Thirsk's overseers paid only £6 to send William Clements and his wife and child to America. In the early 1820s some local parishes paid as little as £3 to get rid of poor individuals.[50] Between 1831 and 1834 Guisborough paid £60 for five families to leave. Some of the Poor Law grants appear to have been quite generous: in 1824 the Robert Ranson family, from Brough, Cumbria, were granted £25 16s 7d to leave.[51] The Muker vestry paid John Pounder £20 to leave, whereas a Grassington miner got only £5 to do the same.[52] And in nearby Alston Moor, in Cumbria, 124 persons left for Canada, their passages having been paid by a subscription fund that raised £311, two-thirds of which was contributed by Greenwich Hospital.[53]

Assisted pauper emigration increased in the early 1840s when the transatlantic depression began. As the depression worsened, Poor-Law-assisted emigration from North Yorkshire rose again. The linen industry was in crisis, the port cities were stagnant due to lack of trade, and agriculture slumped. Conditions were so bad that some people were leaving to escape poverty, even hunger itself. As the *Sheffield Independent* reported in early 1841: "Some idea of the condition of the working classes in the neighbourhood of Dewsbury may he formed from the fact, that a considerable number of persons, driven by poverty and the fear of starvation, have emigrated to the United States, during the past year; and within the last few days 22 individuals have left Earlsheaton for the same destination, and many more are about to follow."[54]

Thus parish-assisted emigration expanded. In the area of the North York Moors between 1841 and 1844, three pauper families were assisted from Pickering, six from Helmsley, and five from the Guisborough area (including Danby and Westerdale). Most were farm labourers.[55] Meanwhile, as we shall see in the following chapter, the lead region of the Dales was experiencing its greatest outward flow, as local newspapers recorded the departure of large groups of families travelling through Hawes on the way to Liverpool.[56]

It is understandable that the Poor Law Commissioners insisted that Poor Rate money be used to finance emigration only to the Dominions, not the United States, a competitor nation that would only benefit from such a gift of human capital.[57] For these reasons they refused to help Grace

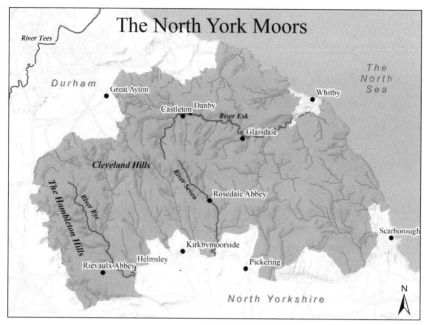

Figure 3.1   Map of the North York Moors, showing main rivers and places where people left for North America.

Brown and her six children, from Richmond, to join their husband and father in New York, in 1842. The commissioners argued that her husband should be able to send money for them, which he did, so the parish only paid her expenses to Liverpool instead.[58] Nevertheless, some parish-assisted emigrants were sent to the United States. In 1830 Muker parish officials provided £20 to John Pounder – paid to him once he was on the ship – to leave for the United States.[59]

Resistance to Assisted Migration

As assisted pauper emigration rose, so did opposition to it. English reformers and journalists were quick to condemn it. The most prominent perhaps was William Cobbett, the so-called "radical" who complained that England needed its poor labour and that shovelling them out to Canada only left England with more idle people and pensioners.[60] Though the critics were making a valid point they tended to underestimate the scale of destitution. And they could not foresee the long-term success of the poor who were assisted to Canada. For, despite some dubious motives behind government-assisted migration to Canada – often based on the simple desire to reduce welfare costs – the overall approach was "generally fair-minded and compassionate."[61]

Assisted immigrants to Canada were visible in the press because of the funds spent on them, attention that was sometimes unfair and misleading. Schemes to help poor English people get to America created an illusion that the English were poorer and more undesirable than they were, and statistically, the numbers of assisted immigrants were insignificant in comparison with the great majority who were unassisted.[62] The greatest resistance to assisted pauper immigration was directed against the Irish, especially during and after the famine years, because of concerns over costs and anti-Irish prejudice.[63]

North Yorkshire migration to North America in the few decades following 1815, then, was sustained and varied. People of moderate means outnumbered the desperately poor who needed parish assistance. Land in the United States or Canada was the big draw for most. But the most significant migration from North Yorkshire in the first half of the nineteenth century was one that affected both Yorkshire and America in profound ways, one that saw the largest numbers of the most skilled people who would contribute to the transatlantic industrial revolution. This was the remarkable movement of lead miners and smelters who left the Yorkshire Dales for the Upper Mississippi.

Lead

A hush is a ravine in the hillside caused by miners releasing dammed-up water to scour away the topsoil and reveal the ore veins.

KELD RESOURCE CENTRE,
KELD, YORKSHIRE, 2014

Lead Mining in Yorkshire

We have already noted the ancient tradition of lead mining in the rugged Pennine landscape that shaped the people who lived and worked there. The harsh, dangerous, but potentially rewarding nature of lead mining was bound to do that. Considering the various kinds of workers and their conditions in an extractive industry, it is no wonder that so many decided to – and were able to – go to America.

The lead industry required a variety of workers, who fell into two broad groups: those who toiled underground and those who toiled above. Underground were the pickmen, who hewed out the ore, and the "deadmen," who dug the shafts and tunnels and supported them with timbers to prevent deadly cave-ins, and who combatted flooding and poor ventilation. Above ground were the smelters, a relative elite, but also ore dressers and washers who prepared the ore for smelting, and various other skilled and unskilled labourers who performed the tasks required to produce the lead and bring it to market.

Together, pickmen and deadmen first had to find and expose the galena – the lead ore. To accomplish this, they often used the ancient mining technique of "hushing," which dates back at least to Roman times. Pliny described the method in terms that would have been familiar to Dales miners nearly two millennia later: turf banks would be constructed to dam up water which would then be released in a torrent to eat away at the top soil and expose the ore. The hushes could be used time and time again, and redirected to carve away large stretches of the moors and hill-sides. To this day the remnants of hushes can be found throughout the Yorkshire Dales and contribute to their unique and dramatic appearance.[1] Hushing was relatively safe but the actual mining could be unhealthy and dangerous.

Even in the best of times the lead miner's life was hard, uncomfortable, and often short. If the mine was not too remote, miners made the trudge each day, hiking long distances in all types of weather. If the mine was more distant, miners were away from their homes for days at a time, living in a mine company's barracks. Once at the mine, the miners often risked life and limb to earn their pay, and as the nineteenth century progressed the mines typically got deeper, wetter, and colder. Miners sometimes found themselves up to their waists in ice-cold water, struggling to breathe the poorly circulated air. Water made working conditions miserable: it dripped from the roofs, clung to the miners' clothes by mixing with clay and often threatened to drown them. In some cases, miners spent six hours of an eight-hour shift bailing out the mine with buckets to access the ore. Rock falls below ground were also a constant threat. In 1839 William Alderson was injured at age seventeen in a rock fall, and had his leg amputated on the spot without anesthesia. But he was lucky to have survived.[2]

Along with hard and dangerous conditions came the threat of disease and debilitation. Diseases took various forms, but "miners' ailment" – a catch-all understatement for a combination of pneumonia and lead poisoning – was especially dreaded. The near-constant inhalation of siliceous dust and the infections it caused were potentially deadly, especially when ventilation was poor. Adequate ventilation was essential and often difficult to achieve. Funnels, screens, and other deflectors could drive the wind down mine shafts, and then fans and bellows could push the fresher air to the miners – all of which required the latest and most advanced skills in the industry. Miners breathed heavily as they toiled; the fumes of candles and gunpowder made this difficult and contributed to "miners' consumption," a form of asthma caused by the inhalation of various noxious particles.[3]

With all these problems combined, many miners died young.[4] Their shortened life is indicated in records for Swaledale, where the average age of death between 1859 and 1861 was almost sixty-one for non-miners, but only about forty-seven for miners. A commission in 1864 discovered that of the eighty-five miners in Swaledale at that time, fifty-five, or 65 per cent, died of chest and lung diseases, compared with only 34 per cent of those in other occupations.[5] Miners under the age of forty outnumbered those over forty by more than three to one because older miners were past their prime, and because too many miners did not survive past forty.[6]

Smelting

Smelters usually earned more than miners,[7] but they also paid a high physical cost. Smelting burned the sulfur out of the galena and changed it into an oxide, which was then roasted further to reduce it to pure lead metal. Smelters not only stoked the furnaces but performed the harder, more dangerous task of collecting the condensed lead by laboriously scraping the flues that were typically built into the hillside. Then they carried the toxic, stinking residues away from livestock and plant life, only to inhale the deadly fumes themselves.[8] Yorkshire Dales miners and smelters certainly earned more than most agricultural labourers and many skilled craftsmen. But when they had to provide their own gunpowder and candles or had to pay someone to break and wash the ore, their earnings were cut considerably. And when paid on a piece-rate system, which was common, they usually earned less as they aged. When they died young, they earned nothing at all and left a poor family behind.

Women and Children

Women and children also worked in Yorkshire's lead mining industry, usually as ore dressers and washers. Washer women were paid a pittance – a mere 6 shillings per month, according to Swaledale accounts.[9] And yet that pittance could make a significant addition to a family's income. Women were also employed to reclaim ore from spoil heaps. Though some women worked below ground in the eighteenth century, they generally did not in the nineteenth. Women could be a welcome presence at the mines. One diary entry from September 1817 reads, "Saw some very handsome girls washing the lead" in Arkengarthdale.[10]

Ore washing was hard, labour-intensive work. It involved cold and wet conditions and required a lot of strength and stamina, but the Dales women were up to the task. The heavier lead ore (the galena) would sink to the bottom of water tubs, called "hotching tubs," which the women rocked back and forth, and then used sieves and troughs to rake the ore away. By the mid-nineteenth century some saw such work as inappropriate for women: as one visitor to the C.B. Mine in Arkengarthdale noted in 1857, "Young women are engaged at working at the hotching tubs, and this is a matter of regret, because the employment of women in hard out-of-door work always implies a want of social refinement."[11]

As the century progressed, more and more companies invested in mechanical ore rollers and crushers, which displaced many women – though some still worked at breaking up pieces too large for the crushers.[12] Thus the numbers of women working at the Swaledale and Wensleydale mines declined: the 1851 census recorded fifty-nine women working on the ore floors there; thirty years later that number had fallen to only six.[13] The reduction of women's employment in the mines can rightly be seen as progress, but this also reduced some family incomes. When impoverished lead miners applied for poor relief during times of depression in the industry, that relief was sometimes granted only if the wives or daughters agreed to work as ore washers.[14]

Miner-Farmers

Most miners in Swaledale worked six-hour shifts underground six days a week. They commonly worked in partnerships because of the inherent dangers of their work and the benefits of fellowship. The relatively short shifts allowed miners to work their farms if they had one. It appears that between a third and half of Swaledale miners also had a farm, often with a cow or two, and surviving records usually show that these people juggled mining and farming effectively.[15] They were used to being flexible in their work and many would use that flexibility in America to combine mining with farming with the ultimate goal of being full-time farmers of their own land.

A common problem for those who combined farming and mining was the lack of adequately sized land. An analysis of eight dwellings above Swaledale in 1841–43 shows that six of them had agricultural holdings, and later the other two did as well. Lot sizes varied from about 3 to 9 acres; most had a cow or two, and some, sheep and pigs. But farming activities were restricted by the limited acreage and the limited number of cattle gaits for common pasture, which made it hard to grow enough hay for more livestock.[16] It was a classic example of land shortage limiting the options of miner-farmers. It did not take them long to realize that the Upper Mississippi region not only had much rich land but rich lead deposits as well, all in the early pre-industrial phase of development, ideal for Yorkshire immigrants who were experts in mining and smelting and who wished ultimately to farm. Given the dangers of mining, emigration for Yorkshire miners and smelters could be not just a means to a "better life," but to life itself.

New Methods

During its many ups and downs the Yorkshire Dales lead industry developed new methods and techniques that were also eventually carried to the Upper Mississippi by emigrants. Swaledale was the centre of lead smelting innovation, and what happened there in the early nineteenth century was truly part of the industrial revolution. Most significantly, the old ore hearths were replaced by the new reverberatory furnace. Old ore hearths were like a blacksmith's hearth, forming a stone rectangular box about two feet square and about a foot deep. The bellows pushed air toward the back, fuel and ore were put in in alternate layers, and eventually beads of molten lead dripped through the fire and into the bottom. It was labour-intensive and inefficient. The reverberatory furnace, invented in the early eighteenth century by the London Lead Company, was not only larger but featured a special roof that reflected heat from a fire in a separate chamber, so that the ore and fuel never blended. This saved labour, reduced waste, and greatly increased efficiency in the use of both ore and fuel. Refinements in the furnace and its flues occurred in North Yorkshire and made it one of England's leading centres of smelting innovation.[17]

Innovations in both methods and investment came early to the Dales. George and Thomas Alderson were among the most important miners of the early century, having already leased the Old Gang Mine in 1811 while prices were still relatively high because of wartime demand. Unfortunately, they hired an incompetent and dishonest agent by the name of John Davies. After only three years the Aldersons suffered a net loss £20,000, fired Davies, and replaced him with Frederick Hall, a well-connected lead manufacturer with great knowledge and experience in smelting. Hall

Figure 4.1   Old Gang and Mill Gill in Swaledale, a rich lead mining area.

had built Arkengarthdale's C.B. Mill, which operated six reverberatory furnaces that incorporated air pumps, roasting furnaces, and a slag hearth. Now working for the Aldersons, Hall implemented the very latest science and methods to both mining and smelting and improved the methods and technology in numerous ways: he installed two water wheels for the dressing floor and new cast-iron rails to replace the old wooden ones for hauling the ore. At great expense he also drove new shafts – one 800 meters long – to access new veins, cut new drainage shafts, and sank new shafts at inclined planes to draw out the ore. Hall's plans did not stop there; he was about to buy two steam engines to pump out water and pull up ore. But in 1818 a quarrel with the Aldersons over the details of his contract led him to sue them for £60,000. The lawsuit failed and the partnership dissolved, but the Aldersons and soon others in the Dales now had the latest methods and technology for the lead industry.[18]

The story of the Aldersons and their Old Gang Mill illustrates the impressive economic scale of these early mining and smelting ventures, as well as the remarkable surge in technological innovation – all of which placed the miners and smelters of the Pennines into leadership in the industry. The location was also an advantage: the miners were perfectly placed to absorb new ideas and techniques emanating from the nearby Tyneside coal fields. Miners who moved between the two areas for work brought back new technology or methods that could be applied to lead.[19] The experience in various mines and locations gave miners and smelters skills and a flexibility that helped them succeed in England and eventually in America. But leaving Yorkshire for America made sense only after a series of blows to their wages and earnings.

Wages and Earnings

Wages and earnings in the Dales' lead mining district varied along with market prices and are not easy to calculate or summarize. Early in the century miners were commonly paid quarterly, or even every six months, and were forced to rely on credit, though from the 1820s on most miners were paid monthly and relied less on credit. The miners' average wages were usually based on a piece-rate system, and the lack of reliable data, and fluctuations in lead prices, further complicate calculations. Wages and earnings fluctuated as widely as the industry that produced them. Average earnings probably peaked in 1810, but then fell to desperate levels within a few years of Waterloo, after military contracts dried up, and the economy slowed down. Lead prices and wages dropped so sharply and suddenly that unprecedented misery hit the mining communities. It was their hardest time.

Details on the plight of the lead miners were presented on 6 March 1818, by Thomas Buxton, a flour miller and dealer in Gunnerside, who came to London to testify under oath on behalf of the Committee on the Miners to the Lord Mayor of London. His account was as shocking then as it is now. Sheer poverty and desperation were bringing people to the point of hunger and starvation. Buxton testified that his wife, midwife Susannah, attended the birth of the sixth child of the Christopher Metcalfe family,

Figure 4.2   Gunnerside, one of the main lead mining villages whose miners settled in the Upper Mississippi region.

also of Gunnerside. Metcalfe mined lead at the Surrender Mine and rented a bit of land near Gunnerside. The poor family "had nothing to wrap the infant in" and "there was nothing upon the bed to cover the poor woman or child, not even a blanket or sheet upon the bed." Buxton reported that "the rest of the children had no clothes, but only clouts (that is rags) upon them." The Metcalfe family was hungry, for "they had nothing whatever in the house but a little of the very coarse bread made of Oatmeal." And the harsh, reactionary British government, led by Lord Liverpool, fearful of the hungry masses rising in England as they had in France in 1789, all but ignored such plights. The maladministration of the Poor Laws only rubbed salt into their wounds: after the Metcalfes sold their only cow to survive, they were now "liable to pay poor rates and other taxes for the support of others," while they themselves were not eligible for aid.

Other Gunnerside miner-farmers were just as desperate. Christopher Bell and his family were "reduced to such distress and starvation" that Thomas Buxton himself intervened on their behalf and secured the paltry sum of 3 shillings a week from the overseers of Abbeyside for their relief. Buxton also testified that the miner Stephen Dinsdale went to work in the Old Gang Mines without having had any supper the night before. Buxton declared that, as a miller with access to food, he began supplying the miners "till he has lost nearly all his property in advances to the poor miners" and that had he not done so, "many people would ... have been reduced to the great misery, if not actually starved to death."[20] The miners would never go through such awful times again, but the memories left scars and could only have contributed to decisions to leave for America.

Recovery came quite soon after this disturbing report, but the lead mining district still had to deal with a highly volatile and unpredictable economy. The years 1815–32 can be roughly divided into three periods of relative depression and prosperity, as reflected in lead prices. After hitting the low point that brought Buxton to London to testify, new demand and an economic recovery arrived in the early 1820s, when Swaledale reached a peak in prosperity. In 1821, a good year, the estimated annual wages for lead miners in Swaledale and Wensleydale were about £37 for a miner. At the same time Muker's population grew to about 1,400, and Gunnerside's Methodist Chapel reached new levels in membership. In 1822 a Methodist writer described the area as flourishing in both economy and religion: "The most flourishing parts of our field of [evangelical] labour are Swaledale and Arkengarthdale. If you were to see the crowds of miners who came pouring down the craggy hills to our places of worship, you would be led to inquire, 'who are these that fly as a cloud, and as the doves to their windows'? Most of our chapels and preaching rooms are crowded to excess, and as the weather becomes warmer, we shall be compelled to turn out of doors ... within the last four months our increase had been astonishing."[21]

In fact, 1824 marked a relative boom for the Dales' lead industry. But then, beginning in 1829 and through 1833–34, there was a continued drop in lead prices, and an "almost unrelieved depression." The opening of new Spanish lead mines was a major reason for the falling prices. With an oversupply of lead on an increasingly international market, prices plummeted as did wages.[22] A related problem was the scale of North Yorkshire mine investment. At times it was too large to be viable, even during times of high lead prices. From 1808 to 1813, for example, the rich

Figure 4.3   Swinner Gill, a "rough and romantic place" linking the lead mines
of Swaledale.

Surrender Mine produced a little over £72,000 worth of lead, but because
of high haulage and production costs, spent more than £75,000. Even
when prices were relatively high, unfavourable geological conditions could
prevent profitable operations, especially when available veins got deeper.[23]
Such were the inherent problems of extractive industries.

Together, high investment costs and the new Spanish mines gave
Yorkshire miners quite a beating during the early 1830s. In Gunnerside,
miners' wages were abruptly slashed by about half.[24] The 1829–33 depression
was in fact the most severe in duration and severity that the Yorkshire lead
industry would ever suffer. Both small and large companies failed. Even
the Old Gang Mine of the Aldersons, which was well established in 1811,
had to call it quits. Already by 1830 some of the formerly thriving Dales

Figure 4.4   Interior of Brandy Bottle Incline Mine. Begun in 1815, it joins the
Surrender Mine near Arkengarthdale.

mines looked like the edge of a ghost town. "Swinnergill is a rough and
romantic place," observed Edward Broderick in 1830, "but now I could
see only two solitary persons dressing some poor waste, a young woman
and a boy, where formerly all was life and crowded with workmen and
washer-women."[25] These depressed conditions and a seemingly bleak future
would prompt the first significant departure of lead miners for America.

Here and there some people adjusted and carried on. Edmund Alderson
Knowles, who mined and farmed in Thwaite, diversified into woolens and
knitting and leased a fulling mill. He and others who knew the local area
and economy intimately were able to survive the depression.[26] But any
general improvement that occurred over the next twenty to thirty years
was limited in scope and duration. Looking ahead to 1851 and 1861, for

example, annual wages were little more than £30, less than what had been paid in 1821. Miners' wages rose to almost £40 in 1871 – approaching the level of smelters, who averaged £43 – but then permanently declined, along with the industry itself.[27] Thus, wages fluctuated widely "according to the luck of the mine," as well as the price of lead.[28] Even at their highest levels, these wages did not adequately compensate the miners for their hard and dangerous work. There had to be more to life than that.

To cope with such wage fluctuations miners commonly formed partnerships of a few men or more to bargain for the price of their work and the ore they produced. This bargain system endured for most of the nineteenth century, and partly explains why Dales emigration was so much a group movement. The men worked and bargained together, they had tight social and professional relationships, their families married into each other, and so many would emigrate together.[29]

An essential and often difficult part of the process of emigration was to make the decision, and the preparations, and say farewell to family and friends, perhaps forever in this world. That profound experience of leaving was shared by emigrants from all backgrounds, and from all over North Yorkshire.

Leaving

The old village ... seemed the most lovely spot upon earth,
and it was like tearing heart strings to leave it.

SAMUEL FOWLER SMITH
ON HIS NATIVE WETHERBY

It is impossible to fully comprehend the transatlantic migration experience of the nineteenth century. Today, people armed with instant global communication feel anxious when parting from loved ones for only a short time. In the nineteenth century the parting was often assumed to be permanent: "We will meet again in heaven." was a common farewell. Though many emigrants eventually had the means and the desire to make a return visit to their old village, they did not necessarily know that at the time of their departure. The act of leaving could leave emotional scars, but it could also strengthen the person in the long run.

Leaving for America involved several daunting and interconnected steps: making the decision and preparations, getting to the port of embarkation, taking the voyage itself, and finally travelling from the American port to their destination. Leaving involved a comparative analysis of a future in England with that in America. Usually there was a calculation of interrelated "push" and "pull" factors. The decision process could look different for every migration decision, but usually it was based on personal information in letters written by family or friends already in America.

Immigrant Letters

Immigrant letters have some bias. Illiterate people were silent, unless they had someone to write for them, as were those who had no one to write to, or those who soon returned to England. The letters of English emigrants may also be biased by a need to justify one's move from a homeland with superior institutions and infrastructure to a place with rougher character and standards.[1] When letters and other sources tell us something about how and why people decided to leave, they almost always reveal "chains" of information, connections, a network of knowledge and associations at work. This was certainly true of those who left North Yorkshire.

We see chains clearly in the migration of Robert and Elizabeth Pannett, who left the area of York in 1852, soon after their marriage, for Clermont County, Ohio. A lack of opportunity seems to have sparked their interest in leaving, for they relied on financial help for their passage and to get established in America. More importantly, the Pannetts had three "ready-made contacts" in America consisting of two extended family members and an acquaintance who had left from nearby Acaster Selby, where Robert's parents had moved. The Pannett family worked hard for many years and suffered personal difficulties. But eventually they did own land, which would have been highly unlikely in the Vale of York.[2] They and so many others relied heavily on the links that were forged by their families and acquaintances within their village. Some counted on multiple layers of connection and support. Information about America, how to get there and find if not pre-arrange work, how to get assistance if necessary – all of this was conveyed in the letters. Letters paved their way.

Perhaps the only more effective influence on migration decisions was a return visit by an emigrant. Those who returned to their village could cast a spell as they described American life in person to relatives and former neighbours. Yorkshire immigrants returned to fetch their friends and relatives more commonly than we might think. A couple of Yorkshire farmers who landed in Quebec in 1839, for example, were actually returning to their homes near Toronto, taking "a number of friends with them who intend to purchase lands and settle in their neighbourhood."[3] But letters were much more common than return visits and ultimately had greater impact, especially when they were circulated among people in the village, who could then write replies for additional information and clarification. In this way prospective emigrants could compare their home in Yorkshire with a potential new one in America.

Some letters contain proof of their influence on migration decisions. Edward Broderick, of Grinton in Swaledale, recorded such a case in his diary on 2 March 1833, concerning his friend, William Woodward, who had received a letter from Metcalfe Bell, who had left for America three years earlier: "About a fortnight ago," Broderick recorded, "Wm Woodward received a letter from Metcalfe Bell in which he describes America in such flattering terms as to induce William seriously to think of going."[4] The Woodwards left for America the following month, and others left soon thereafter. Broderick continues that Bell's letters "persuaded my father to take the land off his hands … and had his sale of stock this day. They sold well. It is so unexpected. I hardly know what to think of it. John Bell is going too."[5]

Other letters show their power of persuasion. When Henry and Elizabeth Hunt left the Yorkshire Dales for Pennsylvania in 1830, they had benefited enormously from the chains and connections established by those who had preceded them. Writing back in 1849, the Hunts encouraged the James Pratt family to join them and offered aid once they got to Philadelphia. The Hunts mention that, when they themselves had arrived in Pennsylvania nineteen years earlier, a Mr W. Spensley of Reeth had arranged for them to stay with one Anthony Barnes, "who treated us like a father." Now the Hunts were offering a similar favour, though they did misinform the Pratts, stating that Galena – their ultimate destination – "is between 2 and three thousand miles [3000 to 4000 kilometres] from here," overestimating the distance by several times.[6]

No Yorkshire immigrant wrote more surviving letters than Matthew Dinsdale, a young Methodist minister who left Askrigg in early 1844 for the Upper Mississippi region to serve as a circuit preacher. He wrote his first letter from English Prairie, Wisconsin, to Askrigg in October 1844, knowing it would be passed around Wensleydale among people who were interested in following him. The letter is detailed, dispassionate, cautious, but ultimately encouraging: "For myself, I have never once regretted that I left home and friends tho' in doing so I felt as Keenly as a person can feel. The views I had respecting America when I left have been confirmed. I thought and I still think that there is a better prospect here than in England for those who have their living to work for … I cannot say yet how it would answer for [brothers] Matthew and Edward but I have little doubt that they would find America to answer better for them than Askrigg."[7]

Though Dinsdale emphasized that he was not trying to encourage others – that "everyone should decide for himself" – his letters seem to have cast a spell. In March of 1847 his brother Edward wrote to him saying, "Dorothy, Elizabeth and myself have thought that we should do much better in America than what we can do in England – by the accounts you

Figure 5.1   Matthew Dinsdale, date unknown. He paved
the way for other emigrants from Wensleydale.

give it is a much better place."[8] Eventually, most of the family made the
move, as did many neighbours and friends.[9]

Another extensive set of letters was written to and by the Matthew and
Jane Longmire Willis family – friends of the Dinsdales, who left Carperby
in Wensleydale for Wisconsin in 1845, in part because they were Quakers
tired of discrimination in England.[10] Matthew's father and uncle had
farmed at Woodhall, near their home in Carperby, and Matthew Willis's
letters back to Carperby were widely read, caused much excitement, and
inspired others to go to America. As Matthew Dinsdale's mother wrote
to her son, "Matthew Willis['s] letter has set the pepel all of talking hear."
Some of the nuances of American life were read with astonishment: "He
says," she continued, "when the Preacher went to one place to Preach they
were playing at cards with Whiskey before them & there is some kind of
a fly you have that flies in to the House and Bits you ... I was surprised
to hear you have no Tea but green."[11]

Figure 5.2   Askrigg, the home of Matthew Dinsdale and other emigrants.

Other Willis letters were excitedly circulated throughout Wensleydale by people dreaming of their own life in America, eager for whatever information they could find. Matthew and Jane appear to have been recruiting them. Willis's brother-in-law, John Humphry, who was still in Low Thoresby (near Carperby, about 10 kilometres from Askrigg) wrote that the Willis family "almost wishes them all to come to him, both his mother and the remainder of his family."[12]

We can see how letters were circulated, and how complex migration plans and arrangements for help were made, in Humphry's letter back to the Willis family. "I send this by James & Thos Lawson of West Burton [in Bishopdale, which parallels Wensleydale] ... They are steady young men ... I hope should they come to your place you will do all in your power to assist them, and it is their intention to proceed to you whereabouts." Humphrey also gave details of the Lawson Brothers' itinerary and how they planned to get to Wisconsin. "They come by way of Quebeck through

Figure 5.3   Matthew Willis, the "mountain minstrel"
of the Dales who struggled on his Wisconsin farm.

Canada where they have some friends and near relations, but it is not
their intent to stay, only but for a short time, but to make their way into
the western states, they start in a few days ... I have written by them to
Wm Richardson. I have given him your directions."[13] In this way letters
forged complex links that encouraged and facilitated migration and led
people to leave one specific place for another, while others stayed behind.[14]
Letters opened the doors and lowered barriers to leaving England.

Letter writers were cautious in their descriptions of America. Their
determination not to encourage the wrong people to go was sometimes
taken to such extremes that readers became suspicious. John Humphry,
for example, suspected that Matthew Willis was overly cautious in his
letters from Wisconsin when he responded, "sometimes I think you seem
fearfull to write your wishes and that you dar not advise anyone to come
to you for fear they should not like and you get the blame."[15]

Conscientious letter writers struggled to balance encouragement and caution. To persuade loved ones to join him without taking responsibility for any wrong decisions, Matthew Dinsdale blended caution and understatement with honest descriptions of America. By mid-1845, a year after his arrival, Dinsdale had accumulated considerable knowledge and perspective on American life and he longed to see his family members join him; but he knew America was not for everybody: "I am aware that a person might come here and do well, who at the same time might not like it and therefore I do not say to anyone 'come over.' Let everyone be persuaded in his own mind," he wrote in the summer of 1845.[16] Five months later he repeated this advice: "If you are doing well and are comfortable where you are I expect you cannot do better than remain ... I think it is better for some to emigrate, and it is better for others to remain, let people judge for themselves."[17]

English immigrants' expectations of America could run wild, especially when not accounting for the fact that whereas land in America was cheap, crop prices were low. As Matthew Dinsdale observed in Wisconsin in 1847, "Some Englishmen find great fault with this country because they cannot turn what they raise into gold or silver at their own door. They err by viewing things comparatively that are quite different. No one ought to expect to purchase land for 5 shillings an acre and sell wheat for 8 shillings a bushel. If land is cheap should not what it yields be cheap also?"[18]

Much of Dinsdale's advice reflected the piety and values of the Methodist preacher he had become: "I would also like to give a word of Caution to intending emigrants," he counselled. "If any one comes here to find happiness that person will be woefully deceived. Happiness in its perfection and fullness is to be found only in Heaven. And a satisfying portion on earth is only to be found in God." Dinsdale stressed that the material advantages of America were not that great, and in any case, beside the point: "I was quite as comfortable and happy in England as I have been in America and in some respects much more so inasmuch as I had my relations and friends near me ... Our local situation is a mere circumstance and does not affect our relation to the Father of Spirits. If we can be at enmity with God in England we can also be so here."[19]

Two years later, despite bouts of homesickness and a deep longing for relatives and friends, Dinsdale still struck the same chord of caution, balance, and piety: "You know I am not disposed to hurry any one from home and country; or to wish any one to come here. You will have to look to God for guidance."[20] And yet at the same time Dinsdale held out an encouraging invitation: "I think myself if you were all here and settled together, we should all be much more comfortable. I have never been sorry that I came and I expect I never shall, I am very partial to America it is just the country for me. If a person is well he has nothing to do but live and be respected."[21]

Sometimes we can see how letters formed multi-level information, not unlike today's integrated social media. In October of 1845, for example, Edward Dinsdale wrote from Askrigg to his brother Matthew in Wisconsin in response to his letters and those of family friend Matthew Willis, who had also left Wensleydale for Wisconsin. Edward starts by announcing that their sister Jane, her husband Barzillai Chapman, and their children "have determined to start for America in the Spring if all is well." They were already making plans to sell their livestock and furniture. The younger sister, Ann, was eager to come along to help with the children and be a companion. But then, "we have heard Matthew Willis['s] letter read which came to Carperby ... a good many things in it quite surprised us." They found Willis "discouraging" though "in some instances he speaks very favourable of America." The Willis family lacked "Good Black Tea" and wanted some from England. Furthermore, America's meat and pork were much inferior to England's; "[T]he swine run in the woods until they are Two years old consequently they are not so tender." Willis also seemed tormented by Wisconsin's hot weather and bug infestations and insisted that "anybody that can get a living in England [should] stay where they are."[22] A disheartened Edward Dinsdale responded "Is this any encouragement for those who are thinking of emigrating?"

Willis's letter was so frustrating for those still in Askrigg because it contradicted Matthew Dinsdale's own reports. "What a difference in descriptions," Edward Dinsdale remarked after reading both accounts. Edward absorbed his brother's caution about living in a new country: "[W]e cannot expect a newly settled place to be like a country that has been in habited many hundred years & where all appears to have reached to perfection ... America wants cultivation & there is an abundance of land to keep the inhabitants ... People who expect to find it a paradise should be disappointed."[23]

In addition to immigrant letters – though less important in deci-sion-making – were the emigrant guidebooks and pamphlets catering to the nineteenth-century mass migration to America.[24] Some contained accurate information and letters to help people make decisions about whether and where to go. It is unclear how influential these guidebooks were, but some immigrants read whatever they could get their hands on to prepare for their life-changing move. Occasionally we see proof that these guides were read. In an 1845 letter to his family still in Wensleydale, for example, Matthew Dinsdale compared what he found in Illinois with what he had read about it in a guide: "I think there is a very fair description of this district of country in the twelfth volume of 'Chambers Journal' entitled 'Eight months in Illinois.' I did think the picture rather too flattering, but I begin to fancy that it may be near the truth. But it applies more specially to the South of Illinois in some particulars."[25] Such references to guidebooks in immigrant letters are rare, but guidebooks would never have been published without a market for what they contained.

Political Factors

Though the main considerations for migration decisions could be lumped together as largely "economic," non-economic factors entered the equation too. One was America's greater political freedom, especially the right to vote.

Like much of England, Yorkshire felt pressure from the combined effects of industrialization and a rigid class system that resisted extending the franchise and created a sense of inferiority. Understandably, some turned to America in part to be free of such a system.[26] In November of 1856, for example, the *Hull Packet and East Riding Times* printed a letter "sent from America by a labourer late of Barton-on-Humber." Though the letter may have served the political agenda of the editor, it does contain an important truth about America's greater political freedom, and how that freedom was often wrapped up with economic prosperity: "I am going to be naturalized so that I can vote and become an American settler. I think to vote is a great privilege, that is, when one man is as good as another. Do you think I should ever have been able to vote in England if I was not rich? But I am rich enough in America to enjoy the privilege of a man, which is what I never should be in England ... Chickens we give away. If a poor neighbour has not got chickens nor milk, nor vegetables, they are welcome to them from those that have them. You are not so neighbourly in England as that."[27]

Preparations

After the migration decision came preparations. One of the most remarkable features of the letters and diaries of North Yorkshire migrants is the frequent reference to selling livestock, property, various goods, and sometimes land, to finance the move. These people were not among the poorest. Most seem to have had assets to sell, and some were even described as "affluent." This may be a bias inherent among the literate letter writers: unquestionably there was much distress, especially in the Dales during the 1830s, when the lead industry was declining most rapidly.[28] But even during distressed periods some did have enough capital to get to America and buy land. We have already seen this in the diary of Edward Broderick and his reference in 1833 to William Woodward's plan to sell his land, and how other emigrants quickly sold their belongings to friends and neighbours. The proceeds were not lavish, but neither were they insignificant. As Broderick witnessed: "John Bell has had his sale, both stock and furniture. I bought the plough, nearly new for 12s 6d … The little money that he has been scraping up to carry him to America, will, I doubt, go fast. William Woodward has had his sale of furniture and I have been writing for him. The sale was uncommonly well attended and the things sold well. They all kept their spirits well up considering they sold nearly all except bedding."[29]

The auctions of departing emigrants were often big events that attracted much attention. When Matthew Dinsdale returned to Askrigg in 1853 to wed Mary Ann Mann and take her and the rest of his family back to Wisconsin, they held such an auction in Askrigg. The published list of items for sale – especially the stock – is impressive: "7 spring calving cows, 1 Heifer, 4 Heifer Calves, 1 Yearling Colt, very promising, 8 Ewes; also, 3 Mows of Excellent-won Hay, 9 Acres of Rich Fog, and the Eatage of the Pasture Land. 2 Hay Sledges, Rakes, Forks, Spades, Shovels, Cow-bands, &c."[30] Though the proceeds of this auction are not known, they clearly put the Dinsdale and Mann families well above the poverty line. At the very least, we see an example of Yorkshire emigrants being quite typical: they had had some success in England – in farming, or crafts, or some sort of trade – and by using some combination of resources they not only got to America but soon bought land and prospered.[31]

Farewell

Once preparations had been made, it was time to leave. For some the parting was the most dreaded event in the entire experience, even worse than seasickness. For the young shoemaker Samuel Fowler Smith, leaving his parents and family behind in Wetherby in 1835 was so heartbreaking that he could not face it. He recounted the sad scene nearly forty years later, and the traumatic event was still all too fresh in his mind:

> The terrible ordeal now came of parting forever with my parents, and my sisters and brother … I dreaded the hour or parting. They had been for some time getting my things ready … The last moment came. We had all tried to keep up our spirits, though sadness was in our hearts. Mother, father and sisters were all sitting by the fireside. I walked backward and forward across the room, when, watching my opportunity I said, "I'm off" and shot out the back door and almost ran down the yard towards the orchard, and the gate that opens into the road. My mother and sisters gave one suppressed scream. The time occupied by that walk was the *bitterest moment* of my life. Truly the concentration of misery.[32]

For Matthew Dinsdale, twenty-nine, the parting was also extremely difficult and emotional. He preached on the Sunday before his departure in the chapel at Askrigg.[33] That night he recorded in his journal, with probably some understatement, that he "took leave of several of the congregation at the Chapel door. Did not go to bed. Was somewhat affected when parting with my friends, as probably the next time we may meet will be at the bar of God."[34] The next morning, he parted from his mother and siblings, visited his father's grave "and upon it implored the guidance and grace of God, and kiss'd the head stone thro' affection for the dead." He left Askrigg on 5 August 1844. His brother Edward accompanied him to Lancaster, where Matthew said his final farewells and took a schooner to Liverpool. "My feelings cannot be described after he had gone out of sight," Matthew recorded, "for I thought that I was alone, to contend against the world, but my God was with me."[35]

The departure was also hard for friends and neighbours who stayed behind. As Swaledaler Edward Broderick recorded in 1833, his friends the Woodward family have been packing up their things and taking leave of their friends and now when parting begins to be so near, we all find it to be very painful … I … found William busy packing the boxes and preparing to load carts. He possesses wonderful resolution … Though I had always thought favourably of America and believed they were acting wisely in going, yet I confess that my spirits were so much depressed at the thought of their long and dangerous journey and the difficulties which they would have to encounter that I felt very much inclined to persuade William to stay. They set off soon after 5 o'clock.[36]

Getting to the Port

After selling their possessions and leaving their village, the next step was to get to the port of departure. Liverpool was by far the most popular port; but Hull and Whitby were also common for those leaving North Yorkshire. For those who lived on the North York Moors or near the east coast, those ports were easier to get to, especially before the days of the railroad, and the route to America was a bit shorter (by going via the Pentland Firth, the straits separating the Orkney Islands from Caithness). Most important, the fares were usually cheaper because ships carrying timber from America needed passengers on the return trip to act as ballast, and most of these ships were bound for Quebec, which demanded more modest fares. About three-fourths of the English who headed for Quebec sailed from northern ports.[37]

Thus, like many English emigrants, those from North Yorkshire heading for the United States often arrived via Canada. British officials sometimes paid careful attention: over half of the 7,000 who disembarked in New Brunswick in 1841 proceeded almost immediately to the United States, where they were recorded by American officials as immigrants from the British Isles. Many others arriving in Canada crossed the border undetected. It is no wonder that immigration statistics for British immigrants to both Canada and the United States are notoriously deficient.[38]

North Yorkshire emigrants often left for their port in small groups, for mutual security and support. The scenes were unforgettable, as groups both large and small marched from their village to their local town, perhaps to buy last-minute necessities, and then say farewell, most likely

Figure 5.4   A shipwreck at the Port of Whitby, a common North Yorkshire port for those leaving the North York Moors.

forever. Sometimes the rest of the village marched with them, even playing music or singing hymns as they escorted them away. Some departures were reported in local newspapers, such as this one in the *York Herald*: "Emigration. – Several families, amounting to be-tween 50 and 60 persons from the Yorkshire wolds, passed through this city last Monday morning, on their route to embark for America; also, a number of families from Rainton, near Ripon, for the same destination."[39]

In 1842 Solomon Harker's group made their way on foot from Keld and over the moors to make the long journey to the nearest port. In 1844 another group of fifty was seen passing through Hawes, on their way over the moors toward Liverpool; it probably included Thomas Robinson and the Fawcett family, all miners.[40] The scale of the departure of people for America was at times huge – at least in relation to the size of local populations. In 1849, for example, Eleazer Chapman reported that "there are about 200 persons coming out of Swaledale to America at the present time."[41] Given that the total population of Swaledale was little more than 6,000 at mid-century, and that the dale was a tight, unified community linked by geography, economy, and culture, the departure of two hundred people at a time was a major event that affected the area. It was a sight that no one would forget, and one likely to inspire more to follow.

The scene of groups of people leaving their village and dale was often sad and touching, highly emotional, and permanently etched in one's memory. In the early years, carts and wagons were loaded up with belongings, and wives and children sometimes rode the cart while the men walked. Many would do the same as they travelled to their destination in America. Liverpool was about 160 kilometres distant and getting there required several days. Getting to Lancaster first and then sailing to Liverpool saved some time and effort.[42]

The route from the Yorkshire Dales to Liverpool was the same that hikers take for pleasure today: from Swaledale they could walk a track from Oxnop to Askrigg. Others at the head of the dale would take an even steeper and more arduous trek over the moors to Hawes in Wensleydale, passing the queer limestone geological pits known as the "Buttertubs." Once in Wensleydale the emigrants had access to the turnpike from Richmond to Lancaster, which was built in the middle of the previous century, and as emigrants they were usually exempt from the tolls.[43] Those who left from Wensleydale likely took the road passing Bainbridge, the ancient Roman military and lead mining base. From there they could walk the surviving Roman road for part of the way to Ingleton. Others would have taken the road to Hawes and then to Ingleton. Once there, the route to Lancaster was relatively easy: they could walk or sail to Liverpool or by mid-century take the railroad. Others got there via Preston. There were a variety of ways to get to the famous port, but each required great effort and expense in time and money.[44]

The sights the emigrants encountered on their way could be grim and depressing. Some walking to Hull passed pathetic scenes of people selling what little goods they had to leave the country. In Driffield, in the East Riding, the spring of 1830 was especially bleak. In March of that year the vicar, Revered Richard Allen, mourned the frequent emigrant sales – "one or two every week" because "the strength of the nation [was] removing very fast to America. Emigration injures the whole." The Thursday market sales that Allen witnessed indicated "extreme poverty."[45] Twenty years later Driffield saw another spike in emigration for America, as reported in the *Yorkshire Gazette*: "A larger number of emigrants are this spring going from every village in the neighbourhood of Driffield than has been known for a number of years past. The floodtide of emigration is to the American shores, principally Canada."[46]

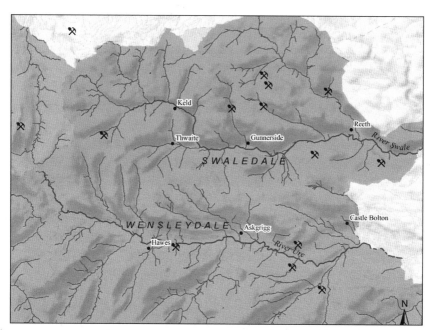

Figure 5.5   Map of Swaledale and Wensleydale, showing main villages and lead mine locations.

Some Dales emigrants got to Liverpool quickly by taking a short sailing from Lancaster, but even that could be an ordeal. When John Dinsdale left Askrigg in February of 1849 to join his brother Matthew in Wisconsin, all started well by getting to Lancashire by 8:30 that evening. Early the next day they got to Lancaster and boarded the "Dutchess" for only 3 shillings and sailed for Liverpool. "We had a rough passage," Dinsdale recorded in his diary, "and were all sick, very sick."[47] But this was nothing compared to the transatlantic journey.

6

The Journey

A ship is worse than a gaol. There is, in a gaol, better air,
better company, better conveniency of every kind; and a ship
has the additional disadvantage of being in danger.

SAMUEL JOHNSON

Like the act of parting, the overseas journey in the age of sail stretches our imagination. Today we cross the Atlantic sitting in cushioned chairs, eating hot meals, watching movies, and still complain about cramped seats on a seven-hour trip. We email messages, pictures, and even live video conversations, virtually erasing the vast distance. What migrants endured to make the trip in the nineteenth century is simply unfathomable today. Their journey meant weeks, if not months, of often terrible discomfort, danger, and too often death. The rigours of the journey say much about the people who made it – their strength and character, and what they eventually contributed to North America. North Yorkshire emigrants recorded remarkably vivid details of their voyage which reveal much about them and the ordeal that forever marked them. The voyage became an essential part of their identity.[1]

Waiting

Just boarding the ship and waiting to sail caused anxiety and frustration. Ill winds and low tides meant agonizing delays. Matthew Dinsdale was distressed not only by "all the confusion on board" but that there was "no Sabbath." Watching "several ships in motion," he and his fellow passengers were "very anxious that the ship should start."[2]

Delays at port also tormented those who followed Matthew to Wisconsin. In early 1846 two of his sisters joined him in Wisconsin: Jane and her husband Barzillai Chapman along with their children, and his other sister, Ann. Another sister, Dorothy, followed in 1847 or 1848 and soon married Thomas Alderson and moved to Dubuque. In 1849 Matthew's brother John and his wife Tirzah (Barzillai Chapman's sister),[3] their two children, and a large group of people, mostly from Swaledale but also Wensleydale, followed, on the detailed advice from Matthew and others. Having booked a passage on the ill-fated American ship *Saxony*, they too had frustrations as they waited to sail. Along with the Dinsdales were Hannah Buxton, fifty-eight years old and widowed in 1825; her son John (listed as a miner), and his wife Mary Buxton; Hannah's daughter, also named Hannah, and her husband John Pedelty and their five children – all from Gunnerside. Other North Yorkshire passengers included George Heslop, James and Jane Heslop, and young Thomas and Peter Walker from Askrigg, who had decided to emigrate after the death of their parents. On the passenger list we also see William Metcalf (misspelled as "Mitcalf"). The Calvert siblings are there – William as a farmer aged thirty-two, Ward as a miner aged twenty-five, Jackson as a miner aged twenty-two, and William's wife Jane, listed as a farmer's wife. In that one family we see how miners and farmers' occupations were compatible and interchangeable. Others from Swaledale and Wensleydale are also there. There is also the Arkengarthdale family of Ambrose and Ann Alcock, and their three children. This group shows how the three dales were connected by a common interest in America. John Buxton reported that "we are all from the neighbourhood of Swaledale except 1 score of Irish."[4] Altogether they formed a tight, familiar community of workers (nearly all farmers or miners), families, and faith, which proved vital for surviving the horrendous and deadly ordeal that lay ahead.[5]

Even before sailing, the party's problems mounted. The group had no idea how much to pay the man who fetched their luggage, and later realized they had been grossly overcharged. Nor were their lodgings acceptable, so they had to pay far more for other ones as they braced themselves for the big day.[6] The shadow of crime and dishonesty was all around them. Liverpool was infamous for the so-called runners, the thieves and con men who infested most ports. They would offer to carry luggage, only to run off with it; or offer currency exchange in phony American dollars; or lead emigrants to boarding houses that robbed guests; or steer them toward unscrupulous accomplices who picked their pockets, and so on. The variety of thievery was endless. Unfortunately, things were not much better in New York or most other American ports where unsuspecting immigrants were easily preyed upon. The only way to fight back was to heed the warnings from other immigrants. The letters and guidebooks almost always warned readers of these pitfalls and advised them how to avoid the crime that threatened their precious savings.

As they waited, the John Dinsdale party gathered to sing hymns, and several men and one woman led the people in prayers. "The Lord was present," Dinsdale recorded. But favourable winds were not: for a full week the *Saxony* was delayed, forcing the passengers off the ship to make their "tin slop pail run" and find hot water for their tea. Singing and praying and "a good prayer meeting" filled much of their time and afforded them some comfort. The singing of songs would reinforce their identity as "pilgrims" on a journey and reassure them that God was with them. But the delay was insufferable. As they waited anxiously, John's young daughter became terribly ill.[7]

John Buxton wrote his own account of the long and frustrating delay. While waiting for favourable winds he observed that "the captain is a steady man and we have a prayer meeting every night in the ship ... we have no candle no fire while we are in the dock but we can go into the Town to get our water boiled."[8] Apparently, each night they held a prayer meeting and walked into town together to get hot water, and perhaps release some of the tension from being stuck in Liverpool. But their religious faith was the most important way they had to cope with the fear and anxiety before sailing: Buxton wrote to his brother still in Gunnerside to "not forget to Pray for us that the Lord might Bring us safe to land ... and if we never meet again on earth may we have the Happiness to meet at gods right Hand."[9] Altogether, then, leaving one's village, family, and friends; journeying to the port on foot, cart, and later on perhaps, train; and waiting seemingly forever for the ship to sail, was exhausting and emotionally draining. It was also a time of intensified religious expression, as fears mounted.[10] Then came the voyage itself.

Sailing

There was some variety in sailing to America. Those who left Yorkshire from eastern ports to Canada took a route north of Scotland, but once on the Atlantic they followed the more numerous ships leaving Liverpool for the United States. And though each voyage had its own set of circumstances, storms and sickness were all but universal and were often terrible enough to create regret about leaving in the first place. Glaisdale shoemaker John Dixon, for example, was so horrified by his nightmarish voyage of 1832 from Whitby to Quebec aboard the *Columbus,* especially after his young niece perished only two weeks after leaving port that he confessed that "if I had known this, I would have begged my bread from door to door before I would have come." More children died on that voyage, but Dixon was also tormented by the ungodly behaviour of his fellow passengers, especially the "filthy language of several on board" and their drunken violence. For another North Yorkshire emigrant on the *Columbus,* Dr John Meburn, a surgeon from Whitby, it was far more horrific: he buried three of his children at sea.[11]

On their 1834 voyage from Whitby to Quebec, William Easton and his fellow passengers endured storms and sickness on an extreme scale: "[A] great number very sick ... the sea runs mountains high, it blew away our fore jib-boom and broke our top gallant mast, and the Carpenters was obliged to turn to and work make a new one Sunday afternoon, and put it up on Monday morning. I never saw men work so hard in my life as the sailors had to do."[12] The following day was even worse: "[I]t blew very hard and the sea very rough, it run mountains high, the ship rocked very much. A great many sick and some were tossed out of their beds in the evening and pots, pans, tins, chamber pots, water barrels, was knocking about in all directions." The voyage took six weeks plus one day.[13]

It was not always as bad as this. Matthew Dinsdale was lucky on his 1844 cabin voyage on the *St George.*[14] For this young and pious Methodist preacher from Askrigg, the foul-mouthed, irreligious American captain and crew were the worst part, as "from the Captain to the Cooks boy they were very much give[n] to cursing swearing two three of them at times were truly dreadful, they could scarcely speak without an oath, this practice was the most unpleased thing I met with on shipboard."[15] But Dinsdale was also sick, like virtually all the other passengers. "I now know what Sea Sickness is ... I was [so] sick that for 4 or 5 days I ate nothing or next to nothing and drank only a little soda water." Eventually his positive attitude pulled him through. Once he recovered, he was thrilled by the birds and porpoises racing along the ship that "appeared to be delighted by attempts to beat us."[16]

Dinsdale also recorded details about his sleeping arrangements and fellow passengers. In his cabin "there were two berths or places for beds in each room one above the other, the one next to mine (I secured the upper) was occupied by a Yorkshireman from near Hull, a medical gentleman who appears to be travelling about for pleasure. He was once in America before."[17] He got to know other passengers in the adjacent cabin as well. They included Americans and English, some who were making return visits, women joining husbands who had gone ahead, and some women who gave birth on board. Astonishingly, he also got to know a woman who had returned to England "to see her friends" and was now travelling again, alone, to her American home. Enduring a horrendous round-trip voyage to see friends may seem astonishing, but it reveals how tough these people were. Throughout much of the voyage all passengers were at times subject to a cacophony of screaming children and babies, the sounds and smells of retching and vomiting, and people slipping on the wet filthy floors of the ship – all of this to see old friends in England?[18]

At times the journey seemed unendurable, even for Dinsdale. After a brief respite he was again "seized with that dreadfull malady – Sea Sickness. I soon found that my best plan was to deliver myself up to my tormentor. My only relief was vomiting, and I was glad when I could freely do so ... I continued for a full week, being most of the time in bed, I believe I was never so ill in my life ... For four days I ate nothing and drank only a little soda water, and I began to fear I should be hungered to death, tho' I had plenty of food, Indeed the thought of eating used to make me sick ... I had quite a loathing for everything."[19]

Remarkably, after landing in New York and perhaps attempting not to frighten off his family from joining him someday, Dinsdale claimed – rather extravagantly – that "I now feel the benefit of the voyage, I have no doubt but that the sickness has been of much service to me."[20] Others claimed that the arduous voyage made them stronger, and more resolute about their decision to make it in North America.[21] The duration, tight quarters, and physical rigours strengthened some, perhaps in the spirit of "what doesn't kill me makes me stronger." The ocean barrier itself, one historian has concluded, "strengthened migrants' original commitment to America and compelled new Americans to look to the future rather than dwelling on the past."[22]

After landing in New York in September of 1844, Dinsdale's positive spin on his journey escalated in his first letter to his mother. In spite of a crash with a schooner early in the voyage, he had arrived safely, and "so far as the weather was concerned," he had a "very pleasant voyage" and "had no storms to encounter." In fact, "most of the sailors declared they had never witnessed such a pleasant voyage from England to this continent." In contrast, Dinsdale's journal, quoted above, recorded the vicious storms and seasickness that had racked his ship. Perhaps he was trying to lessen his family's anxiety and fear of making their own voyage someday. Thus, we see in Dinsdale's letters inconsistencies, some selective memory, and how the voyage could be a bundle of contradictions – ghastly bouts of sickness on a "very pleasant voyage" that was "of much service to me."[23]

The voyage was featured in Dinsdale's other letters and was no doubt much talked about by readers. A half-year after he left Askrigg, Dinsdale, now comfortably settled in Peddlars Creek, Wisconsin, wrote back to family and friends in the village on how to make the voyage, should they choose to join him:

A good and new ship should be secured. Let the emigrant apply to respectable parties in Liverpool. Great caution is necessary in selection of a vessel, and the cheapest is not always the most desirable. I would recommend everyone to keep out of the Steerage. That is the place for the Irish and for filth. Employ the Ships Cook, he will be worth all he may charge; all has to be prepared for him, and he bake's roast's or boil's as the case may be. The Emigrant should find all his own provisions, taking nothing but water from the Ship. Have a good stock of potatoes a ham or two according to family, some fresh meat to last say a week, some fresh baked bread to serve a few days … a little of the best Brandy in case of sickness. A person should have provision for six weeks, it would be better to have a little over rather run short.[24]

Matthew's brother John had no doubt read this letter carefully, and hoped that his voyage on the *Saxony*, which occurred four years later, would be spared some of the trauma. But it was far worse. After the long delay in Liverpool, as noted above, the *Saxony* finally met the right combination of winds and tides, and on 17 February 1849, the captain announced they were ready to go. "We then sailed away so very smooth we scarcely felt ourselves going," John Dinsdale recorded. But at the slightest motion at night some of the Yorkshire passengers got terribly sick. In the morning they recovered enough to notice the fine clear day and praise God for being "present with us."[25] The respite was short-lived.

Soon the *Saxony* ran into a storm that lasted from 27 February to 2 March. "Children crying, men and women praying, tubs and cans rolling about. It was truly dreadful," as John Dinsdale searched in vain for words that could convey the surreal nightmare that was unfolding on a ship reeking of vomit, sweat, and fear. After the first storm abated, the passengers thanked God for deliverance, but they were still "all very sick the next day" and so was the *Saxony*, with bulwarks smashed by the terrific waves.[26] The pitiful group then found that their cooked meat had gone bad, though the bread that the ship's cook had baked was good. The Dinsdales' two-year-old daughter Bessey had "grown very thin" after only a week out, and they had seven weeks to go. The first Sunday sermon on "how shall we escape if we neglect so great salvation" was well attended by the voyagers from Swaledale and Wensleydale.

The *Saxony's* passenger list is sobering: John and Mary Buxton's infant, Elizabeth, was born and died on the voyage. Altogether there were seven births on ship; of these, five died, in addition to three others. They were likely buried at sea, though there was a report in Yorkshire newspapers of at least one mother heading for America who "salted down the body" of her dead infant to bring it to New York "in a state of preservation."[27] John and Mary Buxton's mother Hannah was also "taken ill by shortness of Breath" but recovered. She was tough, having worked as an ore washer after the death of her husband George; but she too was traumatized on the voyage of 1849, recording upon their arrival in New Orleans on 29 April. The voyage was so rough that she was unable to write until they reached America. From the start of the voyage "the majority of the Passengers thought of no les than going to the Botom and many Began to make preparation for theire later end and the confusion made by the tins Pans and Boxes Being thrown from one side of the vesel to the other made it to seem really worse than what it was and we were in more danger of being hurt by the Boxes Being thrown about than of going to the Botom at many time were the Great Danger of Being thrown out of our berths By the vilent movement of the vessel."[28] And all of this before the *Saxony* had even reached the Atlantic.

Being ejected from one's berth by violent storms was not uncommon. Samuel Fowler Smith recorded on his 1835 voyage that "I lashed myself to the upper deck with a rope, and expected never to see the morning."[29] But along with terrifying dangers came the occasional joy. For Matthew Dinsdale's sister Ann, who sailed to join her brother in 1846, the journey was one of the best moments of her life, for on the ship she met a widower and married him later that year.[30] But especially in the age of sail, virtually all voyages were arduous at best and horrific at worst.

During storms at sea the possibility of dying in a shipwreck probably entered the minds of most passengers. Stories of shipwrecks were deeply embedded in the culture and were reported in local newspapers. This report in the *York Herald* in 1850 was typical in some ways, except that the passengers miraculously survived after the ship went down after nearly completing the crossing:

AN EMIGRANT SHIP LOST A shocking shipwreck was reported at Lloyd's last week, namely, the total loss of the ship Bridgetown, belonging to Liverpool, having on board 390 passengers, emigrants for America, whose escape, considering the fearful circumstances of the wreck, was most miraculous … . They had sighted the Banks of Newfoundland, and were bearing to the southward, with light breezes and foggy weather, when about mid-night she went upon a rock at Clam Cove, between Cape Ballard and Cape Race. The violent force with which she struck instantly aroused the emigrants, who rushed upon deck in a stale of great excitement, and the scene that ensued, when it was found that she was fast filling, and most inevitably go down, was painful beyond description. … The poor emigrants lost everything they possessed; many reached the shore with nothing on their persons but their night-clothes.[31]

Disease

As terrifying and deadly as storms were, disease took more lives. Only a week out of Liverpool, having survived their first storm, the John Dinsdale party aboard the *Saxony* now saw children succumb to illness. Dinsdale reported "six children dead since we came on board" and that by 8 April both the Buxtons and Heslops had lost one of their children. And then so did the Thomas Metcalf family, and then their cousin Eden. John Buxton captured a sense of the grief of his sister Hannah and her husband John Pedley: their youngest child "was taken ill by a fit and suffered very much and it was continued by the same till it was weak. But on Tuesday … it died and it was buried the same day."[32] And then, as if to mock them, the sea rose again to gale force winds and became, in John Dinsdale's words, "tremendous, rising at times like mountains and foamed in a dreadful manner," until "a wave – the greatest we had – came over, washed on of the hatchway houses away and some of the passengers got well dipped. Some of them rolled about and thought they were in the sea for some time." The captain would have lost the *Saxony's* top mast had he not "got the sails in, just in time."[33]

Cholera was the deadliest scourge on the ocean, especially in the 1840s when it reached epidemic proportions. The most notorious case voyage was the *India*, which left Liverpool for New York in 1847. In addition to the usual seasickness, a five-night storm shook the ship so violently that cargo and passengers were battered to the brink of destruction. And then, after four weeks of torture, a fever broke out and killed fifteen passengers, after which the captain himself died. Inadequate and poisoned water led to severe diarrhea, and the death toll continued. After eight weeks the *India* limped into New York. Twenty-six of her passengers were buried at sea, and one hundred and twenty-three more were near death and required emergency care.[34]

Two years before the sailing of the *India*, the Matthew and Jane Willis family boarded the *Hottinguer* in Liverpool and headed for New York (it arrived on 5 June 1845). On the same ship were friends and neighbours, including George Metcalf, aged fifty-three, and his sons Giles, aged twenty-one (who was listed as a cooper; George's occupation is not readable), and other sons Matthew and Richard – both in their twenties and listed as miners. Matthew Willis himself was listed as a farmer. He was forty-five years old, and with him were his wife Jane, thirty-three, and young sons John, Thomas, Matthew, and the infant James. It was Matthew, only two, who died and was buried at sea. So great was their loss that when they chose a farm near Mifflin, Iowa County Wisconsin, the Willis family named the farm "Rama," in memory of young Matthew. The name comes from Matthew 2:18: "In Rama was there a voice heard, lamentation, and weeping, and great mourning, Rachel weeping for her children, and would not be comforted."[35] Naming their farm in this way gives some sense of their deep anguish, their piety, and how the tragic voyage became the defining moment of their migration and apparently their entire lives.

Writing from Wisconsin the Willis family realized that their accounts of the voyage (and of their frigid winters) were discouraging their sister

Figure 6.1 "Rama" with the Willises' granddaughter Maggie Thomas Gardner, c.1880s.

Ellen back in Carperby from joining them. As their brother-in-law John Humphry informed them: "[Y]ou will perhaps say, well it might be better for you to come into America, myself think it would, but you send such Horifying accounts you terrify your sister Ellen that she dare not venture over the Sea into a country where the Frost is so exceedingly severe as allmost to Freeze the Kettle to the Fire." And yet Humphry notes in the same letter that others who read the letters were not deterred: "And yet as long a journey by Sea and Land as it is and as cold a climate in winter and a Hot one in summer there are many cases of people coming to your place every year for instance this spring there have set of [off] already from Swaledale and Arkindale [Arkingarthdale] from 100 to 200 persons and I suppose there are a good many more preparing to go immediately, now these persons have all either Friends or relations in our country and to your country they are going that is if providence permit ... a quantity have also set of out of Coverdale and Netherdale."[36]

Meanwhile, at the opposite end of North Yorkshire, others were leaving and boarding ships in Hull bound for Canada. One particularly well-documented case is that of Marmaduke Eckles. He was born in 1811 in Gilberdike, about 27 kilometres west of Hull in the East Riding, and married Hannah Levitt, who was born in 1810 in Bilton, northeast of Hull. Eckles rose to become a "successful manager" of a brick manufacturing industry; but that was not enough for he was highly ambitious, industrious, a lover of books, and aspired to more. He had resources – enough for passages for his entire family of twelve – and a brother-in-law, Benjamin Gates, who was in Illinois, encouraging him to join him as a brick maker and then turn to farming. It seems doubtful that the prosperous Eckles family would have come to Illinois without this family connection.[37]

On 16 May 1850 Marmaduke and Hannah Eckles and their ten children sailed on the American ship *Allen Brown* from Hull to New York. There were fifty-two passengers, all from Yorkshire or Lincolnshire, and as soon as the ship cleared the "Spurn" (a point on the tip of the East Riding north of the Humber Estuary), "all the passengers fell sick; first one and then the other." And though they felt better the following day, some passengers were already regretting their decision to emigrate. Two days after that most were sick again, and Eckles admitted he was "very sick while writing this." After six days at sea the passengers were talking about England, and Eckles believed that "if all had the chance to return, we should have very few left in the ship … Some are so homesick that they talk of coming back as soon as they get there. But I suppose it is a regular thing on board ship." A couple of days later there was "scarce any wind," and yet "the ship rolls most awfully. We scarce can keep upon our legs … Nothing but roll, roll, roll."[38]

On 29 May, in the chaos of one storm, casks of linseed oil broke loose and struck the passengers' berths so violently that "all the passengers jumped out of bed screaming and running in all directions. I never wish to see such a sight," Marmaduke Eckles recorded. "And with the smell of oil and the oil running about the decks and the ship rolling most dreadfully," the rest of the passage had a sickening stench. Moreover, "the decks have been so slippery that we can scarce walk about and everything seems to smell and taste of oil. It is a great nuisance," he recorded with understatement. Little wonder that he concluded, "I do not like the *Allen Brown*."[39]

To make matters even worse, the *Allen Brown* was running out of provisions toward the end of its crossing. Eckles recorded that "our provisions are getting very scarce – all our flour is off and we cannot buy any of[f] the captain or anyone else ... we cannot make anything of the oatmeal, only a little gruel at times ... If I had to provide for another voyage I should do very different from what I have ... We are all well, but begin to be very anxious to see America – our victuals are getting so scarce."[40] And though it was June, it was so cold on ship that "we are almost perished ... We have very poor fare – nothing but coarse bisquits and rice to eat ... the children are all crying from the cold."[41]

Return Voyages

Understandably the trauma of the voyage was enough for some to rule out ever repeating the experience. In fact, there are cases of travellers intending merely to visit America becoming permanent immigrants, so dreadful could the crossing be.[42] And yet some Yorkshire immigrants seemed unscathed by the ordeal and soon contemplated a return voyage just to visit relatives, if not to encourage them to join them in America. Sailing back to visit family may seem far-fetched, but it appears that such return journeys were not that uncommon. As John Humphry wrote from Low Thoresby in 1849 to his brother- and sister-in-law, Matthew and Jane Willis, in Wisconsin: "[A]nd another thing strikes me as strange, that tho' so many emigrate, yet [a] few come back again and most of these few stay a few weeks or months and then return here have been two or three over a while since but they have gone over again into their own western settlement. James Davy of West Witton twice before you went crossed over the Atlantic and twice returned again, he is gone the third time last spring and is doing well."[43]

Others downplayed the ordeal in hopes of transatlantic visits. In 1853 Richard Buxton – the other son of Hannah and brother of John – also settled in Benton. Soon he wrote back to family members in Gunnerside encouraging them at least to visit, with offers by his brother John to pay half their expenses. "Take him at his word and come along," Richard wrote, "it would do you good to cross the ocean."[44] But relatively few were so cavalier about an ocean voyage in the age of sail. And all emigrants on any ship were eager to see land and get ashore.

Landing

Sighting land and disembarking brought intense relief. But unless one intended to remain at the American port the journey was far from over. Except for those landing in New Orleans to take a boat up the Mississippi to the lead regions, most landed in New York. Their first perceptions were bewildering if not horrendous. The infamous runners and other shifty criminals of Liverpool had nothing on those of New York, where they had refined their evil craft to perfection. Marmaduke Eckles recorded in 1850 that even while his ship was anchored at bay, "there came on board swarms of boarding house-keepers, all pretending to be Englishmen, Yorkshiremen, Lincolnshiremen, or from any county they thought you came from. As soon as they knew that the ship had sailed from Hull, they were most of them from Yorkshire, but the truth was they were most of them from Ireland … Those are a set of infernal villains who would rob and cheat you out of the last farthing you had."[45] In addition there were disconcerting signs of poverty and desperation. In Montreal, many newly arrived immigrants were sick and penniless, had no place to go, and ended up sleeping "like dogs" in the streets.[46]

Proceeding inland was often more difficult than anticipated. Going west from New York in the days before the Erie Canal required following nature's route as much as possible and trekking through the wilderness far enough to reach the Ohio River. One early Yorkshire immigrant who recorded his experience was Thomas Hulme, a master bleacher who left to escape England's high taxation and the reactionary government. In 1817 Hulme headed for Ohio to locate a new home for his family of nine children, and his experience was quite typical for the time. "Leave Pittsburgh," he wrote in early June, "and set out in a thing called an ark, which we buy for the purpose, down the Ohio. We have, besides, a small skiff, to tow the ark and go ashore occasionally. This ark, which would stow away eight persons, close packed, is a thing by no means pleasant to travel in, specially at night. It is strong at bottom, but may be compared to an orange-box bowed over at top, and so badly made as to admit a boy's hand to steal the oranges: it is proof against the river, but not against the rain." The following day, "floating down the Ohio, at the rate of four miles [7 kilometres] an hour," Hulme experienced "lighting, thunder, rain and hail pelting upon us. The hail-stones as large as English hazle-nuts. Stop at Steubenville all night. A nice place; has more stores than taverns, which is a good sign."[47]

After the Erie Canal was completed in 1825, the trip west was much quicker, but not necessarily safe or comfortable. In 1833 William and Nancy Woodward and their children, and several others, left Swaledale and after six weeks at sea landed in New York. Then they took the Hudson River to Albany where they hopped on an Erie Canal boat to Buffalo, which usually took about nine days. Then from Buffalo they sailed on Lake Erie to Cleveland, and from there took the Ohio Canal to Akron. There they loaded all they had on an ox cart, which was so crammed full of their belongings and supplies that all but the mothers and babies had to walk, carrying bundles. The Woodwards finally reached the home of their brother-in-law and former neighbour, John Bell (who had married William's sister Ann) in Sharon, Median County, Ohio, but were crushed to find that Ann had just died. Not only that, they found that the Bells were so poor they could offer the exhausted arrivals nothing to eat.[48] Hunger was not something they had bargained for in America.

Other Yorkshire immigrants faced similar disappointments and dangers. Those who took the Great Lakes might not have reckoned how dangerous they can be. Any complacency from having survived the transatlantic voyage could soon evaporate on the Great Lakes. William Coates and his wife and son safely arrived from Swaledale in 1842 and headed to Chicago via the Erie Canal, but on Lake Erie they were shipwrecked and lost all they brought with them. They managed to get to Dubuque where William took up mining.[49]

Some journeys west were relatively easy, even pleasant. For Matthew Dinsdale – who after his arrival in New York in 1844 also went to Albany to take the Erie Canal to the Great Lakes and then to Wisconsin – the journey was an enjoyable adventure. "The scenery on the banks of the River in many places is quite of a romantick kind," observed the native of Wensleydale, "being rocky, steep, and covered with timber ... The next morning I found myself in the beautiful valley of the Mohawk ... The canal ascends this vale for a distance of more than 1000 miles [1,600 kilometres] with the river frequently by its side and mostly in view."

Dinsdale loved the colours of the American autumn and made comparisons with his favourite places in Yorkshire: "The scenery is rich and varied being formed of water, cultivated ground, and hills covered with trees, displaying foliage of various hues. There were also to be seen neat cottages, pleasant farm houses and flourishing towns and cities. Many parts of it strongly reminded me of Wensleydale...the whole distance I travelled along the canal was between three and four hundred miles

[500 and 650 kilometres], leaving at Buffalo. I quite enjoyed this part of the journey, the weather being fine, and the Boat going so slow I could walk as fast along the tow path. And this I frequently did."[50] Impressed by the "vast number of orchards" whose fruit was "ripe and delicious," Dinsdale summed up the scenery by admitting that "it would not blush were it placed beside the fairest portions of England, beautiful and rich as that country is."[51]

For any immigrant lucky enough to take a detour on the way west, Niagara Falls was the highlight of the journey, if not of one's life. It was an experience that defied most descriptions and inspired poetry and deep spiritual reflection. Many English immigrants' descriptions are filled with awe, and once again Matthew Dinsdale's took on a distinctly North Yorkshire twist: "I left the canal at Lockport thirty one miles [50 kilometres] from Buffalo ... and went by railway twenty miles [30 kilometres] to Niagara to see the Falls." At the bottom of the falls he collected "several nice pebbles and should I ever visit England I can treat my Friends by presenting them with one each." Matthew tried to describe the Falls by comparing them to the famous but relatively puny ones near his native village. "The best description I can give you of this view," he continued, "is by saying that the Ure just above Asgarth bridge resembles it, only not on so great or grand a scale ... and no pen is capable of describing it. The immense body of water, the height and extent of the falls, the rich and wiles scenery around, the roar of the water, the dense and immense columes of smoke rushing as from a mighty furnace below, conspire to form a picture too great and too grand to be portrayed." And a bit later in the letter he admits: "I have just read over my feeble effort to describe the falls of Niagara. You must pardon my folly for making the attempt. This task is infinitely beyond my power. And I am ashamed for what I have written."[52]

Going West

Like most Yorkshire immigrants heading west, Dinsdale relied on friends who had gone before him. Three months after leaving Wensleydale, Dinsdale arrived at Kenosha, Wisconsin (which was called Northport at the time) and then walked just south of the border to the small town of

Albion, at English Prairie, in McHenry County, Illinois. Here his friends, including Peter Sill and his family, originally from Askrigg, had recently settled and gave Dinsdale advice and help, just as Dinsdale himself would soon do for others coming from the Yorkshire Dales. Altogether this was a classic example of "chain migration."[53] Matthew Dinsdale benefited greatly from the Sill family at English Prairie. It made his early adjustment to American life easier, and while living with the Sills he worked making rails, building fences, killing hogs, hauling wood and logs, and doing various farm chores. He also preached on Sundays. In Albion, Dinsdale and the Sills surely talked about their native Askrigg, which must have cheered them both.

Albion and English Prairie were founded in 1817 by English immigrants George Flower and Morris Birkbeck, who sought to create a colony in which English settlers could live among fellow expatriates in the new world. This was not the only such attempted colony, the other notable ones being at New Harmony, in Posey County, Indiana, and Englishtown in Athens County, Ohio. But significantly, all these colonies soon dissolved because the English, unlike other European immigrants, already had the language and basic cultural traditions that enabled them to mingle more easily with most Americans. English ethnic communities might have seemed a good idea early on, but soon they were self-evidently pointless. Few saw any need to restrict themselves to colonies, which in any case became diluted by other American settlers. Such was the case with Albion. It was a foothold for English immigrants like Matthew Dinsdale, who then went to other parts of the Midwest to become a magnet for friends and family leaving Yorkshire for America.[54]

Dinsdale's move to America was ultimately religious in purpose and character, and this too channelled him to Wisconsin. Within a month of his arrival he was "received into the quarterly conference of the Methodist Episcopal Church" and admitted as an accredited Wesleyan local preacher.[55] This is a good example of how the religious denominations planted by the English in previous generations flourished and became conduits for later English immigrants. Through the churches, transatlantic communications thrived. Their common theology, liturgy, and denominational organizations allowed newcomers like Matthew Dinsdale to feel relatively at home through a familiar religious expression. And Dinsdale hit the ground running, for he soon joined the Rock River Conference and was

Figure 6.2   Map of the Mississippi River Region.

assigned the Potosi circuit in southwestern Wisconsin. This was the lead mining district where North Yorkshire miners had been thriving and attracting more immigrants to the New World. As we shall see, future emigrants from the Dales wrote to Dinsdale for reliable information to get to the Upper Mississippi.

From New Orleans to the Upper Mississippi

For those miners heading for the Upper Mississippi, landing in New Orleans and steaming upriver seemed the best route. But getting to New Orleans took more time than getting to New York, and the trip up the Mississippi had its own set of challenges – some of them totally unexpected, some ghastly, the worst part of the journey. For the Dales families who survived the wretched voyage aboard the *Saxony* to New Orleans, the river trip became a nightmare. That large group had left Swaledale so optimistically in 1849, only to endure the hellish conditions described above. After fifty-four miserable days at sea the *Saxony's* passengers were nearly out of provisions as they limped into the Gulf of Mexico, and it was at this point – only a day or two before docking – that George Heslop's seven-year-old son died and was buried at sea.[56] They landed in New Orleans on 30 April 1849. Now, on the way up the Mississippi during one of the region's worst cholera epidemics, the nightmare unfolded.[57]

Cholera was terrifying for its grotesque, agonizing symptoms and high mortality, and for the frightening speed with which it attacked and killed its victims. Mid-century Wisconsin newspapers carried stories of how leading citizens of Madison were in perfect health one day but dead the next. In Milwaukee two men were discussing the cholera that had struck their city and within a couple of hours one of them had died and was being prepared for burial. Many could make no more sense of it than to describe it as "The Scourging hand of an Almighty Providence."[58] Victims who panicked and fled spread the disease. This was the world that some of the Dales immigrants were entering at mid-century.

Cholera on the Mississippi had struck newcomers from Swaledale before, even those who had disembarked in New York. The victims included Mary Bonson, wife of Robert Bonson, both fifty-two. They had left Swaledale with their four adult children and sailed on the *Hark Away*, arriving in New York on 9 June 1834. From there it took them three weeks to take the Erie Canal to the Ohio River, and then to the Mississippi up to Dubuque, but it was on the Mississippi that Mary died of cholera. Her husband and children buried her on the riverbanks near St Louis and continued to Dubuque in what must have been an agonizing conclusion to a difficult journey. This story repeated itself only a few years later when Elizabeth Brunskill, from Gunnerside, died on the same journey, her husband Simon and three children continuing to Dubuque.

And the same tragedy occurred yet again for Elizabeth Metcalfe, wife of Lister Washington Metcalfe.[59]

The 1849 immigrants who took the *Saxony* and were now steaming up the Mississippi had arrived at the height of one of America's worst cholera epidemics. In that year a tenth of St Louis's population died of that dreaded disease.[60] As the survivors continued north, those who awaited them in Wisconsin were fully aware of the epidemic and dreaded the worst, knowing that cholera was already claiming victims in their own area. Matthew Willis recorded in his letter of 3 June 1849 that "the Cholera has been in Mineral Point these 2 or 3 last weeks, and a few deaths have occurred from that awful malady."[61] Their sense of relief on the arrival of the survivors was palpable in their letters back to Yorkshire: after the group arrived in Wisconsin, and John Dinsdale and his family had joined his brother, Matthew wrote excitedly to his mother on the safe arrival of his brother John: "It gives me much satisfaction to be able to inform you that John and his family have arrived in Wisconsin quite safe and in good health, and I may add good spirits … I had been to a Bible class we have in operation, and on my return found message had been lost by a gentleman who had passed them that my brother and his family were close at hand … Almost immediately after I heard the approach of a wagon, and going I met John. I hardly dared to expect them all alive and well on account of the prevelance of sickness on the Mississippi." And Matthew continued: "For three weeks at least I was calculating on hearing every day that disease had taken some of them," he admitted, and credited the "mercy of God" for the survivors, while "the Cholera seizes on the inebriate and dissolute and generally carries them off … Several died of the scourge in the boat John came up the river on and has told me the most of them were of intemperate habits."[62]

John Dinsdale wrote his own letters to his mother in Askrigg from New Orleans and another from Wisconsin, and his mother replied with a combined sense of relief and grief: "My dear John, Whe received your welkom letter from New Orleans it was the Best Letter that came … I was in hopes then you had got the worset past but lo in a few weekes your Father in law called and teuld hous one of your childer was dead … but when whe heard you were all alive & safe All Burst into tears Tha whar tares of Joy."[63] Others were not as lucky: Ambrose Alcock from Arkengarthdale, his wife Ann and daughter Sarah, did make it to Galena, only to die in May, almost certainly of cholera.[64]

Some survivors developed second thoughts about their migration. Successful settlement required years of hard work, either mining or farming or doing both in the Upper Mississippi. It sometimes required many years before doubts faded, if they ever did. Adjusting to life and the environment of the Upper Mississippi took much time and effort, for despite some similarities, the region was very different from North Yorkshire.

The Upper Mississippi

[Iowa's] miners, like those of Galena, are worse than savages.

EMIGRATION (1849)

Yorkshiremen were not the first to produce lead in the Upper Mississippi region. Native Americans had been doing that for more than a century, as observed in 1700 by the French explorers who discovered lead in an area on the Fevre River (which was named after a French trader and soon known as the "Fever River," then renamed Galena in 1826 to end the negative connotations and draw attention to the mineral ore by that name).[1] The early miners were few. In 1743 French traveller M. le Guis counted "eighteen or twenty" miners digging in the Fevre River area, each man working for himself and making barely enough for subsistence with their primitive and wasteful smelting methods.[2] But knowledge of the Upper Mississippi was growing. In 1763 a Francis Benton worked there long enough to lend his name to Benton, Wisconsin. And in 1766 a traveller named Jonathan Carver drew a map that indicated the location of crude mines south of the Wisconsin River, which caught the attention of those hoping to strike it rich.[3]

The biggest early strike was made west of the Mississippi River by Julien Dubuque, a French Canadian. Born in 1762, he had worked as a clerk for the Indian trade based in Michilimackinac in Michigan and in about 1783 became the first known European in Iowa. There, in 1788, he met with a full council of Sauk and Fox Nation – collectively known as the Meskwaki – who granted him a permit "to work lead mines tranquilly and without any prejudice to his labors."[4] One of Dubuque's richest mines had been discovered eight years earlier by the wife of Peosta, a Fox warrior. Dubuque successfully petitioned the Spanish governor of Louisiana for a tract of mining land and called it "The Spanish Mines" to honour the

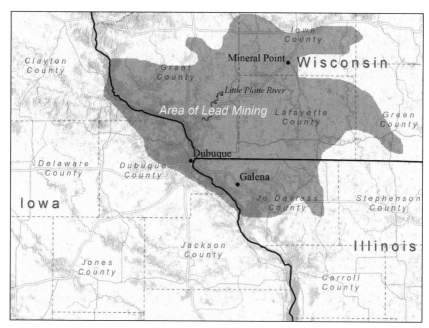

Figure 7.1   Map of the Upper Mississippi, centre of lead mining in the United States, where Yorkshire Dales miners had a great impact.

nation that still had claim to the territory. Twelve years later the French gained sovereignty, only to sell it to the Americans in 1803 as part of the Louisiana Purchase. For twenty-two years Dubuque had lived peacefully with the Native Americans and controlled the lead fields, allowing no other white person to trespass without his permission.[5] In 1808 Governor Meriwether Lewis appointed Dubuque to serve as the Indian Agent for the Upper Mississippi, but he served for only a couple of months because his health was declining. He died in 1810, and naturally, the town that was taking shape on the west bank of the Mississippi took his name.

Native peoples had produced lead for bullets, for use and trade, and even after Dubuque's arrival their methods were basic to say the least: "Large logs would be placed on the ground and smaller pieces of wood piled around and the ore heaped on. The fire would be set in the evening and in the morning shapeless pieces of lead would be found in ... small holes scratched in the earth under the logs; or sometimes in shapeless masses."[6] Dubuque and other French newcomers improved the techniques, but even their methods were very simple, as recorded by an eyewitness in 1819:

A hole was dug in the face of a piece of sloping ground, about two feet deep and as wide at the top. This hole was shaped like a mill-hopper and lined with flat stones. At the bottom or point of the hopper, which was eight or nine inches square, narrow stones were laid across, gratewise. A trench was dug from the sloping ground inward to the bottom of the hopper. This channel was a foot in width and height, and was filled with dry wood and brush. The hopper being filled with the ore and the fuel ignited, in a few minutes the molten lead fell through the stones at the bottom of the hopper, and thence was discharged through the trench over the earth. The fluid mass was then poured into an awkward mould, and as it cooled it was called a "plat," weighing about 70 lbs., very nearly the weight of the "pig" of later days.[7]

Despite other incremental improvements, huge amounts of timber for fuel were still required and most of the lead lay wasted in the slag heap.

Dubuque prospered by expanding and diversifying his labour force. He employed Native Americans to find lead, often allowing them to work the mines for themselves, and he brought in Canadians to help. By the time he died, Dubuque's operations had helped unify the lead region of the Upper Mississippi – in what is now Northwestern Illinois, Southwest Wisconsin, and East Central Iowa – and bring it into early, proto-industrial production. Native Americans remained active in the nascent industry. In 1815 they operated some twenty crude furnaces in the Galena area alone, and their product was bought by French Canadian traders, who used it as a form of currency or sold it for ammunition. In 1820 it was estimated that several million pounds of lead had already been produced by Dubuque's men, both European and Native American.[8]

But changes were already underway. After the US Congress allowed leases to be granted to individual miners in 1807, people arrived in greater numbers, mainly prospectors and squatters from Kentucky, Tennessee, and Missouri.[9] According to a report made in 1826 by the US superintendent of lead mines, Lieutenant M. Thomas, the numbers of people mining in the Galena diggings grew from about 100 in mid-1825 to 453 in little more than a year later.[10] The economy and population grew further when General George W. Jones established a smelting operation about 10 kilometres east of Dubuque, where Native Americans delivered ore by canoe in exchange for blankets and other provisions they desired.[11] Generally, 1822 through 1832 were lead rush years in the Upper Mississippi, a much smaller version of the legendary California Gold Rush a generation later. About 4,000 miners came to the region during this time, especially to Mineral Point, Wisconsin, and Galena. Most were white, but black and Indigenous people arrived too, often mining side by side. There was considerable diversity in the region. The 1830 census recorded for Jo Daviess County, Illinois, and Iowa Country, Michigan Territory (which was soon to be in Wisconsin Territory) showed not only 3,594 whites, but 104 black people, and an estimated 11,400 Native Americans, mainly Winnebagos and Sauks and Mesquakie.[12] In the late 1820s, however, aggressive settlers took over the Native Americans' mines and the resulting tensions helped spark the Winnebago Revolt of 1827 and the Black Hawk War of 1832.[13]

Like the later gold rush, the lead rush gained momentum from reports of miners making hundreds of dollars in a single day. Tantalizing stories were already circulating in the Midwest by 1826,[14] and soon made their way to Yorkshire. The lead rush probably peaked in 1827, when miners swarmed over the region. A female resident of Galena observed that "from the slope of the hill, you could see as far as the eyes could reach, miners' shanties, and windlasses in activity … the store was furnishing tools and provisions to hundreds of miners. Three four-horse teams making regular trips to town every other day, could hardly supply the demand or transport the lead, smelted night and day."[15]

At the same time lead mines were opening in Missouri, but for several reasons they held little appeal for Yorkshire settlers. In 1829 the state stopped granting mining leases to new miners, and its farmland was not as good. Opportunities for combining mining with farming were far greater in the Upper Mississippi. Perhaps most significantly, Missouri had entered the Union in 1821 as a slave state, and slavery made it repulsive to many immigrants, especially the English.[16] There is the exception of Nathan Haley, who left Great Horton, near Bradford, in 1820, went to mine lead in Missouri, and used his earnings to engage in trade. Haley did not see slavery as much of an issue, insisting to his father in 1823 that "Slaves in this part are well off, better than your paupers, and their children is not sent to work in factorys as white children is with you sixteen hours per day."[17]

Mining in the Upper Mississippi briefly stalled in 1830 when future president Zachary Taylor, who was serving as military commander at Fort Crawford, Prairie du Chien (in what is now Crawford County,

Wisconsin), visited the Dubuque mines. Acting under orders from the War Department, he abolished the settlements and ordered the miners back across the Mississippi because they were not yet legal – the treaty with the Mesquakie at the end of the Black Hawk War had not yet been ratified. Taylor sent troops to Dubuque to enforce the order and prevent the miners from returning. Two years later rowdy miners did return, so Taylor sent in more troops from Prairie du Chien to expel them once again. Finally, after the treaty was ratified, in mid-1833, about 500 people rushed to the Dubuque mines. A key date in the mining history in the region was 26 June 1834, when Congress permitted public land in Iowa and Wisconsin lead districts to be sold into private hands. And in the following few years they were joined by hundreds more, so many that in late 1836, a year before Dubuque was incorporated, the population had grown to an estimated 1,300.[18] Among the newcomers were those from Yorkshire, who were already revolutionizing the local mining and smelting industry.[19]

An Alien World

Yorkshire immigrants found a rough, alien world in the Upper Mississippi. They had left an ancient culture that dated back to the Romans for one that was still in its infancy – at least in Western cultural terms. The first impressions must have been appalling: Dubuque had no federal agents to provide order and protection, so it was much like the Wild West, with much violence among brutal men. Lynchings, murders, knife fights, and public floggings were not uncommon.[20] In the summer of 1834, while some of the first Yorkshire miners were getting settled, the Dubuque community was preoccupied with news of a man named O'Connor, who had murdered his business partner. Twelve men were chosen for the jury and found O'Connor guilty. He was hanged in the town centre "in the presence of many hundred people."[21] Miners commonly carried pistols and bowie knives, as did the criminals and gamblers who preyed upon them. Quarrels over land claims resulted in gun fights, and when one man ran off with someone else's canoe loaded with lead, he was caught and given thirty-nine lashes in public not far from Main Street.[22] Between 1833 and 1836, even as early Yorkshire immigrants were trickling in, Dubuque was marked by "wanton outrages of personal violence" due mostly to disputes over mineral claims. Justice and order were capricious: when a Patrick

Brennan clubbed a John O'Mara to death after being provoked, he was only given a public tarring and feathering and expelled.[23]

One especially sensational murder case could not have escaped the attention of newcomers from Yorkshire. Due to a claim dispute, a Mr Woodbury Massey (who was one of the founders of the Methodist Church in Dubuque) was shot and killed in September of 1835 by a Mr Smith. Massey's younger brother then retaliated and shot Smith dead in the street. When Smith's younger brother vowed revenge on Massey, Massey's sister Louisa entered a store Smith was in, and shot him. A thick pocketbook prevented the bullet from killing Smith. He then pursued Louisa, who fled to Illinois. She eventually made her way back to Iowa and became something of a folk hero for avenging her brother's murder: Louisa County, established in late 1837, was named after her.[24]

The lawlessness of other parts of the Upper Mississippi disturbed newcomers from Yorkshire. Edmund Alderson had left Arkengarthdale in 1839 and settled in New Diggings, Lafayette County, Wisconsin. Four years later he wrote to his brother back in Yorkshire that "The only faults [I] find with this place is the wickedness of the people ... [A] mans life is no more valued than the life of a dog Every man cary [carries] his bucknife or pistols, if two men quarrel they fight with Knives pistols clubs axes or anything they lay there hands upon."[25]

But early Dubuque was especially rough. A modern historian describes the Dubuque mining community as "generally restless young people of all social ranks ... Their goal was wealth, excitement, or both ... The women were generally adventurous sisters and wives." This made it "an inflammable region," according to Michigan territorial governor Lewis Cass, when he toured the region in 1827.[26] Drinking and gambling fuelled violence, especially in all-male mining shacks that had been hastily thrown together near the shafts. In 1830 the lead region of the Upper Mississippi had only a few clergy, along with a handful of lawyers and physicians. But there were lots of saloonkeepers. Most of the farmers were Native Americans because whites had only come in to get rich fast by mining lead.[27] In 1836 there was still not a single brick building in Dubuque, and only a few frame buildings. The first district court session was held in a log hut.[28] And not until 1855 did a railway finally reach Dubuque. Galena was just as squalid, if not more so, with its rickety shacks huddled along the river and streets often knee-deep in mud. People there admitted that "Galena was remarkable for its wickedness," and shootings among miners were common.[29] One Dubuque woman wrote to a friend that in Galena "there is no morality ... Drinking, Swearing and Carousing is the order of the day. I have frequently been asked where I thought Hell was located. I think I could answer the question now. I believe it is here."[30] This, then, was the world that the pious, upright, mostly teetotalling families from North Yorkshire and other parts of England were entering.

But North Yorkshire immigrants included some of their own unsavoury, even criminal characters. In 1848 Yorkshire newspapers carried graphic stories of Swaledale miners with surnames common in North Yorkshire and familiar in the Upper Mississippi – Simon Brunskill, William Bell, George Buxton, and George Calvert, as well as Ralph Tiplady and Francis Close – committing violent drunken assaults in Askrigg, and seriously injuring several innocent people. They were convicted, fined, and served two months of hard labour in Northallerton. Unfortunately, it is not possible to know for certain if they then left for America, but this rather shocking episode does suggest it was possible that some violent Yorkshiremen did eventually make their way to North America, where their evil deeds were forgotten, or at least never made it into the historical records.[31] The weight of the evidence we do have, however, indicates that the North Yorkshire immigrants were overwhelmingly law-abiding, honest people with a fierce work ethic and deep religious faith. And for them the lack of religion on the Upper Mississippi frontier was distressing.

Lack of Religion

For the many Yorkshire newcomers the godlessness was the region's worst problem. Dubuque's first formal and public religious service occurred in 1833 – and it was Catholic. The first Methodist church, consisting of a log hut, was built a year later.[32] The lack of institutions, of piety, of much religious life characterized most frontier mining towns, especially those along the Upper Mississippi. Writing in early 1845 from Peddlars Creek, near Mineral Point, Wisconsin, Matthew Dinsdale, who was by then preaching regularly in the area, declared to family and friends back in Wensleydale that "everywhere there is an anxiety to hear the Gospel preached. My prayer is that the great head of the Church may bless my feeble efforts."[33] Improvement did not come quickly enough for the impatient Dinsdale, for a few months later, in October 1845, he again reported that in the area of

Potosi, Wisconsin, where he was now working as a Methodist circuit rider, "I find religion is at a low ebb, and a too general indifference prevails ... There are probably good reasons to be given for the present cold state of the Church; the principle of which is that there has not been sufficient ministerial labour among them of late. They have no Local Preachers and those sent by the Conference for the last two years have not been much with them, owing to sickness and absence. They have been for weeks at a time without any preaching."[34]

It wasn't just the young preacher Dinsdale who bemoaned the lack of religion. As late as the mid-1850s Richard Buxton reported that "with regard to religious maters we are but at low ebb at Benton. I should like to see a better day I fell it is desirable may the Lords help us Brethren pray for us."[35] Thirty years later Buxton was still not satisfied, as in 1881 he wrote to family members in Gunnerside that "I am sorry to say that the society [in Benton] is in a low condition and we need a revival of religion the people are to worldly mind."[36]

Yorkshire Women in the Upper Mississippi

The raw and violent culture of the early Upper Mississippi shocked Yorkshire men and women alike. Nothing could have fully prepared them; but the women seem to have handled it in their stride as they helped transform their new world into what they would have called "civilized." The Upper Mississippi posed new problems. Stories of Indigenous men threatening white settlers circulated widely and were whipped up by prejudice and racism. Women had more to fear from whites. Everywhere, it seemed, there was swearing and drunkenness, and there were cases of women in the camps being brutally raped and abandoned.[37] The English were among the culprits. Dinsdale remarked that the place called British Hollow, "where several English people reside ... [was a] ... notorious place for grog drinkers. Many of the foreigners give themselves up to this vile practice, the English among the rest."[38]

The lack of religion and refinement on the mining frontier of the Upper Mississippi had much to do with the imbalance of women and men. Being outnumbered by about three to one when they started arriving, Yorkshire women could see it was still a rough man's world in most ways and that they could play a part in bringing religion, manners, and domesticity to the uncultured area. It was an uphill battle. As late as 1845, John Hodgson, who had left Yorkshire for Madison and then proceeded to the lead region, wrote back to his parents on the east coast of Yorkshire, giving his early impression of Wisconsin. There was a shortage of eligible women. As he put it: "[Y]ou need not tell my girl not to come for girls are very scarce here. They are all batchelors around about us ... You must give my respects to friends. ... Tell them I could be very much at home if I could have a Misses around. Well, a man is free here and there are several rich widows. I am the poorest man in the territory. You might bring a flock of lassies."[39]

The shortage of women was partly due to a lack of opportunities. As Matthew Dinsdale emphasized to his family back in Askrigg in 1846, "I would not wish that any young woman to come here in search of a fortune; there are in almost all parts of the country, even in the newly settled west, a great number of respectable young females who have little or nothing to do except to attend to family affairs. Needlework, washing, and domestic service may allow some to get along in a way, but if they have to do these think my opinion is that they had best stay at home."[40]

Despite the dangers and roughness of the mining areas, the region did offer certain advantages and brighter prospects to Yorkshire women. Their relative shortage made them scarce and desirable. Single women, so often exploited in Yorkshire, could usually do better in the Upper Mississippi. Here women did not wash or dress ore, as in Yorkshire, but rather filled more appealing occupations. Because domestic servants were in greater demand in America they were typically treated better there. Isabella and her husband Richard Buxton knew this well when they wrote back to Gunnerside around 1855 to encourage families with girls to join them in Benton "as it would be so much better for the family the girls would do so much better and there is so many wanted and I can assure you they are not made like as the girls that is servants are in England. They are made more like their own family ... I do assure you they all eat together and they would not be called servants and they consider they have the Sunday to themselves."[41]

Environment and Landscape

In the Upper Mississippi both women and men from Yorkshire confronted living conditions scarcely imaginable in England. In 1846 a storm forced

Matthew Dinsdale to spend the night in a log hut where he had preached, and the conditions he described in his journal were experienced by other Yorkshire immigrants during their first years in primitive America:

> I am now writing in a log cabin about ½ a mile from the house where I preached and remained all night … my pony is tied to a log with a blanket over him, there being no stable for him to creep into. The family abode is open to the roof, and from the roof in places to the sky allowing the breeze to fan you and the rain to sprinkle you now and then. For a floor the half is solid earth, the other half where the beds are, solid plank. There are several children and one stranger besides myself and the host and hostess … So our room is in turns or all at once used for every purpose. Nursery, eating room, study, &c … The goodwife is baking upon the table where I now write, so if you cannot read you will see the need of being lenient.[42]

Even in more settled mining settlements, housing was rough and often ugly. The shoddy appearance of the Upper Mississippi mattered to settlers from North Yorkshire. They had left ancient villages that, though perhaps poor, were still orderly, tidy, and picturesque. Yorkshire villages meshed delightfully with the dramatic beauty of the landscape, which itself had been sculpted by nature and people, so that the hills, walls, churches, and cottages were made of the same honey-coloured limestone. The special beauty of the Yorkshire Dales was important enough to some that the prospect of leaving it for America was a reason not to go, or at least to hesitate to go. Matthew Dinsdale suggests this in a letter he wrote in 1845, observing that "my sister Elizabeth thinks that America cannot be so beautiful as a certain portion of Wensleydale … There is scenery in my own native dale that probably cannot be surpassed for variety and beauty, and I am quite willing that she should consider it the most delightful portion of the world."[43]

Architecture mattered too, and in this the Upper Mississippi could not compare with North Yorkshire. "We have no cloud-capped towers, no gorgeous palaces, no dismantled castles and monasteries," Dinsdale admitted about his new home in Wisconsin. Of course, his native North Yorkshire was extraordinarily rich in that regard: Bolton Castle, which to this day dominates the village of Castle Bolton and much of Wensleydale, was just one of many local ancient landmarks. However, America did

Figure 7.2   Bolton Castle, a medieval fortress where Mary Queen of Scots was held captive, still dominates much of Wensleydale today.

offer something else. Dinsdale saw Yorkshire's architectural treasures as but "fragments of a former age of superstition and vassalage" while in Wisconsin there were "no narrow fields confined by petty hedgerows as if to prevent their escape. We have no macadamized roads nor marble bridges. And because these are lacking some may not like America nor yet American scenery ... however we have a broad open country that shows its face and is not ashamed to be seen. When you look at it you can see it in all its freshness and strength."[44]

Dinsdale had a point, but he ignored what appalled many other English immigrants: the mutilated landscape that was common in areas recently opened to mining and farming. The clearcutting and burning of virgin forests left a charred and horrid landscape dominated by blackened stumps, which brought to the mind of some the appearance of hell. As one remarked when settling in Ohio: "What a contrast to the beautiful and fragrant hedge rows of Old England do the bare zigzag wooden fences of Ohio present! And how disfigured its luxuriant crops by the half-burnt black stumps that show their unsightly heads in every part! Yet even these are not so alarming as the hollow trunks of trees through which the flames are still bursting; or, otherwise their black ruins present such dubious shapes to the lonely traveller, that it requires but a little superstition to convert them into fiends and hobgoblins."[45]

On the other hand, the landscape around Dubuque did have some vague similarities to the Yorkshire Dales. It had rolling hills and the limestone bedrock that encased the lead veins. These were more than mere visual elements. The commonality of landscape had a deep cultural and economic meaning that invited Yorkshire immigrants: the hills were good for raising stock, as in Yorkshire; the bedrock could be cut into blocks to make stone walls and building foundations, and above all the rock contained the galena that could be smelted into lead. All of this helped create an environment and opportunity for work that drew in people from North Yorkshire. And as they became settled, they transferred not just the latest methods of mining and smelting lead but also building styles and attitudes toward the landscape. To divide their mineral allotments, they built at least one stone wall that resembled those of Swaledale.[46] This was a symbol of their culture as well as a socio-economic tool, as were the lead shafts and mines they dug and the smelter furnaces they constructed. Later, their livestock and dairy farms also harkened back to their corner of England. Thus, in some ways the Upper Mississippi was ideal for prospective Yorkshire Dales immigrants. Much of it was good for both the kind of farming they were used to in England, and the kind of mining in which they were expert.

The immigrants' aesthetic sensibilities can be seen in their buildings. In the 1850s the Grange family, from Dacre Banks, near Harrogate, North Yorkshire, established the Key West community, near Dubuque. There they built a house using building techniques that had come from Yorkshire and that were used in the Dubuque area by other Yorkshire immigrants, hewing the local limestone as they had in Yorkshire. They also purchased ceramics that reflected their English tastes and thereby "successfully integrated a number of locally available frontier cultural expressions while maintaining their British cultural identity."[47] In these and other ways the North Yorkshire immigrants left their indelible mark on the Upper Mississippi.

The First English Settlers[48]

This, then, was the world that many of the Yorkshire Dales immigrants entered. Leaving behind villages and towns that had been around for hundreds, even a thousand years, with ancient churches and a mature social structure, they were now entering a region that had only recently been stolen from Native Americans and opened to white miners and settlers. The region's lead industry was primitive by Yorkshire standards and it seemed to be waiting for the mining and smelting skills and technology that had been developed in Yorkshire and other parts of England to bring it into modern industrial production. The immigrants were coming to a frontier mining culture in the throes of a lead rush, with three men for every woman.[49] Immigrants from North Yorkshire and other parts of England, especially Cornwall, made a difference. By 1850 Platteville alone had about ninety English families living in or around the town.[50] And the Benton area contained nearly fifty lead mines, mostly discovered and opened by the Yorkshire immigrants who also named them, including the Calvert Mine, Cottingham Mine, and mines associated with the names of Hird, Metcalf, Milner, Peacock, Pratt, Raisbeck, Spensley, and Wiseman.[51] They were helping make Wisconsin the state with the highest concentration of English immigrants, 6.2 per cent of its entire population in 1850.[52] Their numbers in the region would never have been this significant, though, without the Yorkshire immigrants' ability to successfully adjust and assimilate.

8

Adjustment and Assimilation

I left my native hills and many has been the ups and downs since that time[.]
I still love my native hills her rocks and gils my heart with rapture fills but
I love America beter the land of the free and the home of the brave.

THOMAS LEWIS WALKER

In North America, North Yorkshire immigrants found adjusting and assimilating to the new country challenging, especially in remote areas. The sheer loneliness and foreboding sense of isolation on or near the vast frontier could be overwhelming, even when other immigrants were nearby. Those from the Dales had left a geography that enforced tight community relationships and a sense of interdependence; their villages and dales had brought them together. In many parts of America, the contrast could be stark, even shocking, resulting in acute homesickness.

The combination of loneliness and the strange qualities of a new country could be debilitating, even in American towns and cities. Samuel Fowler Smith was so homesick after he left Wetherby for America in 1835 that he decided to go back the first chance he got. "My bubbles all melted into thin air," he recalled, "and that most dreadful feeling, homesickness, came on me with crushing effect. It seemed that I should give every thing that I had in the world if I was only back in the place that I had left. And I fully determined, however humiliating it might be, to return as soon as I could earn the money."[1]

Homesickness also apparently afflicted Matthew and Jane Willis on their isolated Wisconsin farm, Rama. The loss of their son was compounded by the absence of family members still in Wensleydale. Evidently they poured their hearts out in letters to their brother-in-law John Humphrey, whose response survives and indicates the Willises' frustrations: "[S]uppose all your Brothers and sisters, and your own family and Friends were situated near or within a few miles of Rama, how then would you like the country?

Would you wish that you were all back in England again? Think you, would it alter the Country any? Would America then be any better than England, or it would not? These are questions Dear Matthew that you alone can answer by just supposing this to be the case, I hope you will ask yourself these questions and then answer me them candidly and without reserve."[2]

The Role of Letters

Adjusting to North America often depended on letters from the old home. Letters kept the immigrants grounded and connected with friends and relatives as they constructed their new lives. It is probably impossible to grasp fully the importance of letters. Matthew Dinsdale seemed desperate for contact from Yorkshire and confided in his diary in 1846 – more than a year after his arrival – that "I have this morning been thinking, as I often do, about home. I looked over some of the letters I have from time to time received. Last Saturday I thought I should surely have either letters or papers from Askrigg. But none came … I hope I am learning to live more upon God, and not expect or desire enjoyment from any earthly source."[3] Sometimes the frustration over the lack of letters boiled over and caused tempers to flare to the point of exasperation: "I must try and write a few lines," wrote Richard Buxton's wife Isabella, around 1855, "but I have often thought I would never write again as there is not one in Gunnerside [who] thinks it worth their while to write to me."[4]

Letters from England were a virtual lifeline. The joy of receiving them could be immense. They were a physical item, touched by loved ones on the other side of the ocean. Matthew Dinsdale felt their magic when he received his first letter from Askrigg in February of 1845, about a half-year after his arrival in Wisconsin: "[I]t breathes a kind and affectionate spirit," he responded, "you can streach [stretch] out the hand of affection even across the wide Atlantic. I thank the Lord that I have still relatives in the world who think about me and pray for me. Perhaps if you had known how precious every word is that comes from home in this 'far west' you would have sent me a few more."[5] For Dinsdale, letters were almost objects of worship, as he himself admitted, pious Methodist that he was: "You cannot think what pleasure your letters afford me," he wrote to his mother in December of 1845. "I am with regard to them almost an idolater; they are perused by me over and over again."[6] A year later, as he was travelling as a circuit rider and preaching on Sundays, Dinsdale wrote again to his mother and siblings, underscoring the importance of writing his journal and letters, and why they should write more letters to him:

> By this futile attempt to write a journal you will see that I still think about you every day. I am inclined to think you will frequently be receiving letters from me as I often write. But I must inform you I do not have as many from home as I desire. Cannot some of you adopt this plan and write a little every few days, or when anything occurs you think would interest or benefit me, or cannot you make a journal and all write by turns ... I am now expecting a letter, or rather letters, from you, as I have not had one since last July. And this is the first day of December.[7]

Dinsdale begged for more letters and agonized over the lack of them, as did others. When feeling especially homesick and not receiving a letter when he expected one, he expressed disbelief and frustration: "Is it possible," Matthew Dinsdale asked in his private journal in 1846, after desperately checking at the local post office, "there is nothing for me? ... I have received nothing from home ... If my friends knew my feelings when I expect letters and papers they would try to take care I should have no disappointment."[8]

More than two years after his move to Wisconsin, Dinsdale was still complaining about the infrequency of letters, which he was measuring with obsessive accuracy: "My Brother Edward has sent me this time a rather meagre letter," Dinsdale complained to his mother. "He thinks himself it is rather deficient and apologized at the close of it. He might have put three times as much in it as it contains and even then he would not have repaid me for some of mine. From the receipt of my letter on the 17th of February till the period of yours left full thirty-five days elapsed, and yet I am to be satisfied with what costs about an hour to write. How is this? I almost feel as tho' I could scold ... My very questions are often unanswered."[9] Dinsdale's loneliness and obsession with letters was compounded by his occupation. As he further explained to his mother, "as a Missionary I have trials that others can know nothing about ... At times I also need encouragement and comfort; you attend to those things and I am thankful."[10]

Letters and packages were especially precious when they contained items unavailable in America, though there was little the immigrants could send back to return the favour. This seems to have weighed on Matthew Willis's conscience. After he received a package, he wrote excitedly back to his nephew in Carperby, Wensleydale. He was so grateful for the wonderful gifts from various old friends and neighbours, but he had little to offer in return. Willis's letter also provides insight into how certain items from England were requested and obtained:

> Your kind favour of 9th 2nd month came to hand in due course, along with a Box of Clothing of various sorts, Iron ware etc. with which, it appears our Friends in England are kindly presenting us. When in a previous letter I mentioned those articles as likely to be useful to us, I had no idea whatever of having them without paying all costs and charges. However, as they are gratuitously sent we cannot do less than return our warmest thanks for the same. We often regret that the opportunities of returning the like kindnesses to England are so few. ... We also wish thee to accept our grateful acknowledgements thyself for thy presents of very interesting Books and Tracts, etc. The Hayseeds were a fine specimen of old English produce. We sowed them on the evening of the 31st. Let the first of our friends that comes over bring along with him a few Goose berry seeds, if it is not too late to get them.[11]

Some items in packages and letters contained things intended to bridge vast distances. Locks of their hair provided literally some physical contact. As William Atkinson wrote from Ingleby Greenhow (on the western edge of the North York Moors, near Great Ayton) to his cousin in Iowa in 1863, "We were also very pleased with the locks of hair but we should have been more pleased if we could have been as near you as we were the lock of hair." Later that year another reply to Iowa announced that "we have sent you a lock of ours (hair) as we have all hair of one colour."[12] Some American mementoes making their way back to Yorkshire were not so common, the rattle of a rattlesnake, for instance.[13] Later on, letters often contained photographs.

The time lag between letters was at least several months, and some ingenious methods were employed to cope with it. Matthew Dinsdale wrote home to his siblings and made the observation that in Wisconsin they were "planting potatoes when your letters were wrote, and when I read them I was eating them – that is eating new potatoes! With you spring was first opening, here summer is almost at an end! Your planting the seed and I eating the fruit and yet we appear to be conversing together at one time, I am now hearing what you then said! Does your voice indeed take so long a time to cross the Atlantic? Tho' the interval is long I am thankful that we can converse together. This privilege is worth more than it costs."[14]

Packages were also commonly carried by immigrants who were joining family and friends. When Matthew Willis left Wensleydale to join Matthew Dinsdale in Peddlars Creek, he carried a package put together by Dinsdale's mother. Dinsdale was delighted: "I have this day received the parcel you sent by Matthew Willis which was heartily welcomed by me, even before I opened it, because it came from Askrigg, and from those who are dear to me there." The prized package contained not only letters from people in Wensleydale – many of them asking specific questions about American life – but also mittens to combat the freezing Wisconsin winters, as well as various seeds. "I am grateful to J. Robinson for the Rhubarb seed," he responded. "I gave half of it to Mr Wasley who I expect has planted it; the other half I retain to give to some other person." It wasn't that Dinsdale did not like rhubarb, but that "I have no garden of my own but if I should have one I can probably procure seed from those I have given it to."[15] Dinsdale responded to his mother that "You may be sure that I was glad to see him … I am much obliged to him for his kindness … Matthew [Willis] appears to be well satisfied with the step he had taken and I think so far likes this country as well as he expect he should before he came."[16]

Climate

Though letters and packages helped people to deal with homesickness and loneliness, other adjustments had to be made on their own. The harsher climate was one. The colder winters and hotter, more humid summers come up in letters with such frequency and detail that this must have been significant. Some of the accounts of the extreme cold were shocking. A few years after Edmund Alderson left Arkengarthdale in 1839 to mine in New Diggings, Wisconsin, he reported back to his brother that: "I believe it to be 5 times as Cold here as ever I found it in England there is some days that before a man Could ride one mile with his ears bare at full trot his ears would freeze hard So that they much be rubbed with snow till they get there natural heat or otherwise they would break of [off] my wife was an eye witness to it by an Arkindale man."[17]

And four years after Matthew and Jane Willis had settled in Wisconsin they complained at length about the winter:

> I suppose you have heard already of the severity of our last winter. The snow began to fall on the 2nd day of Nov. with a southwest wind, veering by the south & southeast to the north-east. After this the ground was never bare till the latter end of March. The snow increased in quantity and the cold in intensity till the 10th of Feb. The mercury in the thermometer running down as low as 26 degrees below zero under a burning noonday sun, and 33 in the shade by the scale of Fahrenheit … it was some time in April before spring work could commence, great quantities of snow remaining till the latter end of March. On the evening of the 18th Feb. a cann of spring water was placed by the stove in our cottage to be ready for morning use. When morning came we found the water frozen to the depth of from 3 to 4 1/2 inches by measurement, and the cann literally shivered to pieces. This will give you some idea of what we have to endure in an American winter. I have not yet seen a man from any part of Europe that does not complain of the cold of a Wisconsin winter. Even the hardy Norwegians complain of the cold being much more severe in this, than in their native country.[18]

Jane Willis's brother John Humphrey received the letter, circulated it to others, and then responded: "I hope … you will be able to write without your Ink Freezing in your pen."[19] Not that Yorkshire winters were always much milder. In late March of 1834 John Jackson of Redmire, near Castle Bolton in Wensleydale, took some cows over the moors to sell in Reeth, in Swaledale. After selling all but one he returned over the high, desolate moors and in a blinding snowstorm clung to the cow's tail, knowing that the beast could find her way back home. He and his cow made it back safely, but later that winter Jackson got lost in another storm and was found frozen stiff in a snow drift.[20]

It is surprising how much winters could bother hardy Yorkshire immigrants who had endured such a punishing journey to America. Even their American-born children seemed annoyed. Richard Willis, born to Matthew and Jane in Wisconsin in 1850, five years after the family's arrival, wrote back to his sister Elizabeth in Wensleydale that "it has been quite cold, and makes me think of England more than once a day. Indeed I think of coming again sometime though it might be years first."[21] At the other end of the climate spectrum, the hot, muggy summers were also a problem, especially the illnesses. Ague and other water-borne, malarial diseases were especially common scourges in frontier regions. In 1845 Matthew Dinsdale noted that in the area of Wisconsin where he was preaching, "All places in the vicinity of rivers are subject more or less to ague and bilious fever."[22] Though not as deadly or horrific as cholera, ague and other American illnesses, as well as the torment of mosquitoes, were new problems for immigrants.

Foods

Another difference in North American life that pops up in the immigrants' letters and journals was the diet. Strange foods and eating habits could be annoying. In the 1870s Swaledale traveller and land agent James Broderick found the beef in Dubuque "very inferior with scarcely any fat upon it. The people here won't buy fat meat, and when they do, they make the butcher take it off. And the hams are trimmed down till they are nothing but lean, the fat being melted down into lard." And observing the Americans' table manners, Broderick noted that "when one dines with the Americans they give one all kinds of eatables and nearly all at once, filling his plate as long as it will hold anything … He is then compelled to eat very quickly or some of his dainties would get cold. Is it not better to have things served up in succession, just as required, and to take a little more time? Of course the Americans live well, on three meals a day, with butcher's meat to every meal; in other words, they live upon 'three dinners, a day'."[23]

Language and Speech

Wherever the North Yorkshire immigrants settled in North America they had advantages in basic cultural traits they shared with most Americans – especially their language. Having the same language as their host country

helped skilled English immigrants – such as those in the building trades –
get jobs readily by word-of-mouth. They communicated easily with
prospective employers, or with others who could help them succeed in
America.[24] This is not to say that sharing the English language made
them "invisible." Although their common language certainly facilitated
communication, it could also expose differences in accent, expression,
and dialect.[25] The Yorkshire dialect had many regional variations, which
probably contributed to some early confusion. Swaledale itself had its
own traditional dialect known as "Swardle," and some of its words were
unique to the area. Not surprisingly many of them related to sheep. For
the people around Keld, "a 'gimmer' is a female sheep, a 'yow' is a ewe, a
'tup' a ram, and a 'twinter' is a two-year-old sheep, since it has survived
two winters." The numbers were also distinctive: yan, tan, tether, mether,
pip, sezah, azah, catrah, honra, dick.[26]

Aside from unique words, there was also the Yorkshire accent, or
brogue, which often made the speaker stand out as a foreigner, though
not necessarily in any malicious way. Samuel Fowler Smith, who left
North Yorkshire in 1835, found his accent a source of friendship and
comic relief in his first home in Cincinnati. There he "soon made friends
and found … that my Yorkshire brogue was against me. I well recollect
asking a gentleman at a musical party if his tuning fork was a hay fork,
meaning was it "A" or "G." He, to make the bull more pointed, asked me
what I said. I could not conceive what they were laughing at, when I, in
all simplicity, repeated the question. I soon, however, found where to put
the "H," and to do many other things.[27] As Smith realized, some native-
born Americans could scarcely understand the northern English accent,
especially the Yorkshire tendency to drop the letter *h*. John Strickland,
of Rosedale Abbey, referred to the "Ickery" [hickory] trees of Ontario.[28]
Some in Ohio thought that a recent arrival from Yorkshire had "forgotten
all his English."[57]

But such linguistic differences were a minor hurdle for Yorkshire immigrants. More serious were anti-English hostilities that lingered after the
Revolution, the War of 1812, and ongoing tensions over the border with
Canada – tensions that were stoked in 1844 by James K. Polk's belligerent
slogan, "54 40 or fight."[29] Noisy, chest-thumping celebrations of the 4th of
July often included pompous anti-English speeches that could spill over
into ugly violence. On their way along the Erie Canal to Iowa on 4 July

1850, some Yorkshire families were hit with insults and rocks merely because they were English.[30] English settlers whose loyalty was questioned resorted to painting enormous flags on their barns or making some other conspicuously patriotic display. Later, many proved their loyalty once and for all by quickly volunteering to serve the Union during the Civil War.[31]

Despite examples to the contrary, most Yorkshire immigrants did blend in and assimilate relatively quickly. Samuel Fowler Smith, whose Yorkshire brogue made him stand out to his friends, nonetheless realized the extent of his assimilation to American life when he made a return trip to his native Wetherby in 1852 – eighteen years after his emigration in 1835. "I had thus become theroughly Americanized in taste, thought and feeling," he recorded, "so that when I landed in Liverpool everything seemed almost as strange as they did when I landed in New York." Yet, his return did trigger powerful emotions: "I had just this mingling of feeling, – strangeness and familiarity," he continued. "Landing on Sunday morning I heard the first sweet chimes of bells that I had heard since leaving that port eighteen years ago. How sweetly they sounded in my ears; what blessed recollections they brought to my mind. They seemed to welcome me home."[32] But after a highly emotional reunion with his aged father – who died a mere few days after his return – and seeing once again his siblings and old friends and neighbours, Smith's "Americanization" struck him more fully as he soaked in the home of his youth. "Though familiar to my boyhood and youth many things now appeared odd and strange," he recorded. "The variations and oddity of the Yorkshire dialect, each town and village almost having its peculiarity."[33] His 1852 journey to America was far less traumatic than the first one in 1835.

In other ways assimilation was eased by a relative lack of linguistic or cultural barriers. As we shall see in the following chapter, some Yorkshire families in the lead region boarded other newcomers from various parts of America, an indication that their common language and culture facilitated interaction with most Americans. Their cultural differences were real but did not get in the way of social interaction and even cohabitation.[34] Yet, at the same time early North Yorkshire immigrants continued to help new arrivals from their old village or dale, and they embraced their own kind, intermarrying extensively and enjoying continued contact with relatives and friends in Yorkshire.

A Small World

Along with letters and packages, other immigrants also eased homesickness and adjustment. The frequency with which Yorkshire immigrants came across strangers who also hailed from Yorkshire is remarkable and seems to have been a source of great cheer. From the start of his time in America, Matthew Dinsdale ran into other Yorkshiremen and at other times sought them out for companionship and an emotional anchor. A month after his arrival in New York he stopped by another local Yorkshire immigrant renting a farm in New York State, John Woodward, and stayed for three days. Dinsdale reported that "I found him in good health, working hard and probably better off than he would have been had he remained in England," and that Woodward and his wife were "very kind to me." On his journey to Wisconsin, Dinsdale went out of his way to seek out old friends and other Yorkshire immigrants, perhaps out of a need for familiar faces and voices. Doing so seems to have been comforting and probably helped him cope with living in a strange land. In one detour Dinsdale stopped by to see an immigrant family from West Burton, a few kilometres from his native Askrigg, and spent the night with them. While he was there, he met a young man named Heseltine, from Thoralby, again, near Askrigg, whose aunt Matthew Dinsdale knew, as well as another immigrant named Wray.[35] It was in some ways a "small world" for Dinsdale, and others, who met people on their journeys in America from the home village and dale, often by chance. And on their way, they picked up advice and encouragement for their transition to American life.

After becoming established as a widely travelling circuit riding preacher, Dinsdale continued to run into other Yorkshire immigrants, quite by accident. In 1845 he found himself performing the funeral service of a person from the same part of Yorkshire, whom he thought was an old friend of his grandfather. In the same letter he refers to meeting many people who had also come from the Dales – from his own Wensleydale but also people from Swaledale, and other parts of England. "There are a great many number of English about this place many of them from Yorkshire," he noted. "The other day I saw a woman, a member of the Church, from Whiteside. She has been in this country for about fifteen years, I think her name was Spencely ... I also heard of one Stephen Dinsdale from Thoralby ... but has gone off for a few days, or I suspect I should have seen him."[36]

That small world showed itself again in 1846 when Dinsdale travelled to preach to the Brotherton Indian Nation. To get there he had to hike in the wilds, sleep on the ground, and then take a canoe made of a pine log – only to find it paddled by a man from Leeds, in West Yorkshire. The surprise must have been both real and enjoyable, at least until he realized his ineptitude. "I expected every moment to be turned into the water as my countryman was a little raw at using a paddle to move and guide a canoe."[37] One can only imagine their conversations, but very likely they included reminiscences of Yorkshire, what they missed about it, what they didn't, how and why they got to America, and what they had in common as Yorkshire immigrants. Other immigrants from places near Yorkshire also popped up in Dinsdale's travels. "The first house I called at this morning is an englishman's he is a native of Cumberland and came from Canada to this part last spring, he has a beautiful farm of two hundred and forty acres, which would cost him a little over £60. I presume there is hardly any land in Wensleydale equally good in quality. He was ploughing with three yoke of oxen."[38] Altogether, Yorkshire immigrants benefited from contact with fellow countrymen and women – not only those from their old communities, but also ones they happened to meet on their travels.

This of course did not dispel all the problems of adjustment. Dinsdale had to travel widely and mingle with strangers in new places. But most Yorkshire immigrants in the Upper Mississippi were busy mining and smelting lead, living and working alongside others they had known in their old village or dale, and interacting with Americans. Their extraordinary success in the Upper Mississippi helped them adjust and assimilate and gave them important roles in the transatlantic industrial revolution.

Mining and Smelting

The rich mineral districts of Wisconsin, as well as its broad and
fertile prairies and openings, offers, either to the capitalist or
operative, the most substantial inducements to settlement.

YORK HERALD, 1854

Having left the world's first industrial nation, British immigrants helped
make the United States the second.[1] They were especially vital to America's
mining industry – whether coal, iron, lead, copper, or gold. British miners
had the experience and expertise that had fuelled the first industrial revolution, and the many thousands of them who came to America in the
nineteenth century helped transform the nation. During the 1850s alone,
about 37,000 British miners came directly to the United States while many
others arrived undetected via Canada. The British dominated America's
coal industry to such an extent, one modern historian has observed, that
"the world of the coal miner was largely a British world" and "every mine
boss in the anthracite region was English, Welsh, or Scottish."[2] In 1851,
miners of all types accounted for about 5 per cent of Britain's male labour
force but 7 per cent of the male immigrants, a ratio roughly similar for the
early 1840s and late 1880s as well. Miners were mobile and had a tradition
of moving to find the best opportunities. The stream of mining skill and
labour from Britain to America was steady and significant, as can be seen
in the Yorkshire lead miners who came to the Upper Mississippi.[3]

In fact, there is perhaps no better example of the industrial revolution
being transferred from Britain to America. Though the first Yorkshire
miners who arrived in the 1830s were entering a lead rush in full swing,
they pushed it into a new phase of maturity, stability, and efficiency. The
new smelter designs they brought from England were key to that process.

The first Yorkshire immigrants to the lead region, virtually all of them
from Swaledale, settled the area that was soon called Center Grove, near
Rockdale (then known as Catfish Creek) in the heart of the lead mines

near Dubuque, in the early 1830s. This community transplanted their
culture as well as their industry, which made indelible and lasting physical
impressions along with important economic contributions. They affirmed
their Yorkshire roots by preserving their aesthetics and values as much as
possible, in the form of building the type of stone walls and gardens they
knew in Swaledale, and by building Center Grove Methodist Church and
cemetery.[4] The leading Swaledale families who founded Center Grove
included the Bonsons, Spensleys, Brunskills, and Wallers. They were
not only pioneers but central figures in the region's mining and smelting
industries. Their names have been permanently etched on the city's maps
and roads.[5]

The Bonsons and Wallers

A few of the early Yorkshire families in the Upper Mississippi were especially significant to the local industry, economy, and community. Of
special importance were Richard and Mary (Harker) Waller, and Robert
and Mary (Spensely) Bonson and their son Richard. As mentioned earlier,
Robert and Mary Bonson and their four adult children left Swaledale in
1834, landed in New York, and then travelled down the Ohio River to take
the Mississippi River north to the lead district. Richard Waller, Robert
Bonson's brother-in-law, also left Swaledale in 1834 but had arrived in
Dubuque a month earlier. The two families were closely tied by marriage
and occupation (Waller had married Robert Bonson's sister, Ann). Along
with them came a nephew, also named Richard Bonson, and his wife
Isabella, and son. Yet another nephew, James Bonson, twenty-eight, was
in the group too. It was a complex, interrelated, group.[6]

Richard Waller and Robert Bonson and his son Richard had learned
and developed the latest mining and smelting technology and techniques
before arriving in Iowa in 1834. Waller was especially knowledgeable in
the blast furnace and in 1835 he, Robert and Richard Bonson, and a few
others formed their own company, Waller acting as the general agent and
engineer and manager.[7] Most significantly, in 1835 they erected America's
first blast furnace for lead, on the Little Platte River in Wisconsin, and then
recruited more skilled immigrants from the Dales to build and operate
more furnaces. The following year they also erected the first blast furnace
near Platteville and then two others as well, including a smelter near

Figure 9.1   Portrait of Robert Bonson, one of the most
important immigrants in America's lead industry. Dated 1845.

Rockdale on Catfish Creek. They used the proceeds to invest in mining properties near Dubuque. Their success and recruitment of people
they knew in the Dales explains much of the surge of North Yorkshire
immigrants in the region for the decade and beyond. Some of them were
already in America and could now make a shorter journey to the lead
region. Joseph Brunskill, for example, had already left the Dales for Ohio
in 1833, but in 1836 he left Ohio to join the flourishing community in
Dubuque. There he mined and in 1845 formed a partnership to build his
own smelter and business, which was so successful that Brunskill became

Figure 9.2   Portrait of Richard Bonson, Robert's
son and leader of Iowa's business and political
community.

one of Dubuque's most prominent citizens.[8] Meanwhile, Waller and the
two Bonsons reorganized as Waller & Company and between 1837 and
1860 they produced an average of 90 pigs of lead per day (21,000 per year),
for a total of 37,220,000 pounds of lead for the period.[9]

For several reasons the new furnaces that the Dales immigrants built
on the Upper Mississippi were a breakthrough. They allowed smelters to
obtain 70 per cent of the lead from the galena ore, instead of the 40 per
cent obtained by less efficient methods. They could also exploit the rich
slag heaps that remained from earlier smelters. Furthermore, they used far
less fuel and were so efficient that, after later improvements, the design was
still in use into the 1880s and beyond.[10] Because their new design extracted
more lead from the ore and reduced the cost of smelting, it was possible
to pay the miners more, which boosted the local economy.

Robert Bonson's son Richard (b. 1814), who had also mined in
Gunnerside, was significant in his own right. He was twenty at the time
of his family's migration and in Dubuque he mined and operated the
furnace with his father and Waller. In the late 1840s, as the lead industry
began to decline in Dubuque, Richard put his earnings into agriculture
and built a farmhouse north of Center Grove. When local land prices
rose in anticipation of impending railway construction, Bonson and two

Figure 9.3   The Bonson/Waller Lead Furnace, the first lead blast furnace in America, 1835.

friends went to the Dubuque recorder and filed a town plat (a scale map showing the land divisions) for Center Grove, composed of about 50 acres of former mineral land located a little more than 3 kilometres from the Mississippi River – some of which had been owned by Joseph Brunskill's company.[11] Because of his experience and ambition he was asked to serve on the executive committee that arbitrated and settled disputes over mine claims. Richard Bonson became one of the most successful of all the English immigrants in the area and married Jane Burton. He expanded his own holdings to some forty tracts of land, and in the 1840s built more smelters and bought up more mining lots nearby from other Yorkshire immigrants, including his father-in-law John Burton.

Not everything was easy for the Bonsons and the others from the Dales. They faced some aggressive competition in the form of the Langworthy brothers – James, Lucius, Edward, and Solon – who had arrived from Vermont and New York in 1833 and 1834, at precisely the time that settlers from Yorkshire were getting established. Forming a powerful partnership and purchasing some of the best lands, the Langworthys "quickly gained control of mining and smelting" and expanded their interests into mercantile, transportation, and banking activity. The Bonsons and other Yorkshire Dales immigrants were doing the same; but at mid-century the Langworthys were the richest family in Dubuque and had laid out

Figure 9.4   Richard and Harriet Bonson.

much of the city, which they considered "their town." Early historians observed that they were so influential they had become a "proprietary shadow government behind the elected powers, using their own 'means and credit' to build the city," according to their own interests.[12] In the 1840s and 1850s they built fancy houses on "Langworthy Bluff" overlooking the town, aiming to create an elite society with refinement and privilege.

The Bonsons and other Yorkshire Dales immigrants were based 3 kilometres west of the Langworthys, at Center Grove in Catfish Creek valley, where they built another blast furnace that smelted the lead mined by other North Yorkshire immigrants. Here they and their fellow Dales immigrants created their own "economic system" that was an independent competitor to that of the Langworthys. Richard Bonson served with the Langworthys as a member of the Mining Claims Settlement Committee, which governed the sale of government lots to individuals for mining, and after buying more lots he owned more real estate than the Langworthys.[13]

Both Bonson and the Langworthys engaged in boosterism to promote the community and local economy and protect their investments. For Bonson, boosting Dubuque meant entering politics. This was apparently related to the mysterious "unpleasant family affaires" he refers to in his diary. His marriage to Jane Burton was not happy, nor was his home life, so he rented an office in the town and engaged with social and political life there.[14] In 1852 he entered the state legislature for Dubuque County, and was soon considered the most important "representative of Dubuque's immigrant culture."[15]

In the mid-1850s Bonson and some Yorkshire friends joined others to form the Dubuque Harbor Company. Their shares "soared" as railroads and the Iowa land grant bill passed to secure Dubuque's future.[16] In 1858 he was elected a director of the Dubuque and Pacific Railroad, only to find it insolvent, like many other railroad companies in the wake of the Panic and Crash of 1857. But Bonson had avoided the worst effects of the depression by diversifying with mercantile businesses, insurance, and local leadership positions. He also served as State Inspector of Banks and then was elected twice to the state legislature.[17] He was one of Dubuque's leading "boosters," as well as the leading representative of the area's immigrant subculture. Richard Bonson, one historian has noted, had "learned how to employ the discourse and behaviors of gentility and collective sociability among lawyers, businessmen, and members of a broader male subculture" and in that role he helped build a "unified booster ethos" that was vital for the economic and social development of the city.[18]

Meanwhile, both Richard Bonson and the Langworthys knew that as production costs rose in their extractive industry, lead prices would become unstable making the extinction of their industry inevitable, as was happening in Yorkshire. Changes had to be made so in the 1850s Bonson began operating his mines and smelters only when lead prices were high. But unlike the Langworthys, who turned to more banking and land speculation, Richard Bonson turned to farming.[19] Given his roots in Swaledale, where mining and smelting were usually seen ultimately as a stepping stone to farming, Bonson's choice is not surprising. Farming one's own land was what it was all about.

The Brunskills and Pratts

A year before the Bonsons arrived in the Upper Mississippi in 1834, Joseph and Elizabeth (Woodward) Brunskill had arrived in Akron, Ohio, and in a few years made their way to Dubuque. Born in Gunnerside in 1811 to a lead mining father, Joseph "became thoroughly familiar with mining." Marrying Elizabeth Woodward in 1833 and "wishing to emigrate to America," he borrowed from his father-in-law to pay for his passage on the *George Washington* and they arrived in New York on 15 June that same year. The ship's passenger list shows that Joseph was twenty-two, enumerated as a farmer and travelling with his wife Elizabeth, who was a year younger. With them were ninety-four other English passengers. Their specific origin is not provided, but on the list we do see William and Jane Alderson, and the John and Mary Bell family, and their ten children, including an unnamed boy born at sea.[20]

After a six-week crossing they arrived in New York, took the Erie Canal to Cleveland, and then came to Akron. There for three years Brunskill chopped wood and worked as a general labourer until he was able to repay his father-in-law. In 1836 he proceeded to Dubuque, began by mining for others, and then started out for himself. In 1845 he built a smelter and conducted an extensive business until 1871, when he retired.[21] His sons James and William had been smelting at Center Grove for five years. William started farming in 1865, and in 1880 they were farming and raising stock.[22]

Swaledalers James and Hannah Pratt also sailed on the *George Washington* and though James had been both a farmer and miner in his native Gunnerside he is listed as a tanner on the passenger list, suggesting that many of these young people had a variety of skills and experience that would suit them well in America. Along with the Brunskills, the Pratts first went to Ohio where for two years James cleared 50 acres of dense timberland and worked for his neighbours for 50 cents a day. But after his farm was established, he left to investigate the lead region of the Mississippi, walking some 800 kilometres to Dubuque. He recalled how he "swam rivers and waded creeks, slept on the ground o'nights, ate in houses when I could, and killed game when I was hungry elsewhere. Sometimes I followed roads, sometimes paths through the woods and over the prairie and sometimes made my own paths I was a great walker in those days!"[23] As an expert miner in his native Gunnerside, Pratt was able to mine successfully in Iowa for a few months and then return to Ohio by boat to sell the Ohio farm and take his family to Iowa. There he and two partners bought the Catfish Mill and then in 1840 with Walter Manson formed Pratt & Manson, a large milling company which for twenty-five years flourished and helped promote farming in the area.[24] It was so successful that the mills were enlarged and rebuilt and became the Rockdale Mills at the economic centre of Dubuque. Pratt became a financier, helped established the Dubuque branch of the State Bank of Iowa, and became director of two other local banks.[25]

When James Pratt died in 1869, the local newspaper reported that he had left an estate worth between $60,000 and $80,000.[26] Meanwhile another Gunnerside smelter, John Watters, bought up part of the Rockdale Mills and helped rebuild them again. The furnace he built northwest of Rockdale was the heart of a family business that operated for three generations. It was probably the last furnace operating in the Dubuque area.[27]

The Spensleys

Another important early North Yorkshire family in the Upper Mississippi was the Spensleys, from Feetham Holme, Swaledale. Its patriarch was James Spensley (1773–1848/9), whose son Richard was married to Robert Bonson's daughter, Alice. Spensley was highly experienced in mining and became a foreman at the vast Barnsley coal mines in South Yorkshire. But, as he recalled later, even as a foreman "the outlook had been very discouraging, with little prospect of bettering his condition," so he left for Iowa in 1839 with Alice and their six children, having to borrow money for the journey, and sailed on the *Roscius*. Landing in New York and proceeding up the Erie Canal to Buffalo, they then took a different route than the one that had claimed Robert Bonson's wife Mary by cholera on the Mississippi. Sailing from Buffalo to Chicago, Richard Spensley "had only money enough to convey his wife and children to his destination in Iowa, he himself walking the entire distance."[28] In Dubuque, Richard and Alice Spensley built a log cabin and lived there for years, indicating their modest means and slow start as Richard worked alongside his father-in-law, later moving to Galena to mine and smelt. Richard's ultimate success was ascribed to the fact that he was "a man of stubborn resolution and indomitable will – traits handed down to him from his substantial English ancestry."[29]

Other Spensleys followed Richard and his brothers to the Upper Mississippi. Richard's sixty-nine-year-old father James Spensley arrived in the late 1830s, as did at least two of Richard's brothers, Anthony and John. Anthony arrived in 1839, but, like Richard, these migration "chains" seem to have offered him little material advantage because for years Anthony and his family lived in a log hut.[30] The 1870 census listed him, his sons, and some boarders as miners. His son William, born in 1842, followed his father into mining on the claim and also had a small farm, truck garden, and fruit orchard, but he was still listed as a miner in 1880.[31] John and Mary Spensley also prospered after getting established, teaming up with James Calvert and others to establish the mining and smelting business of Spensley and Company.[32] The extended Spensley clan in various parts of America enjoyed similar degrees of success and prominence in mining, the smelting business, and the law.[33]

Thus did the Bonson, Brunskill, Watters, Spensley, and other North Yorkshire families contribute to the modernization of the Upper Mississippi mining industry as well as its agriculture. They were joined by others, who will be featured in later chapters, but first we should understand more fully the nature of the Yorkshire mining community and their work.

The Yorkshire Mining Community

Because the 1840 census recorded only the male "heads of families," we must turn to the fuller 1850 census for more details on the immigrants from North Yorkshire. At Center Grove, the heart of the North Yorkshire community near Dubuque, we see Joseph and Elizabeth Brunskill, with Joseph listed as a lead manufacturer. His lead furnace was just south of the Center Grove Methodist Church, on the side of what is now Brunskill Road. John Watters was listed as doing the same as Brunskill, and his furnace site was about half a kilometre north of Brunskill's. James Pratt is recorded as a miller, aged fifty, with $6,000 worth of real estate; his wife Hannah is also recorded, but in their household, there is also Sarah Ann Coates, age fifteen, and a seventeen-year-old labourer born in New York by the name of Robert Bruce. The John and Margaret Spensley family, recorded as miners, follow the Pratts, both in the census and the order in which they were visited by the enumerator, so they were neighbours.

Other members of the Spensley clan – Anthony and Ann – boarded miners who had come from other areas. The 1850 census shows that their household, in addition to their three children, included two English immigrant miners: John Walton, aged forty-six and John McCoy, aged twenty, another miner from Ohio named Ira Timmons, as well as a Virginia-born wheelwright named Washington Morrow. There was also a twenty-year-old woman named Bolivia White, from Missouri.[34] The fact that the Spensleys had such a large and diverse number of boarders living in their household shows their role in offering a place to start not just for other English immigrants, but for Americans born in three different states as well. It also suggests an ability and inclination to associate with Americans. This English community was far from being exclusively English; it was more diverse than other immigrant communities in America.[35]

In this snapshot from 1850 we see a community that was led by the English, especially those from Yorkshire and Swaledale, but mixing comfortably with native-born Americans. The North Yorkshire immigrants were noticed for their accent and dialect, their expertise in mining and smelting, and even for constructing walls and churches in their distinctive style. They also seem to have been perceived as less foreign than other immigrants, especially those who did not speak English or had their own exclusive churches and other places of social interaction. This, at least, was the conclusion of the historian Joseph Shafer: "The foreigners in early Wisconsin ... divided into those who were English-speaking and those who were not. The first class found little difficulty in participating freely with all Americans in all phases of public life ... Germans, Norwegians, and Bohemians appeared much more tardily. Their great handicap was in being limited to an alien tongue. For language is one of the deeper parts of life ... In the competition with the Yankee and Englishman, the German, Norwegian, and Bohemian never had a chance."[36] At the same time, North Yorkshire immigrants were bringing in other families and a sense of order and respectability to an area that still had vestiges of the rough and lawless mining frontier.[37]

Other clues in the census add to this view. The Simon and Margaret Harker family – one of several Harker families from Swaledale and Wensleydale to migrate to the Mississippi lead region – are a good example of chain migration serving in this way. They were part of a large group who had left the Dales together in 1839. Eleven years later the 1850 census shows that Simon was a miner and that he and Margaret lived with their seven children. Their household also included four other men, all miners from England, between the ages of twenty-two and forty-six. Simon died early at age forty-two, in June of 1850, and may have been the first person to be interred at the Center Grove Methodist cemetery, which contains more than forty confirmed English immigrants.[38] This tradition of early Yorkshire miners providing a start for others in America continued for several decades. We see in the 1860 census that the Nathanial and Nancy Simpson household included four other English immigrants: James Raw, a miner, aged twenty-eight; John Wall, a thirty-five-year-old labourer; John Welsh, a nineteen-year-old servant; and James Cuthbert, a twenty-six-year-old smelter.[39]

Smelting

The most important technical contribution made by Yorkshire immigrants was the new smelting furnaces and techniques. Two types of blast furnaces were developed in England and brought to the Upper Mississippi: the Scotch hearth and, later, the more sophisticated horizontal reverberatory system.[40] They were built of brick and stone and could be used as blast furnaces. As in Yorkshire, they were typically built over a stream that turned a wheel to power the bellows to achieve the temperatures required to melt out the lead. After the ore was broken into small enough pieces, it was thrown on to a hearth with just the right slant and enough wood or charcoal. The liquid lead then flowed into a hot reservoir and was placed into iron molds to cool. The resulting "pig" of 70 pounds of pure lead was taken to market.[41] The North Pennines of Britain was an ideal place to use the hearth smelting process because there was abundant peat for fuel and materials to make the hearth. But in America Yorkshire miners and smelters had to make adaptations because peat and coal were not readily available in the Upper Mississippi. Here they had to use wood, usually baked into charcoal, but eventually the timber was exhausted and supplies had to come from farther away.[42] Because the horizontal reverberatory system was expensive to build and needed to use higher quality fuel than the hearth furnaces, it was gradually replaced by ore hearth smelters, particularly the Scotch hearth blast furnaces.[43] Both systems were British and, especially after improvements were made to suit American conditions, Yorkshire immigrants used them to modernize America's lead industry and enable it to meet rising demand.

Mining

Though the Cornish were the most numerous and among the most skilled English miners in the region, Yorkshire Dalesmen and their families were more prominent in terms of the contributions they made to mining and smelting. They had a great wealth of experience in mining lead, which helped them prosper and gain prominence in their community. But mining experience was not always essential, and its importance can be over-stated. In early 1845 Matthew Dinsdale wrote from Peddlars Creek, about 10 kilometres from the lead mining centre of Mineral Point Wisconsin, explaining to his family in Askrigg that: "Many persons about here do well at Mining. Almost every day I hear of some one having struck a rich bed of mineral. But there is some risk in this call as a man may labour for months and even years and find very little tho' this is not usual; the ore being so very plentiful. And no one can tell where to find it so that a novice has quite as good a chance as the most experienced in mining operations. Every one has to make trial by sinking a hole."[44]

Even experienced Yorkshire miners got skunked in the Upper Mississippi, at least for a while. John and George Metcalf were digging as partners but reported they "have been rather unfortunate so far this winter," sinking their third shaft but not yet getting a big strike.[45]

Whatever their level of experience, Yorkshire immigrants in the mines of the Upper Mississippi faced conditions just as hard and dangerous as those in Yorkshire – if not worse. In Dubuque the ore was often found at a lower depth than in Yorkshire, in very narrow seams mixed with clay, and sometimes to the water line, which could run a mere 50 feet below the surface. This geology accentuated the problems and dangers associated with poor drainage and wet and cold conditions.[46] Some of the shafts and tunnels were so narrow that they required a miner to crawl and elbow his way for long distances to get to the veins, getting thoroughly wet and cold before digging could begin.[47] In the Galena district mine shafts usually went no deeper than 50 or 60 feet because of the threat of cave-ins, and because ore veins often ended in water, where sudden flooding could be lethal.[48] Facing such dangerous conditions, Yorkshire immigrants were instrumental in providing better techniques to prevent cave-ins and combat flooding with better pumps and drainage systems.

Some understanding of the actual conditions and environment that the Yorkshire immigrants endured is possible through the words of a contemporary eyewitness after he descended into the mines in Dubuque to watch the miners at work:

[We] were in one of the shafts, 200 feet below the surface. Above and below, the mineral glistened when touched by the dim flicker of

Figure 9.5   Picture of an early lead mine in the Upper Mississippi.

the candles ... After moving along several hundred feet, a strange, weird scene met the eye. A line of flickering, smoking dips, seemed to be struggling despairingly to light up the deep gloom of the place, and for all the world looked like a row of street lamps in a black fog, only that they seemed to be moving ... As the eye grew more accustomed to the dim light afforded by the candles, a number of miners were seen hard at work some making their way further into the drift, while others trundled ahead of them wheelbarrows of dirt, which were to be raised to the top. To reach the workmen, it was necessary to swing over deep chasms, by the assistance of ropes.[49]

Data on accidents and deaths in American lead mines are vague and incomplete. It seems likely that the experienced Yorkshire immigrant miners helped reduce rates of accidents. But they were not immune. In Wisconsin, Hannah Buxton, daughter of Richard and Isabella Buxton, married Christopher Looney, an immigrant from the Isle of Man. Only a half-year after the wedding Looney died a horrible death: a rock weighing several tons fell on him, covering all but his head, shoulders, and arms. His comrades frantically tried to pry off the rock. Hannah's brother William was also there, and after more than an hour of work they managed to free the man, but "all this time the unfortunate man was suffering the agonies of death and it was evident he could not survive." William cradled his brother-in-law's head for only the minute it took for Looney to die.[50]

Not everything was gloomy and depressing in American lead mines. In fact, there could be a degree of contentment among miners, emanating from their belief that their primitive conditions were only temporary and striking a rich vein was only a matter of time. The miners' natural optimism could engender a camaraderie that made the experience endurable. As one recalled at a mining camp hear Potosi, Wisconsin:

We had little shanties made of logs, generally split, and covered with elm bark, and we had bunks two stories high. Our bed and covering was a thick Mexican blanket, but what good sound sleep we did have; not a trouble on our minds; not one of us who was not confident of striking a lead very soon. Each had a tin cup, and we had a common coffee pot. Our meat was mess pork and we made our own bread. The fare, without variation, was coffee, bread and meat. In one hut there were four of us, which was the rule generally. These huts were scattered for a mile along this branch. All told, there were about sixty miners in the camp, and of the whole there was but a single quarrelsome man.[51]

America's Advantages

If mining conditions were somewhat better for Yorkshire miners in the Upper Mississippi, other advantages also made their move worthwhile. In about 1855, some five years after his arrival, Richard Buxton wrote back to his brother and sister in Gunnerside to tell them that he was still mining lead in the area of Benton. Now around forty, he felt his age: "I am not as able to do as much as I was twenty-four years of age," he admitted. But one major advantage in his situation was that he was working much closer to his home than he did in Yorkshire "so near as to go home at noon for dinner." The very idea of coming home for lunch break must have been highly appealing for those who had to walk for hours to get to their mines in the North Pennines, or stay in barracks on site.[52] Buxton also remained optimistic and apparently in good cheer, as he noted that mining was a bit like gambling: "[S]ome are more fortunate than others. If a person should strike up a good digging he soon gets himself a raise as they call it here but there is more blanks than prises."[53]

Even better, Yorkshire miners were able to combine mining with some other occupation in the Upper Mississippi, where the local economy was rapidly developing and offering newcomers some flexibility in their adjustments. For Matthew Dinsdale mining was a convenient alternative occupation to augment what little he got for preaching, his main life calling. In January of 1845 he travelled the 10 or so kilometres from Peddlars Creek to Mineral Point where he "became acquainted with several pious persons," preached there on Sunday, and headed for Galena until friends urged him to stay longer in Mineral Point. There:

I thought I would try mining or rather digging as the employment is very properly called. I went two days in company with a man, as two generally go together. We went to prospect, that is, to try to find mineral, we dug 3 or 4 holes to the depth of a few feet, on the second day we came to a little float mineral, which often betokens a body of it at no great distance ... But two days tired me of uncertainties, for a person may work for years and get nothing ... I am partial to digging or mining but would not like to depend on it for a living. If I had a farm I should be apt to employ myself a little in searching for Mineral. Many respectable persons do nothing else.[54]

Yorkshire miners and smelters in the Upper Mississippi showed an uncanny ability to combine various forms of work, especially when intending ultimately to farm.[55] Coming from the nation with the most diversified economy, they were more likely to have a variety of skills and experiences which gave them flexibility, allowing them to shift occupations in their quest for a farm. Recent research confirms that English immigrants generally were unique for their complex employment backgrounds and ability to shift back and forth between working at various crafts and farming, ultimately to become successful farmers in America.[56]

A good example of these complex employment patterns is Thomas Lewis Walker, another Askrigg emigrant who at age twenty-four left on the *Saxony* and survived the cholera-plagued trip up the Mississippi. He was a stonemason by trade, having learned it from his father, and seems to have left Yorkshire to have a brighter future. After arriving in Galena, Thomas and his brother Peter went to Lafayette County, Wisconsin and mined lead near Benton and New Diggings. But as a stonemason he could choose to do that in Illinois and then return to mining. He then juggled mining, smelting, and purchasing minerals for a furnace near Shullsburg until he had enough cash to buy a 240-acre farm 14 kilometres south of Muscoda, only to exchange it for a different farm in Grant County, starting with 40 acres and then purchasing adjacent lots to expand it. He continued to farm until he began serving in the Civil War and then bought an additional 160 acres in Kansas.[57]

What ultimately allowed such remarkable opportunities for the immigrants from North Yorkshire was America's booming demand for lead, used primarily for paint, printing type, pewter, glass, bearings, ceramic glaze, and later, batteries, toys, leaded windows, and the like. The Civil War sparked new demand: an estimated 80 per cent of the lead ammunition for both North and South came out of Platteville alone. The importance of lead in Wisconsin's history and culture can be seen in its state seal, which has lead bars in the symbol, and in the fact that the "badger state" is named after the "badger holes," the dugouts that those early miners lived in. North Yorkshire immigrants played central roles in this story.[58]

As important as Yorkshire miners and smelters were to the history and development of the Upper Mississippi, they were only a part of the story of North Yorkshire migration to North America. At the same time, many others were leaving other parts of North Yorkshire for Canada, as they had done in the previous century.

Upper Canada

I would be quite willing, personally, to leave that whole country a wilderness
for the next half-century but I fear if Englishmen do not go there, Yankees will.

JOHN A. MACDONALD,
FIRST PRIME MINISTER OF CANADA

While Yorkshire Dales miners and smelters and their families settled in the
Upper Mississippi, people from other parts of North Yorkshire were pouring into Upper Canada. Yorkshire people led the early-nineteenth-century
movement to Canada: from 1820 to 1840, more people left Yorkshire for
Upper and Lower Canada than any other English county.[1]

John and Ann Knaggs

Among the wave of Yorkshire immigrants to Upper Canada were John
and Ann Knaggs, who left the area of Rosedale and Lastingham, on the
southern edge of the North York Moors, in 1830. They knew much about
farming and livestock. In some ways they seem typical. On 7 April they
set sail, probably from Whitby, and were "in company of Thomas Easton
and his wife all the way." They took two full months to land in Quebec.
Predictably, their first letter from Canada focused on their voyage. It was
a "very rough passage of eight weeks and five days." Storms tore off their
"main top mast, part of our sails, part of our bullworks and the seas rould
[rolled] mountains hy [high], it was beyond all humain conception to
conceve for I cannot make you believe without you were to see something
of a similar kind." Sickness and death were no strangers on board: "Ann was
sick about 8 days ... we lost a young woman on the 27th April which
was a shocking sight to see a humain body put into the sea ... we have
had prayer meetings ever since we lost the young woman, but I have to
inform you that we all fell short of provisions."[2]

After landing the Knaggses headed straight for Ontario and reported that they "like the Country very well." John was especially impressed by the "finest breed of horses I ever saw in any place," and that in Canada "they kill very good beef but their mutton is not very good."[3] The family first went to Sandy Beach, Ontario, and on the very day of their arrival John was hired as a farm labourer at 12 dollars a month. Six weeks later they proceeded South to Nelson (named after Admiral Nelson), Gore Township, in Halton County, Ontario. This area had been settled in the 1780s by Loyalist refugees of the American Revolution, and now English immigrants like them were following in their footsteps. Within the year the Knaggses settled on a farm about 50 kilometres west of Toronto that already had grist sawmills and several churches nearby; they rented the land for five years by working for the owner. The Knaggses apparently chose this place because they were only a couple of kilometres from Thomas and Hannah Easton, family friends who had left Danby earlier, along with their two children and mother-in-law. Thomas Easton had most likely arranged for the Knaggses' settlement nearby, though the letters are silent about this.[4] The final surviving letter from the Knaggses ends with mentioning they had Thomas Easton and his wife over for a visit. It appears that at least for the first few years and probably longer, they relied on friends from Yorkshire for company in Ontario."[5]

Writing to John's parents in October of 1830 – about five months after their landing – the Knaggses still seemed shaken by the voyage, recounting how "sometimes nothing but death [was] before us." But in the same letter they raved about their new Ontario home as much as any immigrant who settled in the Midwest, and in much the same tone: "Here you may buy land or you may take land for so much a year or you may take land on shares. Prices of land here is from 2 to 4 dollars an acer as its situated for market and you may take land that is cleared for one dollar an acer by the year. Here are no taxes to pay. Here is the finest breed of cattle I ever saw, in particular Oxen – no such in England." John goes on to describe the quality of the food, prices and wages, clearing land, how neighbours were expected to help each other, in much the same way that immigrants wrote about the United States. Indeed, for the Knaggses and other Yorkshire immigrants, Canada *was* America, with the same challenges and rewards: "A man that buys land in america must not think its all cleared land. When you buy a lot of land you must take your ax and go into the woods and chop down a piece of land and by the help of your

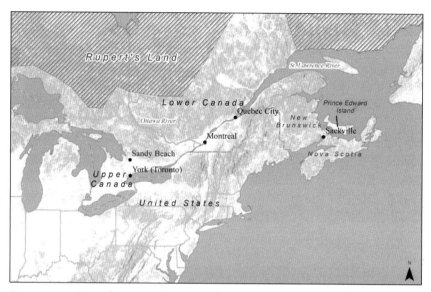

Figure 10.1   Map of Upper and Lower Canada, showing surrounding regions.

neighbours you are able to raise a log house in one day and when this is done you begin to knock down trees … After this is done you invite your neighbours which is call'd a bee day, some with oxen and some without, and they provide meat and whisky."[6] The working "bees" reveal how Yorkshire immigrants helped each other during hard times of adjustment and how their sticking together helped reinforce their identity. Farming bees and similar communal activities ran deep in Yorkshire culture, and to some extent still do.

For the Knaggses, pioneer life in Upper Canada was a mix of blessings and challenges: "No duty on any thing, it is a free country … we can go barefooted and barelegged. Cloging is dear, shoes is very bad, cobling is very light … Indeed here are land plenty and an industerous man may do well here without one copper if he have his health but a man that has got £40 or £50 in America is a gentleman."[7] On the inevitable question of whether or not he should encourage others to follow, John Knaggs sounds exactly like the Yorkshire immigrants in the United States: "I must conclude by saying that it's a pity that theirs so many privledges in America and so many distress in England that they will not come to America, yet I would not press upon any to come without it be chiefly their own mind, and if you dispute anything I have written it is best to come to see for yourselves and you will find all as I have written." And when John and Ann concluded their letter by saying, "Remember us to George Walker, Allen Peirson and all enquiring friends," we see again how immigrant letters were widely circulated in the Moors and made a deep impact.[8]

There was also homesickness.[9] John seemed to adjust quickly, reporting already in October of 1830 that he was "very content since I came," and adding that "if all poor laboring men was here it would be much better for their families."[10] But Ann was struggling. John wrote that she "has not been well settled … she often thinks about her Father and Mother, she would like to see them if she could."[11] A year later little had changed, as John wrote again that "I like America very well and I have had better health since I came than I had in England and Ann has had as good health as in England but not well settled. She is uneasy about you. She thinks she never shall see you again. She wants you to come to America."[12] It was not until yet another year had passed that John could reassure his family in the North York Moors: "Ann likes America very well and now she is better settled than she was. She thinks we can do better than we could at home."[13] John added that "I have no thoughts of coming back again," and he encouraged others to join them: "I want all to come to American that can."[14] By November of 1834 their adjustment seemed complete: Ann "is very content and likes this country well and cannot think of coming home again and I am in the same mind." It didn't hurt that they now had "10 mugg sheep, 12 fat hogs, 11 head of cattle."[15]

As the Knaggses got established, they continued to stay in touch with family and friends in Yorkshire. That network preserved family ties and provided precious items, including grey yarn, a frock and shift, laces, and various other things – all from Farndale, about 20 kilometres northwest of Pickering and not far from Rosedale. There was a strong and enduring link between North Yorkshire and Canada. Like those from the Dales who settled in the Upper Mississippi, those who came from the Moors to Upper Canada knew each other and used that knowledge to obtain items from England and to assist in the arrival of others.[16]

And others did arrive. By November of 1833, Knaggs's cousin Thomas Oxley was working nearby for an impressive £4 10s a month. And a year later others from the Rosedale area arrived. In November of 1834 the Knaggses wrote that John Middleton came to see them. He was hired at £31 5s for the year – an impressive sum – and reported on the good health of three others in his area whom the Knaggses had known in Yorkshire.[17]

Thus migration from the North York Moors to Canada took on a life of its own as family and friends followed one another, their move eased by the chains of information and help that awaited them from people they knew well. And the Knaggses could also say with confidence that "This is a much better Country for poor working men than Old England."[18]

Aside from the few luxuries sent to them from Yorkshire, the Knaggses seemed to want for little and were proud of their self-sufficiency: "We raise plenty of cowcumbers, mellons and pumpkins," they boasted, and "we can make our own sugar, soap and candles."[19] They were also able to defend themselves from menacing wildlife. In 1834 John Knaggs wrote to his parents saying that "I must inform you that I shot a bear. It came to my Indian corn and destroyed it very much. I put up a small scaffel [scaffold?] and sat their one moonlight night and shot him as he came in. It weighted upward of 20 stones. I sold his skin for 15s."[20]

John and Hannah Hutchinson

About the same time that John and Ann Knaggs were settling in Ontario, friends of theirs – the John and Hannah Hutchinson family – left the same part of Yorkshire ending up, not in Canada, but in Clarence, in Erie County (near Buffalo), New York.[21] They are a good example of how Yorkshire friends did not always settle together, and how migration decisions could be capricious. Like the Knaggses, the Hutchinsons sailed to Quebec, arriving on 14 July 1830 – only a month after the Knaggses' ship docked at the same port. Along with the Hutchinsons were others from North Yorkshire, including their brother's family, their father, and very likely other family members. Six additional passengers were members of the Headlams family from Glaisdale, also in the North York Moors, about 13 kilometres west of Whitby. Some were heading for Ontario; others for the United States. The Hutchinsons seemed to be divided along those lines. John and Hannah intended to settle in Canada, apparently close to the Knaggses; but John's father wanted to join others in Indiana, where North Yorkshire immigrants had recently settled.

How the Hutchinsons decided where to settle indicates an ability to improvise when necessary. While four Yorkshire families in the party proceeded to Indiana, the Hutchinsons stopped to rest at Syracuse, where other Yorkshire immigrants had settled. John and Hannah Hutchinson

were so "very weary with traveling. The weather was so uncommon hot
when we first came in the country that it very much affected us. We were
all unwell."[22] The death of their brother's child on 21 July dashed what little
spirits remained. But on the 28th they left Syracuse for Buffalo, arriving
there on 2 August – "all very weary with the hot weather."[23]

Their indecision was resolved when "a Gentleman came and said that
he had a farm to sell. We went to see it this day and we thought it would
suit us very well, we made a purchase of it and removed to it on the 4th of
August." The farm they purchased so precipitously was impressive – proof
that the Hutchinsons were not poor. It had a hundred acres, forty of them
cleared and sixty still forest, and "two dwelling houses and one stable – but
the houses is in bad repair." That was not all: "This we have in the bargain
also, one yoke of oxen, one cow, 10 sheep, 20 bushels of wheat, one barrel
of pork. The purchase money is 12 dollars per acre … the land is very good
and it is a very pleasant place."[24]

The Hutchinsons were not escaping hardship but maximizing future
rewards. They had at least $1,200 in capital and were leaving the Moors
for a better future. Their New York farm was by no means isolated – only
23 kilometres east of Buffalo – and near good roads. And their neighbours
were American-born farmers; they were not dependent on other Yorkshire
immigrants for company: "The houses are cloase by the high road side.
We have neighbours just at hand, one farmer not above 150 yards of[f]
and other two not above 250 yards of[f]and many more not above half
a mile of[f]."[25] It appears that the Hutchinsons fit in well, maybe somewhat "invisibly," with their American neighbours: "The people here are
very kind," John wrote. "They will do any kindness for us that lays in
their power."[26]

The Hutchinsons refer to other people from the Pickering area –
both immigrants and those considering a move to North America. The
Hutchinsons had not heard from their friends the Knaggses and seemed
unaware of where they had settled. This is evident in John Hutchinson's
urgent letter to his in-laws still in the Moors saying "I wish you would
send us word where John Knaggs is … we have never seen them nor
heard anything about them nor do we know where any of them is settled
that went with us. … If there be an account come from them I would
wish you would send us word where they are." The fact that John and
Hannah Hutchinson intended to settle in Ontario – until the opportunity
in New York popped up – suggests that they had some idea of where the

Knaggses were heading but had lost contact. Nevertheless, the lack of communication seemed to work in the Huchinsons' favour. They could not have been more pleased with their New York farm.[27]

The Hutchinsons had learned a lot about Ontario and compared it with New York State. There was much in common but also important differences. Writing back to Hannah's parents, John offered a clear-eyed, comparative appraisal of the advantages of the two places, knowing that others in the Ryedale area would read his letter. The Buffalo area offered bright opportunities for those with capital, but Canada was better for poorer farmers and farm labourers. Near Buffalo, they observed, "there are several farms to sell about here with cleared lots on them. A farmer may do swell here if he have £250 or £300 sterling. He may get 100 acres of land with cleared lots 40 or 50 acres cleared for 12 or 14 dollars per acer but as far as I can learn Canada is better than the united states for farmers and labourers. You can buy land for less money and make more of the produce of the land."[28] But both Canada and the United States offered a better life for most Yorkshire people. "I would say that ingeneral that people may do better here than in England if they have their health and be industerous and willing to work, but those that are not willing to work need not come here. I would say to such as are comfortabley situated for a living to sit still, but those that are not, come to America and if they have a little money they may do very well by coming here." Because the Hutchinsons themselves had considerable capital, they seemed to be ignoring their own advice that people who were "comfortably situated" should stay in England. Perhaps they lacked faith in Yorkshire's future. But the promise of landownership is what lured them to America.

Though the Hutchinsons settled near Buffalo on a whim, they were eager to help others in the North York Moors join them. "You may let us know if any of your neighbours talk of coming," John wrote. And he was not hesitant to recommend improvising their final settlement, as his family had done, as a way of making the best decisions in America:

If Thomas and James should come to America the next spring … it will be best for them to make their way to Canada first and if they can fall in for anything that is likely to suit them their it will be best for them to engage and send us word. If not they can make for us if they should land at New York … You will send us word and perhaps I shall have another opportunity of wrighting to you again before then … You must remember us to all enquiring friends and especially to all Brothers and Sisters and tell them we shall be glad to here of their welfare.[29]

Though the Hutchinsons were pleased with their new farm, they still seemed to need time to adjust. "If any of you would wish to know how we like America," John admitted to family and friends back in the North York Moors, "we do not as yet like it as well as England."[30]

Most who left the North York Moors for America did not have the resources the Hutchinsons had. So, they settled in parts of Ontario where land was cheaper – much cheaper than the parts of New York State that straddled the Erie Canal. They would have to pay the price in harder work. Subduing virgin Canadian land to farming required much courage and strength.

These qualities can be seen in the Lincoln family of Castleton, Danby Parish, in the heart of the North York Moors. Zeborah Lincoln was a widow with two, possibly three adult sons, and in 1837 they decided to leave their old cottage for Canada because her sons had heard "the wonderful news that pioneers were wanted in what was then called The Golden West, that farms of their own could be obtained by the industrious if they had courage to push out and sail to that beckoning country that offered free land to the strong and brave."[31] After auctioning off their few valuable items, they left, Zeborah probably never having travelled out of Danby Parish before in her life. The family was described as "poor in purse, but rich in enterprise, courage, and initiative." Other families in the region showed the same pluck and strength of body and character: at about the same time that the Lincolns left Danby, the Hurst family left nearby Glaisdale and walked all the way to Liverpool for their own voyage. It would be another twenty years before emigrants could take a train from Danby.[32]

The Lincoln family are a good example of poor people making it to Canada. Others got there through assistance, especially those from the Moors, who were more likely than Dales people to receive help. Between 1841 and 1844 five families from Danby, Westerdale, Guiseborough, and Moorsholm were assisted to Canada. The heads of household were farm labourers, and one weaver.[33]

Danby was a hot spot of emigration during this period, even though the local people were "not given to roaming and seldom travelled far

Figure 10.2   Danby, a typical North York Moors village where people left for Canada.

from their old homesteads." But exciting news about land in Canada had fired the imaginations of those who wanted to "become their own masters," and so some left. They were mostly young single farm labourers and some married couples, with poor prospects of being successful tenant farmers – never mind landowners – in Yorkshire.[34]

The Fewster Brothers

Both the Knaggses and Hutchinsons knew the family of Robert Fewster, from High Farm in Cropton, a village and parish a few kilometres northwest of Pickering, in the Ryedale district of North Yorkshire, on the border of today's North York Moors National Park. Three of Robert's seven sons joined the movement to Canada because the "moderate acreage of High Farm offered limited possibility for future employment." They were likely inspired by letters from the Knaggses and Hutchinsons, so all three of these migration stories were connected through friendships, shared information, and no doubt the excited discussions as they made their plans. The three emigrant sons were John, aged thirty-one, Robert, twenty-nine, and William, twenty-one. In 1849 they left for the "developing frontiers of Canada."[35]

After a seven-week voyage the Fewster brothers landed and made their way to Oxford County, in southwest Ontario. Like other Yorkshire families settling in the area at the time, the Fewsters got started by building a rough and simple log cabin and living on wild game. Their adjustment was very hard because the young men had been raised on their small family farm, High Farm, according to the well-developed practices of "high farming" and raising livestock. Apparently, the rigours of the Canadian wilderness split the three brothers up: John went to Cincinnati to work as a blacksmith. But Robert continued to pioneer in the Canadian forests and carve out a new home.[36]

After a year or two Robert Fewster returned to the Moors to fetch his wife, Nancy, and young daughter, Fanny. But he also managed to persuade his old neighbours, the Dodgson family, to come along, and so they sailed together back to Canada. The two families shared the same small cabin in the wilderness, until the Dodgsons could get established. The Fewsters and Dodgsons, along with neighbours, helped each other clear their lands. They held "stumping bees" in which teams of oxen pulled out the tree stumps, while the women held "carpet bees," in which they cut up old rags and created carpets for the early rough cabins. With this kind of mutual, collective help, and the important social interaction that came with it, the Dodgsons were able to establish their own farm right across the road from the Fewsters: as in the North York Moors, they were neighbours once again. The ties between the families remained for a long time: after Nancy Fewster died in 1862, Robert married the Dodgsons' eldest daughter, Sarah Ann, aged about twenty-three – more than twenty years younger than him.[37] The Fewsters prospered in Canada. Robert eventually had six sons to help with the backbreaking work of clearing land, and by 1875 he had come to own some 275 acres. They also associated with other Yorkshire immigrants: the Fewsters not only intermarried with the Dodgsons, but Robert's daughter Fanny married a fellow Yorkshire immigrant, William Smith.[38]

Robert Fewster never lost his North Yorkshire accent. Many years after he had settled in Oxford County a woman approached him to buy some butter, and when he replied, "no mare to spare," the woman responded, "I don't want mare, I want butter."[39] He also continued to enjoy singing old comical Yorkshire songs that he had brought with him to Canada: "I Drove my Father's Pig," and "I came to your Wedding without any Bidding." He never did return to England: by the time he expressed a desire, he was too old, and when his daughters said they wanted to see the old country, he told them "they would not like the place, people or customs." Robert Fewster died in 1893 at age seventy-two.[40]

John and Hannah Strickland

Yet another North York Moors family in Upper Canada was that of John and Hannah (Peirson) Strickland, one of the oldest families in Rosedale. In the spring of 1843, they and their five daughters along with John's mother Margaret left their Gill Bank Farm, Thorgill, in Rosedale, for a new home in Ontario. John was born in Farndale, a few kilometres to the west, but when he was three his parents moved to Gill Bank Farm. After his father died, in 1823, the sixteen-year-old had to care for his mother and six siblings. But in 1830 he was afforded the opportunity of a lifetime: to go on an "adventure tour" of America in 1830 and 1831 with an older companion by the name of John Simpson, who was originally from Rosedale, had moved to Ontario, returned to Rosedale for a visit and was now taking John with him. That John could take two years to tour North America suggests that his was not a poor family.

John carefully recorded his tour, which eventually became the basis for his family's move to Ontario some dozen years later. He and Simpson set out from Rosedale in 1830. To save money they had their luggage sent ahead of them and then walked, often in the rain and "foot sore," to Rochdale. There they took a stagecoach to Manchester, walked a stretch, and then took a "cart" to Liverpool, arriving on Good Friday. Because their luggage had not yet arrived, they passed the time by visiting the Catholic Chapel, "surprised to see what superstision remained in the world." As was often the case, after their luggage did arrive their ship was delayed by bad weather and the two had to wait nervously for the weather to improve, passing the time again by seeing the town and area, writing letters, and attending Methodist prayer meetings.[41]

As his ship left port John Strickland probably summed it up for many others by recording: "I stoped on deck till my head ached looking towards my native shore I then went between decks and with a kind of joy mixed with hope and fear I lay myself down on my bed with the thought of all my old acquaintances in my mind … I then went on deck again to see if I could still see old England but it was then out of sight."[42] And then, of course, there were the storms and sickness: "The waves rowl'd so high," he recorded in his diary, "that when a vessil was passing us we were often out of sight one of the other."[43] Later in the voyage, "I thought at first that the ship was sinking," and "the wind was so violent it tore away the fore sail and threw the man down at the Wheel." To prevent sickness, the ship captain "burnt Vinegar and sugar in the howl."[44] Burying a nine-month-old boy at sea in a cask added to a sense of doom.[45]

Finally landing in New York and touring the city, Strickland and Simpson went to see the legendary Niagara Falls. His description reads like a modern tourist's account: "[W]hen we came within a mile or so of the Falls the ground almost trembled under us with the Falling of the water we arrived in the village about 3 oclock the American Falls is just below the Village we went and took a view of them and then went across the river and went down among the shrubs … till we came to the Canada or horse shoe Falls here we were entertained with Maganeficent view of the Fall all together they are quite as wonderful as I expected … we saw the place were sam Patch leapt down … we went with our umbrella's up and as fast as we could."[46]

Everywhere they went on their "adventure journey" Strickland and Simpson seemed to bump into other English immigrants, including those from North Yorkshire. On 23 June they "Lodged at an English man's house," and the following day they stopped in a tavern for refreshment. "[W]hen we went in they asked us if we were from England and on telling them we where they asked us from what part saying they where from Lastingham," which was just several kilometres south of their native Rosedale. The tavern keepers had left thirteen years earlier, and "they were very pleased that we had called."[47] Not only that, but 3 kilometres further, on the very same day, they stopped in to see John Atkinson, who had left the Rosedale area for Canada years before. By now Atkinson had his own mill, with two stones, "and is seemingly doing well … we got our dinners with him," and then went on their way.[48]

Over the next several days the two travellers continued to make their way, stopping to see people they had known in Yorkshire – people who had been virtual neighbours and friends. Visiting Francis Dawson and his wife, Strickland "got a good talk about Old England and the poor slaves that still remained theirin."[49] Two days later they heard that "John Petch from Bransdale lived not far we went to see him," and later the same day they ran into a woman who had married yet another immigrant from the Rosedale area, and enjoyed their hospitality.[50] The familiarity of it all was remarkable, especially so when they recognized the many Yorkshire and English place names that dominated the region: York (later Toronto), Whitby, Pickering, Scarborough, Oxford, Bradford, Westminster, the Thames River ... the list was almost endless. And when Strickland returned in 1843 to settle permanently with his family, he made his way through Ontario via towns whose names he well knew: especially Pickering, Whitby, and York.[51] Londesborough, in Huron County, Ontario, was named after Londesborough in the East Riding of Yorkshire by an immigrant from that place, Dr Thomas Hagyard, who had chosen the site because he saw its potential for development.[52]

Along the way on their "adventure tour" Strickland and Simpson visited more old friends from the Rosedale area who had settled near Palmyra. They were all "very glad to see us and hear from old England" and treated them most kindly.[53] And toward the end of their tour in New York via the Erie Canal, they stopped in to see Richard Dales, originally from Danby, only about 11 kilometres from their native Rosedale. They continued to stop to see other English immigrants when they could.[54]

The familiarity of North American culture and place names in Canada was striking for English travellers like Strickland and Simpson. Its culture and society had been derived so much from northern England, especially Yorkshire, during the previous century. One Yorkshire immigrant tailor in York (later Toronto) was Francis Jackson, who in 1831 noted that there were "a great many from Yorkshire," and the result was that "the place resembles England the most of any place I have seen."[55] Not only did he enjoy the company of others from Yorkshire, but the shops on the high street were "well-stocked with all kinds of goods – same as in Hull."[56]

From Ontario John Strickland and Simpson crossed into Detroit, on 7 July, and asked directions for a recent immigrant from Kirkbymoorside, a mere 13 kilometres or so from Rosedale. As they continued through Michigan in 1830, they called on more people they had known in the North York Moors.[57] Running short of cash they dug wells: for one well that took five days to dig they each got 20 dollars.[58] They spent much of the rest of the summer working for an Englishman by the name of Cade in Michigan.[59] The work digging a cellar in very hot weather was hard, and on 9 August Strickland "was taken with the Ague." A week later he "sent for the doctor he gave me some physic and a puke for which he charged 2 Dollers."[60]

The travelling duo were particularly struck by differences in America's class system. While digging wells they went to see a justice of the peace and were told that the "esquire" was in the field. So, "as he was the first Esquire I had heard of I thought I should like to see what Esquires were like in Michigan." After locating him Strickland observed that "when I go to him he was pulling flax without either shoes or stockings or hankerchief with his shirt neck sliping over this shoulders," and with classic understatement concluded that "I saw a little Difference between a squire in the Terrytory of Michagan and a Squire in Yorkshire."[61]

Strickland and Simpson were especially fascinated by the Native Americans, who by this time were becoming tourist curiosities. Strickland recorded on 22 July that "this day I saw above 100 Indians of the scoces Tribe & it was the best show I ever saw in my life."[62] In December of that year the two Yorkshire travellers walked in the isolated forests of west Michigan and "heard somebody shouting in the woods so we went by the sound till we came to them it was some Indians that had made afire and boiled some deer we eat some with them and then walked on."[63] But they found the wolves so menacing that "I was afraid to lay down and I did not know what to do the wolves were running on all sides in search of there prey and I was left alone I walked as fast as I could."[64]

Soon after John Strickland's return to Yorkshire he married Hannah Peirson, also of Rosedale, and they farmed Gill Bank Farm and raised five daughters. Now, thirteen years after his tour, in 1843, John and Hannah Strickland and their family were emigrating and retracing the steps John had made in 1830–31. John noticed that Ontario had developed a great deal during the interlude, and that there were far more fellow North Yorkshiremen than before. Now he could stop in for familiar company and refreshment at even more places.[65]

When they departed for Canada, they left Gill Bank Farm, which was a thriving, viable farm, to John's brother William. This must have boosted their resources because within only a few months of their arrival in Ontario they purchased property (apparently improved land) and farmed there until 1854. In 1863 John and Hannah made a return visit to Rosedale to see relatives, and later they moved into Toronto.[66]

Pioneer Life in Canada

Like the Dales immigrants in the Upper Mississippi, North York Moors immigrants in Ontario warned their relatives and friends in Yorkshire that the new country was rough and could be off-putting. In 1834 John and Ann Knaggs admitted to their parents that "we must own that the country look a little rough." Yet, "we must not go at looks for ... it is not the best cleared parts of this country that is best. There is a better chance for a poor man in the new parts of this country and that looks very rough and particular for these that just coming in."[67]

In rural Canada's favour was its lack of impoverished people, due to work being easy to find and neighbours willing to help. This might also be said of the United States, but Ontario did have an additional advantage in that "any that is taken sick and is destitute of support themselves there is hospitals to take them two that is supported by the government."[68] And as for single women, "it is a very poor woman that cannot support herself when in good health in this country."[69]

But cholera was a problem in both the United States and Canada. As early as 1832 John and Ann Knaggs reported "that dreadfull disease called the asiatic cholera has been brought to this country by the emegrants and has been raging throughout America to a great extent. People died so fast in Towns and cities that the living could scarce get the dead out of the way fast enough."[70] Two years later, in November of 1834, the Knaggses reported again that "the cholera has been very fatal in this country, in this summer and has swept very many into the cold clay and it has left a great many fatherless and motherless children and these that has nothing to support themselves with, there is places prepared for them and poor widows to take care of them and is kept by superscription amongst the Gentlemen and they are given out to those that will take them in."[71]

Both the United States and Canada also suffered from ague, which seemed to strike wherever people were pioneering in the forests, and where stagnant water bred mosquitoes. In the Buffalo area in 1830 John Hutchinson reported back to his wife's family still in the North York Moors that "my Brother has had the ague and has got better but he has begun again. And he warned others that before they commit to joining them "you will want to know wheather we have had the ague or not – there is no appearance of it yet."[72]

Successful Adjustment

Despite the hard work and difficult conditions of pioneering in Upper Canada, North Yorkshire immigrants adjusted successfully. Some sound like they did so with relative ease, though this may be a bias in their letters. They often commented on their diet, extolling the superior quantity and quality of food in North America. John and Ann Easton, from the Pickering area, were delighted by the quality of bread where they settled, in Nelson Ontario: "I often wishes you with some of this fine light bread," John gushed to his parents back in Yorkshire. "We never saw a bit of brown bread since we came. We have capital wheat in America but all log houses of wood and wood to burn ... we have plenty of milk for fetching where I work and I never was amongst such good and oblidging neighbours and more kind and mo free as they are. Every neighbour is ready to do any favour we want. Here is plenty of fruit piers [pears] and apples."[73]

The Knaggses also relished their heartier diet. Now they could eat like the richer people of Yorkshire, and this new sense of equality was important to them: "As for this country I can live as well as some of the Gentlemen of your place, for I can have Beef or Pork or fresh meat three times a day and Tea three times a day for I have got both Beef and Pork and wheat and potataos and indian corn for to do for this summer ... I intend to buy a Yoke of Oxen and a cow and I will be able to pay for them all."[74] By late October the Knaggses had their "Yoak of cattle and a Cow and a ... Calf and 2 good hogs to kill and 5 for another year," and they had cleared enough land on the rented farm to sow 9 acres with wheat. They had bought their land when prices were still low and were doing well, so they stressed to their parents, relatives, and friends in Yorkshire that "if you have any thoughts of coming to america you must come soon for land keeps rising."[75]

Isaac Bravender was another North Yorkshire immigrant who seems to have adjusted very successfully in Ontario. Bravender came from Malton, just south of Pickering, and enjoyed old friends and neighbours who had also settled nearby. He wrote glowing accounts of his success to family still in Yorkshire: "I am doing very well," he wrote in 1846, "better than I expected for I have very good friends around me ... we have a cow and a heifer that we are raising and I bought two ewes this Spring ... we have two fat pigs ... I intend to have a yoke of oxen in another year if all is well."[76] Isaac's son added that "we thank God that we are in a fine part of the country amongst old neighbours of the Old Country."[77] Generally, the English were widely seen as Canada's most successful immigrants, with the fewest problems of adjustments, especially on farms. As one observer put it, the English "are among the best, and most wealthy farmers ... They soon become acclimated, and enjoy a degree of freedom and independence not exceeded, if attained, in any other part of the world."[78]

Mid-century

At mid-century Canada's demand for farmers, farm workers, and female domestic servants was growing; but at the same time more of England's emigrants were leaving industrial cities without the farm experience that Canada needed. North Yorkshire, however, with its lack of large industrial cities, continued to provide a high percentage of suitable immigrants.[79] In the 1850s the government agent stationed at Quebec was still reporting that ships from Hull were carrying mainly "farmers and agriculturalists, possessing capital." And in 1857 those leaving from Hull – mainly from North and East Yorkshire, and probably Northern Lincolnshire, were described as "respectable farmers, proceeding to friends in different sections of western Canada."[80] The stream of Yorkshire farming families continued throughout the century.[81]

In the second half of the century, however, some of Ontario's appeal was waning. The best cheap lands were already taken, Yorkshire's economy had improved, and the more diverse opportunities of the United States were proving attractive. Still, Hull saw many local people leaving for Canada. On 11 April 1857, it was reported that "the present week has witnessed hundreds of leave-takings on quays and on board ... from this port for our North American Colonies." They were leaving on the *Fergus*, some two hundred passengers in all, and "the passengers are chiefly healthy young men and women ... and with one exception they are either farm labs or country tradesmen."[82] The women mentioned here were not necessarily attached to men. Mid-century census returns for the North York Moors show that women often migrated independently from men, and they seem to have been as likely as men to leave the Moors for other nearby areas; in fact, more than half the emigrants who left the Danby area for Middlesborough in the 1850s were women.[83] But fewer women left for Canada independently. Canada's rewards and challenges were widely known in North Yorkshire. One Yorkshire immigrant, John Fell, wrote a letter from Cavan, Ontario, to his friends back in Yorkshire, where it was published. Fell's encouragement was more muted than that of earlier writers: "There are some I should advise to come, and others I should not, for instance, I would encourage any laboring man to come whatever his prospects may be at home ... a tenant farmer of small capital may also come here with every prospect of success, if he be robust in health & industrious & especially if he has a rising family of boys ... but I should not advise a man of small means to being farming at first, but to work for hire ... The large capitalist may also improve his means here."[84]

Fell tempered his enthusiasm with warnings that Canada was a rough country, and that in places like Cavan, the Irish were becoming dominant. The result was, according to Fell, "the laws are not so well executed, nor so good order kept in society, we have more rough uncivil characters, & fewer trustworthy respectable men. The disorders are chiefly attributable to the Irish, who form the majority of the population ... they are a clamourous discontented people, & very thriftless in general, & decidedly the worst farmer in America ... nevertheless, they are kind hearted, & will do anything for you only keep in with them."[85]

Other problems were emerging in Ontario in the 1850s, ones that likely alarmed prospective immigrant farmers and steered some to the United States instead. John Fell's letter turned ominous: "[T]he harvests have failed the last two seasons, & the prices have been low, which has caused great distress here. People speculated most extravagantly for some years previously on credit, their payments have come due in scarce times, the consequence is that thousands are seduced from good circumstance to beggary, thousands have sold their bread corn to pay debts."[86]

The problem of low prices was just beginning. As we shall see, after the Civil War overproduction in an increasingly globalized and interconnected grain market presented new challenges to farmers in both Canada and the United States. But still the land beckoned. From mid-century through the rest of the century, it was farming and land ownership that ultimately drew most people from North Yorkshire.

Farming

They say Heaven is a grand spot. But Wensleydale is varra bonnie.

WILLIS FAMILY PAPERS

The history of English farming in America is long and significant. From the earliest days of colonization, the prospect of cheap or even free land drove much of the migration across the Atlantic. And with land came the vote, both in colonial assemblies and in post-Revolution governments. Land meant freedom and social mobility; it even had religious dimensions. For Jeffersonians and many Americans land meant self-sufficiency and independence from the merchant class, and later from the industrial capitalists. Land and virtue were closely connected and formed the backbone of the new republic. For the English, North America – whether the United States or Canada – offered a new start, the means of fulfilling one's potential, and a new environment.

Trends

The first half of the nineteenth century saw a great variety of conditions and trends for English farmers. Agriculture recovered after the Napoleonic Wars. The new Corn Laws limited imports and protected profits for farmers and landlords, with non-farmers paying the cost through higher food prices. In the late 1820s and 1830s, the introduction of new farm machinery displaced some farm labourers and increased hardship. These changes contributed to the "Swing Riots," the destruction of machinery and crops by labourers who saw little alternative but to resist the disruption of their traditional way of life. The 1840s added industrial depression to the mix, and bad weather and crop failures – most horrifically, the potato famine – brought disaster.

But the mid-century was a pivotal time. The repeal of the Corn Laws in 1846 gradually led to falling prices as the British grain market was opened to competitors. Lower prices put pressure on English farmers, especially young tenant grain farmers on marginal lands. They lacked the means and capital to raise production and compensate for the lower prices. Some of these responded by leaving for North America, most commonly the American Old Northwest.[1] And yet the early 1850s also saw the beginning of the "mid-Victorian boom," which ushered in a period of sustained growth and prosperity that benefited many people, including farmers.[2]

Research with passenger lists and the census reveals some interesting trends in agricultural migration. Farmers – including tenant farmers, farmers' sons, and independent farmers – were significantly over-represented among English immigrants, especially before and during the mid-century period. In 1851 less than 8 per cent of Britain's adult male labour force were farmers, according to the census of that year. But about a quarter of the adult male immigrants to the United States were recorded as farmers on the passenger lists. Because they were disproportionately young, some of these were perhaps tenant farmers, or even farm labourers with aspirations who identified themselves as "farmers" to the writers of passenger lists. On the other hand, many had means: they showed a distinct ability to afford multiple passage tickets and migrate as families.[3] Furthermore, there are many documented cases of relatively prosperous English farmers migrating to America at this time. They appear to have been making long-term plans to come to America for land and a better future for their children. The middle decades of the century were a "golden age" for people to acquire fine farms, especially in the Old Northwest, where there were virgin lands and an evolving transportation network, centred on the Erie Canal, that linked farmers to markets.[4] People from North Yorkshire were in the vanguard of this movement.

Though less so than other parts of England, North Yorkshire suffered agricultural hardship in the late 1840s and prosperous mid-century.[5] In June of 1849 about two hundred tenant farmers met in Wetherby to protest repeal and discuss how "to alleviate the present distressed state of the agricultural community."[6] Thirsk had problems too: as late as 1850 the area had "unprecedented depression and privation to those engaged in agricultural pursuits."[7] It would take time for improvement to reach those at the bottom of the economy, so poor people in both North and East Yorkshire continued to emigrate from difficulties – even during the

"boom" year of 1851. In early April of that year, thirty people left Pickering
for America in one week while forty to fifty others were leaving Seamer,
near Scarborough. Some villages lost so many to emigration that net
depopulation occurred. Bridlington, on the North Sea, saw two hundred
of its three hundred people "preparing for America." In the streets of both
Kirkbymoorside and Scarborough in April of 1851 one could see "hundreds
of people likewise preparing for America," and the heads of these departing
families were "chiefly the best labourers found in the different parishes,
who go to America because they have not remunerative work at home."[8]

These examples come from the newspapers, which tended to focus on
hardship cases. Other evidence indicates that the agricultural movement
from England to America was decidedly mixed: there were many who
were indeed poor, but others who were not. Farmers were among the
most able to afford multiple passage tickets and to travel as families.
And though this was a time of adjustment in England, it was also a time
when new American lands were opening with the expansion of the export
grain market. Especially after the repeal of the Corn Laws, farmers were
in effect being invited to leave a precarious situation in England, come
to the United States, and tap the new grain market that was opening in
their mother country. Prosperous farmers saw this as the best time to
become farmers of their own land in America, and many did just that.
Some of the English immigrant farmers who later had their biography
recorded in county histories had clearly been prosperous in England but
moved to the United States to own large farms. Even those who were
leaving hardship were not motivated by hardship alone; most were also
set in motion by opportunities in American farming. Probably most had
considerable resources and ambition. One might conclude that the "pull"
forces (especially the promise of land ownership) were stronger than the
"push" forces of rural depression.[9]

English Methods in America

English farmers in America confronted a new farm environment. England
had limited land but a seemingly inexhaustible of labour to work it.
Therefore, the English had developed "high farming" based on "English
methods" that were promoted by famous agrarian scientists like Arthur
Young. This involved a high ratio of labour and capital to land in the form

of more ploughing, fertilizing, applying lime, collecting and spreading manure, and rotating crops. English farmers also took great care to prevent erosion and soil exhaustion. The land was not to be misused.[10]

America's farming environment was the opposite. It had a seemingly inexhaustible supply of rich land, but not enough labour to work it. Confronted with limited and expensive labour, Americans turned to land-intensive methods that saved labour costs. The result was land exploitation with little of the careful cultivation, fertilizing and manuring, rotation, and other English practices. Better to plant as many crops as quickly and easily as possible and then move on to fresh land if it became exhausted. In America, English methods seemed unnecessary and impractical.

It is telling that some farmers who remained in Yorkshire envied their friends who had gone to America and no longer had to do as much ploughing and manuring. As John Humphrey complained from Wensleydale to Matthew and Jane Willis in Wisconsin in 1849: "[A]nd then there is all Labour besides, that is where you have but one Ploughing we have perhaps two or three, and then we have to manure our Land and Lime it and after that is done and all other Labour, we can only grow corn every other year, and when that is done we can only get light crops say 20 to 35 Bus of Oats an Acre and from 15 to 25 of Wheat."[11]

English immigrants who had been steeped in "high farming" were often horrified by American farm practices. Some even stuck with their English methods and prospered enough to convince their American neighbours to adopt English methods themselves.[12] Over time, however, most were forced to abandon their old methods, face the realities of America's agricultural economy, and adopt American methods to save labour costs, especially as production and labour costs soared after the Civil War.

Whether retaining English methods or adopting American ones, English immigrants still made notable contributions to American agriculture. Some became known for importing finer breeds of cattle, sheep, and pigs.[13] Furthermore, the English were among the first to go out to the Prairies, challenging the traditional assumption that treeless lands were not fertile enough to produce abundant crops. As we shall see, this was true of the Old Northwest and Texas. The English showed Texans that the prairie soils, far from being sterile, could grow abundant crops of wheat and cotton as well as support livestock.[14] In these ways the English played important roles in American agriculture.[15]

Combining Farming and Crafts

Another distinguishing feature of the English was their remarkable ability to use craft work as a stepping stone to farming, often combining craft work with farming to buy land.[16] Some resorted to their old craft, such as carpentry or blacksmithing, and hired someone else to work their farms.[17] A surprising number without any apparent experience in agriculture plunged straight from skilled craft work in England into farming the American wilderness. New data show an ability among people from a variety of non-agricultural backgrounds to do just that.[18] Especially in the Old Northwest, the English commonly shifted from crafts or other kinds of work – even the professions – to farming. Because so many had a background in crafts they could fall back on, the English may have been more persistent than others when it came to meeting setbacks on new farms and staying on the land. They also seem to have been less restless than their American neighbours, seeing rising living standards not in rising land values and selling for a profit, but rather in farm life itself.[19]

North Yorkshire Farmers

Generally, the farmers who left North Yorkshire for North America during the first half of the century fit these broad patterns, but with some distinctive characteristics. As we have already seen, those who left the Dales for the Upper Mississippi found a landscape and geology ideal for starting out in mining and then switching to farming, or to farm straight away. The region had familiar minerals and the rolling hills and relatively cool weather that suited their form of agriculture: pasture perfect for livestock but not as good for row crops. Some of the immigrants sought out land in Wisconsin that most resembled the Dales.[20] In the Upper Mississippi and other parts of America, Dales immigrants naturally practised diversified agriculture – raising chickens and cattle and growing the grain to feed them – but also growing a cash crop, like wheat, to purchase what they could not grow. A bit later in the century, dairy products became a source of revenue.[21] The parallels with the economy of the northern Yorkshire Dales are striking. The people and their socio-economic culture seemed to flow naturally from one part of the world to another – to places with similar geological and geographical features.[22]

People from other parts of England enjoyed this good fit and shift to farming as well. Center Grove, for example, was also the new home of George Mollart, a miner from Staffordshire. By the 1870s he had acquired a farm of over 100 acres by putting together old mineral lots formerly owned by Joseph Brunskill. And in 1881 he bought town lots owned by Swaledaler Richard Bonson, on gently sloping land that was perfect for raising livestock. In 1882 he bought additional lots from Bonson, making him the largest landowner in Center Grove.[23] Thus the shift from mining to farming occurred in various timings and strategies. Though most began by mining and smelting lead before purchasing farms, others jumped right in. They had chosen the region for its minerals and farmland, and because other Dales immigrants provided a community.

Farming without Prior Experience

Some North Yorkshire immigrants without farm experience also took up farming. In 1832 and 1833 a group from Swaledale that included William Woodward and his son John, John and Metcalf Bell, William Waters, George Cottingham, Joseph Brunskill, and James Pratt, all settled in Medina County, Ohio. They were miners described as "unaccustomed to farming, but soon adapted themselves to the necessities of their surroundings." They were ambitious: Pratt said he emigrated because he "wanted to be his own boss."[24] Recent research highlights many cases of English people from an astonishing variety of backgrounds – but without agricultural experience – successfully farming in America. They included lawyers, judges, accountants, sailors, grocers, and engravers. And if they could do it, surely Yorkshire miners could.[25] In the Dales few were completely detached from agriculture: even those without direct farm experience were still close to the soil and observed farming. Probably most Dales miners had done at least some farm work in their lives, so they were well suited to make the shift from mining to farming in America.

Some Yorkshire craftsmen went directly to American farming. One was Benjamin Beevers, born in Snaith, East Yorkshire in 1811. He was apprenticed as a carpenter for seven years at Thorne, in South Yorkshire, and then worked at his craft for seven more years. But in 1846 he left for America with his wife Mary and came to Lenawee County, Michigan, where Mary had relatives – illustrating again the network of information that determined destinations – and the Beeverses plunged directly into farming, raising fruits.[26]

It surely helped to have farm experience, and farm labourers had the most to gain by going to America. William Wetherall, for example, was born 13 kilometres from York in 1824 and raised by his uncle after his father died. At age fourteen, "with no moneyed capital, but an abundance of energy and determination," he first worked on a Yorkshire farm for six years to get the capital he needed to buy land, like many other young Yorkshire farm labourers. He then sailed to New York and proceeded to Allegan County, Michigan. There he eventually owned 230 acres, raised livestock, and earned a reputation of one of the county's best farmers.[27] One can imagine people in York excitedly reading his letters and being inspired by his rise from poor Yorkshire labourer to owner of a large American farm.

Choosing Land

One of the most significant decisions any immigrant could make was choosing the right land. Usually a great deal of planning and investigation was involved, through letters and sometimes immigrant guides and pamphlets.[28] But some virtually improvised their settlement decisions, another indication of their ability to adapt to new and changing situations. We have already seen this with the Hutchinson family, who chose a farm near Buffalo even though the family was heading for either Ontario or Indiana. But there are other intriguing examples. After being cheated out of his inheritance by his stepfather, Sampson George faced a bleak future in North Yorkshire and so in June of 1836 he left the village of Galyes (near Newsham and Earby Hall – about 13 kilometres northwest of Richmond), with his wife Ann and five children for America, where he hoped to buy land and hunt game.[29] After a seven-week voyage to fulfill their "great ambition," the George family landed in New York with the intention of settling in Connecticut near a friend who had recommended it – only to find that the friend had mysteriously returned to England. So the George family decided then and there to try out Illinois because they had heard good things about it. They took the Erie Canal to Buffalo and then a boat to Chicago, and from there headed to the Fox River Valley. But upon arrival, they heard reports of disease in the area, so they changed their plans yet again and came to Rockford, which was said to be healthier. Not that it was more developed: they found that Rockford consisted of a hamlet of three log cabins with dirt floors, one of which the family rented. The damp conditions were unhealthy: after a hunting trip Sampson George developed lung fever and died only five weeks after their arrival. Ann and the children struggled just to survive in a strange, undeveloped area, and they suffered great hardship and privation.[30]

To the Prairies

America's prairies appealed to North Yorkshire immigrants, who helped open the prairies to farming by being the first to settle on them. Among them were Joseph and Susannah Bugg. Married in 1833 in Leven in the East Riding, the couple lived close to a canal connected to Hull, so it was easy to get to that port from which they sailed for Quebec in 1834. Spending the winter of 1834–35 with relatives in the Toronto area, the couple then left for a farm several kilometres northeast of Terre Haute, Indiana, and then four years later moved to Christian County. Here they were the first to settle on the prairie, a kilometre from the nearest forest. All other settlements in the area were "along the timber, and the Bugg family was the only one which had ventured out on the prairie."[31]

The significance of this event was recorded forty years later: the area where the Buggs settled was "an uncultivated prairie, which people in those days had little expected would develop into the fine farms which now may be seen in that part of the county." Five years later they moved even farther out on the prairie, and "at that date there was no settlement on the prairie in their neighbourhood. For eighteen miles [30 kilometres] the prairie extended toward the east without a single house or improvement of any kind. People wondered at their choosing the prairie for a residence, when they might have located in the timber."[32] Americans critical of their decision were not their only problem; in this isolated area there was a very real threat of wild animals: "Wolves were abundant and troublesome, filling the night with their howling, and carrying away pigs and fowls."[33]

The Bugg family struggled – but not because of the prairie soil. Both Joseph and Susannah suffered from chills and fever associated with ague, and their cows and horses died. Susannah Bugg later recalled that they "almost wished that they had remained in Old England, or at least were back at their former home in Indiana." And yet they persevered, gradually improving a farm of 380 acres with the help of their eight children.[34]

The Marmaduke Eckles family also came to the United States prairie, via chains laid by relatives who had preceded them. They came from about 16 kilometres out of Hull, where Marmaduke ran a brick yard and with his wife Hannah raised seven children. Wishing to make more of their lives and secure a better future for the children, Marmaduke and Hannah wrote to her brother Bennie Gates, who was in Dixon, on the Illinois prairie, who agreed to sponsor them. So, the family sailed from Hull in 1850 aboard the *Allen Brown*,[35] a terrifying voyage. Other difficulties followed them all the way to Illinois. Taking a train from New York to Buffalo for the Erie Canal, Hannah hopped off at a stop to get food for the children and the train left without her. Her son Richard jumped from the moving train to be with his mother. Though they reunited a day later, Lake Erie proved as rough and terrifying as the Atlantic. Finally arriving in Chicago, the family hired a wagon to get to Dixon, the boys walking much of the way because the wagon was not large enough for them and their belongings.[36]

When the Eckles family arrived in Dixon they happily found that Bennie Gates had prepared a small house for them, and with such a good start the family prospered on the Illinois prairies. Marmaduke's sons made it possible with their combined effort of hard work. And yet Marmaduke "was dreadfully homesick." It did not help that the roof leaked, nor that his intention to practise his brickmaking trade was stymied by unsuitable clay that produced poor-quality bricks. Failing at brickmaking, he soon turned his full attention to farming, but tragically, three years later when Marmaduke and his son Joseph were working together, Joseph got his clothing caught in a threshing machine "and his life [was] instantly wiped out."[37] To add to the tragedy Marmaduke's health failed and he died in 1855. Not long afterwards the family lost their house and most of their belongings in a fire.[38]

Clearing Land

Clearing land was the most physically challenging task. Prairie land demanded much work to prepare it for planting, but wooded lands demanded even more. Most English immigrants chose land that required at least some clearing. In fact, surprisingly many chose virgin wooded land with no prior clearing at all. Clearing land was generally not what farmers did in England, but astonishingly, they seemed up to the task in America. In a sample of 421 English immigrants in Michigan, Ohio, Illinois, and Wisconsin, 105 clearly specified that they had cleared unbroken prairie or forested land. (Others did not specify, but many of them likely had to clear a considerable portion of their land – if not all of it. A mere 17 of the 421 specified that they had purchased farms already cleared and improved.)[39] English immigrants were willing and able to turn forests into farms.

And yet, few could have fully comprehended the sheer amount of work and privation that came with clearing land and putting up a home. Letters from America could hardly capture the scale of the task, and emigrant guidebooks were often rather idealistic. A popular guidebook from 1849 simply titled "Emigration" was perhaps rather too encouraging for those wishing to become pioneers on virgin land. Readers must have been dazzled by the images here, and they were likely underestimating the difficulties as well:

> A good log-house for dwelling in may be erected and finished in this county, say thirty feet long by twenty in breadth, two stories high, with stone or brick chimney, covered with shingles, completely finished for about 300 dollars, or a frame one of like dimensions, lathed and plastered, for 350 or 400 dollars. Buildings for cattle, sheep, hogs, &c., may be built for a mere song, as any labouring man can build such buildings without employing mechanics, as they are generally built of small logs, and covered cabin fashion, that is, with clap-boards fastened with rib poles. The clearing of land in this county is from three to ten dollars per acre; it depends upon how you have it cleared; if you take off all the timber, it costs more; if you deaden the large timber, and remove the small, it costs less.[40]

Some letters give us a glimpse of just how much time and work it took to clear a farm. Andrew Morris, a Lancashire weaver who bought land in Ohio took three years to clear only 13 acres, while another weaver took thirteen years to clear and fence 40 acres. One English cabinetmaker with little farm experience managed to break and clear only 2 acres of prairie in southern Ohio. The most impressive case we know of is John Fisher, who had learned farming from his father in Norfolk. With the help of at least two hired men and ten bullocks, he cleared 20 acres of Michigan prairie in just one year. Within five years he had cleared 75 acres.[41] And in 1849 Jonathan Richardson, a Yorkshire shoemaker with some farm experience, came to Kane County Illinois where he "purchased eighty acres of land, on which not a furrow had been turned or a rod of fence built. He at once erected a log cabin and in true pioneer style began life in America." The nearest market was Chicago, still a small town, "and many were the hardships and trials of frontier life which the family endured." Richardson worked at his old craft of shoemaking to acquire capital, and then devoted all his attention to his farm.[42]

Assimilating to American Agriculture

The shift to American farming came naturally to some Yorkshire immigrants. Though Matthew Dinsdale came to Wisconsin to preach, he also did farm work with the company of other Yorkshire immigrants. Writing to his mother and siblings from Pedlars Creek, near Mineral Point, Wisconsin, Dinsdale recalled working for his old friend from Askrigg, Peter Sill, who had helped him get established at English Prairie in Illinois:

> I think if you could sometimes have seen me at Peter's you would have thought me in a fair way for becoming an American farmer. Sometimes you might have beheld me amongst the timber dealing destructive blows upon a sturdy oak. One while you might have seen me with an immense whip a little ahead of a yoke of oxen hitched to an American Waggon, then again I was perhaps running at the rate of six miles [10 kilometres] an hour having an half bushel of grain in my hand and perhaps thirty hogs at my heels, scattering the grain to give them a little employment.[43]

Adopting American farm methods involved more than what Dinsdale described. In addition to the tight farm labour market, the immigrants had to contend with America's different climate and farm culture. A clearer picture of their adjustments in the Upper Mississippi is found in the correspondence of Matthew and Jane Willis and their extended family back in Wensleydale. As already noted, the Willis family left Yorkshire in 1845 aboard the *Hottinguer* and on that terrible voyage they lost their son, which seems to have cast a long shadow of guilt and self-doubt on them. Matthew Dinsdale helped get the Willis family established, and in the summer of 1845, he visited them and made some optimistic observations:

> [H]e [Matthew Willis] will be able to make an excellent farm. One that might be envied even in Wenlseydale. And then he has room to stir ... He has a very pleasant situation for his house near one of the groves, which shelters it from the east and is close to the water. ... There is nothing to hinder him. He will have to labour hard but his reward will be with him, not behind him. He intends to call the place Ramah in memory of this little boy who died on the Atlantic ... He has bought a small log house hear his place, where he will reside for the present.[44]

In October of the same year Dinsdale wrote to his mother in Askrigg and reported on how the Willis family was doing in this their first year in America. They were off to a good start but like others from the Dales were disgusted by the rough mining culture. Indeed, they seemed shocked by the violent, hard-drinking mining community in nearby Mineral Point:

> I went by Matthew Willis's place ... I found them as emigrants to this country often are found at first, with a house in its infancy, which could not boast of ability to keep outside either rough weather or fine, either light or darkness ... I found them all cheerful and content and in good health with the exception of the youngest boy which is only feeble. I told them by way of consolation that they had no rent to pay. Matthew smiled and said he had been talking about that just before, I am glad they have removed from the place they were at before as I suppose its moral state is most desperate. The people are notorious whisky drinkers ... I do think that there is not a worse place in Wisconsin.[45]

Letters continued to flow from both Dinsdale and Willis. Some were published in the *Wensleydale Advertiser* in 1846 and reveal an argument that caused a feud between them. Dinsdale found Willis's account much too positive and feared it would encourage unsuitable immigrants. Accordingly, Dinsdale wrote a polite response to the *Advertiser* questioning Willis's account, which greatly upset Willis's nephew who remained in

Wensleydale and no doubt Willis himself.[46] Their new antagonism was also fuelled by emerging differences over religion: Willis, a Quaker, had joined a free-thinking sect whereas Dinsdale remained a staunch Methodist.[47]

Matthew Dinsdale's assessment of farm life on the Wisconsin mining frontier proved to be more accurate, for soon after Matthew Willis wrote his rosy account in 1846, he and Jane lost their crops and nearly their house to a raging prairie fire. When Jane's parents, Thomas and Jane Longmire, heard the news they responded in a letter from Stainmore (near the North Yorkshire-Cumbrian border) saying, "[W]e were sorry to hear that after you had labored and toiled in cultivating your land that a great part of your crop should be destroyed" by a wildfire that "nearly destroyed your property" as well. "We should like you when you write to give us an explanation how they originated. We think it is quite unsafe to live in such a place." The Willises seemed to agree, for the event shook Matthew so much that his letters to Wensleydale now took on an opposite tone: "I am far from advising anyone to leave their native land for anything in Wisconsin," he now declared. "I believe farming in England, bad as it is, is much better than in America." Even the promise of land ownership faded into insignificance, it seemed, for "farming in Wisconsin is a poor business. You can scarcely meet with a farmer that can pay ready cash for 5 bushels of seed potatoes."[48]

In early 1847, two years after their arrival, Jane Willis still "did not like America as well as England." And yet, as bad a year as this was for the Willis family in Wisconsin it was worse for people in Britain. Jane's father – John Longmire – continues, "It has been a hard winter for poor People many are labouring under the pinching hand of Poverty in our own country and in the sister Kingdom of Ireland they are in a miserable state dieing by scores and hundreds for want of the necessarys of life."[49]

The Willis family held on by leasing land to lead miners for cash, but their struggles continued, both on the frontier and with their migration decision. Matthew was haunted by the loss of his son and held that against America, and perhaps himself, for leaving England in the first place. He seems never to have stopped considering returning to Yorkshire.[50] By mid-century he concluded that English farming was better than American, but that owning land was most important: "I believe farming in England, bad as it is, is much better than in America. However, we have one advantage here, we can have land of our own to cultivate and improve. And there is a peculiar pleasure, I confess, in working upon ones own soil."[51]

The letters to and from Matthew and Jane Willis show that, while the United States did not necessarily offer much improvement to Yorkshire farmers, English agriculture could be dreary. Jane's brother, John Humphry, wrote from Low Thoresby to them saying that "Times are very bad here at present that is Farming." And then, after listing the low prices that were the main cause, he continues, "so you see if you have times bad in America we have them bad here." England had additional problems that tipped the balance in favour of America: "Rents is as high as ever and then there is Highway Rates and Poor Rates, and then there is all Labour besides," by which he meant the more labour-intensive farming methods required in England. But, as Matthew himself had also noted, the chief difference was that in Yorkshire farmers rented land, generally; in America they owned it.[52]

Altogether, the Willis family experienced a series of highs and lows – of near ecstasy over their lands and unrealistically high expectations about the future, and then what looks like depression and homesickness. This is again revealed in the same letter by John Humphry:

> You tell me in your last letter dated 7th last May that you have a
> beautiful Estate of Land as the Eye could wish to look upon and
> that it is your own without being any Landlords kickabout, and that
> you have no Rent to pay, you seem to think that in one year more if
> all was well you could perhaps live without working much, and then
> the finest of all is you all possess tolerable health and have had no
> serious sickness since your settlement at Rama, it appears to[o] that
> you could sell your produce tolerably well, and for cash, and
> that you thought you had been fortunate in settling where you now
> live ... [but] in your letter to Nephew P. Willis your spirits seem to
> have undergone a change for the worse the winter is cold and severe;
> I understand by an account from America that they have had a
> rigourous winter, has this dipressed your spirits or are you unhappy?
> Could you like to be in England again or you would rather stay
> where you are ... could you be more contented if you had some of
> your relations near you.[53]

Willis responded to Humphrey a couple of months later, on 3 June 1849. It was hard to farm in Wisconsin with such low prices, even with such excellent soil: "I have already told you that farming in Wisconsin is a poor business. You can scarcely meet with a farmer that can pay ready cash for 5 bushels of seed potatoes. In fact I have never met with one unless he had something better than farming to depend upon ... And yet the soil is, in a general way, much better in Wisconsin than in any county in England, as far as my knowledge extends. The quality of the soil here is, I believe, much better than any European can conceive before he sees it."[54]

The Willis family also struggled with high labour costs and the longer winters that limited the working seasons: "But one thing that makes farming bad in this country is, the price of labour. For 5 or 6 months in winter nothing can be done in the farm. Consequently, the sowing of seed, the attending of the growing plants, and the gathering in of the crops, make a hurry of which you can have no conception. I oft think of the advantage you possess in being able to work all the year round."[55]

Willis also complained that weeds forced farmers onto new soils and prevented the application of manure: "Another advantage peculiar to England is, that you can keep the land in cultivation any length of time. We, on the other hand, are obliged to take up fresh and every few years, on account of the impracticability of keeping the weeds under in old ploughing land. This, in all probability is the reason why manure does not get into general use in America. In fact by the time it begins to want manure it becomes unmanageable from its proveness (!) to the growth of weeds."[56]

Finally, Willis thanks his brother-in-law John Humphrey for sending him a plant that could thrive in Wisconsin and provide a bit of badly needed income: "The Rhubarb you sent us does well; especially the giant sort. It is much admired. We sell it in Mineral-Point & Franklin for 5 cents a leaf!"[57]

The Willis family were not the only Yorkshire immigrants struggling on their Wisconsin farms. In 1849 *The Hull Packet and East Riding Times* published an immigrant letter written by temperance advocate John Hockings, known as the "Birmingham Blacksmith," now located in Burlington, Racine County, Wisconsin. It echoes Willis in several ways, particularly on the effect of long winters and the poor prices for crops:

In the spring and summer I work my farm, for I do not keep a hired man; my crops will not pay me to have one, except in harvest time (the crops here do not average more than fifteen bushels to the acre). The seasons here are so short that there is not time to cultivate the land like that in the old country … we have always about five months of winter; this year we shall have six months or more. The long winters make the farmer's life a laborious one, for to sow wheat before the winter sets in, the frost is so severe that it has invariably killed one half the produce … By the time the corn is hoed, the wheat harvest is ready; and although I work from sunrise to sunset the longest day in summer, I scarcely find time to get in my hay; and by the time I have got my hay, winter is on me again.[58]

Along with the longer and colder winters and hotter and humid summers came new kinds of vermin. From Wisconsin, Peter Walker complained to family and friends in Askrigg that "we are troubled with chinch Bugs In our grain. In this part of the country they destroy everything they come at barley wheat oats corn and at the fore part of the Season had drought and kept things from growing and then the bugs get in. I halled ten acres of Barley in at three loads … wheat and corn is suffering likewise with the Bug. So if England has not got Enough of Bread this year She will not get any from America."[59]

The bugs and droughts seem to have worn Peter Walker down, for in the same letter he talks about selling one of his two farms and offering it to his relatives in Askrigg: "I have got one Hd & forty Eight acres of land Eighty under plow twenty of Bottom [?] with timber & which I offer to sell for less than cost if you want to go a farming come and buy mee out as we have got another farm to go to We want to sell if we do not sell we will rent it."[60]

During the 1850s, which were generally prosperous years for both American and British farmers, the Willis family grew tired of Wisconsin and made plans to return to England. After their intentions became known in Wensleydale, Matthew's nephew Thomas Jr, from Manor House, Carperby, responded in 1859: "We were all truly glad," he writes excitedly to his uncle, "to hear you had at last come to the intension of selling out your property in Wisconsin & returning again to your native land. I doubt not but if you are favoured with health & strength to reach here in safety you may yet do well. I believe all your relations are unanimously of opinion that it is by far the best course you can adopt." This encouragement to return was bolstered by improvements in England. It was a good time to come back home: "I do not think there ever was a better opening for honest industry than at present in the old world. Here is a great demand for labour and wages of all kinds are higher than I ever knew." Thomas was referring to local work in milling, and this is where Wensleydale offered more to Willis than farming. But if the Willises wanted to remain landowning farmers, Yorkshire could not compete with Wisconsin, and both Willis and his nephew Thomas knew it: "[I]f you prefer farming I doubt not but some of us could assist you in a situation, farms are bad to meet with in Wensleydale that are good for anything, but in some other parts of England … they are more easily obtainable and as we have got a very extensive circle of acquaintance thorough the breeding of Shorthorns I think our recommendation might be of some service to you. If I were you I would sell out the first opportunity … Let me hear from you at an early date to say when we may expect you here."[61]

Here the network of information was working in reverse – paving the way for a convenient return migration. But though Matthew and Jane continued to think longingly about returning to Wensleydale, they never did. And though they struggled with low prices and farm debt after the Civil War, they did acquire a large Wisconsin farm. The land compelled them to stay, while inviting others to come. For some, southern and western Iowa proved especially compelling.

Iowa

IOWA ... is very healthy, very beautiful, very fertile, abounding in fair
uplands of alluvial soil. But its population are rude, brutal, and lawless,
and possessing no settled institutions or legislature, it is obvious that
it will be avoided by all persons of character and orderly habits.

EMIGRATION (1849)

By the time this description of Iowa was published, in 1849, some of it
was already out of date, at least in Dubuque, where immigrants from
North Yorkshire were helping to develop "settled institutions" and civility.
But Dubuque was just a relative pinprick in Iowa, a vast territory of
over 90,000 square kilometres that became the nation's twenty-ninth
state (the first in the Louisiana Purchase) in 1846. It did not take long
for people from North Yorkshire to turn their attention from Dubuque
and other parts of the Upper Mississippi region further west toward
Iowa's seemingly boundless fertile lands, most of which had been seized
from Native Americans by the United States in 1842. By 1850 there were
nearly 200,000 white settlers in Iowa, and of these 3,785 had been born
in England.[1]

Early historians recorded that on the frontier of Iowa and other states
and territories the English found a familiar culture that enabled them to
fit in and assimilate because the local American-born population "were
as English as the English themselves had been when the first migrations
were made, they were never able to escape from their origin."[2] There was
some truth to this, but it was not the whole story, as we can see in the
attempts to build English colonies in Iowa's more remote places.

The English Colony in Clinton County

Aside from the miners and smelters in the Dubuque area, the most notable
examples of North Yorkshire people settling in early Iowa are the attempts

in the late 1840s to establish two English colonies. The first involved people mainly from North Yorkshire and Lincolnshire who formed the Iowa Emigration Society and settled in Clinton County, south of Dubuque, on the Mississippi River. Their leader was George Sheppard, a newspaper editor from Hull who first visited the area in 1843 and returned to create the Society. He saw the United States as ideal for its "national greatness ... peopled by a race having all the good qualities of the Anglo-Saxon character," and his description of Iowa as a good place for English settlers was deemed accurate and objective in immigrant guidebooks.[3] Sheppard published encouraging letters in his paper, the *Eastern Counties Herald*, and gave public lectures to recruit settlers. Sheppard was inspired in part by Charles Fourier's plans for cooperative settlements and was determined to help England's struggling working classes by relocating them on cooperative farms in Iowa, where they could continue their trade and supplement their earnings through farming. The plan would also supposedly help raise wages for those who stayed behind by reducing the local labour supply. Participants would invest in the scheme and in return receive village plots according to the amount of their investment.

On 15 May 1850, the Society's ship *Columbus* left Liverpool with about fifty members whom the *Hull Advertiser* described as "chiefly agriculturalists."[4] Six weeks later they arrived in New York and went up the Hudson River to take the Erie Canal westward. It was on the canal, on 4 July, that the party had their ugliest experience, when Americans celebrating their independence swore at them and pelted them with rocks merely for being English.[5] That must have soured the group's early perceptions of America as they continued to Iowa. They originally intended to settle in Scott County, but failing to find suitable lands they proceeded to the centre of Clinton County, some 30 kilometres west of the Mississippi, at a place called Wright's Grove. Here they settled on about 2,000 acres of prairie and oak timberland. Writing promotional letters back to his newspaper, Sheppard described the spot as "excellent. It is composed of oak openings studded with small but valuable timber and rich fertile prairie ... many of our members are loud in their praise of the beauty of the location. Some see in it a close resemblance to the finest parts of the Yorkshire Wolds."[6] Here they divided the land according to how much each person had invested in the project and built the village they first called Sheppardsville, and then renamed Welton, probably after the village of that name just west of Hull.[7]

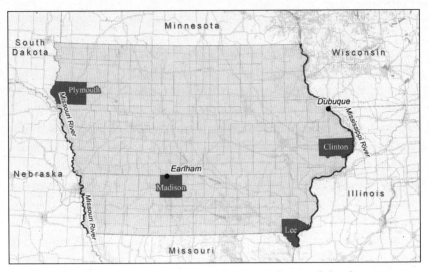

Figure 12.1 Map of Iowa, c. 1860, showing counties where English colonies were attempted but failed.

At first things seemed to go well. In August 1850 Sheppard wrote back to Yorkshire extolling the promise of the project: "The scene of our operations is in Clinton county, which … is on the banks of the Mississippi. Its features are high, rolling and fertile and perhaps the most healthy of all the river counties. Its beauty is unsurpassed … Land speculators are watching our movements and I feel certain that within twelve months from this not an acre will be purchasable near us except at double the government price."[8] At this time letters appeared in the *Hull Advertiser*, including one by a Mr Cortis, whose son had joined Sheppard's colony. Its aim was to recruit more settlers: "The ease with which the people get their living here is truly astonishing. They sit down on the land without anything but a wagon, a pair of horses, and a good axe. All they buy for the first year is on credit; yet, in four years, they are able to enter the land, and are then independent for life. Hard work they know nothing of ever after."[9]

Such accounts were too good to be true, as some readers must have suspected. Even as Welton was being built – with a hotel, stores, and shops – problems arose. The main issue was that, contrary to the earlier report of the settlers being "chiefly agriculturalists," few actually were because "these men did not take kindly to pioneer farming, all of them having been trained to mechanical employments."[10] According to county histories, the Yorkshire and Lincolnshire immigrants in this colony were woefully ill-suited for subsistence agriculture, especially those who were by trade furriers, tailors, bookbinders, painters, paper-hangers, and so on. Some knew how to thatch a roof, but that skill was not required on the prairie. Iowa needed settlers who could subdue virgin prairie, not bind books.[11] Local Americans saw these newcomers as arrogant because some had served apprenticeships and considered themselves above the hard manual labour required for pioneering and subsistence farming.[12]

Another mistake was Sheppard's miscalculation on the size and quality of land. The lots were too small for cash crops and the land was poorly drained and not very fertile.[13] In late 1850 Sheppard suddenly announced in the *Herald* that he was ending his involvement in the project, "without having been enriched one farthing by its formation."[14] The reason was not just that the scheme was poorly planned, but that the English settlers (as one of them soon admitted to the *Herald*) "grumble and growl at everything – comparing all things with the state of things at home – forgetting that this is an entirely new country."[15] With all these mounting problems, as reported back in England, most of the English settlers in Welton "grew homesick," and read and reread letters from England in a desperate attempt to maintain a link with the old country. "It became easy to weep," family members recalled, "to shed tears of both joy and sadness."[16]

Without Sheppard (who ended up working for the *New York Times* and then as a railroad land agent in London to organize settlements in Minnesota) the settlement quickly fell apart. At least one member returned to Hull and spread damning reports, while others who remained in Iowa glossed over the problems with upbeat letters for the *Herald*. But then, even as the settlement was dissolving, a group of forty-nine others arrived from Hull. Though reports declared that they were "highly pleased" with what they found, most ended up going to other places in Iowa or other states to use their skills in crafts.[17] Ultimately, Sheppard's colony was neither viable nor necessary. Newcomers from North Yorkshire and Lincolnshire could choose their own lands and settle where they wanted. They did not need the company of other English immigrants because, according to contemporary observers, their language and culture were similar enough that they could assimilate more quickly and not be so dependent on English settlements. As the Greater Sioux County Genealogy Society concluded about English settlement in the region:

The clannishness so characteristic of German, Scandinavian, Dutch, and Bohemian settlements in Iowa has not been duplicated by the British born to any noticeable extent: the latter have always been more thinly diffused throughout the state, perhaps because the language difficulty never seriously differentiated them from their English-speaking American neighbours. The problem of adjustment and adaptation to the New World quite naturally possessed no terrors for those who had no linguistic handicap to overcome, whereas in the case of all other foreigners the same difficulty very much retarded the process of Americanization.[18]

Meanwhile, people back in England lost interest in the settlement project and soon the town of Welton "all disappeared."[19] By 1879 only one of the original settlers was left, Christopher Buck, who had amassed 1,000 acres, earning him the local title "Lord Buck."[20] Though the colony dissolved, it did bring more attention to Iowa. So did another English colony, in Lee County.

The English Colony in Lee County

At about the same time the Clinton County colony was getting started, another English colony was budding in Lee County, which forms the southeast corner of Iowa, also on the Mississippi River. The initial idea for this colony, under the auspices of the British Emigrant Mutual Aid Society, was hatched by J.B. Newhall, a lawyer from Massachusetts who had settled in Burlington, Des Moines County, just north of Lee County. Newhall travelled to England to lecture and got to know John Lightfoot of Manchester, and William Bateman, a blacksmith who had served in the British navy and settled in London. It was Bateman who organized and led the society and served as its president.[21]

By 1845 ninety-four persons (including adults and children) had become members of the society by purchasing shares. All were from England, mainly from the north, though we know the precise origins of only a few. Most prominent among them were the James and Ann [Wilson] Ware family, from Rosedale, their four children, and James's brother John and his wife Margaret. On 14 February 1845 Bateman, his wife Sarah, and the rest of the group boarded the three-masted sailing ship *Washington of Baltimore, Maryland* out of St Katharine Docks in London for New Orleans, arriving one day less eight weeks later.[22] After three days in New Orleans they boarded the *Big Louisiana* and for twelve days steamed up the Mississippi. They intended to go to Burlington, Newhall's home in Des Moines County, to establish their colony, but because of shallow waters they could make it only as far as Keokuk, which then consisted of only a few log buildings on the riverbank, in Lee County. But here they realized they could purchase the land they wanted. They chose a place called "Big Mound," about 6 kilometres west of La Crew, in Cedar Township, in the northwest part of the county.[23]

Like the colony in Clinton County, the Lee County colony seemed doomed to fail. The basic problem was the society's assumption that 10-acre plots were enough to support each family. In Yorkshire and most other parts of England 10 acres did suffice because of its thorough cultivation, use of labour-intensive "English methods" of rotation and fertilization, and higher productivity. But this was not the case on Iowa's virgin prairie. At $1.25 an acre it seemed a bargain, but the lots were too small to grow crops for market, and the lack of timber for dwellings initially forced the group to camp in tents. Equally serious was the fact that of all the member families only one had much farming experience. Almost all the others were people in pre-industrial crafts: mostly blacksmiths, building trades workers, shoemakers, saddlers, bakers, tailors, miners, and even a bell hanger. They "knew nothing about farming."[24] Quarrels and the shockingly cold prairie winters added to the misery and the colony soon dissolved. Most left for other places nearer woodlands. Few had the means to return to England.[25] Like the Clinton County colony, the Lee County colony had not considered the nature of farms and markets in America. And such colonies simply did not make sense in a country where English immigrants could blend in quite readily with Americans in churches and communities. A few did hang on in Lee County, including the Ware family from Rosedale.

The Ware Family

James Ware was born in North Yorkshire in 1799 – most likely in Rosedale – and at age seven began working in coal mines until 1843, when "ill health compelled him to abandon this occupation." So he turned to peddling for a couple of years, but "he was not satisfied with his condition or prospects ... and resolved to emigrate to the United States, which seemed the 'land of promise' for the enterprising and energetic young man."[26] James's brother John, born in 1797, was also a key player in the story: he was a stone mason and worked on the British Museum in London on and off for about twenty years. Apparently it was in London that John met Bateman and heard about the British Emigrant Mutual Aid Society, and it was John who "had more means and paid the passage for the rest of the Ware family."[27] James and his wife Ann joined the Mutual Aid Society and with their four children (William, Charlotte, John, and Isaac) and brother John and his wife, Margaret, journeyed with the others to Lee County in 1845. By this time, James had become a leader because he, along with Bateman and one other member, had chosen the land for the colony.[28]

In 1851, John Ware caught "a cold" working as a stonemason on walls and new buildings and died.[29] James died only two years later. However, the other members of the Ware family remained and succeeded, for several reasons. James's son John, who was born in Farndale, Low Mills, Yorkshire and like his father worked in a coal mine for 28 cents a day, was fifteen when the family moved to Iowa. There he found steady work with a sheep farmer, saved his money and invested it shrewdly by purchasing 80 acres of virgin land, improving it, selling it "at a good profit," and repeating the process to support the rest of the family.[30] John seemed gifted in real estate, for he "soon found himself possessed of sufficient means to become a real estate proprietor." Already by 1853, he owned a homestead of 195 acres on which he became a "first-class agriculturalist."[31] Meanwhile, in 1846, daughter Charlotte Ware, also born in Rosedale, had married William Atkinson, who was born near Scarborough in 1811, and had moved to Canada in 1835, and then to Lee County in 1840.[32] Charlotte Ware Atkinson and her mother Ann Wilson Ware were in contact with Ann's brother Jonathan back in North Yorkshire.

In a letter from Farndale (about 8 kilometres north of Kirkbymoorside) dated 30 June 1851, Jonathan and Esther Wilson described their current local conditions to their sister Ann Wilson Ware, and Ann's daughter Charlotte Ware Atkinson. While members of the Lee County colony struggled to survive, people in the North York Moors struggled to farm. "Farming is not much better than it was 3 or 4 years since," they reported. "Cattle is only worth 1 third to what it was. Wheat is worth from 5s to 5 and 6."[33] At the same time there were reports of large numbers of local people leaving for North America: thirty persons were leaving Pickering, fifty leaving Seamer (several kilometres southwest of Scarborough, North Yorkshire), and hundreds of others were preparing to leave the area between Kirkbymoorside and Scarborough. They were described as "the best labourers to be found in the different parishes" and they were sailing mainly from Hull.[34] The year 1851 was generally prosperous, and yet local English newspapers continued to compare the attractions of the New World with the misery of the Old. In April 1851, for example, the *Hull Advertiser* reported that "A number of small farmers, during the past week have arrived in this town from the surrounding districts, intending to emigrate to America; and we are assured, by many who are about embarking, that the advices received from friends already settled in the New World are most cheering; that labour is abundant; that poverty is the exception."[35]

Though English agriculture generally prospered after mid-century, farming was still hard and often unrewarding in the North York Moors. But so too was it in many parts of America where North Yorkshire immigrants had settled, including the area of Lee County, even among the Ware family.[36] It seems the work was harder than expected, and that farm life was not as easy as had been envisioned. Farming one's own land in Iowa did offer an independence that eluded most people in Yorkshire, but it did not necessarily bring happiness or satisfaction. This was true of other Yorkshire immigrants in the areas. In Jefferson County, just northwest of Lee County, one West Yorkshire weaver lamented in 1864 that, after thirteen years of backbreaking work clearing fifty of his eighty acres and ploughing and fencing forty, his brother was "not more than making a living," and failed to find farming as an improvement on his old craft.[37]

Le Mars

The English colonies in Lee and Clinton Counties involved ordinary settlers who wanted to acquire a self-sufficient farm. Elsewhere in Iowa, in the 1870s, British aristocratic gentlemen attempted to establish a colony in Le Mars, Plymouth County, in the northwest corner of the state. Younger sons of English aristocrats who would not inherit land in England saw this project as a way of achieving an aristocratic lifestyle through owning large estates and living lives of leisure – or so they thought. The scheme was hatched in 1876 by William Brooke Close, an accomplished Cambridge oarsman who through a chance encounter with an Illinois businessman and land speculator bought up the lands with his three brothers and other investors and organized the Iowa Land Company. They established their colony in 1879 with offices in London and Iowa.

At first it seemed to work, as the population of English immigrants rose to about 500 in the 1880s. Le Mars became famous in England as a notable tourist destination. Golf, polo, steeplechasing, and other pastimes were introduced, and a couple of English-style pubs were built. Raising sheep was the main form of agriculture, and the English hired local people at handsome wages, which endeared them despite their strange, refined manners. New arrivals from England – many of them athletes from the universities of Oxford or Cambridge, and none we know of from North Yorkshire – showed up in their fancy clothes, one family arriving with eighty-two pieces of luggage. However, like other colonies for aristocrats in Kansas and Minnesota, the Le Mars colony was doomed because of the unrealistic plans of young Englishmen attempting to carve out a life of leisure in a forbidding environment, and an economy that simply could not sustain them. And, like the colonies in Clinton and Lee Counties that did include North Yorkshire immigrants, Le Mars was founded on the faulty assumption that the English needed to live among other English immigrants. Though the Close brothers made a profit from land sales, the settlers themselves left for other parts, or returned to England. The only important remnant is St George's Episcopal Church.[38]

The scenes of elite English families on the Iowa prairies were especially striking and incongruent because at the same time these and other frontier areas were witnessing the forced removal of Native Americans, which began in Iowa in the early 1840s. Many of the North Yorkshire immigrants arrived during this rapid transition from Indigenous to European culture and some observed Native peoples first-hand. They were, of course, part of the force that was removing Native Americans to the west. This did not stop the immigrants, however, from interacting with the Native Americans and recording their impressions and experiences.

Native Americans

[T]hey boldly demanded what we were, and what we would;
after many circumstances they seemed very kinde.

CAPTAIN JOHN SMITH

From the very beginning of their settlement in the North America, the English viewed Native Americans with a mix of fascination and fear. Myths of their nobility, generosity, and potential threat loomed large. Native Americans saved the English from starvation, but in 1622 the Powhatan nearly wiped out the Jamestown settlement, killing 347 men, women and children – about a quarter of Virginia's total settlement population. Other massacres followed and the English responded in kind. It was, of course, the wholesale takeover of Indigenous lands that prompted these attacks. But after the British empire was safely established in North America in the wake of the Seven Years' War, the imperial government was more inclined to keep the peace between Native Americans and white settlers, especially as the latter kept moving west past the Appalachians and taking Indigenous lands. To limit white expansion and conflict with Native Americans, Britain drew the Proclamation Line of 1763, and in adjudicating disputes between settlers and Native peoples the imperial government was sometimes more sympathetic to Native Americans than to aggressive white settlers. The hope was that a more balanced policy would keep the peace and the costs of empire down, and that eventually Native Americans might be brought into the body politic.[1]

The American Revolution changed all of that and unleashed unprecedented numbers of white settlers pouring into lands that for generations had been the home of Native Americans.[2] Among them were people from North Yorkshire. By the dawn of the nineteenth century the English image of Native Americans had already become a staple of travel literature and published diaries, as well as newspaper reports. Occasionally the English were taken captive, some later appreciating the adventure of living in a kind of "middle ground" between the two cultures.[3] When the redcoat Robert Kirk, for example, found himself a captive in Ohio, he lived with a foot in both cultures and later described his astonishing adventures in a published account.[4] Thus when Yorkshire immigrants entered America's Old Northwest both during and after the ongoing removals of Native Americans from their lands, they were aware of Native Americans and had various levels of information about them. Some made contact with them and wrote accounts that hint at empathy, even admiration.

Few if any North Yorkshire immigrants had such extensive and intimate contact with Native Americans or wrote about it more than Matthew Dinsdale. His first encounter with Native Americans occurred on his journey westward on the Erie Canal. At Buffalo he saw four Native American women: "They looked as though the whole of their property was on their backs and probably this was the case. They were well but cumberously clothed. Two of them I observed had men's hat on, with broad girdles such as livery servants wear." Then, travelling on the Great Lakes he went to Mackinac Island, which lies in Lake Huron between Michigan's two peninsulas. It had long been a British, then an American fur trade depot, and by the 1840s it was already noted as a centre for tourism and the whitefish industry. Native Americans had long lived there in various degrees of harmony with white settlers, and now in October of 1844 Dinsdale visited the island on his way to Wisconsin. His impressions of Native Americans on the island were based on local reports and biased by the Native Americans' growing dependence on whites: "At Mackinac between Huron and Michigan there had been a short time before I was there four thousand Indians, Men, Women and Children to receive pay from the United States Government for some of their lands … The Indians are quite in their element and made speeches expressive of their pleasure at having the white man for their friend. They are a very indolent and when not ill-used very harmless race of people. I would quite as soon sleep in a wigwam of a Red man as in the House of a white."[5]

After leaving Mackinac and proceeding to Wisconsin to begin his duties as a circuit riding Methodist preacher, Dinsdale had repeated and close contact with Native Americans. This was a time when the United States government held councils with the Menominee to make treaties and payments for land. Of course, Native Americans ultimately had no choice in the matter. Government officials were merely creating the appearance of fairness and volition. One such council was the Treaty of the Cedars, in 1836, when Oshkosh sold over 4 million acres, including what they possessed in Michigan's upper peninsula, for a mere $620,000. Another was the Treaty of Lake Poygan, in 1848, when Oshkosh, Chief of the Menominee, sold their remaining lands in Wisconsin.[6] In November 1844 Dinsdale met some local Native Americans on his travels. He seemed quite impressed, recording in his journal "A light cover of snow" and that he "Met four Indian hunters about noon returning from the grove. Spoke to them but they did not appear to wish to enter into conversation. They stood till we passed them and then moved on. Two of them had their faces painted which had not a disagreeable appearance."[7] Then, while walking with a friend on Christmas Day, "we saw a little to the right of us journeying east along one of their trails a party of Indians men and women and children, they had a few of their Poneys along with them and had they been in England they would have looked like a set of respectable Gypsies."[8]

Like most white newcomers Dinsdale was not fully aware of how Native American culture had been undermined by the force of white expansion and settlement, and how alcohol was used as a tool to pry away lands, with the government serving settlers' interests. Nor was he free from prejudice. On a Monday after he had preached at Lake Winnebago he had a sad encounter, as he recorded in his diary: "On going to the Post Office met an Indian who was drunk. Such a sight I do not wish to see again. He could hardly stand, and appeared to have a bag of potatoes on his back. His long hair shook about with his staggering, which with his blackened and stupid looking face made him a frightful object. On coming up to him he put out a long red tongue and made his face still more ugly by distorting it. On returning I again met him when he tried to whistle. There are several Indians about here at this time. They are on their way to receive their annual payment from the government."[9]

A month later Dinsdale visited the Menominee where they had assembled to collect their annual payment from the United States government, about $20,000, plus a few hundred for provisions. Dinsdale did not have much sympathy for them because, "after having sold a very extensive and beautiful tract of country, they still possess an immense quantity of very valuable land ... about twelve miles [20 kilometres] from Winnebago Lake." There seemed to be enough land for all. But, more to the point, Dinsdale was like most white settlers in his concept of land ownership, as conceptualized by John Locke, that true land ownership entailed a

European style of cultivation.[10] Thus when Dinsdale reflected on the Native Americans' use of land, he concluded that "Would they only cultivate it there is enough to make every one of them wealthy ... the tribe now consists of about twenty five hundred persons, and is I am informed decreasing fast every year. It appears to me that the Indian race is doomed to utter extirpati."[11] And, for the pious Dinsdale and others like him, the displacement of Native Americans by whites was part of God's plan, and part of what was being called "Manifest Destiny":

> This I think is a judgment from God in consequence of their thriftless idle habits and the debasing and demoralizing influence of their indolence. The Almighty designed the Earth to be cultivated, the Indians as a general thinking will not do this, consequently they are removed by Heaven, that another race may occupy. In this God is righteous, as it cannot matter what race of mankind inhabits the Earth so long as the Divine purposes are accomplished. But the Indian tribes ought to have, (and must have, if we do our duty) our sympathies & prayers, and Christ labors. I feel for them in kind tho not in the same degree as Christ felt for the Jews when he lamented and wept over their city.[12]

Dinsdale's other observations of Native Americans are for the most part perceptive and dispassionate and reveal an understudied part of Indigenous history through English eyes:

> I went to the council room first thing where I was informed the chiefs of the tribe were to meet the Government Agent. About 9 o'clock the chiefs one after another assembled, tho they appeared in no hurry. On entering each one shook hands with the agent and then took his seat on the floor. Oshkosh (Brave Man) the head chief sat first. I noticed they all appeared in good humor during the conference that took place and frequently smoked using their tomahawks as pipes, which are made to answer a double and oppos-ite purpose to Kill and Make alive. The Agent had to bring before them some complaints made by some of the white settlers, and ask for damages for property stolen or injured by some of the tribe ... The Agent also heard their complaints against the whites. ... Some Mormons had erected several saw mills on their land and some

white people were cutting some of their timber. These were the principle complaints the Indians had to make.[13]

Dinsdale's description of the actual meeting was as effective as any painting or photograph could have been: "Imagine yourself a temporary house made of boards nailed to posts with a roof of the same kind, dimensions about 18 feet by 22. In the centre was a stove. In one corner against the only window sits at a table covered with paper &c. the Agent and his Secretary, beneath the table stood several kegs filled with money (silver) facing the stove forming a half circle sat the chiefs on the floor across legged in turns smoking, talking, and laughing behind them stood or sat other Indians as lookers on."[14]

Dinsdale then turned his attention to Oshkosh, the Menominee Chief: "The head chief appears to be about 45 years old, he is a little below the middle size, spare of flesh, but with a good frame and is evidently an active man. He appears to be a good and fluent speaker. He always looks grave and thoughtful, I do not remember to have seen a smile play over his broad and strong featured face."[15]

Like other English immigrant observers, Dinsdale seemed especially fascinated by the Native Americans' dress and physical appearance, playing a part in the English tradition of curiosity in the American "noble savage." Stories of Britons held captives by Native Americans had circulated widely in the press. Like Robert Kirk, who was held captive in the 1780s but lived quite amicably with his captors and seemed fascinated by their dress and dance, Dinsdale saw the Menominee dress as somewhat familiar, or at least he tried to describe it by comparing it with fashion in Britain: "The Indians' dress as to the fashion of it is similar to that of the Scotch soldier the material being different, the upper garment is generally made of printed calico the lower of buck skin, and a blanket is always worked over all. In the article of dress I discovered no difference between the chiefs and others. Some wear ornaments on the head's & person's but they are not distinctive of rank. But frequently of wealth, for an Indian – if he is vain – and who is not? will carry all his treasure on his body. Some of the women wear very expensive and highly ornamented apparel."[16]

Another facet of Native American culture that grabbed Dinsdale's attention was the Menominee villages and society. The images he conjures add to our understanding of these people at a time of profound change – soon before their removal to the West. And to fill out his descriptions

Dinsdale used comparisons with other British adventure stories: "I took the pains to go thro this temporary town which I suppose is over a mile from one end to the other, and made an attempt to count the wigwams, but from their irregularity and grouping it was a work of considerable difficulty, however I got an idea of the number and suppose there was about two hundred. The second altogether reminded me of Capt. Cook's visit to the island of the Pacific. Groups of half naked brown children, crying infants, growling lank dogs, wild looking Indians, standing in bands, or walking and riding about, & laboring squaws reminded me that I was in a simple world, and far, far, from the place I once called my home."[17]

Dinsdale also described the Menominee method of making canoes – both birch bark and dugout. And, fascinated with their bearing and social characteristics, he could not help being judgmental, as he himself admitted: "While walking about I noticed one group very much in character – on one side there was the dark forrest on the other the open lake above the dark and threatening sky and around the cold wind was blowing and there was the picture before me – a huge blazing fire at the extreme end of one of the logs just facing me stood a Menominee covered with trinkets as ornaments … And on each side of the fire stood several others with their blankets drawn close round them typical of their forlorn moral and social state."[18]

Dinsdale relished the many opportunities to see and experience nature that had not yet been subdued by white settlers, and he highlighted his experiences in his letters. A letter to his mother in September of 1846 was preoccupied by his commune with nature and especially his observations of the Oneida, who originated in New York but had been forced onto a reservation near the Green Bay area in 1838: "Some of the pleasantest feelings I have ever experienced I have had here while riding from one settler's cabin to another," he exclaimed. "There are several tribes of Indians about here, and that is one reason I am glad I am here as I want to make the Indian a subject of study, some of them are in their wild state some are halve civilized and other are wholly so."[19] Spending time at the former territorial governor James Doty's house on an island in Lake Winnebago, he delighted in observing nearby Native Americans hunting and cooking and fishing from birch bark canoes, all "very picturesque." Other Native Americans on the opposite shore were "pious Christians belonging to the M.E. [Methodist Episcopal] Church … they speak only the English language ... To hear the Red men talk of Christ and heaven was truly delightful and refreshing to my spirit."[20]

Dinsdale's fascination with the Native Americans seemed endless and he admitted that "if I was to write you all I saw and felt" at a meeting with several Oneida Indians "I could fill a small volume." His vivid descriptions of the Native Americans were relished by his sister and mother and no doubt their friends and neighbours, as his sister Elizabeth responded in her letter of 23 January 1847: "I should like to have been with you when you were with the Indians the account of them is very beautiful."[21]

Native Americans in California

Dinsdale's interaction with Native Americans in Wisconsin instilled in him a lifelong fascination with and sympathy for Native peoples. But in the West, the Native Americans seemed more threatening than those he had met in Wisconsin. While prospecting for gold in California's Sierra Nevada in 1850, Dinsdale reported that "considerable alarm has been felt in some part of the mining regions on account of hostile Indians. There have been and still is danger from this quarter. We heard much of their depredations and murders and at last we travelled through the country where their conduct had been most violent and injurious. At one place, the day before we got there, a man had been shot by them and seven oxen stolen. And one night we were told that several hundred warriors were only three miles [5 kilometres] off." Perhaps because of his experience with Wisconsin Native Americans a few years earlier, Dinsdale was aware of the long-term injustices meted out to them, understanding that they had more to fear from whites than whites from Native Americans: "I must however, say in behalf of the Indians that much provocation has been given them. A treaty of peace has lately been made with them, and I do not think they will be the first to trample upon its provisions. I had the pleasure of seeing the principal chief carrying it about with him to show the Whites. He was accompanied by three or four other Indians bearing white flags."[22]

Later in the month, shortly after turning thirty-five, Dinsdale did express some fear of Native Americans: "At noon while resting several Indians came up men and women and children. The men were well armed with bowes and arrows the women carried on their shoulders a large blanket each. Felt some little fear as not one of us had arms along. They all however went quietly away. One man remained with us talking some time."[23]

Matthew Dinsdale was not the only North Yorkshire immigrant to interact with Native Americans. George Heslington, a grocer who left Ripon in 1833 at age thirty-four, and his wife Ann and four children, were among them. After a "very pleasant" voyage they arrived in Illinois and took up 80 acres of government timber land and 80 of prairie in Niles Township as true pioneers. As Ann Heslington recalled, they frequently entertained their Native American neighbours, and in return Heslington "was the recipient of many favours at the hands of the red men. He continued an honored and highly-respected citizen of this community until his death."[24] Surely there were others who interacted amicably with Native Americans but never recorded that, and probably others still whose relations with Native Americans were not positive. But, through the eyes of Matthew Dinsdale we get a detailed glimpse of how at least one North Yorkshire immigrant viewed and interacted with Native Americans. It was with a mixture of fascination, appreciation, and sometimes trepidation that he experienced and described the Native Americans, as well as looking at them through the lens of European values, including concepts of land ownership. Ultimately, especially for the Methodist preacher, it was religion that shaped his attitudes toward Native peoples, and most everything else, for that matter. For most, if not all, North Yorkshire immigrants in North America, religion was the most basic and important foundation of their lives.

14

Religion

Whither am I going? To the New World. What to do? To gain
honor? No, if I know my own heart. To get money? No: I am
going to live to God, and to bring others so to do.

FRANCIS ASBURY

In nineteenth-century England and America, religion was "the greatest
common denominator of life."[1] It defined most people and their society and was a kind of glue that held communities together. Like most
English immigrants to North America, those from North Yorkshire were
highly religious. Religion was at the core of their existence and of many
migration decisions. The common religious foundations and traditions
in England and America facilitated migration and offered advantages in
assimilating and adjusting to life in the new world.[2] And by taking their
religiosity to Canada and the United States, North Yorkshire people were
playing their part in bringing Christianity to the anglophone world.[3]

Because America's main Protestant denominations had been planted
by colonial English immigrants, the churches were now both English
and American in character and still familiar to newcomers. Quakers,
Congregationalists, Baptists, Presbyterians, Anglicans, Shakers, and of
course, Methodists, all originated in England and Scotland. The first
Methodist Chapel was established in America in 1766, and in 1771 Francis
Asbury arrived to spread Methodism there. So, unlike other immigrants
of the nineteenth century, the English did not have to bring along their
churches and worship apart from Americans: their churches were already
there, as American churches, where they could hear familiar sermons
and hymns, practise familiar liturgies, and worship alongside both
Americans and other English immigrants. Though churches did take on
some American characteristics, especially on the frontier, they remained
essentially English in their foundations, basic beliefs, and liturgies, and
often remained connected with their denominations in England.[4] Any

differences were outweighed by essential similarities. Matthew Dinsdale observed this fact in 1844 when he recorded in his journal that "A Lovefeast was held this morg. at nine o'clock which was a good time. Methodism and Religion are the same in character and power and value in America as in England."[5]

Denominations

English immigrants were overwhelmingly Protestant, and significantly over-represented by various kinds of Methodists. This was especially true of those from North Yorkshire.[6] Methodists were more likely to move to America than others because the national ties holding them back were weaker: early discrimination that kept Methodists out of the major universities, civil service appointments, and that sometimes ended their land tenures undermined their sense of belonging in England. Also, the long tradition of Methodist migration to America had created an information network that channelled in more newcomers. Throughout most of the century contacts and visits between evangelicals in America and Britain were thriving.[7] Methodism was especially suited for the American frontier because it was highly organized, eager to help others get established, and held popular doctrines. The lack of interference from religious authority in rural America was appealing as well.

Anti-Catholicism was another common characteristic of English immigrants in both the United States and Canada. The attitude was not just a hangover from centuries of Protestant-Catholic conflict, but also a reaction to massive Irish immigration to both Britain and North America. Ironically, anti-Catholicism served as a connection – another point of commonality – between English immigrants in both the United States and Canada who shared hostility toward Catholic immigrants and were alarmed by the rising tide of Catholics from both Ireland and Germany in the 1840s.[8] This was one reason why the English also voted largely for Whigs and Republicans, many of whom shared the anti-Catholic bias that had formed the old Know-Nothing Party.

Thus, Methodism was a powerful force in the ongoing British-American relationship. In the 1840s influential English Methodists, including some from Yorkshire, came to the United States and helped make American Methodism more sophisticated by developing its educational base, redirecting it from the heart and more toward the mind. Some helped establish theological colleges that tied revivalism to the abolition of slavery.[9] For many, faith and piety were at the centre of their whole migration experience. From their first thoughts of leaving to taking the arduous voyage and then settling in America and adjusting to a new life, immigrants depended on their faith in the Almighty.

In their letters and diaries North Yorkshire immigrants exhibit many of the traits seen in the more general English immigrant population, expressing a deep and abiding religiosity that placed them solidly within transatlantic evangelical culture. They frequently used biblical references in their letters, and surely their conversations, to help them see and understand order and security in their lives. When Thomas Shepherd wrote back to his family after settling in Platteville, Wisconsin and described his new farm, he exclaimed that "I and our Lads set off in the name of the Lord to seek for a Farm like Faithfull Abraham not knowing where to go, but Glory to God he directed our steps."[10]

Primitive Methodists

The commonality among English and American Methodists is especially clear in the variant called the Primitive Methodists, who originated in England in the wake of early camp meetings. Though most commonly associated with America's Second Great Awakening, camp meetings also occurred in England, another example of their similar evangelical cultures. After one such meeting in Staffordshire in 1807, under the leadership of Hugh Bourne, the participants were condemned as "Ranters" for their highly emotional behaviour, and the name stuck. Bourne was then expelled from the Methodist Conference, so he formed the "Camp-Meeting Methodists," who in 1811 merged with others who held similar revivals to form the Primitive Methodist Church.[11]

Primitive Methodism reached America in the 1820s when Teessdale convert Joseph Grieves settled in Galena, Illinois, where Yorkshire Dales immigrants soon arrived to mine lead. Other Primitive Methodist missionaries appeared and led revivals and services that the immigrants found quite familiar and participated in.[12] Although some Americans saw the English Primitive Methodists as foreigners, there was much commonality as well.[13]

Primitive Methodism thrived in the Upper Mississippi, especially in Galena and Mineral Point, where Yorkshire miners and smelters had settled. Mostly raised as Methodists, they found it easy to make the relatively minor adjustment to Primitive Methodism. In 1848 the *Primitive Methodist Magazine* featured an article by a Mr T. Jobling, an English immigrant minister from Preston, Lancashire, and it underscores the scale and dynamism of the denomination as well as the continued close links between English and American preachers:

The Primitive Methodist cause is making progress here, and at our quarterly meeting, held yesterday, all our affairs were found to be doing well. A fortnight ago we had a camp meeting, in a grove adjoining the Primitive Methodist church ... the congregations were large, and the feeling which pervaded the services was delightful. Persons were present from places, twelve, fourteen, and sixteen miles [19, 23, and 26 kilometres] distant respectively, and had come purposely to the meeting. Our beds were all occupied, and sumptous provisions were made for as many as wished to partake of them: indeed, we had to look out expeditiously for persons to eat with us, as there were many householders desirous to entertain strangers. We have lately received a preacher, Mr. Hewitt, from the Birmingham circuit, Old England, and we are expecting another daily from New York. After his arrival we shall have four travelling preachers in this circuit (besides one at Louisville), twenty-four local preachers, and three or four exhorters.[14]

Two years later the same magazine published an article featuring Mineral Point, which was also part of the Galena Confederation of Primitive Methodists. It was written by John Sharpe, a reluctant English Primitive Methodist missionary, who arrived unannounced in Galena in the fall of 1848. He caused much excitement, because "this sudden and unexpected appearance of a regular traveling preacher in good standing from England was hailed with pleasure, and his company and services were in much demand."[15] Sharpe observed the community there, which was composed largely of Yorkshire lead miners, including a "Brother Alderson": "The thoughts of leaving my native land, and my friends and acquaintances, and of travelling to this Far West, filled me at times with sorrow; but when I had arrived I rejoiced for the course I had taken, and

more especially when the friends here gave me such a hearty welcome ...
I was appointed to labour in and about Galena until the Conference of
1849. In December, 1848, Brother Alderson and I visited Mineral Point, –
a rising place, principally inhabited by lead miners."[16]

Other kinds of Methodists joined the Primitive Methodists. Among
them were dissatisfied Episcopal Methodists:

> In February, 1849, a number of persons left the Episcopal
> Methodists, and offered themselves to us. They had long been
> dissatisfied with the manner in which the society was governed,
> and a dispute arising from a choir of singers, they thought they
> ought peaceable to withdraw from the episcopal stock. After having
> read and approved of our rules, they wished to be taken into our
> Connexion; and though we neither rejoice to see unnecessary div-
> isions, nor to recognize schismatics, the case of the separatists here
> seemed to demand our sympathy, and to justify a reception of them
> into our fellowship.[17]

In March, Sharpe attended a quarterly meeting at Mineral Point and
found the area "very prosperous," and the congregation thriving and
growing: "We had seventy-seven approved members, and nine on trial. ...
we reported one travelling preacher, seven local preachers, six preaching
places, and 123 members. Praise the Lord: On Christmas-day, 1849, we
opened our new chapel at Mineral Point. ... The congregations were large,
the collections liberal, and one soul was converted after the evening's
service."[18] Sharpe was particularly proud of the new chapel, which was
"built of stone" at a cost of $2,000, measured 50 by 40 feet, and "stands
in a good situation." He also reported on New Diggings, where "there
has been a great revival; nearly one hundred souls have been converted.
Thank God! You will see that Primitive Methodism in this western country
is prospering, and its friends are expecting still greater things. We have
confidence that our brethren in England will sympathize with us, and
pray that our expectations may be abundantly realized."[19]

New Diggings received further attention from John Leekley, who was
known as "the founder of Primitive Methodism in America."[20] One of
the earliest Primitive Methodist converts in Teessdale, Leekley arrived in
Galena in 1842, established the denomination there, and in 1851 published
an article in the *Evangelist*, Canada's Primitive Methodist magazine. New

Diggings was also the home of many Yorkshire lead miners, and it is hard to imagine a more prosperous, thriving, and happy immigrant community:

> The annual festival of the Primitive Methodist Sabbath School, was celebrated at New Diggings, Lafayette County, Wisconsin, in the Primitive Methodist church, on Saturday, July 26th, in the afternoon, when the Scholars, about 100 in number, with cheerful hearts and smiling faces, repaired to the church, and was regaled gratuitous with pies, cakes, and delicious tea, after which, the teachers, parents and friends, sat down to a very superior repast, which as to the quality of the provisions, and excellency of the arrangements, reflected great credit on the females and other friends connected with the management.[21]

Leekley continued by extolling the community's devotion to temperance: "the importance and necessity of abstaining from all intoxicating liquors; the benefits that would accrue to the world and church; the misery that would be prevented, and benefits realized, if this principle was universally acted upon." As we have seen, the Upper Mississippi mining communities were a logical target for the temperance movement, and it seems to have responded well to it. The local church was thriving so much that it was "crowded to excess," and "Thirty Dollars were collected on the occasion in aid of the funds of the Sabbath School. This has been one of the best anniversaries that was ever celebrated here," Leekley continued, and "the singing of the choir, the energetic addresses, and praiseworthy recitations of the children, produced a happy effect, and afforded a delightful treat to all present. The crowd that assembled on the occasion, and the liberal collection that was taken up, are evidences of the confidence of the Christian public in this neighbourhood, as to the utility of Christian education and Sabbath schools."[22]

Reverend Leekley wrote another article for the *Primitive Methodist Magazine* in 1851 in which he focused on the nature of the lead mining industry around New Diggings and how it differed from England's: "This is a lead-mining district, extending over sixty square miles [155 square kilometres]; that is to say, you may find patches of digging to that extent. The strata is limestone. The veins are weak, nothing like the old country veins; they are more like the stringes or leads that run by the side of a main vein. They are also very numerous, and easy to come at. The average depth is about fifty feet, flats from two to twenty feet high, and from four to forty feet in width: but some are rich, others not so. I have known large quantities of mineral got under the clay, on the rock, about twelve feet deep."[23]

Leekley also compared the region's landscape with that of his native Yorkshire, revealing more of what the immigrants had experienced by leaving one area for the other:

We have no large mountains, as in the north of England. We have hills and valleys, what we here call ridges and ravines ... Wisconsin is an excellent farming as well as mining state. We live on the line between Illinois and Wisconsin. Newdiggins is about ten miles [20 kilometres] from Galena, which is in Illinois ... There are a great number of Teesdale people here, and several from Arkendale, Weardale, Allendale, and other parts of England, besides a great-number of Irish. It seems that a notion has been entertained by some who have emigrated from England, that the people of this part are an heterogeneous mass of uncivilized Europeans and Indians, living in the woods amongst wild, voracious animals. But as for Indians, they fly back as the whites get up ... The people are in general intelligent and enterprising, though of different nations. ... It is true there are some poor people here; but meat is plentiful, and I have never seen those poor creatures in this country who are so numerous in England.[24]

But soon the Primitive Methodist communities in the Upper Mississippi suffered a setback, when the California Gold Rush pulled away many miners and caused a sudden slump in the local churches. By June of 1850 the English immigrant preacher W. Tomkins had arrived in Shullsburgh and he "felt rather discouraged at the state of things. There were only thirty eight members in the town society, and many of them in a low state; the prayer-meetings were almost deserted. Several of the leading men had gone to California, and the cause had suffered much from the Californian excitement."[25] Not only that, but "the cholera appeared; a few adults and many children died; three of our children were swept off in a few days. This was trying indeed, occurring so soon after coming into a strange land; but I trust the Lord overruled it for my good and for his glory."[26]

But then the following January Tomkins's spirits were lifted because his preaching had a great effect at a camp meeting "lovefeast": "[A] woman was powerfully awakened under the preaching, and was in an agony two or three days till she found mercy. The next Sunday her brother cried aloud for mercy, in the lovefeast, and was made happy in a few minutes. We then held a protracted meeting three weeks, during which time about forty persons found peace in believing. We then had some blessed seasons, which more than compensated me for leaving my friends and country."[27]

When Tomkins left Shullsburgh in June of 1851 he was paid his entire salary of $230 and more. The congregation's generosity and ability to build the church was a testament to their faith but also their success in the Upper Mississippi lead mining region: "The people kindly subscribed 37 dollars towards buying me a horse, which cost 54 dollars, or eleven sovereigns; and they subscribed 12 dollars for timber, &c., to build a stable, and I did the workmanship. There was a debt of 300 dollars on the preacher's house when I arrived, but we paid off 125 dollars during the year I was there, and purchased lamps for the chapel which cost 20 dollars. So that we might truly say, the Lord hath done great things for us, whereof we are glad."[28]

Matthew Dinsdale's Methodism

Matthew Dinsdale provides a more personal look at English Methodism in America. As a preacher, Dinsdale is not representative of all Yorkshire Dales immigrants. But his piety and religiosity were widely shared by others. Dinsdale saw American and English Methodism as essentially the same[29] but some interesting differences stood out when, after a year on the Potosi circuit, he was assigned the Lake Winnebago circuit. This was a mission district with duties that included preaching to the Brothertown Indians near Oshkosh and other nearby places. Like other circuit rider Methodist preachers, Dinsdale "virtually lived in the saddle, going from cabin to cabin, and gathering the settlers together for a Sunday service."[30] As one who had left the ancient village of Askrigg, with its medieval church and fine buildings that still stand today, he had to adjust to the primitive American wilderness and its Native peoples. Often, he had to sleep along the roadside or in the woods, which took a toll on his health.

As a circuit rider on the move meeting strangers, Dinsdale relied ever more on this faith. In October 1845 he reported a "good time" at a

"Lovefeast" and wrote to his mother to that "I have again removed" from Pedlars Creek to Potosi, where he was "received on probation by the Rock River Conference of the Methodist Episcopal Church." His emotions were mixed as he was "again amongst strangers. But I look to Heaven as my ultimate and eternal resting place and home."[31] For devout Methodists like Dinsdale, religion was paramount. It would bring not only eternal life in the hereafter, but comfort in life on earth.

Dinsdale's pay was meagre. Though he was not preaching in Wisconsin for the money, he still had a right to complain in a letter to his mother in 1845 saying, "The people pay their servants better than they pay their preachers. I have been about here for three months and I have not received a single cent from the Church, and I do not know when I shall. Coming here has almost been a hundred dollars out of my way already. But none of these things move me. I am willing not only to suffer but to die for the Lord Jesus … I can procure no money as a Preacher," he continued, "I am ashamed to beg but not to dig." Matthew dug lead to make ends meet, and later in California, gold to thrive.[32]

Dinsdale's financial struggles were matched by religious and professional ones: it took him time to hit his stride and learn how to preach effectively. At times he seemed obsessed with sin and his own inadequacy. "I find that without God I am nothing but sin," he confessed in 1846 to his family in Askrigg, "and can do nothing but sin, I am truly the chief of sinners and the least of saints." His dark mood seems to have been rooted in his lack of experience and perhaps a need to adjust to America: "I try to preach Christ, but I find that I know not how to preach him," he reflected. "I strive to be a Christian but alas I only become convinced how far I fall short of being one."[33]

Things soon improved. As the Primitive Methodists' reports indicate, religion was thriving. Dinsdale observed that by early 1848 a local revival was underway, and he was apparently contributing to it. "We have at this time a powerful and very interesting revival of religion here," he told his mother in January.

We have had meetings for two weeks, and they will be continued for at least another week. Every evening during last week … and almost every one in the week previous penitents have come forward for prayer and advice and encouragement, and most of those who have done so have been washed from their sins in the blood of Christ …

So much of the Divine Presence has been felt I never before experienced ... Praise our God ... I was never so happy in my life before.
Never so full of love of Jesus ... If I only had language to express
myself I could write to you for a month.[34]

Mormons

The centrality of religion in English migration and assimilation is especially
evident in the history of The Church of Jesus Christ of Latter-Day Saints,
or Mormons. This distinctly American religion resonated deeply with the
English because of their shared evangelical culture. In 1837, only seven
years after Joseph Smith published the *Book of Mormon*, Mormon missionaries arrived from America. They targeted England's poor, unemployed
textile workers and others facing hardship, and by 1840 English converts
were arriving in Nauvoo, Illinois. Soon the Church established shipping
agencies in Liverpool and other ports, where church leaders chartered
their own ships and prearranged lodging and meals before they set sail
as a group. The Church also funded many converts' passage tickets and
often escorted them to Utah, maintaining cohesion and discipline on the
long overland journey.[35]

Between 1853 and 1856 alone about 16,000 British converts arrived.[36]
Many were skilled and had been recruited by the Church to help build
the settlement; their common faith and worldview helped them blend in
with American Mormons. By 1870 almost 100,000 British people had
converted to Mormonism, and more than a third of them had migrated
to the United States.[37] In 1870 nearly 38,000 English-born people were in
Utah, forming nearly 20 per cent of the recorded population, the highest
concentration of English-born people in any state or territory.[38]

Generally, Mormonism had a bad press in England, especially as more
people converted and left for America. Mormons, like any people, were
capable of treachery and bad behaviour. But the tone of some letters
published in English newspapers smacks of an anti-Mormon bias that
was perhaps "enhanced" by editors. The Mormon practice of polygamy,
the murder of Joseph Smith, and their expulsion from Nauvoo to Utah
under Brigham Young's leadership all exposed the group to scurrilous
and vicious attacks in the press. One article, published in the *Hull Packet
and East Riding Times*, was putatively written to a son by "a workman,

a decent respectable fellow," named John Knaggs.[39] After a dozen years working in Hull, Knaggs "got acquainted" with the Mormons, "who persuaded him to join them in their journey to the Great Salt River Settlement." But Knaggs was so revolted by what he experienced with the Mormons that he left:

> Dear Son, you desired me to give you some account of the reason why we left the Mormons ... We found them to be villains of the worst sort, for all they wanted was young women and money. H—, W— and G— selected young women out of the camps, and took them to their own wagons, where they themselves slept. We have a great many respectable people who have told us of many most awful crimes which the Mormons were known to be guilty of, as they were eye witness to many of these awful deeds, for which they were driven from Nauvoo and other places ... when we got to St Louis, we were surprised to find so many orphan children, whose parents, being Mormons, had died, and they were left desolate, no one to protect them but strangers ... This more strongly convinced me of the character of the Mormons ... We never got one farthing of our money back.[40]

At roughly the same time, newspapers in York were also condemning Mormons, especially in their treatment of women and their miserable lives in America:

> The Mormon delusion still it appears induces English people to leave comfortable homes and face a perilous and painful voyage, to a strange land. The ... Iowa papers give some details of the passage of a band of Mormon emigrants through that place. In the broiling sun these poor creatures, the majority of whom are women, moved along slowly in Indian file, dragging behind them in little carts the necessaries for the journey, sometimes two women dragging the cart, at other times a man and woman together. The company was from Europe, and mostly consisted of English people, who had left their comfortable homes ... and here, with a journey of more than a thousand miles [1600 kilometres] before them, of which two hundred would be through a perfect desert, without shade or water, these miserable, deluded people were trudging forward.[41]

The Longstroth Family

The story of Mormon migration from North Yorkshire is told in remarkable detail in the fascinating letters of the Longstroth family. Their spellings are phonetic, allowing us to hear how they spoke in their Yorkshire dialect (though making the letters challenging to read). Born in 1789 in Langcliff, near Settle in Ribblesdale, Stephen Longstroth married Ann Gill at St Oswald's Church in Arncliffe, where they also raised their first eight children. In 1833 the family moved to Clitheroe, Lancashire, as did other poor Dales families for work, and there within five years Stephen had converted to Mormonism. Soon he was authorized to preach and in 1839 was ordained as a priest. It was in Clitheroe that Longstroth met Willard Richards, the Massachusetts-born cousin of Brigham Young who led a four-year mission to Preston and converted people like Stephen Longstroth. Richards would not only lead them and a large Mormon party to Utah but would become the Longstroths' son-in-law – three times over – by marrying their three daughters. Though Stephen Longstroth had prospered spiritually in Clitheroe he suffered materially. He was mired in poverty, probably labouring in the textile mills, and by 1841 two of his eight children had died.[42]

Ann Gill Longstroth wrote the first surviving letter from Clitheroe on 12 December 1841, to their brother, about two months before their departure for America. The beginning is as tantalizing as it is cryptic, referring to a "crime" committed by some relative or acquaintance who was "captive by the devil," and which severely disrupted the family.[43] Ann also sheds light on their dire circumstances when she writes that "their is great distress in Clithero and has been for several weeks … the factory has been standing nearly 3 weeks and they want a fortnights wage and some 3 weeks and i[s] doubtful they will ever get a penny. The factory is to be sold in January so there is a long time to looke forward … I do not know what will be the consequences." The very next day Stephen wrote another letter, making final arrangements to emigrate through the Mormons' extensive network of connections.[44]

There were other problems in the Clitheroe mills that probably precipitated the Longstroths' move to America. The work environment was tense, as suggested in the biography of another worker there who also emigrated in 1842. He was John Spencer, a weaver who was blacklisted after a quarrel with his employer. "John seems to have been of a very

Figure 14.1a and b   Left: Portrait of Stephen Longstroth, a Mormon convert who took part in the great trek to Utah. Right: Portrait of Ann Longstroth, Stephen's wife and writer of many of the family's letters.

independent and spirited nature and this quality got him into trouble with the foreman," it was later recorded. "This foreman blamed him for some mishap to the loom and since John felt that he was in no way to blame he refused to accept any responsibility for fixing it. The quarrel grew so bitter that John was discharged and the foreman threatened to blacklist him which meant that no mill in region would hire him."[45] Spencer, who was not a Mormon, fled to Fall River to continue his work. Meanwhile, Longstroth had suffered some additional, unspecified problem in the mills so in 1842 the family left with other Mormons for America, and eventually Utah.[46] When they sailed from Liverpool Longstroth had left "with nothing, having given away all his possessions" except a feather bed. Somehow – probably through church assistance – they bought eight passage tickets to New Orleans, and from there went up the Mississippi.

Over the next dozen years in America Stephen and Ann Longstroth wrote back to relatives in the Yorkshire Dales, documenting their difficult and adventurous lives in America, and their eventual settlement to Utah. Starting at Rockport, Illinois, they wrote to their "brother" on the first day of 1844 to report on their circumstances and impressions of the new country: "This land as [has] the advantages of England for working people and they may get a good living all most everywhere. The only defecelty hear is that money is very scarce." Stephen himself got work and planned to build a proper house that summer "some where in Ilinois wheare the Saints have settled. They have got a maney lockations now."[47]

Many of the Longstroth letters are engrossed with Mormon theology, attempting to convince relatives that "the gospel of Christ [has] been revealed from the heven by almighty God to Joseph Smith" and perhaps lead them to conversion. As the family gradually made their way from Illinois to Missouri and to Utah, they wrote glowing letters that seem designed to convince family members and others to join them. But not everything in America was positive. Like many English immigrant letters of this period, American slavery was a frequent topic – especially when witnessed first-hand: "The conterey vareys, allmosting every state, this state Missouri is a slave state and is not a good place fore emergrants fameleys in general, on account of so many black people. The masters or owners of them, hire them out for every place where there is aney work. The black women in service and black men to all kinds of labour so not good for white family." But Missouri's slavery was also a foil that made the free states sound even better: "Illinois is a free state wheare we intend to settle wich is better for white familieys and much pleasanter." The Longstroths were concerned about not hearing from one who "professed to be a frend and relative" in Settle and had offered help, so they tried to maintain links by asking that their letters be circulated among family and friends still in England.[48]

Like other English Mormons in America, the Longstroths had two primary, interconnected goals: to enjoy religious freedom among fellow believers and to acquire land. The importance of acquiring land, and the independence and self-respect that came with it, was difficult to disentangle from religious motives. In both Missouri and Illinois, the Longstroths reported that "we can have land out in the countery from 1 ½ to 2 ½ dollars per acor. the towns lots sell tollerabely high for building on and gardens a good situation will sell for 100 dollars an acor. Cattle is verey cheap hear, and good cow will cost about 10 or 12 dollars. Pigs we might have had more given than we could keep, I never heard eney amount of pork being so cheap as it is hear."

The family had a good situation in Rockport: they lived close to the Missouri River and could "see all the steam boats passing up and down with all kinds of produce from the counterey and furs from the Rocky Mountains." Adding to their interest, they could "see some of the whilde Indians with chiefs com down on the boats in sommer to trade and receive the yearly pay which they have granted to them for som exchange of lands."⁴⁹

The Longstroths participated fully in the Mormons' epic stage migration to the West, their "sojourn to Zion," and they witnessed and participated in some famous events. On 26 March of 1844 the family left Rockport, took the Missouri River down to St Louis and then the Mississippi River up to Nauvoo. There they bought a new home and attended a conference led by Joseph Smith himself. "We made it hour business to get hear before hour conference, which commenced on the 6th and lasted 4 days." There, "in a grove shaded with trees" they sat at the feet of the great, charismatic prophet himself: "we herd maney good and glories from the mouth of the prophet Joseph Smith and other elders of the church." Stephen estimated that about 1,500 people attended the conference and about 300 were "sent ought on mission to preach the fullness of the gospel." Stephen was still struggling to convince his brother and sisters in England of the truth of his religion, and knew his letters were read with skepticism, if not downright hostility: "This woorke is rowling on in majesty and great power," he insisted, "but whilst I write I suppose you will stager at the word prophet but I tell you that he is a prophet and receves revelatones from god as much so as Moses so [that?] when he speaks it is with authority and power and he is honored by all as such."⁵⁰

The Longstroths had come to Nauvoo in early 1844 not only to attend Smith's conference but to live permanently – or so they thought. When they arrived, they bought, for $100, one acre "with a good log house on it and a whell which supplies us with water." Stephen added a workshop to get established as a joiner. He also planted a garden with an impressive array of vegetables, some familiar to his relatives in Wensleydale, but others that were indigenous to America and still exotic or only vaguely known in Yorkshire: "I have planted my acer lot with all kinds of seeds such as potatoes, indean corn, peas, beans, turnips, carrits, beets, cucumbers, water and much melons, pumkings and squaches and rice corn and coffe, corn, sugar corn and all other seeds such as you sow in your garden." For an additional $12 the family also bought a cow and calf, which could graze freely "ware the land is not fenced in." And though they had to be fed in winter, "the cow supplies us with milk and butter." The Longstroths, like many other English immigrants, took pride and pleasure in the fact that "we have no house rent to pay" and that "together with our great garden" they had "taken a great burthens of[f] any shoulders [h]our living amount to verey little hear [here]."[51]

The Longstroths arrived in Nauvoo just as the town was booming with the influx of other Mormons; they seem to have timed it just right. They bought their home quickly, for a good price, and Stephen spent the first eight weeks "fitting up my place all the time and I have made it tolarable comfortable." "People are taking up this land verey fast," he reported, "but it is very extencis [extensive?] this land is fenced by ditching and all wood land little with railing." One drawback was the scarcity of money in circulation, which necessitated the barter system common to many frontier regions: "[M]en can bye houses and land, horsed and cows and provisions without money. It is done by exchanges hear is a nother thing that will look straing to you that is to build houses with out money."[52]

For the Longstroths the highlight was the erection of the Nauvoo Temple. Stephen reported excitedly that "the saints are building a large tempal of splendid work of nearly all of wite polished stone." He describes the stone as similar to the limestone of the Yorkshire Dales and that the temple "will be 3 stories high, the bottom or bacement stroie as the baptismal fount fitted up, which stands upon twelve oxon of fall stacher and exceeding well rought and is intended to be over laide with gould." Stephen's pride of being part of both a religious movement and a cultural force in America is evident, as is his excitement for how the structure was to be financed: "Now this temple which will be of so magnificent a structor, it is supposed that it will be one of the finest buildings in all America and it will be completed nearly without money. The means for raising this great building is done be everrey man giving a 10th of [h]is propherty and work every 10th day or carryin provisions or propherty to that amount. Som people give in horses, cows, lands, furniture and all kinds of provishons, this is the way the bulding will be completed it is 3 years since the foundations of the tempal was laide, and are expected to have the roof on this fall."[53]

But the Longstroths also had to address some of their more curious theological practices. Particularly difficult to explain was that "the baptismal fount is for the baptisms of the dead that is which your berthing service says on the words of Sant Pall when he says only then are we baptized for the dead, if the dead rise not ye but you will know more of this there after." They also struggled to set the right tone to their family back in Yorkshire. Despite America's many appealing advantages, their plea to convert to their faith was falling on deaf ears. And then there was the fact that American life had its own hardships: "Now I have given you an out line of the prosperity of this city and now I must tell you … that all new settlements have a maney hard things to encounter … hear is no manufacterey to employ, no boys or girls and together with a scarcety of money makes it once in a while hard getting a long. Be sides maney things come to try the faith of the saints for we have to be tried as by fire."[54]

Stephen Longstroth could have had no idea just now tragically accurate his words were. In June of 1844, a mob attacked the Mormons in Illinois and killed Smith. The Longstroth family were likely eyewitnesses to this appalling event because their son-in-law, Willard Richards, was in the same prison as Smith on the night of the murder. How the Yorkshire family coped with the vigilantism against Smith – bizarre even by American frontier standards – is hard to fathom, until one remembers the centrality of their faith and their understanding of themselves as people persecuted for their religion. Stephen finally got around to writing these events back to his "brothers and sisters" in Arncliffe, in Littondale, on 6 July 1845. After reporting on the family's health and thriving livestock, he got to the heart of the matter. Perhaps it was the stress of the recent events that made him rush and use spellings even more challenging to modern readers than in his previous letters: "We have got an hoast of henermies [enemies] in Illinois and in joining countries. They have [illegible] hard to prise us from the state by threttening to drive us but we are boath regardelas and unconcerned abought them. We are still building up the city and the temple, I am working all the time at the temple and it is to be one of the splendedist building in the states." The details in Longstroth's description of Smith's murder suggest he had seen it happen: "The prophets Joseph and Hiram is brother, where serve with a rit under false accusation to get them bought at the city and they whear taken as prisaners to gaill and before the trail came on thear was abought 150 men in disguise with there faces blacked and came up to the gaill and brook through the gardes and doors to the prison room and comenced firing through the door and shot Hiram dead a bullet [in] the eye. The prophet then made [h]is a cape to the window and droped down on outside into the crowde and they set him up against a well … and 4 men where celected and shot him there."[55]

Non-Mormon Yorkshire immigrants observed these events too but from a very different perspective. Matthew Dinsdale paid close attention and reported the news back to Askrigg; he thought the episode a bit overblown:

> Lately there has been considerable disturbance near the Mormon settle at Nauvoo, the particulars will probably have reached you through the paper … the Mormons have promised to leave Nauvoo in the Spring, if so the inhabitants will be satisfied as the Mormons are not desirable neighbours. Several persons were killed and considerable property destroyed by both parties. Outbreaks of this kind are generally magnified by distance … I have conversed with several different individuals from the neighbourhood where the disturbance has been, they come and go on business as tho' nothing had happened.[56]

For Stephen Longstroth the messianic nature of Smith's murder only enhanced his holy status, as he emphasized to his relatives back in England: "Now theas men whear prophets in deed and 2 finer men and good men can-not be found upon the face of the earth. You will also understand that a prophet's natteral death is to be a marter [martyr], now this prophet, when going to Carterig gaill [Carthage Jail], he said I am going as a lamb to the slother but my mind is clame [calm] as a somers morning. So by the los … all things are wright and according to the order of heven. Another thing wich the prophet said on the morning they whent ought, I shall die innocent and it shall get said of me he was murdered in cold blood, this prophesie will allway be remembered."[57]

Longstroth continued by explaining in more detail the theology of baptizing the dead and asking his brother for the names of their father's parents "and also hour half sisters naimes that is dead and the names of all our uncles and ants" so that he could have that sacrament performed on their souls. "Do not fail to give me all the names that you can," he pleaded, "for this is a work of redemption by the words of Jesus when speaking to Necadimas 'except a man be born of water and of the spirit ye can not enter the kingdom of heven'." He also confidently predicted that "in twelve or fifteen months from this time you will hear the fullness of the gospel and then you will be with out excuse and I pray that my brothers and sisters will obay the gospel and be baptized for remichen of your sins, that you may be reborn in the Kingdom of Christ that is on this earth when Christ will be king over all the earth."⁵⁸ The end of this letter is also interesting because Ann takes over "as my husband says he has got no more to say" and refers to their brother Joseph Longstroth and some unspecified thing he did – so terrible – that it produced a "cancer in his soul." This is probably again the unspeakable event that Ann referred to in her very first letter from Clitheroe. And then she says she was "expecting a letter from Arncliffe a long time in answer to one I sent six months ago and I am afraid it has been lost."⁵⁹

By March of 1848, the Longstroths and the rest of the "saints" had moved to St Louis and were preparing for the Great Trek to Utah. Stephen again wrote to his family in Wensleydale to make sure his brothers and sisters were not being misled by biased reporting: "[T]he people of God and the people of the world are at variance and we as people called Mormans have had all the lyings and fals accusations that chould be invented by news papors, pamphlits and reports laid to our [door?] falsely." He also recounted the details of how they were driven out of Nauvoo after the murder of Smith, and why they were going to head for the Far West. The scene he describes was one of war:

[T]hey commenced burning the farmers houses that was in the counterey. Burning about fifty or sixty houses and the inmates obliged to flee into Nauvoo ... if we did not leave the city befor a set time they whould come and either drive us or massacre. Acordingly we agreed to leave the city, when abought ten or twenty thousand of our people had left the city and crossed the river Missippi we had only then a bought two hundred able men left and the mob came and encamped a little way of the city with a bought nine hundred men and all well armmed. We had then but a short-time to prepare our selves for the seage, the canon bools began to fly from boath sids ... 900 to 200 and we made them to retret two or three times. We only lost two men, and it is said that a bought one hundred and seventy of our enemies wheare killed, so you see that the name of the lord was in this, so they sent in an Ambasetor giving us three mor day to quit from the city. Whilst we remaining they came into the city plondering houses taking aney thing that suted them and driving som from there houses. In this way we was drove from our hoames, lost our property.⁶⁰

The Longstroths themselves lost everything: "When we was driven out from Nauvoo," Stephen recalled two years later, "I lost my property my house and shop and 1 ½ acors of land wich I planted as garden I had a number of fine peech trees in the garden I lost all and never got the first reed cent for it."[61] The solution was to carry on to Utah.

After about a year and a half in St Louis the saints were busy preparing for their journey across the Great Plains. Stephen Longstroth wrote a final letter before setting out. Though they were heading for Utah he called the region California. The anticipation of the challenges and dangers must have stunned his family still in Wensleydale. The images of a vast land so different from Yorkshire, the isolation, the natural wonders, must have seemed fantastic – as they indeed were: "We are going to California, a journey of a bought seventeen hundred mils ... On our way we have to go through a wilderness countery and amonst wild Indians. I suppose we shall be abought one thousand in company. The name of the place The Great Salt Lake Valey, in this valey a number of our brethren are settled and commences building a city ... Ann is now preparing our wagon covers and a large tent for the journey. In the valey there is a hot spring of wather verey hot and also warm springs, on the east side of the valey is a high mountan caped with perpetual snow and the valey is very pleasnt and firtile, it is about 20 miles wide [30 kilometres] and 30 miles long [50 kilometres], there is no inabitans near the valey only the Indians."[62]

The Longstroths set out with the party on 3 July 1848 and arrived in Salt Lake on 15 October.[63] They not only survived the journey but by the mid-1850 were thriving in Salt Lake City, having established their home and farm in remarkably little time. As Stephen wrote, "[W]e have been greatly blessed I have got a good house with 3 rooms and 6 ½ acrors of land in good cultivation."[64] They were anticipating a bountiful harvest and a rapid development of their society, especially as more converts headed their way, but also as miners heading for California passed through their town and stimulated the economy. Stephen was earning money, presumably as a joiner, and the city was cashing in on the gold rush, which was pulling in people with plenty of spending money: "[H]ere is thousands of men going to the gould mines which pass through this way and a great maney have dyed som drownd in the crossing the water ... and others by the ... gould mining ... have made ... our city plentiful place for money we coine all our owne gould money ... I am herning [earning] fifteen dollars a week when at work."[65]

The Longstroths contributed to the legendary success story of Salt Lake City and remained devoted to their faith. Yet Stephen seemed haunted by the prospect of his brother and sister never converting and risking eternal damnation: he begged his siblings and extended family to join him in his faith – if not in Utah then at least in England, so they could at least meet again in Heaven. He prayed that "you may obey the gospel of Christ and go down into the waters and be baptized for the remishans of your sins and … for the gift of the [h]oley ghoast and continue faithful to the end that you may have a part in the first reserection for I would say probaely that bee the first chance that I whould have to see me."[66]

The next and final surviving letter from the Longstroths to their siblings in Arncliffe, in Wensleydale, is dated 1 May 1854 and acknowledges the "long time since I have had aney knowledge how you are getting along." After four years of settling and getting more established, Stephen and Ann were still "in tolarabl health" but also "feeling a little of the infirmities of hould [old] age coming upon us."[67] They boast of the thriving settlement and how they had plenty to eat and that "almost every family have got a house and garden that lives in the city." Merchants were finally bringing in all the goods they needed and with new clothes the "people hear are all well clothed and a more respectable people there is not upon the face of the earth."[68]

As an ordained bishop, Stephen was busy attending conferences and building the church, for "Mormonism is spreading all over the world, with an increase of many thousands a year. I will say in spite of all henemys." And he still clung to the hope that his siblings might see the truth as he saw it, or that through late baptisms at least their parents might also be saved: "I have no argument to ofor to you for not obaying the gospel of Jesus but the time will com when you will know of ashurty that Mormanism is true … Baptizam … will secure to me eternal life and exaltation and I shall have great work to do for father and mother and also for maney of my ancestors … of why then are we baptized for the dead, I leave this subject for your further meditation."[69]

Finally, Longstroth commented on the delicate matter of his children, particularly the marriage of his daughters, Alice, Sarah, and Nanny. He was highly circumspect, for all three married Willard Richards, "one of the great men of the earth," who was also "the second Councelor to the presedent." Richards, as already noted, was an American-born Mormon missionary in northern England. The two had met before leaving England

and Richards escorted them and other converts to America and eventually led them to Utah. Apparently, the marriage arrangements for the first two daughters had already been made in 1843 – before their migration – and were sealed in Nauvoo. Stephen's third daughter, Sarah, married Richards too, after her first husband died in Utah.[70] Perhaps these arrangements were what Ann was cryptically referring to in her letter before departing England. It was polygamy that had incited the distrust and hatred of Mormons in the first place. And it was likely polygamy that had made Longstroth's siblings suspicious of their brother. Stephen ends with one last elegy to his new home, never giving up hope that his brothers and sisters might join him: "While I am writing I look hought of my window and see the white capt mountains and hear in the valey it is as wharm as is comfortable and in 2 or 3 weeks it will be as hot as we can have and our vedgation will spring up in a hurey … I remain yours as ever Stephen Longstroth."[71]

The Longstroths and thousands of other English immigrants in Utah were part of an extensive migration to the Far West of the North American continent. Religion and independence drew people like the Longstroths to Utah. Gold and riches drew many others to California.

Figure 14.2   Portrait of Willard Richards and his family, American Mormon missionary in Yorkshire who converted and led many to the United States.

The Gold Rush

Doctors go to digging & diggers or persons unfit go to doctoring.
I believe California has an interesting & important future.

MATTHEW DINSDALE

The California Gold Rush was mythical in its own time. News of ordinary people finding huge gold nuggets in streams and rocks in the West spread like wildfire, not just in America but throughout the British Isles and other parts of the world. Almost immediately, Yorkshire newspapers contained fantastic reports that were read excitedly throughout the region. On 16 January 1849 – less than a year after James Marshall's discovery at Sutter's Mill – the *Wensleydale Advertiser* was already reporting that "The gold hunting mania has reached Hawes. On Saturday last, large posters were struck on the doors of the old Shambles, announcing the sailing of vessels from Liverpool to California, with passengers, and also a 'California Gold Mining Company' is advertised."[1] A couple of weeks later the *Yorkshire Gazette* added compelling details: "Letters from California state that further discoveries had been made in the gold region, which yielded even a more abundant supply than the previous diggings. According to the latest accounts the gathering amounted on the average to about 100,000 dollars daily, and was constantly increasing, without apparently any exhaustion or any limit to the supply."[2]

Letters about the gold rush flowed both ways. In February of 1849 Eleazer Chapman wrote to his brother Barzillai in Wisconsin about how gold mania was spreading in the Dales: "America is much talked about at Askrigg just now. But wherever you go the principal topic of conversation is California & its gold. We continue to receive the most extraordinary accounts. There are scores gone from Sheffield, & I myself feel half inclined to make a start … I should think that the discovery of this gold region will be of great benefit to you in causing a market for your superabundant produce."[3]

By this time English immigrants were already flooding in, and Yorkshire lead miners from the Upper Mississippi were among the first to arrive. Despite an overland distance of some 3,000 kilometres, which took on average about six months to cross, they were eager to dig for gold in California instead of lead in the Upper Mississippi. The temptation grew as lead mines in the Upper Mississippi became less productive and approached exhaustion. In fact, so many Yorkshire and Cornish miners left the area for California that the local economies crashed. So did the churches. In Platteville, the English immigrant preacher W. Tomkins reported in January of 1852 that the local congregations, which included many Yorkshire miners, were struggling because so many had left. Roughly a quarter of the population in the Upper Mississippi's lead district went to California, he estimated – including nearly half of some 7,000 Cornish miners. Because so many had left, lead prices rose and some who remained took advantage of the short boom. But the lead district never fully recovered.[4] Reverend Tomkins added that some of those who left for California were successful, while others had little to show for it:

> [Our] cause has suffered much from the Californian excitement; many have gone to California, and many more are going thither. I do not know what will be the termination of this Californian mania. People who have done well, and might do well here, sell or mortgage their farms, and leave their wives and families, and make great sacrifices, and expose themselves to great dangers for gold. Many have died in California, or on the journey thither; and several have returned thence quite debilitated. A few have returned with a considerable amount of the precious metal; but it has unsettled them, and they are far from being-happy."[5]

Yorkshire newspapers reported both the failures and lucky strikes in California. The inconsistencies may have frustrated readers, but they did reflect the wide range of experience to be found in California's mining frenzy. Sickness and inflation were unforeseen problems:

> There was great amount of distress among the diggers from the want of the common necessaries of life, and attended with very extensive sickness and mortality. Men loaded with gold appeared like haggard vagabonds, clothed filthy garments of the meanest kind. To show the value at which liquors are estimated it is stated that one man

who had two barrels of brandy sold them at the mines by the small wineglass at rates which realized him 14,000 dollars in gold. Everything, and particularly articles of food and raiment, were at most unheard-of prices; for gold was so plentiful in the possession of every one, it seemed to have lost its value. Daily additions are being made to the numbers employed in digging.[6]

Inflation had already reached unprecedented levels in early 1849, as did the influx of people of dubious character, who caused others to rethink their decision to go to California: "According to the New York Herald … Common clerks and salesmen in the stores about town often received as high as 2,500 dollars and their board … The principal waiter in the hotel were board paid 1,700 dollars per year, and several others from 1,200 dollars to 1,500 dollars! … gambling and drinking have already become very prevalent among the gold washers; also that many deaths had occurred; but that the seekers were so intently occupied that the bodies remained without burial."[7]

Yorkshire Dales lead miners had advantages over the parvenus pouring into the region, in the skills, attitudes, and discipline they had honed over the years. They embraced the Gold Rush because of their ongoing sense of adventure, their somewhat restless character, and their relatively high earnings, all of which combined to give them both the means and attitude to leave for California. They were joined by many other English. By 1850 California was third behind Utah and Wisconsin in its recorded English-born population (9.3, 6.2, and 3.3 per cent, respectively).[8]

The Gold Rush also attracted Yorkshire immigrants who had not been miners. Though a man of the cloth, Matthew Dinsdale needed a break from his arduous circuit riding life and meagre pay, so he left Wisconsin for California in early November 1849. Deciding against crossing the vast continent by foot and wagon, he took the longer (by about 6,500 kilometres) but faster (by a month or two) water route: The Great Lakes to Buffalo, the Erie Canal to Albany, down to New York, then to Panama to cross its infamously deadly isthmus, and finally up the Pacific coast to San Francisco.[9]

For Dinsdale the water route was the adventure of a lifetime. Writing to his mother from New York on his way to Panama, he was proud to report that "I had my Daguerreotype taken at [Matthew] Brady's in this city as a present for you," as he had "long purposed to send you my likeness."[10] And twelve days later, still in New York, he wrote again to her saying he had "spent my time very pleasantly while I have been in this very bustling City." He was paying $5 a week for room and board at the Tremont Temperance House on Broadway, which "is sustained on strictly temperance principals." Temperance was still a vital cause for Dinsdale. One evening it was his "good fortune to hear J.B. Gough the celebrated temperance lecturer." Gough was himself an English immigrant from Kent, who by mid-century had become an international celebrity, eventually credited with inspiring 200,000 people to pledge to never again drink alcohol. Dinsdale also took time to hear anti-slavery lectures – the most important reform for Northerners, and especially English immigrants.[11]

The worst part of the journey was sailing to Panama. "I was very sea sick," Dinsdale wrote, "and felt unwell all the time."[12] But Central America fascinated him. Writing to his sister from Panama in December, Dinsdale struggled to keep cool while he described the town of Chagres and all the sights, sounds, and smells, and the flora and fauna that he had never seen before. Local religion did not escape his attention, of course: "The religion of the country so far as there is any is Popery, desolating destructive Popery." On the other hand, "it is the easiest thing in the world to live here, almost every article of food used growing spontaneously and in great abundance ... Oranges, lemons, plantains, bananas, pie apples, yams are found in abundance of the best kind." Furthermore, "I have seen several parrots some of the very rich plumage."[13]

By 12 January 1850, Dinsdale and his party had crossed the Isthmus, sailed north and landed in Mazatlán, Mexico. He reported "a delightful day" and wrote in his diary "How manifold are thy works O God in wisdom thou has made them all."[14] But then, sailing up toward the California coast, seasickness returned with a vengeance and the weather got cold and wet, triggering in Dinsdale an intense homesickness for England. "This day reminds me of home, more than any day I have seen for some time ... cloudy with some rain and the coast just to our right is a gentle slope with the green and brown grass in pleasant harmony like a well eaten pasture overshadowed with clouds but bright in places with sunshine ... Dear old England, shall I see thee yet again? When looking on land I can almost fancy myself in Wensleydale looking about from A[skrigg]." Three days later they landed in San Francisco.[15]

Dinsdale was impressed with San Francisco, rightly predicting that the city "will become a great place. Its location is good convenient and pleasant and more still is healthy."[16] And he was practical, preaching on Sundays and mining during the week. But the mining environment was much harder than Wisconsin's, as he recorded in April of 1850: "After three or four attempts descended the big canyon and made a claim. Took us all day and had to encamp before reaching the summit. Dined in a ravine on a small island near the bottom. Found just on the edge of the Canyon stream a very good stick for a cane marked by a vine. I called it her rod of God and received it as a sign of his blessing and protection. While in danger felt no fear, but trusted in my God."[17]

Discouraged by miners who failed to find gold, Dinsdale soldiered on. By 18 February 1850, he was "digging half the day" at Weaverville, the newly founded gold rush town in Trinity County. Snow and rain made it dreary business. So did the living conditions, which were rough, to say the least, and must have appalled readers back in the Dales. "The first house I lived in was a tent," he recorded with emphasis, and "the second a cabin without a floor, and not wholly without a roof, nor yet destitute of sides, but they were open … I have slept in turns on the plain the mountain and close to the stream in the deep valley. By the day I have walked thru falling snow and rain with nothing waterproof on except boots."[18] Furthermore, the hard snows of mid-March "makes me think much of home." "Shall I ever see the dear old place of peace?" he wondered.[19]

To make matters worse, there was the notorious violence of gold rush mining towns like Weaverville. "Saw a man on the floor dead who lost his life thro' being ducked the evening before on the supposition that he had stolen a watch," Dinsdale noted on 17 March. "One man shot another at Mr. Seward's," he noted just two days later.[20] Travelling as both prospector and preacher, Dinsdale observed a lot of violence. "Two murders committed at this place to day over cards," he recorded in April. "One man shot another, when the brother of the dead man stabbed the murderer."[21] On the 27th, "A trial today. A man for stealing a mule. Sentenced to 30 lashes given by a boatswains mate."[22] In July Dinsdale witnessed a trial at camp: "It was a true California style and without expense … A man was accused of stealing a mule. The case was heard both sides, each party having chosen six men. The criminal was found guilty and condemned to receive thirty lashes which were inflicted by a Jack Tar." And on 5 July he recorded that "today a Mexican woman stabd a man at the forks, he died in ten minutes after. She was tried by the people found guilty by a jury and hung on the bridge in the afternoon. Both were interred side by side today."[23]

These scenes would have shocked most readers back in Yorkshire, and yet Dinsdale insisted that "I believe life and property are as secure here as in any other part of the world ..." On the other hand, "Moral and domestic restraints on natural human passions hardly exist here," he observed. "I am almost surprised that matters are not much worse. However the prevalence of profane swaring does astonish me."[24]

Alongside the violence and sickness Dinsdale saw some of the riches that were luring so many people to the area. Travelling toward Georgetown he saw a "piece of gold weighing two and a half pounds. A beautiful piece." And then, passing through Sutter's Mill, where the original strike was made, he set up camp with his partners for some serious digging.[25] Combining preaching with gold mining seemed to work for him. Writing to his brother John from Upper California in April of 1850, Dinsdale revealed his success as both a preacher and a miner. "There is much wickedness in the land," he said of the local mining population, "but there are a few whose hearts are right with God," and these were the ones who attended his sermons. And, prospecting on the "lower slope of the Sierra Nevada ... the diggings have been good." They "always found some gold though frequently but little." And, while mining near Weberville "three of us made about 90 dollars each the most of it in old diggings."[26] "On the whole," he concluded, "I am well satisfied that I came here and at present would rather be in California than anywhere else on earth."[27] But Dinsdale did not intend to stay in California: "I have seen no part I like so well as Wisconsin & if providence permits I hope to return there to live & die." By this time, he was working with two men who had arrived from Mineral Point "and am very comfortable."[28]

Just how "comfortable" Dinsdale was is revealed in his letters. In July, after only a half-year of prospecting, Dinsdale reported his methods and level of success to friends back in Wisconsin. "I will give you last week's earnings which is about average of our labors. Monday eight men working: $132. Tuesday seven men: $80. Wed. seven: $104 ... This is reconing gold at $16 an oz ... we make ten or twelve dollars a day and hope to do still better. The most I have made in one day was $37.25." As for their methods, "we throw off about three feet of surface to find gold deposited ... in clay or gravel which we wash ... We have used a quicksilver machine, a rocker, and a 'long tom' as it is called. That is a trough about twelve feet long by one and half wide."[29] Altogether it added up to an impressive sum: Matthew Dinsdale's assay of gold amounted to $4,094.13.[30]

When Dinsdale finally left California, he retraced his steps but sailed to Philadelphia for a return trip to England. Just sailing to Philadelphia was awful: "[N]othing uses me up like sea sickness," Dinsdale admitted. So horrendous was the ordeal that he had "serious thoughts of giving up the idea of crossing the Atlantic, from the belief that I could not stand it."[31] This was not uncommon – bad voyages could make return trips unthinkable. Dinsdale had to find the courage for his return visit to Askrigg, and he had two weeks to stay in Philadelphia before boarding the dreaded transatlantic ship.

Ultimately, what brought him back to Yorkshire was Mary Ann Mann. The two had scarcely known each other but had developed a relationship through letters and by Mary Ann's friends meeting Dinsdale in Wisconsin and reporting back to her. As Matthew wrote in February of 1853: "You are somewhat acquainted with me and my family, I have given your friends the opportunity of seeing me. I believe I have no questions to ask, but in all candor I say will you become my Wife?"[32] In April of the same year they married in York, where Mary Ann had lived a comfortable life, with servants. Significantly, Dinsdale described himself on his marriage certificate as a merchant, as he had engaged in that activity along with his preaching.[33]

The return to Wisconsin would be a family adventure. Matthew's mother and sister left Askrigg first and waited in Liverpool while Matthew and Mary Ann made their final preparations. "I came away without one sigh or regret about anything excepting the poor old cat," Dinsdale recorded. "I left her in Mrs' Daskin's care but she made no attempt to settle in her new home." He walked all the way from Askrigg, via Leyburn and Bedale, to York to fetch Mary Ann, who was making her own preparations, with some trepidation. From York they took the train to Liverpool and then sailed for America with the other family members.[34] In Wisconsin, Mary Ann faced some serious adjustments: their home was still a log cabin and there were no servants to help with the work. As the couple raised five children, Matthew continued to preach in various parts of Wisconsin, including Highland, Washburne, Platteville and Potosi, Lancaster, Mineral Point, and finally in Madison in 1875. (He died in 1898.)[35]

Though Matthew Dinsdale was only one of many North Yorkshire people to mine in California's Gold Rush, we can surmise that others shared many of the core experiences: making the arduous journey, seeing glimpses of California that triggered memories of the Dales, experiencing crushing homesickness in such a faraway place, and being jarred by the violent mining culture in an alien landscape. The extensive depopulation of the Upper Mississippi mining region suggests that many were successful in California. Most would return to the Upper Mississippi or go to other places and invest their earnings in their farms. But those who remained in California helped develop the territory and push it into statehood. Ironically, California becoming a free state in 1851 raised the tension over slavery and contributed to secession and the Civil War, and here too the people of North Yorkshire were at the centre of events and played important and sometimes unique roles.

Politics, Reform, and War

The cause of temperance is a high and holy cause.

MATTHEW WILLIS, JR

Politics

As has already been observed, English immigrants relished America's greater social and political equality. Some based their migration decision partly on that. Many English immigrants to New England were class-conscious, especially mill workers who had been members of trade unions and embraced Chartism to cope with the onslaught of industrial capitalism.[1] Other members of England's working classes were aware of America's political advantages and hoped that by emigrating they could free themselves from England's class-ridden culture. Meanwhile some English labour leaders and intellectuals shared the conviction that Britain could learn much from America's experiment with democracy. The English "radicals," John Bright, Richard Cobden, and others, held up America as a model for reform at home, and encouraged people to migrate to America to benefit from a government not dominated by aristocrats.[2] English immigrants in the United States were quite knowledgeable about America's government; some surviving letters contain news about both American and British politics. Eager to take their political rights and responsibilities seriously, they were often among the first in American communities to get involved in politics and serve in a variety of offices and functions, such as postmasters and justices of the peace. Participating in American political life contributed to their assimilation.[3]

Their voting patterns also indicate assimilation and commonality with Americans. Most immigrants from other countries supported the Democrats, who generally welcomed immigrants from non-British backgrounds, used them politically at the city and state levels, and opposed social reform movements like temperance and abolitionism. But the English voted overwhelmingly for the Whigs (who formed their party in the 1830s) and Republicans (formed in 1854 by absorbing Whigs and others who distrusted the Democrats, and those who wanted to limit slavery in some way). Whigs and Republicans were dedicated to reforming society and raising moral standards through government action and churches. Yorkshire immigrants, especially the dominant Methodists, agreed wholeheartedly with that agenda. As the only immigrant group voting Whig and Republican, the English fit in with voters in northern states.[4]

There were interesting exceptions. Those who had converted to Mormonism were mostly Democrats, as were most Mormons at this time, because of their distrust of a powerful government that might usurp God's authority on earth, and because of the social hierarchies they allegedly promoted.[5] This perception and behaviour among English immigrant Mormons was explained by Stephen Longstroth in a letter to his brothers and sisters in England, not long after the assassination of Joseph Smith: "You wanted to [k]now how the saints stand in relation to politicks ... we give our voats to Demmecrats and by hour great numbers we can gain the voat, for we all give our voats oneway. As for politics we believe that governments were instituted of God for the benefit of man in making laws for the good and safety of society. We belive that everyman should be honoured in [h]is staition, rulers and magistrates."[6]

Canada's English immigrants also voted in patterns that meshed with those of the dominant British cultural group. At local and provincial levels, they supported people and parties dedicated to maintaining the imperial connection, love for Queen Victoria, and building the nation. North Yorkshire immigrants were quickly absorbed into the political status quo.[7]

Temperance

Throughout the nineteenth century, reform movements in both Britain and the United States flourished, often by working together through transatlantic ties. Temperance was one of the most important. The English had their gin and the Americans their whiskey, and their low prices and easy availability contributed to widespread abuse. Yorkshire immigrants, especially Methodists, were active in or at least sympathetic to temperance events. In Yorkshire, lectures, concerts, and teas dedicated to the cause were important social occasions in which people could demonstrate their social respectability. And when people left Yorkshire for the mining camps of the Upper Mississippi, they could see the havoc that cheap booze could bring. Occasionally we see glimpses of alcohol affecting their new lives in America. Writing to his brother and sister, Richard Buxton remarked that their sister's husband, John Pedley, "don't deserve the tittle of brother he is nothing but a drunken sot ... his whisky he will have he has drunken himself into the horors a good many times I think if he goes on he soon will kill himself."[8]

Many nations struggled with alcohol, but Britain and America had a shared evangelical and reform culture that responded effectively. A linked British-American temperance movement emerged in the United States in the late 1820s, when Lyman Beecher's lectures for the Massachusetts Temperance Society inspired Henry Forbes to establish England's first society, in Bradford in 1830. Soon there were many other branches.[9] Maine's liquor laws became a model for Britain's United Kingdom Alliance of 1853.[10] The transatlantic temperance movement was connected through the extensive exchange of people and ideas. Sometimes migration and temperance were coordinated. In 1842 the British Temperance Emigration Society was formed in Liverpool and by 1850 it had assisted nearly 700 Britons to Wisconsin to attempt a cooperative society based on temperance principles. Though this community and others like it soon disbanded, they nonetheless got English people to America.[11]

Slavery and Abolitionism

The central pillar of the British-American reform movement was abolition. Slavery was so repulsive to most English immigrants that it drove many to the North instead of the South. Abolitionism was launched in England by Quakers and Anglicans, and then Methodists, Presbyterians, Congregationalists, and Baptists – denominations brought to America by immigrants in the eighteenth century and strengthened by later immigrants.[12] Other English evangelicals joined the cause and headed for America. By the 1830s English and American abolitionists were working closely together and travelled back and forth in coordinated movements.[13] In 1833 William Lloyd Garrison visited England to pay homage to William

Wilberforce on his deathbed, and the following year he invited George Thompson – Britain's most celebrated abolitionist – to the United States for a lecture tour financed by English abolitionists, and to be commissioned as an agent of the American and New England Anti-Slavery Societies. Thompson's uncompromising speeches inspired many Americans. Lecture tours occurred in the other direction too. In 1845 the former slave Frederick Douglass, his freedom purchased by English supporters, began a nearly two-year lecture tour of Britain and packed the halls with his mesmerizing oratory. Douglass developed a lifelong admiration of Britain and returned to the United States in 1847, telling Americans the irony that he had to "seek a refuge in monarchical England from the dangers of republican slavery."[14] And during the 1850s and the Civil War years, other African Americans – some refugee slaves like Douglass – toured England to lecture and drum up support. Few parts of Britain were left untouched by their efforts, though they did not always get along with the British anti-slavery organizations.[15] English women also played important roles in transatlantic abolitionism by raising funds and publishing and circulating information and petitions.[16] The English and Scots also helped establish American educational institutions dedicated to abolitionism.[17]

English interest in American abolitionism peaked when – during its first year of publication in 1852 – Harriet Beecher Stowe's *Uncle Tom's Cabin* sold 150,000 copies in the United States, but over a million in Britain: a ratio of seven to one. The book brought Queen Victoria to tears; the prime minister, Lord Palmerston, claimed to have read it three times. Stowe toured Britain as a celebrity in 1853, 1856, and 1859.[18] And in 1863 she published *A Reply to the Affectionate and Christian Address*, a warm response to English women who were supporting abolition during the Civil War. Stowe addressed them as her "sisters," related by culture, religion, blood, and abolitionism.[19]

Prominent Yorkshire immigrant abolitionists included Thomas Vickers, who worked closely with Wendell Phillips, William Lloyd Garrison, and others before becoming president of the University of Cincinnati in 1877. Garrison introduced Vickers to English abolitionists on one of his return trips. Vickers probably knew the family of Henrietta Ramsden, also natives of Yorkshire, who were leaders of the movement in Salem, Ohio. Ramsden's passionate fight against slavery began while she was still in Yorkshire, where she sold the first book on the life of Frederick Douglass. Like Vickers, she worked closely with Phillips, Garrison, and others, and provided them lodging in her home. And Edward C. Benson, from Thorne, Yorkshire, graduated from and taught at Kenyon College, which had been established by Lord Kenyon as a college dedicated to abolitionism.[20]

But North Yorkshire had its own links to slavery. As late as the 1820s local landowners like George Metcalfe, from Hawes, still owned African slaves on his estates in the Caribbean, and arranged for their sale only at the time of his death.[21] Thus, there was a strong local and moral dimension to abolitionism among people from North Yorkshire, who carried this passion to North America. Like most Methodists, Matthew Dinsdale despised slavery. While serving as an itinerant preacher in Wisconsin in 1845 he stayed with an elderly Methodist originally from Virginia and described him as "the owner of several slaves and considerable property." But, Dinsdale recorded approvingly, "Slavery he could not do with so he liberated his Negroes (I think 26 in number), sold his estate for 20 thousand dollars and removed to the west."[22]

The Civil War

The political and diplomatic relationship between Great Britain and the United States during the American Civil War was complex. In some ways the war divided the British public and government. At the outset Queen Victoria's government granted belligerent status to the Confederacy, an act that temporarily put England back into favour in the Southern mind, after years of disenchantment over England's hostility to slavery.[23] And when the US navy boarded the British packet ship RMS *Trent* in late 1861 and arrested two Confederate envoys, the two nations seemed headed for war, and Britain's sympathy for the Confederacy rose even higher. Meanwhile, British shipyards built the warship *Alabama* for the Confederacy, which reassured many Southerners of a forthcoming alliance.[24] Some English conservatives and aristocrats supported the Confederacy because of a perceived cultural affinity and the assumption that a division of the United States would enhance British international power – that an independent Confederacy would serve as a buffer against growing American power in the Western hemisphere.[25]

English radicals, liberals, and the working classes, on the other hand, tended to support the Union, as did most English immigrants in America. They saw the war not only as a tragic necessity to end slavery, but also as a symbol of a larger struggle for universal political equality. They agreed with John Bright and other labour leaders that the struggle for black freedom was linked to their own, that in the words of historian John Morley, "the triumph of the North … was the force that made English liberalism powerful enough to enfranchise the workmen, depose official Christianity in Ireland, and deal the first blow at the landlords."[26] As the war escalated, most English on both sides of the conflict condemned the war for its wanton carnage. And for some English observers, the war confirmed the superiority of their political system and the dangers of mass democracy.[27]

For other reasons England's stake and interest in the American Civil War was high. The war devastated England's cotton industries. Lancashire's "cotton famine" brought widespread unemployment and unrest. Even so, textile workers still sympathized with the Union, as did most members of the business class. The British government acted cautiously: because the war was still only about preserving the Union, it could continue to acknowledge the Confederacy's legitimate belligerent status. But when the Emancipation Proclamation brought a moral purpose to the war at the end of 1862, British support for the South evaporated: Britain could no longer be hostile to a Union government that was now fighting to end slavery. In northern states England was being associated with emancipation, and English immigrants celebrated the "Yankees" who were following the English example of thirty years before by working to end slavery.[28]

A surprising number of English soldiers and officers came to America to join the conflict, mostly on the Union side, to fight slavery.[29] As for English immigrants already in America, they distinguished themselves for volunteering for the Union in the greatest proportions of all immigrants. At least 54,000 English-born men served in the Union, many of them recent immigrants, some even signing up upon their arrival. Their motives varied but fighting to eliminate the "great stain" on American liberty and preserve the Union was probably the most common and deeply felt. Some, however, were motivated more by the pay than by slavery. Quite a few were determined to dispel lingering doubts about their loyalty to the United States, or suspicions about their loyalty to Queen Victoria. These motives were often mixed and hard to disentangle. One certain fact is that the English felt no need to form their own regiments, as all other immigrant soldiers did, but served comfortably in ordinary American regiments. As with the larger society, they could blend in with the Union forces. They served in virtually every capacity in the Civil War, in every major battle. Whatever their role, many later identified the war as the event that made them complete Americans.[30]

These characteristics of the English in general also apply to those from North Yorkshire. They seemed well informed about the issues behind the tensions between Britain and America and within America itself. Matthew Dinsdale did not join the military but did serve on the "Christian Commission," which went to hospitals in the South to help the survivors of the battlefields.[31] Others seemed eager to serve in military capacities. Having left Askrigg in 1849, Thomas Lewis Walker was prospering on his farm in Wisconsin, and like others used his skills as a stonemason and miner to finance his growing farm operation. But in February of 1864, at age thirty-nine, he left his comfortable life and wife and four children to enlist in Company H, 7th Wisconsin Volunteer Infantry. Within three months he saw his first combat in the Battle of the Wilderness. And then at Petersburg four bullets hit his cartridge belt, which became his prized possession for saving his life. He was also at Appomattox to witness Lee's surrender to Grant.[32]

Thomas's brother Peter did not fully understand why Thomas had volunteered to fight in such a ghastly war. Perhaps it was the bounty for enlisting, which Thomas would not have received had he been drafted. As Peter speculated in his letters back to family and friends in Askrigg, "Tom went to the War why I can not say he was not compelled to but Enlisted for three years left a wife and four children ... they have been talking about drafting or pressing men into the Service ... I think Tom thought he would be drafted so he would rather go as a volunteer ... When Tom went they got 300 dollars from government."[33] At thirty-nine, Thomas was not likely to have been drafted, and was probably motivated by nobler reasons.

Peter Walker also expressed a reluctance to serve, which seems to have been based on his uncertainty over the war's aims and strategies, as well as his conviction that more black soldiers should fight before more whites were enlisted: "I do not know if I will go or not I want government to get Every ... Black man and let them fight for their freedom before they take any more white men as this is a Negro War and they ought to have a hand for fighting Every one of them If government had commenced at first to take the blacks Into arms this War would of been over with two years ago but our rulers hesitated too long about it but we have got a great many of the blacks in arms now ... When this is done I am Satisfied for the whites to fill up and help put down this ungodly Rebelion."[34]

Peter Walker was deeply troubled by the war, especially as casualties mounted. Among them was his brother-in-law (Thomas's wife's brother), who served in the same regiment as Thomas and was killed at Petersburg: "Tom's wife lost a brother he was killed in a charge a fine young man rose to be Lieutenant."[35] Peter seemed depressed and admitted to having "the ups and downs" since he last wrote to Askrigg. He was especially upset that "they never answer my letter yet and now I do not know where they live." He was also still mourning the death of his first wife, which had occurred three years previously. Though he had remarried, his health problems were frequent and severe.[36]

Immigrants from other parts of North Yorkshire fought for the Union. Charles Eckles, who immigrated as a boy with his father, East Yorkshireman Marmaduke Eckles, served in Company D, 34th Illinois Volunteer Infantry, which was also known as the "Rock River Rifles." He quickly rose to sergeant then lieutenant and fought in the battles of Shiloh, Lookout Mountain, and others. His brother Thomas also served, in the 140th Regiment of Illinois Volunteer Infantry. In 1888, as a distinguished veteran and successful farmer in Iowa, Charles Eckles was elected to the Iowa House of Representatives.[37]

Not all North Yorkshire immigrants were eager to join the military. In addition to Peter Walker's hesitation there was that of the Matthew Willis family. As Quakers, the Willis family were pacifists and the four sons felt no compulsion to volunteer to save the Union, free the slaves, or for any other reason. They were determined to avoid being drafted. The sons were John Willis, born in Preston, England in 1837, twenty-eight; Thomas Carter Willis, also born in Preston, in 1841, twenty-four; James Willis, born in Wisconsin and about twenty, and Richard Willis, born in 1850 and at fifteen probably too young. Their mother wrote back to her daughter Elizabeth, who remained in England and had married into the Longmire family, and tried to explain the complicated system of hiring substitutes for those subject to the draft. The Willis family was already making payments to keep their sons on the farm, but they were not necessarily in the clear yet, and were considering dodging the draft by sending their sons back to England:

In our township we have hitherto hired men to fill the quota, for which we raise a Tax of a few thousand dols which tho'expensive, does away with the danger of a draft. Every volunteer has a government bounty allowed of 300 dollars for a term of three years; while those who are drafted have nothing allowed; And from this time forward it is not unlikely that our rulers will demand men by draft which will do away with the necessity of giving bounties. In this case it is not unlikely your Brothers Thos and Jas will be force into the army, or compelled to hire substitutes which will cost in all probability 1000 dollars each which is much more than we shall be able to raise unless times should improve a great deal. A draft is coming off in about ten days … and unless we can raise volunteers to fill the quota for the township of Mifflin we shall have a draft and we fear this is the last time we shall have the privilege of raising men by enlistments. … Your Brothers have paid in about 53 dollars bounty tax for this call … I want them to come over to England to stay till the close of the war. It is uncertain however, whether we can persuade them.[38]

The Willis family wrote again to Elizabeth in February of 1865, indicating their relief that the boys had not yet been drafted, and revealing their past associations with General Grant, who had lived in Galena: "As yet none of your Brothers have gone to the wars. Several calls have been made for young men and vast numbers have been drafted or have enlisted, few of whom have returned … we had not much knowledge of Genl Grant although we sold him our best hides when he was tanner in Galena before he entered the army. He always seemed a prompt straightforward upright trading man always willing to give the best price for whatever suited him."[39]

As the war raged, letters back and forth between Yorkshire and America carried details of the effects of the conflict on both sides of the Atlantic. From Farndale in the North York Moors Henry Wilson wrote to his cousin Charlotte Ware Atkinson, who, with her family, had joined the Colony in Lee County, Iowa. It was mid-1863, and the raging war was the main topic: "We … were all very glad to hear you are in good health but are very sorry to hear in England of the war in America, it is causing great distress in England and we hope sincerely that the war will close and cause you no more trouble in your own family … If the war discontinues and you think of coming to England you are welcome to come and stay at my house."[40]

President Lincoln's strategic plan to keep the border states in the Union by not ending slavery there, even after the Emancipation Proclamation took effect, was also a topic in letters, but it was either too obscure or unconvincing for Matthew Willis. Writing from his farm in Iowa County, Wisconsin two years after the war ended, he was convinced that, "had the Negro population of the South been proclaimed free when the rebellion broke out the war could not have continued longer than a single year at most; but the pride of the North would not do it, and the consequence has been the loss of thousands of men and millions of money an everlasting loss to the country never to be redeemed."[41]

North Yorkshire immigrants, then, paid close attention to the war, especially the now-legendary battles, and how the war affected their daily lives. Some seem to have been tuned into the war's political ramifications for the British-American relationship. The potential for Britain to support the Confederacy to protect their cotton supplies, or to limit America's political and economic might in the Western hemisphere, was never as great as some thought. Many Southerners had nurtured the illusion that the South was still an informal part of Britain's empire, and that Britain would therefore ensure her independence. But the possibility of Britain or France interfering in some way concerned some Yorkshire immigrants. Keenly interested in Britain's reaction to the war and the potential for an alliance with the Confederacy, Peter Walker wrote to his cousin and aunt still in Wensleydale: "[T]here is Some Rumors that the South is a going to turn over to England if this is the case you and I may meet face to face in Civil Combat together but god forbid ... It will be worse than now son against Father Brother against Brother."[42]

And, showing his comprehension of the cultural affinity between Britain's aristocracy and the Southern slave-owning planters, Peter Walker recognized what working-class leaders in Britain were saying – that the freedom of blacks and of whites was ultimately connected: "If England does go In with the South She will show to the world the dog coming out [of?] her but I do not think she will as France may pay her a visit at the same time although it would just suit the Aristocracy of England they are like the Southern Slave holders which brought on this war. When We the people of the United States has to be ruled by such god pity the poor; the black man will be kept in Slavery and the white men will not be much better … they say would not you fight to free your posterity from Such rulers [?]. Enough about this awful war which has sent many a father from his children and made many orphans and widows."[43]

The war also affected Yorkshire immigrants' local economy. On their farm "Rama," in Iowa County, Wisconsin, the Willis family benefited from higher crop prices and were able to send money back to Wensleydale, apparently to settle a loan from their daughter's extended family. But the war had also distorted the labour market, making it impossible to find builders to build a better house to replace the ramshackle one they seemed stuck with. Furthermore, the banking crisis and the federal government's ending of specie payments, along with its issue of paper greenbacks, fell heavily on them, particularly when they sent money back to England. As Willis wrote in early 1865, as the war was winding down:

On the first prospect of war, specie payment were suspended by the banks and since then there has been no chance of getting any kind of money except paper money which we understand will not pass in England without a heavy discount. I spoke to the Bankers in Mineral Point a few weeks ago and they told me that to send four hundred dollars to England I should have to deposit with them, (I think) something over eight hundred in American currency. If your Uncle could have confidence in us he shall certainly be paid with interest; but to have to do it now there will be unavoidably, a heavy loss.[44]

The stress of the war, the precarious economic situation caused in part by the suspension of specie payments, and perhaps above all the looming threat of having their boys forced into the army all weighed heavily on the Willis family. A continuing frustration with the changing American farm economy was accentuated by a deep longing to be back in Yorkshire:

In case specie payments should be resumed by the banks I should like exceedingly to sell our property here and return to my native land. The great mischief is, that property in America sells for a trifle in comparison with what you would think it worth. For instance Land partly cultivated sells for about the sum that 2 years crops would be worth. Thus our place if 400 acres were in cultivation might raise grain worth ten thousand dollars annually (which is the calculation of some experience farmers) crops averaging 60 bush oats per acre, which has been our average hitherto, might not sell for more than twenty thousand dollars sterling which I would not like.[45]

After the War

The Civil War was indeed a formative catastrophe that affected the entire American population, including those from North Yorkshire. Some, like George Buxton of Company I, did not survive and "died of wounds."[46] Even for the survivors, the physical effects from injuries could linger forever. Thomas Walker survived, unlike his wife's husband, but he still paid a heavy price. Though thankful when his cartridge belt had saved his life by deflecting four bullets, he then became ill at the Battle of Hatcher's Run and suffered severe lung and respiratory problems that plagued him for the rest of his life.[47] In January of 1871 he wrote to his aunt in Askrigg that his doctor found "the catarrh had got to my lungs this being the case it will sooner or later terminate my life with consumption." Yet he continued farming, even though 1870 was "a poor year for farming in this country." Walker ended his letter with a summary of his life as a Yorkshire immigrant in America, one that surely many others would have agreed with: "I left my native hills and many has been the ups and downs since that time[.] I still love my native hills her rocks and gils my heart with rapture fills but I love America beter the land of the free and the home of the brave."[48]

Ultimately, the American Civil War was a crucible out of which emerged a new nation and people.[49] With the war's end and the dawning of a new era, the Anglo-American relationship was changing but it continued, and North Yorkshire immigrants remained part of that relationship. The Civil War also marked a new era on how to get to America: the widespread use of new steamships, which revolutionized the transatlantic passage and American immigration.

The Steamship

Since the invention of steamships distant countries
have become like those that are near at hand.

TOWNSEND HARRIS

After the Civil War, the ongoing transportation revolution on both sides of the Atlantic transformed migration and allowed unprecedented numbers to arrive. Railways were expanding everywhere, including in North Yorkshire, making it much easier to leave. In 1856 railways linked Leyburn to Bedale and Northallerton. And in the 1860s and 1870s new railway lines penetrated Wensleydale's villages, including Hawes, which became connected to the Settle and Carlisle line in 1876.[1] Long walks or bone-crunching carriage rides to a seaport were a thing of the past.

Steamships made the biggest difference. Early models, hybrids of sail and paddle steamers, were used in the 1850s; but soon better and faster ships were designed to serve the emigrant trade. By 1867 more than 90 per cent of all passengers leaving English ports for America were taking steamships. Seasickness and shipwrecks were still common enough, but instead of the five and often ten or more weeks that sailing ships took to cross, steamships made it in only ten to fourteen days. And though steamship tickets were roughly double the cost of the old sailing ship tickets, passengers actually paid less in lost wages and costs for provisions. Thus, steamships lowered the "migration threshold" – the physical and psychological barriers to emigration. The decision to leave was no longer so daunting; one could "try America out" and return to England if it failed to meet expectations. The new ships also made repeat migration, or seasonal migration among the so-called birds of passage, common – even routine. In fact, between 1860 and 1914, about 40 per cent of England's total emigrants to America returned – a total of about 2 million people – the highest rate of all return migration.[2] That could never have happened in the age of sail.

But steamship voyages could still be daunting. This is clear in a letter that Rose Willis wrote from Wisconsin to her sister Elizabeth in Wensleydale in 1875: "Do you ever think of coming over ... although I should be very much pleased to see you here, yet dare not encourage you to come for fear of the Ocean."[3] And no matter how fast the new ships were, seasickness could make the journey seem an eternity. When James Broderick sailed for America in 1876, he claimed his ship had broken the record and had made the crossing in a little more than seven days. He also enjoyed being "extremely well fed and attended to while on board." Yet much of the time he suffered debilitating sickness.[4]

Because of steamships more English immigrants made return journeys to their old home, sometimes to find a wife. In 1868, for example, Elizabeth Longmire Willis, who had remained in Wensleydale and lived in Woodhall, a small hamlet a few kilometres from Askrigg, wrote to her brother Thomas, now twenty-seven and living in Mifflin, Wisconsin, that "we have had a man from America in Askrigg he has however now gone back and taken a young wife with him his name is Preston. I daresay you will have heard of him as he only lives some miles from you he was a native of Askrigg and has six children by a former wife. I saw him in Carperby one day and he told me that he lived so near you."[5] Here we see how even decades after leaving England migrants still returned to their native village to find suitable spouses. But steamship tickets still required resources in both time and money, and the Willis family appeared to have little to spare. In 1869 Thomas Willis wrote from Wisconsin to his sister Elizabeth to report that their parents, Matthew and Jane, "are getting rather feble" and to say that "I would like very much to come over & see you & all our relations but I see no chance of that at present." Without the means for a return trip, immigrants had to rely more than ever on letters and mementoes: "it would be a great treat to have you come over," continued Thomas Willis. ... "you might send me your picture ... & a little braid of your hair ... please write more often than you do."[6]

John Flounders Dixon

A vivid sense of what Yorkshire migrants experienced in the age of steam is recorded in the detailed account of John Flounders Dixon. Born in 1844 at Crathorne, near Yarm (near the western edge of the North York Moors),

Dixon emigrated from nearby Great Ayton in 1871 at age twenty-seven, along with his younger brother, Charles, and Frank Standing, a teacher whose uncle had a farm in Earlham, Iowa – the trio's destination. His father was a farm labourer. Both parents had experienced prior moves because they were not born in Crathorne Parish. Dixon's mother, Eliza, came from a Quaker family that had a tradition of movement within England. Her father had worked at various trades in various places, including blacksmithing in Northallerton, before settling in Yarm. In fact, some time before 1820, Eliza's father Joseph Flounders, his wife and two of his four children, emigrated to Philadelphia, leaving behind two other children – Eliza and her sister – to stay with Joseph's brother, William Flounders, who had taken over the family farm. So, the family was well acquainted with stories of America. By 1851 William Flounders was farming 185 acres and employing four farm labourers, which made him a prominent farmer in the parish.[7] He may also have employed Eliza's husband, William Dixon, but by 1851 he too was a farmer of 99 acres and employed three farm labourers. William and Eliza Flounders Dixon had ten children, including John and Charles. But opportunities were limited in this part of Yorkshire, especially for farmers after mid-century, when prices were falling and agricultural opportunities for their children were vanishing.

After being educated at the Quaker North of England Agricultural School in nearby Great Ayton, John Flounders Dixon worked on the family farm until they moved to Great Ayton itself. Here ironstone miners and quarrymen lived and prospered and a new railway, flour mill, brewery, and a couple of tanneries boosted the economy. This combination of uncertain prospects, family experience with migration, family connections in Iowa, as well as resources from both sides of the family (including £200 from an uncle for land purchases) set the stage for Dixon's move to Iowa. Thus, in 1871, John and Charles Flounders Dixon and their friend Frank Standing set out for America.

Liverpool

Getting to the port was much easier than before. At their hometown of Great Ayton, the Dixon party hopped on the train to Darlington, where John converted the £200 of bank notes given to him by his uncle into gold and bought a leather money belt to keep it safe. It seemed that everyone they met in Darlington wanted to chat about America. One warned Dixon that "we should find things very rough & that we were leaving all the comforts of England, & that the Yankees were a very quick, cunning & advantage taking class of people."[8] But in no time they were in Liverpool.

Though getting to Liverpool was easy, the plague of thieves and runners seems only to have worsened. The three lads were swarmed by con men pretending to be agents for the steamship, but intending to steal their luggage. Other swindlers tried to force them into dubious boarding houses where their possessions would be an easy target, but they had already decided to stay at Lawrence's Temperance Hotel because it had been recommended to them. The frenetic harassment over luggage made the Dixon party suspicious of everyone, including honest men who actually were employed to take care of luggage: they were "quite vexed, because we would not let any of them have a shilling.[9]

The Dixon party boarded the *Cuba* with second-cabin tickets, which meant they were to share a cabin of twenty berths with others. Determined to get the best possible situation – top berths – they rushed to their cabin door, found it locked, but forced it open, causing "a complete scuffle & a tremendous pushing by those fellows behind us, for the top Berths. Some of them were old hands, & tried to pitch their beds & tins over our heads, so as to get them tossed into the best of the top Berths, but we succeeded with their pushing & our scrambling to secure the three best top berths out of the ten." When the stewards arrived and demanded to know how they had got into the room cabin without their permission, a bribe by those on the top berths secured their favoured situations. Though far better than steerage, second cabin was still a far cry from the best cabin rooms: the berths "were just like a shallow box – a board between, parted us from each other – you may fancy how unhealthy it was, for 20 people being in those little places, to sleep at night & to rest there, if stormy on deck."[10]

Though the North Yorkshire trio had taken some of their own provisions, the shipping company provided "plenty of food, but pretty coarse, & the bread ... was generally very sour." The water "was so nasty ... as a substitute we had to buy of the head steward at great cost, Ginger Beer, Lemonade, Soda Water & Ale ... we happened at times, to get a bit of Ice from the ice house, which was grand for us ... Soda Water was the best drink for me, when Sea Sick."[11]

The faster, bigger, and more sanitary steamships were certainly no guarantee against seasickness. As Dixon recalled: "We each had a good share of Sea Sickness ... I had only about two days out of the twelve, to feel myself a bit better, & seldom slept much, as every toss of the vessel smacked us to one side of our Berths against the partition boards, unless we managed to wedge ourselves in, with coiling up, & and fixing our knees & feet against the partitions – each roll & toss of the Vessel left a very sickly, dizzy sensation through ones whole frame ... I on one stretch went without [food] for about 60 hours & after that I forced myself to eat a little."[12]

Friday 12 May was the worst day on the *Cuba*. Dixon's account sounds as bad as that for a sailing ship:

[I]t was a fearful day & night & the waves of the ocean rose mountains high & tossed the vessel about in all kinds of ways ... just as tho' it was a cork – the waves rolled fast & heavily over the vessels decks – we could not look outside, to wash ourselves, or our plates & tins – in fact, people flew about in all directions, & got pretty well battered & bruised, the poor women and children fell in for the hardest fate. We had to cling with strong grasp to posts, ropes, doors & our Bert boards, or else we should have been beaten & knocked up & and down, to and fro, like beans passing thro' a steam Thrasher ... food, coffee, plates, tins &c. &c. whirled about like fury – it was a sad time for us & others, who were just at the worst stage of seasickness.[13]

Whatever the miseries in their second cabin, at least the three companions were spared the steerage: "[T]he stench of the place ... was awful," John recalled; "we used to dread going down off the decks in the Hatchway on this account." When the sea was calm, however, they enjoyed "plenty of Music from various instruments" being played by the Irish immigrants in the steerage. But, at last, "we caught sight of land, which afforded us true joy." At noon on 18 May, the *Cuba* arrived at Castle Garden, and "we were pushed forward like a drove of Sheep to the centre of that large building." The exhausted Dixon party slowly made their way through customs, dodged New York's own gangs of thieves and runners, and boarded a train bound for Iowa.[14]

On the train John noted that "the Railroads in this country are mostly, single lines, like your Ayton branch." Living mostly on bread and cheese, the three "longed for & needed a comfortable meal, a good wash, & a good nights rest." But if they assumed that their trouble with swindlers and runners was over once they got out of New York, they were sorely mistaken. Stopping in Chicago, Dixon not only found the city infested with runners, but the people running the trains fully in league with them: "When we got to Chicago, the Sharpers & Swindlers gave the Conductors & Engine men, cigars to bribe them, so as to get admittance into the cars among the passengers. These sharpers which abound prodigiously in Chicago, can talk different languages, & catch foreign Emigrants grandly, with their kind brotherly manners & tongues – they can do their business with style & artfulness … we have watched them … how they have got to the soft side of some parties, especially the Germans & Dutchmen they would fleece them."[15]

Not that Dixon sympathized with the German and Dutch passengers. They were "the most filthy, stinking & disagreeable set of men, women, & children, any one could ever come in contact with." It was so bad that Dixon and other English immigrants on the train begged the conductors to "put us English folks in good cars by ourselves," for the Germans and Dutch "had such an abominable stink with them, & were excessively dirty & disagreeable, in person & manner … They were a simple, fond set: we detested them."[16]

Not until the three reached Des Moines could they wash and rest properly: "This was my first time of having my clothes off & a whole nights rest and sleep since leaving L'pool," John Flounders Dixon reported.[17] And then, at last, they arrived in Earlham, Dallas County (now Madison County), in central Iowa, where Standing's uncle farmed. Earlham was founded in 1869 and named after Earlham College, a Quaker college in Indiana, so the Dixon party was choosing their location because of family links and the religious connections between Quakers there and in Great Ayton. Their timing was good: Dallas County had grown from 854 persons in 1850 to more than 12,000 by 1870, and ten years later it would grow again to almost 19,000, so they arrived in the midst of a boom. There were surprisingly few English in the county: of the 12,000 total people recorded in 1870, a mere 91 out of 880 foreign-born were English. But the prospects for farming and owning land were much better there than in North Yorkshire.[18]

When John and Charles Flounders Dixon and Frank Standing arrived in Earlham they were literally among "Friends," that is, the Quakers who dominated the settlement: "They were going to call the city of Earlham 'Quaker City,'" remarked Dixon, "there are so many Friends in it, & about the surrounding country… there are no Liquor or Beer house of any kind in it, the inhabitants are great temperance folks, & have houted & driven all those that used to sell intoxicating drinks, out of the place, & mean to keep all such like away."[19]

However, the three did not stay in Iowa for long: after only about a year Charles took on factory work in Cincinnati and then with a mining company in Wyoming. John, frustrated with the kind of land he could afford, (see chapter 19) soon moved to Baltimore to farm near his mother's sister. And then in 1872 he returned to England (apparently to marry), only to return to the United States. Such repeat migrations were now common, but Dixon was far from finished: in 1875 he again returned to England to help execute his great-uncle's estate, and then for ten years he and some siblings ran a confectionery business in Birmingham. Then in 1885 he again moved to America and did some market gardening near Baltimore. Yet another return trip found him stranded in England when the Great War broke out, but then he emigrated – one last time – to New York, where he died in 1921.[20] He had crossed the Atlantic at least seven times, on steamships.

Dixon's many crossings may seem surprising, given the sickness he endured on the first voyage. But, as he explained, the first journey prepared him for the later ones, making them easier and less daunting: "Many parties in Ayton used to tell us, that it was nothing, now a days, to go to America – but I could tell them now, that it is something to perform the first journey, & more so, when a person is inexperienced in the things of a strange place & country ... but when you once get thro' you are at home whenever you perform the same, or a similar journey ... Chas. & I ... think it a comparatively trifling matter, to go to England & back again to America now ... it is a small matter in our estimation, & we are now able to give information & hints to others."[21]

And at least for Dixon it was the English language that made it easier: "[I] think it now," he recalled, "a little undertaking to travel such a journey over again, to any part of the world, where the English language is known."[22] It was in the age of steamships and rising immigration from new parts of the world – especially southern and eastern Europe – that English immigrants like John Flounder Dixon could feel somewhat "invisible" among native-born Americans who shared their language and some cultural traits. But the transportation revolution was only part of the great economic transformation of the Atlantic economy. England and North America were going through new, interrelated phases of development that would shape migration for the rest of the century and beyond.

The Post-War Economy

It isn't the sum you get, it's how much you can buy with it, that's the important thing; and it's that that tells whether your wages are high in fact or only high in name.

MARK TWAIN

Britain

The transportation revolution was just a part of a vast transformation of Britain and America that followed the Civil War. As the world's first industrial and urban nation, Britain continued to lead the world economically, but competition was rising. A newly united Germany in 1871 and a fantastically growing United States challenged Britain's dominance. In the final quarter of the century, crises in Britain's traditional industries – including coal mining in the 1870s and iron production in the 1880s – gave elbow room to the newer powers. Britain's decline was relative, not absolute, but its confidence and supremacy in industry and empire were waning.[1] England's biggest crisis was in agriculture.

The Great Agricultural Depression

The two decades between 1851 and 1871 were in some ways a "golden age for British agriculture," one of "high farming" and high profits, with investment in new farm buildings and drainage and larger herds of animals to fertilize the soil.[2] But this was followed by a period known as the Great Agricultural Depression, usually dated from 1873 to 1896. The depression was largely a result of the falling prices that followed the repeal of the Corn Laws in 1846, worldwide grain overproduction, and Britain's growing reliance on food imports. As the United States and Canada subjected their endless prairies to new ploughs, the McCormick reaper, and other clattering machinery, wheat production soared, and prices fell.

The Crimean War (1853–56) and the Civil War temporarily boosted prices, but then peace and more agricultural expansion depressed prices to new depths. American railroads – funded significantly by British capital – made it possible. The United States had about 50,000 kilometres of railways by 1860, about 85,000 kilometres by 1870, and 150,000 by 1880 – all of which, along with transatlantic steamships, facilitated grain shipments to England and further reduced market prices. Poor English harvests and wet weather in the 1870s did not help.[3]

The shift in grain production from Britain to America was dramatic. Between 1872 and 1902 Britain's wheat production fell by nearly half while American production increased seven-fold.[4] By the 1890s the American West was providing 70 per cent of Britain's grain imports. In effect, Britain was outsourcing its food supply because the manufacturing nation could no longer feed itself. One can even see Britain's exploitation of American grain as a form of colonization.[5] Britain benefited from cheaper grain, but English farmers, farm workers, and landowners paid the price. By the end of the 1870s over 100,000 English farmers and farmworkers had left their farms, mainly for towns and cities in Britain, but others to North America, often to farm their own land.

What we see after the war is a deepening economic symbiosis between the two nations, an Atlantic economy that involved the movement of people as well as capital and goods. The flow of British capital overseas was enormous, much of it directed to America: during the 1870s alone Britain invested £458 million in foreign government bonds, and of this £160 million was American. Britain also invested £175 million in overseas railroad securities, and of that £40 million was American. Between the Civil War and the First World War, Britain invested more than $5 billion in the United States, more than in Britain itself.[6] This was a boon for the United States and for some individual investors, but not for Britain itself, whose aging industrial infrastructure lacked adequate investment. In fact, the United States was now investing in Britain: the first American-owned factory in Britain – the Singer Company – opened in Glasgow in 1876.[7]

The United States

For the United States, agricultural expansion and grain exports to Britain were part of a larger transformation. The Civil War had finally settled the issues of slavery and states' rights and unified the federal government under the control of northern industrialists instead of southern planters. This ushered in an age of astonishing economic growth, expansion, and change. In terms of sheer economic power and industrial output the United States was catching up with Britain and poised to surpass it. The two nations' comparative population growth is a good gauge of this change: between 1871 and 1901 Britain's population grew from 26 million to 37 million (42 per cent), whereas the United States' population grew from under 40 million to 76 million (90 per cent).[8] The two economies were intertwined, and British immigration was one reason why. The continuing "free gift" of British technology and talent through immigration and investment helped the United States to outperform Britain in many ways.[9] By the turn of the century, economic leadership had fully swung from Britain to the United States.[10]

But American growth had come at a high social and moral cost. Its cities grew so fast and teemed with so many of the so-called new immigrants from southern and eastern Europe that they had become almost unrecognizable from the pre-war period. Appalling conditions in slums and ghettoes, and the inhumane exploitation of immigrant labour created the potential for social unrest and revolution. This and widespread political corruption made this the "Gilded Age," as Mark Twain dubbed it in his 1869 satirical novel by that name. Political corruption was not as widespread in Britain, but social injustice was, as were gaps between rich and poor, urban squalour, and a failure to spread the benefits of Britain's immense wealth and power. Both nations had developed a chasm between their vaunted ideals and the hard realities. It was a transatlantic Gilded Age.

Migration Patterns

These changes and developments affected, and were affected by, changes in British migration patterns to North America. British immigration to the United States began to rise even before the Civil War was over. Between 1861 and 1870 over 600,000 British immigrants arrived – more than a quarter of all of America's immigrants. In 1870, more than 100,000 people left England, about three-fourths of them for the United States. Another peak of 75,000 to the United States was reached in 1873, and then another in 1887 and 1888, when about 130,000 Britons entered the United

States directly. For the entire 1880s about 800,000 people left the British Isles and around 80 per cent of them went to the United States, forming about 15 per cent of all immigrants to America.[11] In the 1890s the figure approached 550,000 – 20 per cent of all American immigrants.[12] As in previous decades, the British were still choosing the United States over other destinations by about four to one.[13] But Canada was the second favourite, and would replace the United States as the favoured destination in the early twentieth century. Like the United States, Canada offered vast lands for farming and growing opportunities in towns and cities, with the added attraction of still being politically attached to Great Britain.

The occupations of English immigrants also shifted after the war: from farmers (who made up about 20 per cent of all English immigrants at mid-century but a mere 10 per cent in the 1880s) to members of the building trades, who could thrive in America's burgeoning cities, as well as unskilled labourers. The surge in the 1880s was not caused by England's agricultural depression but rather urbanization and industrialization in both Britain and America. They were leaving mainly from urban and other places of rapid economic change and responding to America's rising demand for skilled and especially unskilled workers.[14] About 30 per cent of the English immigrants of 1875–90 were classified as unskilled labourers – still a far lower percentage than other immigrants of that time.[15] But even many of those apparently without agricultural backgrounds took up farming in America. Perhaps the most remarkable fact about English immigrants in late-nineteenth-century America was the continuing desire and ability of many to become farmers, with or without much previous farm experience. North Yorkshire immigrants continued to show a keen interest in farming.

The destinations of English immigrants also shifted after the war, as the mid-Atlantic states (especially New York) and even the Old Northwest lost ground to the Far West, including the mountain and Pacific states. By 1890 some of the highest concentrations of English immigrants were in the silver mining counties of Silver Bow County, Montana; Nevada County, California; and Gilpin County, Colorado. The highest concentration of all was in Salt Lake City, with its many English Mormon converts.[16]

Lead Mining in the Dales

The globalized markets that linked England and the United States affected lead prices in North Yorkshire. In the 1860s lead prices continued to fall because of new production in Spain, Germany, and especially the United States, where Yorkshire immigrants had settled. Miners in Yorkshire must have been struck by the irony that they were now competing against their kin who had gone to America. One possible remedy was new technology and science to exploit the remaining ore veins, which were getting deeper and nearing exhaustion. But even the boldest attempts could fail. In 1870, for example, Sir George Denys tried to persuade the Old Gang Company in Arkengarthdale to use new air-compressed rock drills that were powered by waterwheels, and when the company refused to fund it, he went ahead and contracted it himself. After three years of expensive effort he had "neither won nor lost a five pound note."[17] Denys then convinced the company to install new hydraulic engines, dressing floors, and crushing machines.

But ultimately, the continuing fall in lead prices drove the company into debt and the miners to desperation. In August of 1879 a reporter from the *Ripon Gazette* visited Arkengarthdale and recorded that "miners are starving on half wages; lost-looking men, in ragged clothes, are roaming about for employment; and athletic, enterprising men are leaving the Dales for a happier sphere of action."[18] A modest recovery in 1880 enabled Denys to convince the company to construct a new underground engine house, and from 1887 to 1896 the Old Gang Mining Company combined with other companies and actually made a profit. But the writing was on the wall. Lead prices continued to fall as Nevada and Colorado expanded their production in the late 1870s, with the help of North Yorkshire miners who had started out in the Upper Mississippi. The United States was now exporting lead to some of England's old markets in China, Japan, and Australia.[19] The combination of new American competition and mine exhaustion was too much for the industry in the Yorkshire Dales.[20]

The collapse of the Dales' lead industry is mirrored in stark local population figures. Between 1801 and 1860 both Swaledale and Upper Wensleydale lost over 90 per cent of their natural increase in population. Lower Wensleydale was not quite as hard hit: it lost a little more than half of its natural increase because it was less dependent on mining. Swaledale's depopulation was significant in the 1820s when the boom faded, but during the 1880s Swaledale lost nearly 40 per cent of its population, as recorded in 1881.[21] This drastic decline undermined the local economy and was seen in the abandonment of many houses and other buildings. Local crafts and industries suffered along with farming and trade. Most of those who left settled in other parts of England, but some did make their way to America, where their arrival had the opposite demographic effect that their departure had had on Yorkshire.

Lead Mining in America

Like North Yorkshire, the Upper Mississippi had passed its peak in lead production and opportunities for miners. Dubuque did enjoy higher lead prices during the war because of the inexhaustible demand for bullets. But afterwards the lead had been mostly worked out and the miners and others working in the industry moved West for fresh opportunities. In 1881 Richard Buxton reported from Benton that "the mines here are only poor and mineral is bad to find and a low price and this is a moving country. A good many people are going west and taking up land and young men going to the mountains some do well and others do not."[22] In Dubuque, zinc was now more profitable than lead, so the lead mines gradually closed and some converted to zinc. In 1882 Buxton reported that zinc production had far outpaced lead.[23]

In his visit of 1876–77 James L. Broderick saw problems in both farming and industry around Dubuque. "The land all round here is very uneven and, when ploughed, washes badly at times," he recorded. And though the land was "capital," there was a danger from the "numbers of lead ore shafts which are often left open by the heedless miners, and cattle and horses often get into them. Joseph Reynoldson has lost a cow in that way lately." Broderick also observed that some Yorkshire immigrants still showed a lingering affection and loyalty to the Crown, while also becoming Americanized.[24]

In the late nineteenth and early twentieth centuries the Dales immigrants and their children continued to play important roles in the mining industry of the Upper Mississippi – not as miners or smelters but as industrial organizers who shifted from lead to zinc and other minerals. In 1906 there were still thirty-six mining companies in the Dubuque area alone, and six of them were headed by Dales immigrants or their sons.

Wisconsin enjoyed a brief recovery in both lead and zinc during this time, and the state was now second in the nation in deep mining, with some 440 companies. Prominent here as well were Yorkshire Americans, including the Calverts, the Spensleys, and others, who had built considerable fortunes and reputations at home and abroad as directors of companies and developers of modern machinery.[25]

The North York Moors

Meanwhile the North York Moors were undergoing changes and developments that also triggered emigration. In 1861 the arrival of a railway going through Castleton made it easier to get to a port, and during the decade Teesside became more industrial, providing people with wages that could finance migration. With industrial changes, higher wages, and improved transportation, local people began considering moving to Canada or the United States.[26] At the same time local farmers were frustrated with new problems, like cattle disease. On 22 March 1866, the Wilson family of Ingleby Greenhow (a village about 5 kilometres south of Great Ayton, on the northwest edge of the North York Moors) reported to their cousins and family members in Lee County, Iowa that:

> The cattle plague is very bad in England. It has made a great havoc in the country but I think it is getting a little better. Some of the farmers and some of the milk sellers have lost all the cows they had and there is some places about York where they have not a beast left. No one knows what kind of disease it is but they think it is the smallpox inwardly and cannot get through the skin. But there is two kinds of disease and one is very fatal and the other not so fatal. The laws are very strict. They will not allow anyone to remove live beasts on the high roads and they wont let anyone remove their sheep or pigs without a pass, not even the hides of their beasts. ... the Butchers have to kill the beast where they buy them. Father had to go about six miles [10 kilometres] to kill one yesterday and beef, mutton and bacon is very dear.[27]

North Yorkshire agriculture had advantages in its diversity and variety of conditions. Farm labourers benefited from the high demand for industrial labour in West Yorkshire, and women and children could earn more than their counterparts in southern and eastern England. The custom of "provision of allotments and cottage gardens," which was more common in North Yorkshire than in other counties, helped alleviate poverty and raised living standards, particularly in diet. This helps explain the fact that rural crime and protest movements like the Swing Riots were relatively rare in North Yorkshire. This improvement for farm labour – which should not be exaggerated – continued into the early 1870s. It helped that the labour supply was being limited by migration, by the West Riding's thirst for labour, and by the development of North Yorkshire's ironstone industry.[28]

Ironstone

The North York Moors ironstone industry paralleled the Dales' lead mining industry in several ways. A sedimentary rock rich in iron compounds, ironstone was mined and smelted in North Yorkshire quite extensively around Rievaulx Abbey as early as the Middle Ages. Remnants of furnaces and forges date back to the sixteenth century, and for a long while most of England's iron had come from ironstone, before shortages in charcoal led to its decline. In the mid-1850s, with the new use of coal for fuel and the discovery of new seams near Grosmont, Eston, Great Ayton, Farndale, and Rosedale, there was a resurgence. Railroads were extended to the new mines, new settlements were built to accommodate the rural labour, and the local economy blossomed.[29]

Where the lead industry of the Dales stagnated in the 1860s and 1870s, the ironstone industry of the Moors peaked. The American Civil War sparked a boom, which was described in 1862 by William Atkinson, writing from Ingleby Greenhow to the colony of local people that had established itself in Lee County, Iowa. Atkinson reported that the Rosedale area was now humming with activity, especially the ironstone mining industry. "You would be astonished if you had a look into Rosedale to see the work that is going on," he wrote. "There will be betwixt two and three hundred hands employed getting ironstone. They are sending perhaps five or six thousand tons a week. They are building a little town at Rosedale."[30]

In 1863 the ironstone industry continued to thrive. As Henry Wilson reported to his cousin Charlotte, who had left Farndale years earlier to join the English colony in Lee County, Iowa: "At present in Farndale there is a Railway and engines running daily past Blakey House on the moor. Rosedale is a very populous place in consequence of the iron-stone being found there and it is now found in Farndale. It has been found 13 feet thick above Mr. Isaac Garbutt's Red House intake."[31] The good times continued through the decade: in March of 1869 Elizabeth Wilson reported to her aunt and uncle, who had left for Iowa in 1845, that "if you had to see Rosedale now you would hardly know it, it is very nearly turned inside out since you were here. There are Railroads both sides of the Dale now and here are two great big iron stone kilns to burn iron stone. The ground is hollow for many a mile under the ground and houses build in all directions. It's like a little city now."[32]

But decline came suddenly. William Atkinson blamed events linked to the Franco-Prussian War of 1871, which disrupted markets. In February of that year he wrote that "the Iron trade which is the chief support of Middlesbro has not been too brisk for the last six months on account of the dreadful war between France and Prussia." In fact, the war was interfering with industry and trade in other areas, as Atkinson acknowledged "but the Iron trade is not the only trade effected for I think that nearly every trade has been effected more or less. I suppose trade will have been effected in America to a certain degree."[33]

The decline in the ironstone industry was not the only reason for discontent and emigration. Like lead mining in the Dales, ironstone mining in the Moors was inherently dangerous. Elizabeth Wilson reported from Rosedale in 1869 to her aunt and uncle in Iowa that "both men and horses are getting killed and lamed every day. When I am writing this letter they are carrying a man home past our house either killed or badly hurt."[34] At roughly the same time, William Atkinson wrote to his cousin, also in Iowa, that during the previous summer "Farndale, Ingleby and Baisdale moors were set on fire and the two latter nearly all burnt. The fire broke out in Farndale Head. It is supposed it was set on fire by the [railroad] engine, for engines run across the moors to Rosedale for Ironstone."[35] Along with the physical dangers were unreasonable working conditions. Elizabeth Wilson's husband "often has to work Sundays as (well as) week days at the kilns."[36] It is not surprising that, like the lead miners from the Yorkshire Dales to the Upper Mississippi, ironstone miners from the North York Moors wanted to get out of mining and into farming. Though farming had its own dangers, they did not match those of mining underground, and farming in America was a viable option.

Agricultural Decline

Problems in the ironstone industry were magnified by agricultural depression, which by the mid-1870s was becoming more visible in North Yorkshire. Farming now seemed hopeless for those who wanted to take it up in the region. In the summer of 1871 the *Ripon Gazette* reported that "emigration is occupying so much attention" because "farms are at a premium," and "farmers' sons and intelligent farm servants cannot hope to rent a farm, much less possess one."[37] Local newspapers reported farm workers suffering poorer housing conditions and urgent calls for "more and better cottages and substantial allotments."[38] In 1872 the *Yorkshire Gazette* called the workers' cottages "scandalous – the horses and dogs are more comfortably housed. The tenements are mere hovels, dangerous to health." Two years later the same newspaper observed that though North Yorkshire farm workers were better off than those in the eastern counties, "a great work remains to be done … as regards the labourers' cottages."[39] There were other problems. In the dry summer of 1870, poor hay and corn crops and raging wildfires started by sparks from railroad engines hauling ironstone made bleak farming conditions even worse. A particularly hard and long winter that year contributed to rising food and fuel prices.[40]

In 1872 farm workers in Lastingham – where a large percentage of people had left for Canada earlier in the century – demanded better conditions. It was probably no accident that they were close to Rosedale's ironstone mines, where workers tended to be more militant.[41] Arson was a problem in other nearby areas. In 1872 haystacks were burned near Northallerton and Yarm, and in the following year Helmsley and Malton witnessed more incendiarism. In 1874 near Richmond, ricks (stacks of hay) worth more than £500 were set alight.[42] Also in that year two labourers were charged with incendiarism near Pickering, and other such reports were made near Kirkbymoorside. In 1875 the southern part of the Vale of York was targeted. But this spate of farm violence was short-lived. Generally, the North Riding saw little violence and discontent in subsequent years, and the reason for the relative calm was probably the better wages and working conditions that prevailed in the North Riding.[43]

Emigration from Rosedale

Because of these changes there were new reasons to leave the North York Moors. Elizabeth Wilson wrote to her uncle and aunt in Iowa in 1869 about her new plans. She complained about the rising price of food in the Rosedale area, due in large part to the booming ironstone mining and influx of miners, which created a higher demand for local resources. "Meat is very dear here," she reported. "There is no sort of fresh meat under 8 the pound and bacon is 10 pence … My husband is sick of Rosedale so we are coming to America. The money is so little and everything so dear that we had to look sharp around the corner this winter. But things is looking a bit better now so our intention is to leave this country in the course of either nine or ten weeks from this if we have our health."[44]

Like Dales miners, many ironstone workers had been raised doing agricultural work and only turned to ironstone work to supplement their income. For them, settling in North America to farm their own land was a natural goal. This was true for the Wilson family. Continuing her 1869 letter to her uncle and aunt in Iowa, Elizabeth Wilson wrote that "my husband has been working here at Rosedale about two years at the kilns but he has been brought up with farming work all his life and he wants to know if you can inform him where is the best place to come to in your country." She then asked, as probably all prospective emigrants did as they began to plan their move, for the information necessary to make the move possible: "We should like to come to where you are if there is a chance of a livelihood at all to be got, and what is the most usefullest things to bring with us, and what sort of conveniences there is for a man and wife without children, and how the wages run, and I should like to know how much it will cost from New York to your place as I should like to come to your place the first until we get a place to settle down in. My husband is a good worker."[45]

Sadly, as the Wilsons were ready to sail, tragedy struck. Elizabeth's cousin, William Atkinson, reported the following year that Elizabeth "got set off out of Rosedale and had got to her sister's to bid farewell and she died just before going on board. She was poorly when she set off for the doctor told her that crossing the water would do her good. Her husband has come back to Rosedale again."[46]

The decline of farming and ironstone production in North Yorkshire continued. As William Atkinson wrote in January of 1878, "The farmers in England have had a very trying summer this last year for the weather was so bad that many of them did not get their ha [hay] until it was time to cut the corn and some never got it at all. Trade is very bad in England just now."[47] This is not to say that all of the farmers who emigrated had been suffering. Robert Best, born in 1860 in Hutton-le-Hole, learned blacksmithing from his father and worked on a farm. He became rich: in 1888 he left for New York City with eighteen fine horses and for the next seventeen years traded horses between England and the United States, moving back to England between 1901 and 1908 before settling in Illinois to combine farming and horse trading for a large firm.[48]

For most people in the North York Moors conditions worsened in the 1880s, especially as the ironstone industry collapsed. The *Malton Messenger* reported on 21 May 1887 that the Rosedale and Ferryhill Iron Company "ceased to be and the great depression followed."[49] The Tom and Mary Wilson family had avoided these hardships. Twenty years earlier they had left Rosedale for Texas and became successful land agents and farmers. On a return visit in 1893, both seemed shocked by how much the village had deteriorated: the economy had all but collapsed after the demise of the ironstone industry, local living standards had seriously eroded, and smallpox had been reported in three local communities.[50] The Wilson family's migration to America was a remarkable story of how people under economic threat in North Yorkshire could rise to fabulous success in North America. They showed what was possible, after adjusting to changes in American farming after the Civil War. Their story is told in chapter 21.

Farming after the War

A pioneer should have imagination, should be able to enjoy
the idea of things more than the things themselves.

WILLA CATHER, *O PIONEERS!*

After the Civil War, English people contemplating a life in American
agriculture had to be cautious. American farming was changing, not
necessarily for the better. As with England's Great Agricultural Depression,
grain prices spiralled downward as worldwide production rose and modern
transportation systems forced American farmers to compete in a global
market against farmers in Canada, Argentina, Australia, and other parts
of the world. Some survived by diversifying into dairy, livestock, and
garden produce, but many others could not, especially those without the
right soils or the capital necessary to increase production and compensate
for falling prices. Those who did raise production were part of the cycle
that only exerted more downward pressure on prices. And those not well
connected to railways suffered indiscriminate rates.[1]

In addition, the Civil War had in some ways been a revolution: a
"Victory for Industrial Capitalism" according to Charles Beard and
other historians.[2] As industrial titans and the commercial and manufacturing sectors took more and more power and influence in national
and local governments, many farmers felt squeezed. They fell back on
tenancy when they could not afford mortgage payments, and would
eventually attempt to take back their country and livelihoods through
the Granger and Populist movements. Post-war changes, then, hit miners
and farmers hard.

Farming in the Upper Mississippi

Like other farmers in America, Yorkshire immigrants often struggled after the war. The economic boom had passed them by as falling prices threatened them with debt. And the early independence they had achieved seemed to be slipping away into the hands of middlemen. This, at least, was the situation of the Willis family. During the war Matthew and Jane Willis feared that their sons would be drafted into the front lines, and though that did not happen, they seem to have had little to celebrate after Appomattox. Writing back to their daughter in 1867, surely knowing that the letter would be circulated in Wensleydale, Matthew Willis complained about "how entirely the merchants in the employ of Eastern Men have us in their power in regards to the prices of our produce."[3]

Matthew and Jane Willis cannot be assumed to represent all Yorkshire farmers – after all, Matthew Willis found it easy to complain about most things – but they do identify problems and issues that others would have recognized. America's lower taxation had always appealed to the English, who at times were among the most heavily taxed people in the world. But taxes were not low enough for Willis, who in 1867 complained that "another evil is heavy taxation, the bitter fruits of a blundering government." Here Willis was not imagining things, for taxation was still relatively high two years after the war had ended, and those who came to America to escape high taxation found the change worrisome.[4]

There were other problems. John Dinsdale's wheat crop was wiped out by chinch bugs in 1875, and other pests and weather extremes took similar tolls.[5] But there were also booms and busts, investment bubbles, and panics – there being no central bank to moderate the swings. The combination of falling farm prices and rising labour costs posed serious challenges. As Matthew Willis complained in 1867, "another great drawback to settlers in this country is the high prices of all sorts of shop goods a consequence of which is high wages and high charges of all sorts of Handy-crafts men and men of different trades. This makes it next to impossible to raise buildings, so necessary to the comfort of every body, especially in a country like this."[6] This problem was acute for the Willis family because their dwellings were quite shabby and in need of improvement, a factor that kept Matthew Willis disenchanted with American life for years to come.

As if falling grain prices and rising labour costs were not bad enough, a spate of bad weather was added into the mix. Writing back to Wensleydale, Willis summed up the situation in a somewhat contradictory and convoluted way: "The war is now ended as you will long since have known but times for farmers are very bad. The last summer we raised no wheat in consequence of the wheat crop having failed these 3 seasons previously to the last one." The poor harvests did seem to boost wheat prices the following year: "Wheat, however was pretty good last summer, and the price tolerable … Oats are selling at 12 ½ cts and white peas no sale." But otherwise it was hard to turn a profit, and the uncertainty of prices was irritating: "What we sold last year went at 2 dollars such is the uncertainty of farming in Wisconsin. Fat Hogs are well sold and fat cattle are rather higher in price than last year. Times for farmers are decidedly worse than we ever knew them. Farm labourers wages higher, and farm produce low."[7]

In fact, the Willis family was so discouraged that they considered leaving for Canada or returning to Wensleydale, but they seemed trapped by debt with no means to move. Part of the problem was the "greenback" paper money that was issued during the war; it still dominated the local economy and as its value relative to gold fell it depleted their net worth. As Willis wrote to their daughter, Elizabeth, who had stayed in Wensleydale:

> If we could sell out our property here I would like very much to come over to settle our affairs in England. It is likely however, we shall have to see out badly although our place is accounted by many the best in Iowa County, and by others the best in the state for the size of it. One evil of selling now, is this we can get nothing here but Paper Money. And to get it exchanged for Gold will reduce it about one third. I would like, however to sell out 'tho' at a heavy sacrifice as I am now getting old and I do not want to die so heavily in debt. Possibly it might be best to trade with some Canadian for a small place in Canada if we could get as much to boot as would pay our debts. In that case I might come over to see you and to settle our affairs in a comfortable way.[8]

If Matthew and Jane Willis were expecting an encouraging reply to lift their spirits, they were deeply disappointed. When Elizabeth reported the death of her uncle, Willis responded saying he felt "downcast" without knowing "how to muster the energy to make a response" for "I had long fostered the hope that we should one day be permited to see each other again in the 'land of the living.' This hope however, is now blasted ... Writing is to me a burden ... Your Uncle was a Gentleman in every sense of the word."[9]

Two years later, after a quarter-century in America, Matthew Willis was still struggling, and he instructed his daughter in Wensleydale that "[i]f any one should ask what your Father's opinion of America is, tell them candidly that it is much worse than England for a farmer, but better for a tradesman." He explained that around Mineral Point "the crops are lighter," probably a reflection of the soil exhaustion that often resulted from the harsh American methods of farming, which tended to wear out the soil. "This," he continued, "makes me say Trade is better than farming." Willis was also incensed by the merchants and bankers who were manipulating prices for their own benefit. "Farmers are an exceeding poor race of men; while the tradesmen and merchants are amassing very large fortunes. In the fall, when the farmers have their taxes to pay the markets are run down to almost nothing, so that farmers in many cases have to borrow ... of their richer neighbours to put them through till the next harvest."[10]

Some of their bitterness had something to do with a series of illnesses that struck the family: "[W]e have nearly all been sick this spring," they reported. "Your sister Margaret Jane had a severe attack of Inflamation of the chest and plura which brought her so low that she could hardly bear to be stirred in bed for 14 days." Others were nearly as sick, and Matthew reacted with more doubt and dissatisfaction with America.[11] His frustration and regret were only magnified, it seems, by the remarkable success of his brother, Thomas, who had stayed in Wensleydale, becoming famous for developing the Wensleydale breed of sheep and for winning numerous prizes for other agrarian achievements. Hearing about his brother's exploits only brought out Matthew's frustrations more sharply, so it is little wonder that he often doubted his migration decision, thought of his old home, and dreamed of returning there.[12]

What brought some measure of consolation and reassurance was the community of other Wensleydale immigrants in the area. With such a tight community the immigrants from the Dales perhaps did not blend in fully with American society. Writing back to his daughter Elizabeth in Wensleydale, Willis emphasized that "we have some circumstances and blessings that tend to cheer us after all. We have a few families amongst us who deserve our respect, say first some from Askrigg, Thompsons, Dinsdales and others which we hold in great esteem." Matthew and John Dinsdale were social anchors who brought a sense of community and stability to other Yorkshire immigrants in the area.

It was not just fellow expatriates from Wensleydale that provided community. Immigrants from other Dales were nearby and any differences between them were insignificant in contrast with Americans and immigrants from other places. Willis commented that "We have also a few individuals from the Sister Dale," by which he probably meant Swaledale, and he mentioned the Hirds from Craven – "All of which are friendly and well disposed."[13] Craven was near Skipton, Airedale, the very southern edge of the Yorkshire Dales, roughly 50 kilometres south of Willis's native Carperby. It was a serious journey by foot or stagecoach in the mid-nineteenth century. So, the distances and differences between the Dales and their people, formidable in Yorkshire, shrank in America.

Much of the connection between immigrants from various Dales came through religion. Willis reported that "we have a valuable old primitive Methodist Preacher and his wife, from near Thirsk; of the name of Haw. They have been in this circuit two years, and we regret to say they are now going to leave for some other location. I believe Mrs. H. Whitehead of Aysgarth is his sister."[14] Again, one is struck by the network of associations that was established in Yorkshire and transferred to America, in this case the Upper Mississippi where distances were great but nonetheless bridged by common acquaintances and religious traditions.

A Rough Society

Another of Willis's gripes was widely shared by other Yorkshire immigrants: the unrelenting roughness of American society. Development did not seem to help much; in his eyes, immigrants were changing his corner of Wisconsin for the worse. Willis even seemed irritated by Yorkshire lead miners. Perhaps some confrontation with his former countrymen had ignited his resentment. Writing to his daughter in Wensleydale in 1867 he commented – facetiously, it seems – that "in this country we have people from almost every christian clime. We have the polite French, the upright

Scot, the peaceable German and Dutch, the industrious Bohemian, the ardy [hardy] Norwegian and Swede, the independent Swiss, the wild Irish, the proud Cornish, the acquisitive Welsh; and worst of all the overbearing and avaricious North Yorkshire Miners. In addition to which we have a few people of colour, good, bad and medium." Apparently, the problem was the kind of people that the mining industry attracted – the dregs of foreign people, for he continues: "With a floating population medley ... [illegible] The weeds and chaff driven from almost every civilized nation are found here, all tending to make up the proud American Republic ... I often think how happy you ought to think yourselves in England where almost every villain is driven away ... and where you have a large majority of those who think that a good and honorable character is always worth maintaining even at a little sacrifice."[15]

Willis blamed some of the sad state of society on a government that was too limited and lenient. "Of all the evils of which we complain," he concluded: "we must not forget the want of a righteous population, and a righteous government. The state of society being bad, we have the greater need of a strict government. But the laxity of the laws make matters worse than otherwise they might be ... our laws are bad and badly administered, and in too many cases not administered at all."[16]

Living conditions remained stubbornly rough and crude as well. Though the Willis family had a large farm that must have been the envy of many, their dwellings and standard of living were still rather dismal. This was observed by James Broderick, who was raised on a Swaledale farm by his father Edward, who stayed in Gunnerside. James had become a land agent and was touring the Upper Mississippi in 1876–77 to seek out the best places for fresh Yorkshire immigrants. He spent most of his time visiting Dales immigrants like Matthew Willis and reported extensively on what he had found in a detailed diary.[17] He was likely shocked by what he saw on the Willis farm:

> Mr. Spensley hitched up a light wagon with two horses, early in the morning, and drove us out to see Mathew Willis and his farm. The roads were excessively muddy all the way ... we were almost up to the hub in it and apparently in danger of throwing over. Mr. Willis had a very fine farm of 470 acres besides some 40 to 80 acres of timber at distance. His land looks well tilled and clean but his house and outbuildings are nothing more than an old rookery.

In fact when Mr. Spensley stopped the team at the house, it is a
fact, I had not the slightest idea that it was a dwelling. I thought
it an outbuilding of some kind. It was raining fast so we got inside
as soon as possible. The old gentleman and his sons and daughters
made us very welcome. They took us into the parlour and cooked us
a good dinner.[18]

Still living in an "old rookery" after thirty years of hard work was one
reason why the Willis family never stopped thinking about returning
to Wensleydale. In their story we see some of the worst experiences of
North Yorkshire immigrants. What finally carried them through was
their fortitude and determination – common traits of North Yorkshire
immigrants in the area.

James Broderick's visit to the Upper Mississippi was well-timed.
Though Swaledale's lead industry had recently seen a brief and modest
recovery, it was now in another phase of decline, heading inevitably to
extinction. Thus, the new hard times in Swaledale sparked a new, smaller
wave of emigration to America, and it was partly for this reason that
James Broderick was travelling in the Upper Mississippi. It was his job
to find the best places where the new Yorkshire immigrants could take
up farming.[19] Broderick's diary, which was circulated in Swaledale before
it was eventually published, was generally encouraging, as one might
expect from a land agent. Broderick notes that a Mr Cleminson, son of
a lead mining agent who had left Fleetham in Swaledale nineteen years
previously with virtually nothing, now had both mineral and timber lands
that he rented out profitably each year.[20] Swaledalers facing hard times
would have taken notice.

Broderick also noted that recent Dales immigrants found "few problems with language or social customs" because they could both blend in
with Americans and live among earlier Dales immigrants. They were both
assimilating and behaving "ethnically" by associating with other Dales
immigrants and staying in close contact with friends in Yorkshire.[21] They
also retained their dialect and tended to marry other Yorkshire immigrants.[22] At the same time they were absorbing the cultural contributions
of other immigrants. On Thanksgiving Day 1876, Richard Bonson invited
a large group of other Dales immigrants, including the Burtons, Wallers,
Spensleys, and others. As Broderick recorded in his diary, they "dined
off Roast Turkey and Plumb Pudding and various other things amongst

which was sour Krout, a German Dish made of fermented cabbages. Mr. Bonson particularly wished me to try the krout saying that he never met with anyone who liked it as first. I surprised him by telling him that I liked it, which I did tolerably well, and he promised me the receipt."[23]

Dales immigrants could hardly have avoided other immigrants had they wanted to. An Iowa census held in 1885 recorded the country of origin of foreign-born residents; Dubuque County had 6,825 people born in one of the many German states or principalities, 3,109 born in Ireland, but only 980 in England. A reasonable estimate of how many of these English were from Swaledale is "probably no more than a few hundred," or a third to half.[24]

Into the 1870s and beyond, Yorkshire immigrant families stayed in contact and watched each other age and assimilate to American life. In 1870 Rose Willis, the second daughter of Matthew and Jane, reported from Wisconsin to her sister Elizabeth in Wensleydale that "we saw M Dinsdale last fall he is not keeping store now but is a supernumary preacher." She also reported that their father, Matthew, was failing in health and that "he talks much about England," but that he was "getting too feeble" to make the return visit to Wensleydale that he longed for. Jane was in better health "but is beginning to look elderly," and their brother Thomas "often talks of England he would like very much to come and see his relatives and the country."[25]

From this look at farming in the Upper Mississippi, then, we see some frustration with and resignation to American life, but also a broader success. Most recorded outcomes of English farmers in America's Old Northwest were happier than those of the Willis family,[26] but there was plenty of room for discouragement too. The best affordable lands in the Old Northwest had already been taken up, so it is not surprising that when some North Yorkshire people looked to start over in America, they turned their attention across the Mississippi, to the vast plains and prairies of the American West.

The Great Plains

As I looked about me I felt that the grass was the country,
as the water is the sea.

WILLA CATHER, *MY ANTONIA*

After the war, the appeal of the American West grew for many English. The trans-Mississippi West was widely promoted in England as a place of opportunity for miners, ranchers, and settlers of every sort, and this promotion seems to have had some effect. In 1860 there were over 55,000 English-born people living west of the Mississippi River. By 1900 there were nearly 145,000.[1] Free land to homesteaders, new railway connections to markets, new silver mines in the mountains, ranching on seemingly endless lands, and the myth of the West – all of this and more fascinated English people and turned many into immigrants. Among them were members of the elite who hoped for lives of leisure on large estates. Some wealthy English immigrants became highly successful ranchers and cattle barons.[2]

The heyday of Yorkshire Dales migration to America was over. The Upper Mississippi offered fewer opportunities: its lead industry was in steep decline, as it was in Yorkshire, and the best cheap lands were already taken. Thus, some looked farther west, to the plains and prairies, where virgin land was cheap and available but living conditions more primitive. Some were drawn to these remote areas by the schemes of territorial governments that recruited English people and sent them back home to promote their lands and encourage settlement. For example, in 1873 Reverend G.M. Binks, who had left Castle Bolton for Dakota in 1868, was sent back there by the Dakota government to "represent the advantages offered by that government to any who choose to go and settle in the New World."[3] On 13 June 1874 Binks lectured "to a very respectable audience of working people" at Preston-under-Scar, about 3 kilometres west of Leyburn, in Wensleydale. After describing the geography and huge expanse of Dakota Territory – "three or four times as large as the United Kingdom" – Binks explained the Homestead system, "whereby every man above 21 years of age who goes to make for himself a home, is entitled to a farm of 240 acres of good land, ready for the plough, with a healthy climate and plenty of pure water." He also informed them of the prices and wages, and the "free school system," all of which made Dakota unsurpassed "by no country upon earth as a home for working men … and best of all, it is open to all men on equal terms."[4] Binks's lecture was enthusiastically received, and "many left Wensleydale" for Dakota or Canada, though the exact numbers are unknown.[5]

Iowa

As we have seen, Iowa had attracted North Yorkshire families before the Civil War, some to colonies in Clinton and Lee Counties. After the colonies collapsed most stayed in Iowa or went to other places. By 1870 there were 16,660 English-born people in Iowa, and some served as magnets for others from their home village. We have already introduced John Flounders Dixon, his brother Charles, and friend Frank Standing, whose uncle had settled in Earlham, Iowa, and to whom the three were heading. They had left Great Ayton and wanted land, but this part of Iowa was already getting crowded and the land expensive, particularly near settlements. Dixon observed in 1871 that near Earlham, "the private owners asks from 40 dollars & upwards per acre … & an English £1 at par, is 480 … other lots of Prairie land, 2 ½ or more miles [4 or more kilometres] from the City, they ask from 8 dollars to 18 per acre, according to the Situation." Furthermore, "all the choice Prairie land in this part, for 50 miles [80 kilometres], or so around, has been taken up."[6] But Dixon was still impressed with America's relative equality. He observed enthusiastically that "no man, or woman, in any position (that is at all respectable) or circumstances, need for a moment suppose they are above or below anyone else. All are looked on the same & equally, whether prince, or peasant – no man however costly & grand his apparel, or his gold trinkets & jewelry, or great his possessions, & let him try to assume what he will, he's no more looked on, or considered, then anyone else, whoever they may be."[7] This was on a farm, of course; Dixon might have seen things differently in Chicago or New York City.

As Dixon found, purchasing prairie land was not easy: it required a lot of investigation and patience, and rushing into purchases without carefully considering the obligations that came with certain lands could lead to failure. While working for his friend's uncle in Earlham, Dixon spent one day a week looking for suitable land, and in 1871 he described to relatives back in Great Ayton the 200 acres that he went excitedly to see. At $8 per acre it was the cheapest he had come across, and it was a bit nearer to Earlham than the farm he was working on at the time. But it was cheap for a reason: it was "much twisted in form, with hills & hollows, which would make it tedious & inconvenient to bring into a state of cultivation." Furthermore, Dixon found that to enclose it with a fence to keep off the "cattle, horse, sheep & pigs that stray & feed on the Prairie land" would cost about $1,800.[8]

Dixon was frustrated that "mostly all the nicest Prairie lands in this part have been picked up," and the farmers who had good improved land would sell only at a profit, at around $12 an acre. Buying improved land was of course more expensive, but the rewards were more immediate. Dixon was strongly advised to buy improved land, if he could afford it, to "get straight away, with our crops & cattle & with good management, make plenty of money." Those who advised him were perhaps acting upon the notion that the English wanted "to make money as quick … as they can, that is, after the English farmer gets a start, either to toil & break up Prairie land, or have the means to get an improved farm."[9] There were about a dozen farmers in the immediate area offering improved farms for sale, and one of them offered 160 enclosed acres, with an orchard, well, cropped "splendid new land" but with "little … dwelling house on it," for $40 per acre. Dixon, like most young English immigrants, did not have the $6,400 to spend.[10]

One reason for rising land prices was the common American practice of buying land, improving and selling it for a profit, and repeating the process with the aim of getting rich. The tendency to be speculators, and "flip" farms, was especially common in Iowa. Dixon was appalled by the speed and thoughtlessness with which Americans bought and sold farms for short-term profit. He wrote back to his family in Great Ayton about the Americans' "mode of doing business":

They make up their minds about doing anything, all at once, they
never appear to think or care about what they are going to do, or
what they do do – they will make up their minds all on a sudden
to sell their farms, & see off & away they go, farther back in to the
Prairie countries, & start to make a new farm again & again, they
are fond of variety & changing about – they sometimes buy farms,
of what we would think at random, just from what they hear about
a farm, or farms for sale, & never go to see the farms until after, they
have bought & paid for them, & sometimes never see their purchase
at all, but sell off again immediately – win or loose ... they are such
a go ahead lot.[11]

Such reckless speculation in land was matched by its reckless cultivation. Though the more labour-intensive English methods usually fell by
the wayside in America, Dixon and the English farmer he was working
for in Iowa believed that their methods were still the best way to make
their land pay. "I find on calculation," Dixon reported, "(not taking into
consideration, the difference between an Englishman's careful farming &
the Americans careless & disorderly carry on) that it must be an exceedingly profitable life – tho' to take & break up a piece of Prairie land, &
put into cultivation, it is, 3 years or so before a man, who must work as
hard as the English farmers do, in England, before he can begin to realize
a sufficient profit so as to lay by & save."[12]

Still, Dixon was "rather perplexed what to do." The £200 his uncle
gave him was insufficient to buy much without also taking out a loan,
and interest rates were high. Advice flowed both ways: local farmers were
eager to sell improved and unimproved farms, so there were many options
on what and how to buy. Dixon mainly regretted "that I had not come to
this fine & healthy country 6 years ago. How very different, my position
would now have been."[13] It was probably this uncertainty and lack of capital
that ultimately led Dixon out of Iowa, back to England for a time, and
to New Jersey where he took up market gardening.

Clearing the Prairie

Dixon's hesitation about buying uncleared prairie was understandable.
Though largely void of the dense forests that many had struggled with in

the Midwest or in Ontario in earlier decades, prairie land still required enormous effort. "The hardest work on starting to cultivate the Prairie," Dixon had learned, "is stubbing up the oak roots that have spread," which he compared to "stubbing whins" in his native North Yorkshire – removing native prickly shrubs or gorse before planting crops. The process "tired out" his companion's uncle George Standing, who had "a man with three horses & a breaking plough, turning up the wirey sod." After the "stubbing," which the Iowans also called "grubbing," the land was ploughed up using a "Breaking plough," which was "much different to our English ploughs," broad and sharp, drawn by three or more horses, which "cuts thro' roots, as thick as a roll of butter." Stones were not the problem they were in Yorkshire.[14]

Like other English immigrants before him, Dixon was horrified by the Americans' mutilation of nature as they cleared land. He described "hundreds of acres of land that had had timber cut down … they cut the trees off, about a yard from the ground … but what a number of years it must stake to rot, or move those great tree stumps, & how very inconvenient to work amongst & cultivate. Some lands that were in corn, & some in grass, looked very funny, with the rank black tree stumps sticking up above the greenness of the crops – the tree stumps are burnt, to prevent them shooting & growing – this gives their Negro colour."[15]

Climate

After the Civil War the harsh American climate and weather patterns remained and, in some places, seemed to be getting more extreme. This was the opinion of Matthew Willis, on his farm in Iowa Country, Wisconsin. According to him the climate was "certainly getting worse … The winters get longer and the summers shorter." Willis ascribed this to "the wild lands being brought into cultivation," and the problem of fire: "While the lands were in the wild state the grass went dead in the fall, and millions of acres were burnt with fire; which not only dark'ned the atmosphere with smoke but also rendered the air considerably milder than otherwise it would have been." Willis was convinced that the winters were getting longer because he observed that "the blossom of the wild fruit trees which was sometimes as early as the first of May, did not come out this spring till the 27th of that month."[16]

But if the summers were getting shorter in Wisconsin, they seemed to be getting more extreme farther west. Iowa's hot summers surprised John Flounders Dixon, who drank lots of water to cope with the heat: "[S]o do the Americans – it never does any harm & no one could do very long at a time without," and during hay harvest, "we cannot bear at most, more clothes on, then a thin pair of trousers & a shirt, tho' you soon get used to the heat & feel the effects of it, no more, then the summer heat of England. The farmers['] children round here, always go barefoot, because of heat & oftens we see the farms & their assistants, working away barefoot, no matter what they are doing, or where they go."[17] Exposure to the hot American summers also changed the appearance of English immigrants. As Dixon wrote back to his family in Great Ayton, "you would see some difference, already, in our appearance if you now could get a look at us. The sun is burning us like the Americans, very brown & swarthy – the people here don't look at all so rosy, plump & healthy as the English do, tho' in reality they are exceedingly healthy, tall & wirey to the English."[18]

Another common concern for Yorkshire immigrants in the West was the shabby and primitive buildings and farms. Coming from English villages and buildings made of local stone, they seemed stunned by the rough appearance of buildings and the "untidiness" of Americans. Dixon saw this even in Earlham, which had long passed the frontier stage. In his view, the Americans were an "awful untidy, careless, easy going set in general – few of them have the least idea of tidiness, or economy on their farms – in fact, they know it not. Some of them only scratch, not plough, their land over once in two years."[19] He also complained of the local people in Earlham that "their houses are mostly, little wood huts, & how some families do, seems a mystery. Their out buildings (if I many use the word, "Buildings") for their houses are just little wood buildings, thrown together in such a rough fashion, that I could well give you an idea of, the roof is just a few small trees, tossed on to the top, & a bit of dried grass or straw thrown over – never thatched."[20]

How Americans treated their livestock also appalled Dixon, as he observed: "[I]n those stables (which they call "Barns" here) … there is little shelter for the horses in the severe winter from cold, wind, ran or snow storm. I don't think they have any place, or shelter at all for their cattle – their pigs are just in a square pen, composed of a few stakes & rails. The pigs are, in the winter season, generally frozen to the ground thro' the nights, & most likely, numbers frozen to death. They take no thought, or care of stock or anything else; Indeed they are complete strangers to anything of the kind."[21]

Dixon's own living conditions were cramped to say the least: "There are 12 of us in family in a little wood house of 3 rooms – two downstairs & one up – there is their own family of 7[,]a man & his brother breaking up the Prairie … all living & lodging in a little wood house, & only George's wife to manage for all." Dixon worked four days a week at a dollar a day, including room and board, and must have enjoyed spending the other days "exploring the country & looking at a few improved farms that are for sale."[22]

Dixon also noted that "George's wife" had to "manage for all." The relative scarcity of women on the frontier prairies, due to so many single men – like Dixon and his friends – setting out to establish their farms was another difficulty. Getting a farm under cultivation was next to impossible without women, and immigrants like Dixon saw a need and market for more English women: "[W]omen here are rather scarce & not at all managers, or such useful folks as the English women – they have from 3 to 4 dollars a week, including board & lodgings."[23]

In addition to harsher winters and shabby buildings were strange and potentially dangerous forms of life. "These Prairies abound with all kinds of harmless & dangerous Snakes … & kill them whenever we have a safe chance of doing so," he wrote. "We have the skunk, which I have seen – when irritated, they make an awful smell, that people can, to their horror feel it 3 miles [5 kilometres] off. They call it here the Pole Cat … there are wolves & deer … we have a bathe in a Beck, close to George's farm, nearly every day. They call a Beck a "Creek."[24]

But Dixon remained optimistic: "Any man, young or old, that can work & has some knowledge of farm work, can get from one dollar to two per day, with board & lodgings, according to the season of the year … In harvest … we each can get two dollars a day, with board & lodgings, at least." A man with three horses and a breaking plough could make 4 dollars an acre, "himself & horses kept, & live altogether on the farm, until the work is done, & a man & three horses, can break up in a day (10 hours) from one & a half, to two acres, & and sometimes more. They turn over a very broad furrow at a time."[25] By Dixon's calculation, therefore, such a man could earn from 4 to 8 dollars a day, and if nearby land was going for $8 per acre, the vision of earning up to an acre of land a day would have sounded fantastic to most people in Yorkshire.

What helped immigrants like John Flounders Dixon to stay positive was the richer American diet, especially eating meat three times a day. The Americans had other culinary habits: "The Americans have an endless variety of dishes to every meal, always coffee, & the potatoes are boiled with the skins on, & each person has to strip their own. They do in a great degree, do all things opposite to the English." The quality of American food, however, was not always up to English standards: "American beef & mutton is not so nice as the English, perhaps owing to the carelessness of the way the Stock is treated. We get bacon instead & like the Americans, we have potatoes at every meal. The American meals are always the same each time, they have not one meal better than another, but the description of food, differs a little according to the season of the year."[26]

The Wilkinsons in Nebraska and Wyoming

As John Flounders Dixon noted, the best affordable lands in Iowa were already taken by farmers who behaved like speculators. Those who wanted cheaper land, and lots of it, had to go farther west, and North Yorkshire immigrants were among them. A good sense of what was possible for Yorkshire immigrants on the Great Plains after the Civil War – and what had to be endured – is captured in the remarkable story of the Wilkinson family. Anthony Wilkinson was born in 1838 at Howgill Thoralby, near Aysgarth and West Burton, in the heart of Wensleydale, to Anthony and Alice (Sayer) Wilkinson. After working as a gamekeeper in Scotland for six years, he returned to the Dales to help his father, a prosperous stock and dairy farmer. But in 1873 he boarded the *S.S. Europa* and went to Saline County, Nebraska, and over the next decade his parents, seven siblings, and some extended family members followed him. In the meantime, Anthony homesteaded and operated a meat market in Nebraska. He then moved on to Wyoming where he again homesteaded and raised sheep and cattle, while still owning his meat market. He married Lavinia Varney, who was from New York; they had no children. Eventually, Wilkinson was so successful that he became one of the state's largest property owners, with some 8,300 acres at his home ranch, 16,000 acres at Big Horse Creek, and an additional 8,000 acres nearby. For people back in Wensleydale, one of their local lads becoming the owner of 32,000 acres in the American West was a fantastic confirmation of its promise. When he died in 1919 at age eighty, Wilkinson left more than a half-million dollars in his estate. His brother John, who followed him in 1882, also became highly successful in Wyoming.[27] If the Wilkinsons did not represent what was typical of Yorkshire immigrants in the West, they did show what was possible.

The John Wilkinson family's success was neither quick nor easy, as remembered by his daughter Alice. She recorded that the family trekked across the plains from Illinois on an oxcart and started life in Nebraska in a simple dugout home carved out of a bank of dirt:

> [O]ur homestead house consisted of two rooms, partly dug in the side of the upper rim of the creek bank. It was … more like a hill side where the house was made. All around the wall of the dugout, part was sodded up to make the walls the right height. The roof was made by first putting a ridge pole over the centre, then laying poles from that to the walls and putting brush over these poles, laying the brush the opposite way, and on top of the brush, sod was carefully laid thick (sod mud) the wall were plastered with mud and had the effect of something like a stucco wall. A chimney for each room was built up from the wall and from sod.[28]

The Wilkinsons slowly built up their homestead and sheep ranching operation in the middle of the Nebraska plains under extremely harsh conditions. Their sod house dugout had dirt floors. But that did not deter their English relatives and old friends from Wensleydale from joining them. "When ever any one came from the 'old country'," Alice remembered, "it was our home they came to, and they were always welcome until they could get located." Eventually, "all of father's brothers and sisters who came to America" got started with the help of the Wilkinsons; among them was her father's sister, Agnes, who had married Adam Robinson of Starbotton, in Upper Wharfedale.[29]

Just what these people from the area around Wensleydale and Wharfedale found on the Great Plains, and how they coped with the drastic change from an English village to a sod shanty they called "soddies," is hard to fathom. They were desperately poor: Alice recalled that "there were times when we did not have too much to eat, or to wear … there were times when we did not have shoes when we lived in the soddie … I had been wearing a pair of moccasins made out of rabbit skins." Alice herself marvelled at the shocking change the English had to confront: "What an experience it must have been for mother coming from England to such a wilderness. There were weeks that she did not see a woman's face. For months they were the only settlers on the creek. Mother had been used to going to church every Sunday where there was a lovely choir and pipe organ." This was in West Tanfield, an ancient village just north of Ripon that was mentioned in the Domesday Book.[30] After leaving such a village, living in a dirt-floor "soddie" with no church within many kilometres could not have been easy.

The Wilkinsons and Robinsons nevertheless persevered and built more dugouts, and after more homesteading families came to the area the little town of Westerville was established. Like other English immigrants on the Great Plains frontier, the Wilkinsons and Robinsons sometimes feared possible reprisals by Native Americans, even though the Indigenous people had more to fear: sometime in the 1880s the Wilkinsons were told that the Native Americans were "on the war path" and so they took refuge at Kearney, Nebraska, some 80 kilometres south of Westerville. They stayed there about two weeks, until the military found that the Native Americans were part of a hunting party and posed no threat.

The Russells in Nebraska

Though Yorkshire families like the Wilkinsons and Robinsons started out in the American West under harsh conditions, they were not escaping desperation in England. Something else was enticing them, an ambition to become large landowners, something impossible to achieve in England. The John Russell family is a good example. They were well off, but John wanted more – to acquire enough land so that when his sons came of age, they and their own families could farm next to him. The Russells were from Castle Bolton, Wensleydale, and emigrated as a family in 1881. But John had already been to America as a young man in his late twenties. The son of a coal miner, he had to grow up quickly after his parents died young, and support his younger siblings by mining lead. Each morning he had to walk great distances to get to work, no matter the weather. It was news of the California Gold Rush that first lured him to America. After the Atlantic crossing he sailed around Cape Horn and up the Pacific coast to the gold fields, where he made "a very substantial amount of money." Returning to England with the intention of taking the rest of the family to America, he instead stayed in Castle Bolton as a mining agent while doing some mining on the side. Then in 1857 he married Hannah Jackson and together they farmed and prospered. By 1871 they were living in a fine house and were farming 190 acres in Wensley, employing a domestic servant and a farm labourer. But John and Hannah were renting that land and house from Lord Bolton, and they wanted more land for their five growing sons. John's adventures in California provided him some knowledge and confidence, so it seemed natural to go back to the American West.

In 1881 the Russells packed their things, which required eight large crates, and sold their remaining property. Their savings were very substantial, amounting to about $15,000. They also took along their domestic servant, two boys from another family, and the family dog. This was hardly a poor family. John was sixty-one, Hannah fifty, and the five sons between ten and twenty-three. Though crossing the Atlantic had much improved by the 1880s, seasickness still tormented them. Landing in Quebec and taking the train to Detroit, they were not enumerated by the American immigration commissioners and thus entered the United States undetected in the official statistics. By this time America's infrastructure had improved, but the family was still surprised by the rough and crude trains, which were inferior to the ones they knew in England.[31]

The story of the Russell family is especially interesting for how they got to Nebraska. They intended to settle in Allison, Iowa, where a friend of John lived and was ready to help them choose their land. But upon arrival they found that the friend had died, and that there were no other contacts to offer help. So, they improvised: they decided on the spot to head for Lincoln, Nebraska, and rent a house until they could decide what to do. From their base there, John and his eldest son William travelled to the Pawnee Indian Reservation Office at Grand Island to see what land was available. The Pawnee had owned the land until they were forced by the federal government in 1857 to exchange it for inferior lands in Oklahoma. The Russells benefited enormously from this forced deal. They were shown land in Fullerton, Nance County, paid cash for a plot at Horse Creek, and then returned to Lincoln to fetch the rest of the family. They had plenty of cash left over to buy four horses (which cost from $130 to $165 each), harnesses, wagons, and other equipment. Then the family travelled for the few days it took to get to their new, unbroken land.

The living conditions of frontier life in this part of Nebraska were appalling. Though they perhaps should have known, the Russells were horrified to find that most of the scattered homes in the area consisted of sod huts or dugouts – mere holes or caves carved into hillsides. Fortunately, they had resources to travel to Central City to purchase wood for their first house. Inexplicably, Hannah wrote that she found the countryside like that of Yorkshire, which may have been wishful thinking, perhaps a coping mechanism. But soon the Russell family became independent, largely self-sufficient farmers, raising cattle (mainly English breeds), hogs, grain, and vegetables, not unlike what they had raised in England, but now on their own land. John and Hannah Russell were thus able to achieve what they had longed for in England – not just their own land but, eventually, large farms nearby for their five sons as well. In 1890 Hannah made a return trip to England, and the sons bought other farms and took up banking.[32]

The Far West

Farther west of Nebraska and Wyoming lay the Rocky Mountains, which also attracted immigrants from North Yorkshire. In Leadville, Lake County, Colorado, the 1870s were a boom time for silver mining, and Yorkshire lead miners came in to take advantage of the new opportunities. Situated at some 10,000 feet above sea level, Leadville was especially promising: networks for employment and social interaction were being laid by lodge members, who dominated the industry there and made it especially easy for Yorkshire immigrants to settle and get started.[33] In 1883 Robert Carter of Arkengarthdale, son of William Carter and Hanna Stones, arrived in the footsteps of his cousin William. Robert was recorded in the 1871 census as a sixteen-year-old labourer, and in 1881, a wagoner. He married a German immigrant widow, Johanna. William Carter had come to Leadville because he knew he could use his lead mining experience to mine silver. He died there in 1884, and his family members who remained in Arkengarthdale erected a headstone in their churchyard commemorating his life.[34]

California had been a legendary magnet for English immigrants ever since the gold rush, and now in the latter part of the century more arrived. George Francis Langrick was a butcher in his native Yorkshire and came directly to his uncle in Sturgis, St Joseph County, Michigan. After a few years of schooling he left for California in 1860 and worked as a butcher in Placer County. He then went to Austin, Nevada, and established a meat market there for nine years. After working for eight years in Visalia,

California, in 1878 he started two butcher shops, but at the same time he bought and improved 420 acres for raising grain and cattle.[35]

Some of the later Yorkshire immigrants in the Far West came from wealthy and privileged backgrounds. Captain Henry Ernest Boyes was born in Hull in 1844, the son of "a large landed proprietor" of an estate that was sold to Lord Londesborough for $250,000, and the owner of fine homes in Madeira, London, and Yorkshire. In 1858 Boyes began serving in the Indian navy, was stationed in Bombay for about four years, and then sailed on a troop ship throughout the world. After retiring from the navy in 1872, Boyes managed an Indigo plantation in India, where he also hunted tigers and travelled widely. After ten years, in 1883, he returned to England and married Antoinette Charlotte Edwards, whom he had previously met in India. That same year they emigrated to California, came to San Francisco, and bought the most ideal and beautiful section of the valley, which included an old mineral hot spring long used by Native Americans. They developed the property as Boyes Hot Springs, which became the most famous mineral hot springs resort in California. The Boyes's home became famous as well, because of its vast gardens and its "typical English gentleman's home and an air of refinement" with a large library and "many ancestral and family portraits, dating back to the time of Oliver Cromwell." Captain Boyes was known as "an English gentleman of the old school, cultured, refined, genial, having proved loyal and true to the land of his adoption and is well trained in the exercise of those fine intellectual qualities that are the Englishman's heritage and pride."[36]

The western prairies, mountains, and California, then, saw immigrants from North Yorkshire and other parts of England play important roles in their settlement and development. In the southern plains, Texas had long been of great interest among the English. From its earliest times as a Mexican territory to independent republic, and then as the twenty-eighth state of the Union, Texas was also shaped by English immigrants, including those from North Yorkshire.

Texas

I must say as to what I have seen of Texas it is the garden spot of the world.
The best land and the best prospects for health I ever saw, and I do believe it is
a fortune to any man to come here. There is a world of country here to settle.

DAVY CROCKETT, 1836

Like the West, Texas was mythically familiar in England. Englishmen
were in Texas before they were in Virginia. In 1569, three sailors (David
Ingram, Richard Twide, and Richard Browne) walked through southern
Texas on their way northward after being set ashore with others in Mexico
as a punishment by their commander, John Hawkins.[1] By 1800 English
farmers and traders had settled in Texas, and in the 1820s at least six
English immigrants received *empresario* contracts for settlements, as did
Moses and Stephen Austin, though they failed to attract other settlers.[2]
During the 1820s and 1830s English immigrants were among those stirring
up trouble in Texas and were fully involved in the Texas Revolution:
of the 187 who perished at the Alamo, 16 were English or Welsh.[3] The
English were also said to have blended in easily there: "So quickly and
thoroughly were early English immigrants assimilated in the mainstream
of America culture," one historian has written, "that it is now impossible
to determine just how many Americans who came to Texas prior to its
revolt against Mexico were native English."[4]

The Texas Revolution alarmed Britain's government and business
leaders for its potential to destabilize Mexico and threaten their extensive
investments in the region. After independence in 1836, Texas became
an early diplomatic flashpoint between Britain and the United States,
when Britain advocated continual independence for Texas rather than
annexation by the United States. British abolitionists and Whigs, especially, feared, rightly, that, as part of the United States, Texas would tilt
the precarious balance of the Senate in favour of slave states. Britain also
preferred an independent Texas so it would remain a good trading partner,

a safe place for investment, and a reliable source of cotton, as well as a convenient buffer against further United States expansion. Concerned that recognizing Texan independence would jeopardize their relations with Mexico, Britain nonetheless did so in 1840, while opposing annexation by the United States. Many Texans were in debt to British creditors, and Mexico seemed willing to absorb some of that debt as long as Texas remained independent. Meanwhile Americans complained that Britain was attempting to dominate Texas and interfere with the contentious issue of slavery.[5]

Tensions over Texas relaxed a bit in the early 1840s when Britain turned its attention northward over the unresolved borders between the United States and British North America. Lord Palmerston, the foreign secretary, was not going to risk a conflict over Texas when so much more was at stake in Oregon. Insisting that the two nations were "joined by Community of Interests, & by the Bonds of Kindred," Palmerston temporarily back-peddled on the issue of an independent Texas, and went so far as to say that "we should have no objections to see the whole of Mexico belong to the United States," though he hardened his position when the United States headed toward annexation of Texas and war with Mexico.[6]

Between independence in 1836 and its annexation by the United States in 1845, Texas saw increasing English settlement and investment. Some English families were among the 800 who had settled between the Rio Grande and Nueces Rivers by the Rio Grande and Texas Land Company, led by the English immigrant John Charles Beales and the Scottish immigrant James Grant.[7] And in 1839, the Texas Emigration and Land Company was founded to promote and sell land to prospective English immigrants. In 1841 land grants were also made to twenty American and English investors, led by the English immigrant William S. Peters, and arrived in the United States in 1827. Though primarily a businessman, Peters also had philanthropic goals to settle English industrial workers. Some of the American investors married into Peters's extended family.[8] By this time Yorkshire people were reading tantalizing accounts of Texas in their local newspapers:

In Texas, emigrants will be sure to find, not only a comfortable home on their arrival, but immediate, constant, and profitable employment. Mechanics, such as carpenters, smiths, tailors, printers, painters, shoemakers, brickmakers, bricklayers, labourers,

&c. &c., at this moment earn from three to four dollars a day. Bookkeepers, lawyers' and merchants' clerks, receive from 89 to 100 dollars a month. Dress-makers, milliners, straw-bonnet makers, and plain needlewomen, get from two to three dollars a-day. Labourers earning from 13s. 6d. to 18i. a-day What an El Dorado this would be to the starving peasantry of merry England![9]

Settlement Projects

It was also at this time that various guidebooks were published to attract English immigrants and investors to Texas, often as part of a settlement project. One of the important early ones was William Kennedy's *Texas: The Rise, Progress, and Prospects of the Republic of Texas*, published in London in 1841 to promote a project to settle 600 families. Born near Dublin and educated in Belfast and London, Kennedy had first come to Texas in 1839 as the secretary of the Earl of Durham and then served as the Texas consul in London. He then returned to Texas as British consul in Galveston. Though the book failed to attract families, it did attract attention, especially that of his friend William Bollaert.[10] Bollaert, another English immigrant, had trained as a chemist under Michael Faraday but turned to a life of adventure travel and came to Texas to write about it for English magazines. Encouraged by Kennedy's book, Bollaert attempted his own colony in 1850 in Bosque County, which he called Kent. It was located on the Brazos River in modern Bosque County as the base for the Universal Emigration and Colonization Company of London. Here settlers would work cooperatively to produce grain for export. Kent was promoted as the "Philadelphia on the Brazos," with navigable links to the Gulf of Mexico, and in September of 1850 thirty English families sailed for Galveston, with more to follow. The colonists included tailors, bakers, shopkeepers, and bank clerks. In charge was Sir Edward Belcher, born in Nova Scotia and knighted seven years earlier for his service in the Royal Navy.[11]

Things got off to a bad start. Cold and wet weather made travelling and breaking the sod all but impossible, and some abandoned the project. In January of 1851, the town of "Kent" was officially founded on a site of about 40 acres, but it did not even last the year. Settlers died of disease and bad weather. Others fled. By 1852, only one immigrant remained. Because of a

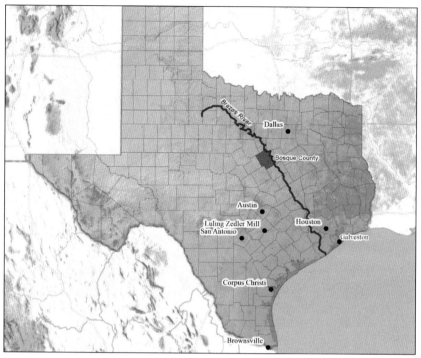

Figure 21.1   Map of Texas, showing places of attempted English colonies and the area of Luling, where the Thomas Wilson family from Rosedale served as land agent for other Yorkshire families.

lack of planning and resources, settlers were forced to live in mud dugouts. Furthermore, the English knew almost nothing about farming – certainly not for conditions in Texas. They were mostly educated persons said to be of "delicate habits," and had never confronted such miserable conditions before. Like other English colonies on the plains and prairies, Kent was doomed. The settlers were poorly chosen, as was the environment, the plans were unrealistic, and Kent soon faded from the scene.[12]

The emigrant press was understandably cautious in their portrayal of Texas. *Emigration*, a popular and evidently balanced guide published in 1849, included warnings about Texas made by the Colonial Land and Emigration Commission. Because the Commission was biased toward steering English immigrants to the colonies rather than the United States, it is not surprising that it presented a rather dim view of Texas. But its warnings were nevertheless fair, considering the disaster that was about to unfold in the colony of Kent: "Emigrants are warned that the statements recently circulated, respecting the salubrity of climate, the fertility of soil, and the richness of the mineral productions of Texas, are reported by authority to be greatly exaggerated, and that British subjects, who may be induced to emigrate to that country, are likely to fall into sickness and destitution."[13]

The guidebook also warned that Texas was "peopled by the scum and refuse, the daring, adventurous, and lawless, of all other countries." Even so, Texas held out some promise: "When fully peopled, well settled, and placed under the vigorous controul of permanent government, and institutions, its natural capabilities will render it a desirable place of settlement. It abounds ... in fine land, extensive prairie, game, and fish; it is well calculated for cattle, sheep, rice, cotton, and other tropical productions. It has scarcely any winter, and is not subject to the sudden changes or great extremes of climate which form the defect of the North American continent."[14] In short, Texas needed development and more settlement before it could be suitable for English immigrants: "[A]t present it does not hold out that security for life, property, and the quiet pursuit of industry which is essential to the happy condition of a colonist ... Rhetoric aside – Texas is a miserable country and its inhabitants a miserable population."[15]

After the Civil War, as the economy boomed, and land companies proliferated, Texas was now deemed good enough for the English. Railroad companies and the popular press boosted the state and made it appealing to the English – especially those with means – by underscoring its promise for hunting and sport and its largely imaginary similarities with the nicest parts of England. Texas, in the 1870s, was:

> a hunter's paradise, on account of its multitudes of game and
> fish, the absence of fences, by which sportsmen are too often
> confined ... its free pasturage, bracing health-giving climate, and
> excellent water ... The country may be compared with the loveliest
> of English parks. Magnificent live-oak groves rather than woods
> divide the region in almost equal portions with rolling prairie lands,
> whose short mesquite grasses will compare in greenness and velvet
> surface with any English lawn ... The rivers, which are numerous,
> swarm with fish ... the waters are of crystal purity and reveal a teem-
> ing of life that would have rejoiced the heart of good Izaak Walton.[16]

The Thomas Wilson Family

The connection between Texas and North Yorkshire is illustrated by the family of Thomas Wilson (introduced in chapter 18). He was born in the North York Moors village of Rosedale in 1846 and was the son of a Primitive Methodist preacher who also farmed about 50 acres. As a youth Thomas worked at the local brickyard and for a farmer, and then entered an apprenticeship for a "slave whipper" of a joiner by the appropriately Dickensian name of "Isaac Garbutt," of Rosedale Abbey. As Wilson remembered, it was misery, "five years a slave" performing unrelated menial tasks, such as cleaning fourteen pairs of boots per week during his "leisure time" and making coffins.[17] He spent most of his days hungry; even his Sunday dinners consisted of broth. It was a "doglike treatment," Wilson recalled.[18]

Nevertheless, the "doglike treatment" seemed to have some benefits. Wilson earned 13 shillings a week plus his board and became a journeyman joiner. After marrying Mary Magson in Nunnington in 1866, he thrived as a cabinet maker and in 1877 expanded his business. On Thorgill Road he built four "nice homes" he called Primrose Cottages, one of which became the family home in which he and Mary raised eight children while Thomas continued to work at his craft.[19]

In Rosedale, Thomas Wilson was also a member of the Shepherd's Retreat Lodge, Rosedale, a friendly society for working men. But in 1877, as president of the lodge, Thomas had some serious unspecified altercation with the circuit preacher and was accused of lying. Thomas insisted he be "put on trial" to clear his name. He won the church court case, but the dispute and anger lingered for "months." Meanwhile, by the late 1870s the local ironstone mining industry was declining and dragging the local economy down. Wilson saw a bleak future: in the words of his ancestor, "He realized that the economy of the Rosedale region was doomed to wither away,"[20] so he decided to "seek his fortune" in America.[21]

Texas became the solution to Wilson's problems. After considering New Zealand, he contacted the London-based immigration agent for the Galveston, Harrisburg, and San Antonio Railroad Company and in December of 1877 sailed to New York where he was interviewed by the company's officials and no doubt made an impression.[22] They immediately hired him as their immigration agent in Luling, about 65 kilometres south of Austin, to promote the company's lands and persuade some of the immigrants pouring in to choose that part of the state over others. After getting established in Luling and working there for about a year, Wilson returned to Rosedale to fetch his family and bring the first batch of immigrants with him.[23]

Upon returning to Rosedale, Wilson prepared his family for leaving Yorkshire. First the Wilsons auctioned off their lovely Primrose Village property, and apparently donated much of the proceeds to the church at Rosedale Abbey. The property was very considerable, as described in the *Malton Messenger* of 15 June 1878:

> To be sold or let with immediate possession. General dealers shop and dwelling house doing a good trade… rent £22 let or lease if required. The owner is retiring from business and going abroad. Also five cottages to be sold. The whole of the above property situated at Primrose Village Rosedale Abbey Yorkshire … The whole of the property has been recently built and will be sold cheap. The shop is suitable for a tailor, draper, grocer, ironmonger, furniture dealer and boot maker as all the above trades are at present carried on in the premise. Such an offer is seldom in the market … also for sale a black retriever dog price 30 shillings Capital house dog.[24]

In the North York Moors the departure of emigrants could be a momentous, religious affair: when the Wilsons left in 1880 the people of Rosedale turned out along with a brass band and a choir singing hymns to bid them farewell.[25] Sailing from Liverpool, the family took a full eight weeks to get to Galveston and from there to Luling, where Wilson resumed his work as an emigrant agent for the Galveston, Harrisburg and San Antonio Railway Company. He also built a new home modelled after an English castle, complete with ramparts and the "English embellishment of crenellations" and named it "Primrose Villa," the same name as their old home in Rosedale. Here Thomas and Mary produced five more children. They also raised roses they took with them from Yorkshire, which would make a long-lasting impact on Texas: this was the famous Yorkshire white primrose, after which they had named their Yorkshire houses, and their new home in Luling. When trimmed, the white primrose was perfect for Yorkshire's hedges and fences, and it thrived in Texas as well. Wilson himself became known as the "English Rose of Texas."[26]

Figure 21.2. Thomas Wilson family in Rosedale.

Wilson was not the only one who brought the primrose and other plants from North Yorkshire to North America. In 1883 Matthew Dinsdale received a letter from a friend in Blackpool who thanked him for the maple seedlings he had sent to him in England. And in return, the friend sent "a dried flower that I gathered in your native valley in the early summer of the present year it is a very rare flower at Ripon but grows plentifully at Wensleydale. It is the Birds' Eye Primrose."[27]

Figure 21.3. The Wilson family home, "Primrose Villa," in Rosedale.

Wilson's rise as a landowner was impressive: in a letter dated 12 April 1880 – only months after the family's arrival – Wilson claimed that "I now own three important farms, three city lots [in Luling], and mortgages on other properties. I have just bought six acres to build myself a home upon, just outside this city, close to railroad, with a lot of splendid shade trees upon it, and close to the public highway. I have given for it fifty dollars per acre. I have now property here that will bring me in over one hundred pounds a year, and my salary for this office is over one hundred a year, with house and … all expenses paid."[28] Wilson also boasted that "all my farms are paying 18 per cent on the investment."[29] But the Wilsons' rapid rise did not necessarily mean extra leisure: Wilson's daughters worked as domestic servants: Mary Ellen served the head druggist in Luling for 4 dollars per month, and Hanna the town's baker for 3 ½ dollars.[30]

The Wilsons were cashing in on the cattle boom of 1887–88, which was centred on the Panhandle but also benefited places near Austin, like Luling.[31] Much of the boom was supported by extensive English investment: by late 1886 the English had invested roughly $25 million in ranches and controlled about 20 million acres within the Panhandle itself, the largest investor being the London-based Capitol Freehold Land and Investment Company. So vast was English investment and ownership that Texans sought protection from large English corporations. They finally got it in 1891 when the Texas government passed the Alien Land Law, which allowed immigrants to hold lands only if they became United States citizens. Because of these restrictions, and rising overproduction and falling prices, English settlement and investment fell.[32]

As part of his job Wilson wrote promotional letters back to the people of Rosedale. Some were published in the local Yorkshire newspapers under the title "A Rosedale Man in Texas." He also made several return trips to Yorkshire in the 1880s to recruit more English settlers. His efforts paid off.[33] "One day I am locating emigrants," he boasted, "another drawing plans of land and buildings, another galloping through the woods, hunting up places for emigrants, another riding 200 miles [320 kilometres] on our railway, another meeting land commissioners and presidents of railways, another writing land titles … another answering letters, and so on all the time … nothing comes wrong to me, and I am giving general satisfaction."[34] He then reported that by April he had already "located here 250 emigrants since I returned from England, and I do not hesitate to say this is the best part to emigrate to."[35] Wilson was said to have settled "over 1000 families" in his part of Texas between 1878 and 1883, though how many were from Yorkshire is uncertain.[36] Over the next few decades English immigrants helped develop Texas; they were among the first to introduce new breeds of cattle and to use steel windmills and barbed wire. They also paved the way for more settlers.[37] Wilson resigned in 1883 to pursue his own business in real estate and hotels.[38]

Wilson's was a classic American immigrant success story with a twist: it was not "rags to riches," because he did not leave Yorkshire as a poor man. Rather, he emerged from poor and oppressive circumstances in Rosedale and became a success there, before anticipating the decline of its local economy and using his resources to leave for America and reach loftier heights: "I was a wild lad when young," he admitted, "but to-day, where can you pick out a man, ever bred and born in Rosedale, who has been promoted, and set up before people in foreign countries as their advisor?" Wilson was proud that he was a professional man, in contact with agents throughout Europe, and dressed to play the part: "I am not only writing to our agents in London, but to our agents in Germany, France, and Switzerland. I am about to have my duties and my salary

increased, and to have a clerk to do my correspondence. I am dressed
up with starched collars and cuffs every day, and in a Sunday suit. I left
England honourably, and I hope ever to remain honourable here in all
by dealings."[39] Thomas Wilson died on 18 July 1918.

English immigrants like Thomas Wilson were the type to inspire the
Texas Sun to declare in 1880 that the English in Texas "are true heroes,
fighting daily the battle of progress, and making for themselves happy
and independent homes. Their names will be inscribed on the pages of
our state's history as the people who made this section 'blossom as the
rose'."[40] And yet such praise can mask the difficulties of loneliness and
struggle in a new environment. North Yorkshire emigrants who made
their way to Texas late in the century faced an environment that was
strange in many ways: the climate and soil were very different, as were its
methods of agriculture. The people were also different, feisty and fiercely
independent, a reputation that remains to this today. Texas required a lot
of adjustments from North Yorkshire immigrants. So it is not surprising
that in the late nineteenth century and into the twentieth, far more of
those leaving North Yorkshire for North America chose a place with a
climate, economy, and culture more like their own, and a place where
they could remain British subjects.

Canada

Peace, Order, and Good Government

PHRASE FROM
THE *BRITISH NORTH AMERICA* ACT, 1867

Although Thomas Wilson and others left North Yorkshire for Texas and other parts of the United States, the migrant tide was turning toward Canada. Familiar places in Ontario, where newcomers from Yorkshire had been settling since the 1820s and 1830s, were the biggest draw. But new options were also opening in Canada's prairies, mountain provinces, and coastal west. Early in the twentieth century Canada overtook the United States as the favourite destination for the English. From 1905 on, more British immigrants went to Canada than the United States, and other parts of the Commonwealth were also increasing their share.[1]

Assimilation

In Canada, late-nineteenth-century English immigrants could expect to find a familiar culture and feel welcome, especially when they settled among other English immigrants or their descendants. Those in Canadian towns and cities, especially, had fewer adjustments to make, because in some ways the urban areas were becoming increasingly English in culture and character.[2] Even more than the United States, which was rapidly changing because of millions of immigrants from new origins, Canada was a place where the English might feel "invisible" because they could blend in. This was one reason why so many were now choosing Canada in the first place – that and the fact that in Canada they would remain British subjects.

The commonality, even invisibility, of English immigrants in Canada was widely accepted as self-evident in the late nineteenth century. In 1897 Toronto's *Mail and Empire* began a series of articles on immigration titled "Foreigners Who Live in Toronto," and those from England were not even included. As the editor said of the English: "These people are … so nearly akin in thought, customs, and manners to the Canadians themselves, in fact so indistinguishable from them in most respects, that in speaking of a foreign population they have generally been disregarded altogether."[3]

Early historians of Canadian immigration agreed. In 1958 Arthur R.M. Lower wrote that, compared with even the Scots and Irish, the English were "almost without feature and untraceable" with "little clan sense."[4] A more recent historian also agrees: "The unassuming miners, carpenters, tailors, labs, domestic servants, farmers, settle workers, shoemakers, and other workers were all part of the invisible immigrant stream that furnished Canada with a large part to its population. They did not wave flags or sing anthems … left few outward signs of their Englishness along the way. They were the silent majority who simply faded into the background."[5]

This was also the view of the St George's Society, which was active in Canada promoting English immigration and aiding those who needed assistance. The Society emphasized the cultural commonality and ease with which the English could fit in.[6] They did not have to change their national identity. As one of the members put it, "the English race proper, when transplanted from their native homes, do not see any especial need for asserting their nationality."[7] Whereas St Patrick's Day was widely celebrated by the Irish in both the United States and Canada, and St Andrew's Day was celebrated by the Scots, St George's Day was hardly noticed – much like it is all but forgotten today.[8] At the same time, publications and promotions of Canadian lands emphasized the similarity of culture. It is not surprising that English newcomers assumed that Canada's society was little different than their own.[9]

But this assumption was not entirely valid. In the late nineteenth century, Canada was developing its own sense of self, with distinctions that had not existed earlier. The "John Bull" patriotic culture and air of English superiority, which marked some English immigrants, offended Canadians.[10] English paupers who needed assistance also created distance between the English and Canadians.[11] And members of the English elite who attempted to carve out estates in the Canadian West invited scorn when they failed and complained, when it was their unsuited qualities that were to blame. Many English simply did not have the qualities that Canada needed in its workforce. Astonishingly, in some parts of Canada the English immigrant's reputation was so tarnished that signs read "Englishmen need not apply."[12]

Some Toronto newspapers picked up on these changing perceptions of English immigrants and, unlike the *Mail and Empire*, did not see much evidence that they blended in easily. One paper noted that some recent English immigrants were met with hostility, and in 1907 it devoted several issues to exploring the reasons why. It found that the recent influx of English was not all the "best quality." Ontario needed experienced farm workers and too many unemployed and unskilled urban industrial workers were arriving with little to contribute. Also noted was the tendency of some English to "grumble" and complain, due in part to the unrealistic expectations that had been planted by aggressive immigrant recruiters. The English could indeed be conspicuous and being English was not necessarily an advantage. Yet, at the same time there were positive remarks about the English in Toronto because they were of the "same stock."[13] For some Canadians, culture and identity trumped any skills an immigrant had to offer. Altogether it was a mixed bag. But whatever the level of anti-English rhetoric, it was modest compared with that meted out to other immigrant groups in both Canada and the United States. In Canada, the English continued to enjoy the advantages and privileges that came with their familiar culture.[14]

Ontario

For the last few decades of the century, Ontario remained the favourite destination of Canada-bound immigrants from England. Ontario's mature economy offered more opportunities, as did its abundant lands. At the same time, in the mid-1870s, England's agricultural depression had begun, and with it rising agricultural trade unionism. So, both British and Canadian authorities began offering special cheap passage tickets for poor English farm workers to get to Ontario. The scheme had several complementary objectives: to help the poorest workers achieve a better life, to help Canada acquire needed labour, to reduce the perceived glut of farm labour in England, and to pre-empt poverty and social unrest in the English countryside.[15] At the same time, Ontario was promoting the northern part of the province to English settlers by offering free grants of 100 acres as long as they cleared it, in a manner similar to the Homestead Act in the United States.[16]

North Yorkshire Immigrants

Immigrants from North Yorkshire were no longer as numerous as they had been. North Yorkshire had already endured the most disruptive adjustments associated with industrialization and globalization, especially in lead and ironstone production. Meanwhile, there were fewer opportunities in the United States, especially in the Upper Mississippi and the Old Northwest, where minerals were virtually exhausted, and the most affordable good farmland already occupied. In this context Canada's appeal was growing, especially as the British and Canadian governments offered assisted passages and cheap or free land to draw English immigrants to Canada rather than the United States. These later English immigrants to Canada included people escaping unemployment and squalid living conditions, but most were "sufficiently affluent" to finance their migration.[17]

Among the North Yorkshire immigrants to Ontario at this time was Robert Watson, of Rosedale, who in 1850 at age thirty-five married his next-door neighbour Hannah Strickland. After living in Kirkdale for a while they left for Canada and by 1881 were farming at Stanley, Huron South, Ontario, the same area where many other people from the North York Moors had settled in the 1830s and 1840s (see chapter 10).[18] Apparently, the links of people and information formed by earlier emigrants from Rosedale were still alive forty years later and influencing migration decisions. It was also at this time, around 1880, that Eliza Jane Anakin and Richard Cape married and left Bridlington in East Yorkshire and went to Chatham, Ontario, hoping to work in bonnet-making and coopering, respectively. Like many of those preceding them, they had a relative, in this case Eliza's uncle, who was also a bonnet maker, eager to help them get established. He must have been a godsend to the young couple.[19] By the late century some North Yorkshire men and women were going to Canada to work for a while and perhaps learn a new trade, and then returning to Yorkshire. Robert Ford, for example, who was born in Rosedale in 1860, went with a local friend to Upper Canada "in about the 1880s" to work as a lumberjack and on the railroads. He returned to

Rosedale to farm and work as a stonemason and then moved to Glaisdale, where he spent the rest of his life.[20]

John Cherry

The general pattern of North Yorkshire migration to North America was that those from the Dales and Vale of York preferred the United States, whereas those from the Moors and eastern regions tended to go to Canada. This difference was based on both tradition and economic backgrounds, since those from the Dales naturally went to the Upper Mississippi to mine lead and farm, and those from the Moors and the East relied more on assistance and other inducements to Canada – a tradition that started in the eighteenth century. But in the late nineteenth century people from the Dales were also finding Canada more attractive. One exceptionally well-documented case is that of John Cherry, of Swaledale. He left his native village of Fremington (adjacent to Reeth) in May of 1894, along with his cousin, also named John ("Jno B." in Cherry's letters). The two intended to work on a farm near Toronto before heading out West. Cherry and his cousin were not the only ones leaving the area for Canada: in Thirsk, on their way to Liverpool, they met a group "of about 10 or 11" emigrants leaving nearby Bedale who were also bound for Canada. Together, these young North Yorkshire men boarded the train for Liverpool where they checked in at the Temperance Hotel – a common hotel for Dales emigrants leaving through Liverpool. After purchasing their passage tickets Cherry deposited his money at the local Canadian bank and got a draft for £16 that he could draw upon in Canada. Then they boarded their ship.[21]

Leaving England was now far easier than in earlier decades, and the voyage quicker and less traumatic. But it was still challenging. Even on the first short sailing to Londonderry, Cherry was "very sick."[22] The Atlantic crossing was far worse, Cherry recounting "a tremendous lot of sickness on board. We were both very bad all the time … both very bad all day on Sunday. Couldn't eat anything."[23] The following day the ship was "at a complete standstill on account of the immense fog … Cannot travel for fear of icebergs." Like John Flounders Dixon, who had left Great Ayton for Iowa more than twenty years earlier, Cherry and his cousin were "both very pleased we didn't go steerage as there are so many dirty looking foreigners, Chinese, Norwegians, Irish and others." Their cabin featured "comfortable beds," each of which held four passengers, which they shared with a Welshman and a Scot from Edinburgh – "both very kind." They also met two other young men from Bedale, apparently in addition to the ten they travelled with to Liverpool, who were heading to Canada's "Far West." The voyage had its perks. Every day on board there were organized physical exercises, and on at least one day they were served roast mutton, soup, and sago pudding.[24]

Having recovered from seasickness by 11 May, Cherry and his cousin enjoyed the rest of the voyage and became acquainted with their fellow emigrants. The group was quite diverse, but most were going to Canada to work on farms. As Cherry recalled, they were on "talking acquaintance with most of the young men on board as we have all sorts of games on deck. Most of them from all parts of England and have been workers in various branches of business and are going out for farm work." Perhaps these were some of the unsuitable English immigrants that Canadians had complained about. Near the end of their voyage Cherry once again exclaimed, "thank God we didn't go steerage." They landed in Quebec on 13 May.[25]

In Quebec Cherry and his cousin John boarded the train for Ottawa, where they had friends ready to help them. They had formed such a close bond with the other North Yorkshire immigrants, he recalled, that bidding them farewell was like a second parting from home. But a couple of the "lads from Bedale" joined them on their train to Ottawa, and they surely reminisced about the land they had left behind and what lay ahead. At Ottawa, Cherry drew his money out.

John Cherry and his cousin were using chains and links of information forged by Swaledalers who had gone before them and offered help, but when they called on their friends in Ottawa, they discovered they were gone. Now they had to find work. First, they searched at East Templeton, near the Quebec-Ontario border, and not finding any there, returned to Ottawa. In a few days they found hard, unskilled work "cutting drains in the street for laying gas pipes." It was not an auspicious start. As Cherry reported in May, "Work is not very good to get here, and trade on the whole is only slack at present." But soon they found work for a "Big Farmer" on Greenbank Farm, some 8 kilometres out of town. This was a dairy farmer whose hundred cows provided milk to the city, and who offered the two lads room and board and winter work as well.[26]

In early June, before starting their work for the "Big Farmer," John Cherry wrote back to his parents and siblings in Fremington, expressing his delight with their letters and reporting that he and John were still working in the city: "We both have got fairly well used to the work and the work-mates ... he has about 40 men working in different parts of the city." But in three weeks they were to start their farm work. Cherry had gained three pounds since leaving Yorkshire, and the clothing they brought with them was not only getting tighter but unsuitable for the hot Ontario summer: "far too thick and our boots far too heavy for this climate. We are nearly smothered in them," he said.[27]

Things were going well for Cherry and his cousin but not for their two new friends from Bedale. They had intended to go to Canada's Far West but were "turning round and going right back home to England." Apparently, they did not have adequate information or resources, for "times are very dull out there unless men have money to take up land."[28] Cherry and John may have abandoned their plans for the Far West at this point.

While adjusting to Canada, John Cherry's mind was often on his native village in Swaledale. He took special interest in its local news. New activity in the local mines energized him: "[V]ery pleased to hear you had cut some ore at Hard Level, hoping it continues to improve and soon opens out to take a lot of men." He was also glad to hear that Reeth had a new minister. Cherry's frequent thoughts about Yorkshire were probably induced by homesickness. Ottawa seemed strange and unsettling, even for an Englishman like him. There were new races of people he had never seen before: "You should see the Chinese with their long pig-tails down behind and all the different kinds of dress," he remarked.[29] And though there were "lovely parks" and "bands playing," he still found himself overwhelmed by the strangeness: "You cannot imagine how everything is so strange and different in this country," he wrote.[30] Yet, he sounded encouraging to young women like his sister Jane, because "steady girls can do well here."[31]

Like others who struggled at first, Cherry seemed desperate for news from back home. In June he begged for more letters, photos, anything that could provide a more consistent connection with his real home: "You might send me a paper now and then," he suggested. "Send me a photo as soon as you get them ... Everything in this country is quite different to home." He ends this long letter plaintively: "You can guess how anxiously I am wanting to hear from you." At the same time, though, he could write that "We are both very content and comfortable."[32]

After a letter and newspaper arrived from Swaledale, Cherry responded. He was especially excited about news of the upcoming brass band contest at the annual music festival at Hardraw Scaur, a dramatic waterfall and natural limestone amphitheatre on the outskirts of Hawes near the Green Dragon public house, and which still thrives today.[33] "Tell me all particulars and don't forget to send me a newspaper sometimes," he demanded of his sister Jane, who was to attend the festival. When "Hardraw Scaur day" arrived, Cherry felt he was back in Hawes and "could imagine I saw everything at Hr/Scaur."[34] The festival triggered deep emotions and memories: "I hope you enjoyed yourself at the H Scaur and had a good Midsummer." John also read in the newspaper that Jane had "a big time at Draycott Hall," a large house in Fremington open for social occasions: "I see by the paper you have had great times in Swaledale since we left … Let me know who was there and everything and who you saw at Hardraw Scaur and if anybody asked about us."[35]

Farm Work near Ottawa

By 8 July 1894, John Cherry was working for the "Big Farmer" on Greenbank Farm, where his partner and cousin John had preceded him by three weeks. Leaving Ottawa was sad because the two had "got to know the city and got acquainted with some nice English people." Ontario farm work seemed to suit Cherry, though his mind was often back at the Dales. Comparing the "Big Farmer's" cattle to those of Yorkshire he found them wanting: "The cattle I have seen in this country are little cross-bred things, not nearly as good as our English cattle." Cherry's younger brothers were still back in Fremington tending their highly prized cattle. As he later remarked to his brother James, "you say you have sold the rowan heifer for £10. Well cattle are worth far more money at home than in this country."[36] But Canada was better for growing fruit: "[T]his is a favourable country for fruit, particular apples and grapes and every other think they can grow. Grapes in the garden and apples hang on the tree like ropes of onions. I never got any like them at home."[37]

Work was hard on Greenbank Farm. Cherry and his cousin were

two of eight workers, all of whom had to rise at four in the morning to begin their tasks. Cherry was a "cow boy," one of six responsible for milking eighty-seven cows, with more on the way. "You would laugh if you saw me coming in with all them cows," John wrote to his sister in July. "You wouldn't know me," he insisted, "in a pair of blue light thin pants with legs as wide a hay sacks and a straw hat as big as an umbrella and two dogs as big as donkeys."[38] After milking, Cherry and his cousin spent the rest of their day cleaning out the stables, feeding pigs, and so on. They usually finished their work at seven and went to bed at eight thoroughly exhausted. There were also the bugs and the more extreme Canadian climate: "It is very warm. Sometimes we cannot sleep, it's so warm and the flies and mosquitoes really worry us. We lay on the bed without a thing on and the sweat runs of[f] us."[39] It is little wonder that some English immigrants found themselves not up to the hard tasks and harsh environment of Canadian farming.[40]

In addition to the bugs and heat was the lingering impact of the Panic of 1893, which had pulled both the American and the Canadian economies into a slump. "Times are not as very good in this country at present," Cherry noted that July, and furthermore "the crops are not so good here this year as it has been too much rain."[41] But the crops did well enough, for two months later, in September, John Cherry wrote again to his father and mother during the busy harvest time. Cutting Indian corn with scythes was very hard work: "You have no idea what it's like," he complained. And though he and his cousin John were "getting on very well" and were in good health, there were now ninety-eight cows to be milked. It was hard work – harder than milking cows in the booming dairy industry around Liverpool, with which he was familiar through the many Dales people who had gone there to work.[42] "You think cow keepers in L Pool have hard to work," Cherry exclaimed, "how do you think I manage all that lot. After milking in the morning, we come up to breakfast ... Sometimes its dinner time before I know where I am, no sitting down for a moment to rest, or the work is there at night to make up." Not only that, but, "Here it's Sunday and workday all the same. I am beginning to be rather afraid of my eyes with so many cows' tails slashing all the time. Sometimes they are very sore."[43]

During harvest season the two young Swaledalers were frequently reminiscing about Yorkshire: "You will I know often talk and think about us," Cherry acknowledged to his parents, "so do we often talk about home when we are together alone. I thought about haytime and the shooting every day," presumably referring to the grouse hunting season now underway, and which his family participated in. "The shooting pretty well nearly be ready for leaving by the time you get this letter. Have you gone with them as usual. I hope you have had a good time." That his family went hunting suggests they were relatively well off, as does Cherry's reference in a November letter to his brother becoming a cycling enthusiast.[44] Yet the family back in Swaledale were still doing hard work as well, as Cherry also wrote that "I was please[d] you had got on so well in haytime but you must all have worked hard."[45]

John Cherry was working very hard indeed, clearing "the manure out with a big grey horse and sled," and performing other backbreaking farm tasks. In November of 1894 he wrote to his brother James and described himself as a "cow man on a big dairy farm and the milk is sent into Ottawa city every morning ... We have to work from 4 am in the morning till 6 at night."[46] But the men said they ate well, had a comfortable room, and were "doing very well as regards making money. I have not been at much expense and I am worth over 100 dollars altogether," he proudly reported. "That's not bad in a little time but depend on it, I have earned it."[47]

John Cherry remained on the farm through the end of the year. His cousin John, however, was let go because there were too many men for the winter months, so he moved to Ottawa to work on a section of the Canadian-Pacific Railway, and then he found work again as a milk driver, leaving John Cherry alone.[48] "Though I felt alone the first few days after he left," Cherry recalled, "it's every man for himself in this country and a man's got to be pretty smart and able to hold his own or he will soon be put on."[49]

As winter set in John Cherry confronted new problems. "There is always something going wrong among so many cows," he wrote in late November. "I often get it into my head to leave in the summer ... There was one week three cows badly hooked, two of them badly ruptured and one got a great big hook in the bag and there was about 22 have thrown their calves since I have been here its some kind of disease among them. We have now 104 head to look after. Quite plenty for two men."[50] Cherry ends his last letter responding to news that an acquaintance near Hawes died of alcohol abuse, and that there was a new "Gold Cure" that seemed to work in Ottawa. And then he asks for more letters and newspapers from home.[51]

The Canadian Prairies

Though Ontario continued to draw most English immigrants, the Canadian West grew in its appeal, especially for miners. Gold rushes in British Columbia in the late 1850s and early 1860s attracted attention, but they were short-lived, and in any case dominated by miners from California. Yet, some English immigrants made – and others made and lost – fortunes there. An early surge of English miners to British Columbia began in 1871 when coal companies recruited miners from Cumberland to mines west of Comox, calling the settlement Cumberland, after their origins.[52]

But it was the opening of the Prairies from 1867 to the First World War in Manitoba, Saskatchewan, and Alberta that attracted more English settlers to the Canadian West. The railroads were the driving force, and the Dominion Lands Act of 1872 offered free homesteads. The following year the North-West Mounted Police was established to provide safety. In the same year the Department of the Interior was created to entice immigrants, especially from England.[53] As Canada's Prairie provinces were opened to settlement, English immigrants arrived, especially in Manitoba and Saskatchewan.[54] Until the 1890s their numbers were small, but in the early 1900s their numbers steadily grew.

The settlement of Western Canada depended on schemes to lure English immigrants who otherwise might have chosen the United States. Some were aggressive railroad promotions of land sales. The completion of the Canadian Pacific Railway in 1895 made the journey to Canada's seemingly boundless western lands relatively easy, and that clinched the decision for some. The fact that they would be living in part of Britain's empire was especially alluring. So, the CPR sent its agents to travel throughout England to lecture and distribute publications extolling the rich lands of Western Canada, just as the Galveston, Harrisburg and San Antonio Railway Company had come to London and lured Thomas Wilson and others to Texas.[55]

Alberta and British Columbia

In the late nineteenth century, Alberta and British Columbia became more popular destinations. Alberta, especially, was being touted as a place where people could reinvent themselves. Whether from dismal urban backgrounds or professional careers in London, Alberta offered promise, or so it seemed. There was a booming cattle industry. Ranches grew to enormous size, and some of the ranchers had egos to match. Here again, Canada and the United States had much in common for prospective immigrants from Yorkshire. Many, like John Cherry's friends who left Bedale in 1894, spent the first years in Eastern Canada to work and get adjusted. Others were the descendants of the earlier Yorkshire immigrants to New Brunswick and Upper Canada. For some the destination seemed fluid: Yorkshireman Richard Pilling originally settled in Utah but in 1889 headed north to the Cardston area, in southwest Alberta, along with a hundred head of Durham cows and fifty horses.[56]

Both the American and Canadian Wests were being promoted by an array of transportation and land companies, though the noisy promotions were not as effective as the companies had hoped. Prospective migrants trusted letters and connections from relatives already in North America more than railroad corporations.[57] But some did respond to the advertisements, which often exaggerated the glories and minimized the challenges of pioneering in the West.[58] Some Yorkshire farm workers left for Canada in groups under the leadership of steamship, railroad, or land companies. In 1882 James Miller, agent for the Dominion Steamship Company, led a group of thirty-nine people said to be "of the agricultural class," from the East Riding, to the Driffield train station, and then on to Canada.[59] This group would have been welcome in the Canadian West, but farmers with capital were more suitable. Like the English in the American West, some were misfits, often poor and unskilled urban workers. They may have been exploited by government agents who simply listed them as farm labourers to keep their bonuses.[60]

There were also members of the middle class, whose work had become stagnant in England, or who were simply bored and felt limited by life in England.[61] And similar to the Wilkinson and Russell families, who left comfortable circumstances in the Dales for sod huts in Nebraska, there were those who left comfortable lives in Yorkshire for "a log cabin on the prairie" of Canada.[62] On both the American and Canadian prairie frontiers, there were also elites who bought large estates on which to hunt and play cricket, like the aristocracy. They were soon disillusioned. They had neither the ability nor the inclination to do hard work.[63]

More significant in numbers were those sponsored by charitable colonization schemes designed to help unemployed tradesmen, the deaf, and other people with special needs. Between 1868 and 1925 some 80,000 children, who were either orphaned, abandoned, or abused, were sent to Canada, under schemes associated with philanthropists like Thomas Barnardo.[64] But again, most were urban people who did not necessarily have the desire or ability to become farmers.[65] More suitable were those who came to Western Canada as individuals or family groups, relying on the same sort of "chains" of information and contact that earlier immigrants had used, ever since the original group left Yorkshire for the Maritimes in the eighteenth century.[66]

Other English immigrants were assisted to Canada in the late nineteenth century by the Sons of England Benevolent Society. Established in Toronto in 1874 to help poor and needy English immigrants, the Sons of England augmented the efforts of the St George's Society, established some forty years earlier, to help poor or sick English immigrants. The Sons of England were more than a charitable organization. They sought to maintain cultural ties between the motherland and the English throughout the world by promoting collective memory through events and even large-scale tours back to England. Loyalty to both the Crown and Protestantism, in a country with large Irish and French Catholic populations, gave this organization a political flair. Thus, the Sons of England, like the St George's Societies, showed the maintenance of an English identity in Canada and the need for many English immigrants to rely on their cultural tradition in their adjustment to life in North America.[67]

Into the Twentieth Century

In the early twentieth century, more urban workers came to Canada, even though farm workers and farmers with capital were what the country needed.[68] But the demographic impact of English immigration on communities in the Canadian West was clear. The 1911 census revealed that over 80 per cent of the people of Magrath, and over half of those in Cardston and Raymond (all in Alberta) claimed an English ethnicity.[69] In 1921 Manitoba's largest ethnic group was English, comprising 28 per cent of the population.[70] The English also dominated the immigrant population of British Columbia for some time – in 1921 they formed 42 per cent of its entire population.[71] Some were assisted. In 1905, the Leeds City Council funded a group of two single men and six families under the Unemployed

Workmen Act, passed that same year.[72] There were many Bolton cotton workers too, about 500 between 1912 and 1926.[73] And a Harvesters' Scheme of 1928 brought some 8,500 British miners to the Prairies for harvest season. Most were English, though few settled permanently.[74]

New Patterns

In the early twentieth century, English migrants to North America continued to prefer Canada over the United States. In the first decade of the century 525,950 people arrived in the United States from England, Scotland, and Wales (with peaks in 1903 and 1907). During the following decade that number fell to 342,000 in large part because the English were going to Canada instead. By the First World War, a mere 18 per cent of all English and Welsh emigrants were choosing the United States. The 1920s saw even fewer total numbers and lower proportions. The Emergency Quota Act of 1921, which restricted all immigrants to 3 per cent of their numbers as recorded in the 1910 census, was not the main reason why. The Act favoured the British along with other northwestern Europeans, but the British filled their quota only twice, in 1923 and 1924. They simply preferred Canada and other parts of the Commonwealth.[75]

English immigrants to the United States were not only falling in number but also increasingly likely to return to England. Of the roughly 33,000 English who arrived in the United States in 1921, about 8,000 – nearly a quarter – returned that same year. In 1928 alone about 7,300 English arrived, and roughly 6,000 returned – an astonishingly high ratio. Many of the returnees had intended to do so all along as seasonal migrants, but opportunities were also dwindling for the more traditional occupations that had characterized the immigrants of the previous century.[76] The 1930s were marred by the Great Depression, and in the entire decade only 61,813 English, Scots, Welsh, and Scots Irish arrived, and record numbers returned to Britain.[77] The era of extensive English immigration to the United States was over, though the cultural and economic relationship they had helped create between Britain and the United States remained.[78]

One important reason why increasing numbers went to Canada, Australia, and New Zealand was the British Empire Settlement Act of 1922, which offered fresh incentives to settle there instead of the United States. The Empire's expanding economies and cheap or free land, along with assisted passages, could not be matched by the United States, which by this time had less demand for foreign labour. In fact, the great majority of all English immigrants to Canada arrived in the twentieth century: nearly two-thirds who arrived before 1950 did so between 1900 and the early 1930s – the era of Canada's greatest period of industrialization, in which the English played a vital role.[79]

As the twentieth century proceeded and Canada overtook the United States as the primary English destination, people from North Yorkshire continued to cross the ocean with hope for the future. Those leaving for Canada in the years preceding the First World War included Rosedale natives Watson and Hannah Mary Hicks, who left sometime between 1913 and 1916. In 1913 Allin Swales left Applegarth Farm in Fryup, about 8 kilometres north of Rosedale, and settled in Nutana, near Saskatoon, where he had friends to help him get work for a farmer for $30 a month, on his "little Garden of 160 acres." Swales remarked on the beautiful country, the gardens and views that went for miles, as well as plentiful work.[80] In August he wrote again and made comparisons between English and Canadian crops and livestock, and, indicating how rapidly things were changing in the new century, reported that he saw "an areoplane which flew beautiful."[81] And the family of J.W. Robinson of Danby were very lucky indeed when they left in 1912: they were all booked on the *Titanic* but arrived in Southampton too late to board the doomed liner. They took a later ship and settled on a farm in Saskatchewan.[82]

That the Robinson family narrowly escaped disaster aboard the *Titanic* is a suitable last case of North Yorkshire migration to North America, because the far greater disaster of the First World War was just around the corner. That war marked the true end of the century, and an end to the long pattern of English migration. For after that war the numbers of English immigrants plummeted, especially as the Great Depression took hold. And though English migration resumed after the Second World War, it was of a far different nature altogether.[83] And North Yorkshire had entered a new modern phase of its history, as did North America, in no small part because of the people who had left one place for the other.

Conclusion and Epilogue

My thoughts often go to Askrigg I should like much to see it once again, it will ever be dear to me, more so than any other place on earth.

MATTHEW DINSDALE

Our portrait of North Yorkshire people in North America offers some noteworthy findings and conclusions. It reveals that the precise place-to-place migration patterns from Britain to America, which defined British migration during the colonial period, persisted to a considerable extent well into the nineteenth century.[1] Most left specific parts of Yorkshire for specific parts of North America, those leaving the lead district of the Yorkshire Dales for the Upper Mississippi being the most conspicuous. Here they applied their skills at mining and smelting to become landowning farmers, and later, leaders in business and politics. Those who left the North York Moors and eastern coastal areas were also quite place-specific in their destinations, choosing mainly Ontario, where they could settle near past neighbours and acquaintances.

As the United States and Canada expanded and developed, they offered fresh options. Newly available areas in Iowa, the Great Plains, Texas, and the Far West meant more diffusion in settlement. But essential migration patterns remained. Like other largely agrarian immigrant groups settling at the same time – such as the Dutch in West Michigan and Iowa, or the Norwegians and Swedes in Minnesota – those from North Yorkshire followed relatives and friends to specific places.[2] Chain migration through personal information was the norm. Unlike other groups, however, they never formed lasting ethnic communities. The few and feeble attempts at doing so were short-lived and abortive. Like other English in North America, those from North Yorkshire had enough cultural similarity with most Americans to render such settlements or colonies restrictive and unnecessary.

Yet, our story also cautions against assuming an English "invisibility" in America, because North Yorkshire immigrants did behave ethnically. Though they did not form ethnic communities, they did associate with others from North Yorkshire when they could. Those who went to the Upper Mississippi were noticeable in their accents and dialect, their looks, behaviour, leadership in the lead industry and business and politics, and so on. Others stood out for their farming methods and prejudices against America's rough character and social habits. And others, especially those from industrial and urban backgrounds and members of the elite, were visible for their unsuitability on the frontier – even in well-settled parts of Canada.

At the same time, it is also clear that North Yorkshire immigrants – like most English immigrants – enjoyed significant cultural and economic advantages, especially in their religious and social traditions, relatively high levels of skill, a tradition of occupational mobility, and perhaps most significantly, their language. While it is true that their accent and dialect could make them conspicuous, that peculiarity was often more amusing than problematic and overshadowed by a more profound similarity. They could communicate and associate immediately with Americans and could move more freely and confidently to seize opportunities. In the United States they seemed less foreign than most other immigrants and assimilated relatively speedily. Those who went to Canada had even greater similarities and advantages, for there the culture was even more English in character, and Canada was still politically attached to Britain. Though some English in the late century were resented in cities like Toronto for not having the right skills and temperament, most – including the cases we have seen from North Yorkshire – enjoyed cultural similarity and affinity, if not invisibility. This was also largely true of those in the United States. Looking at this portrait of North Yorkshire people in North America, it is hard to argue with Charlotte Erickson's early assertion that "perhaps no other immigrants came so well prepared psychologically as the English," and that it is difficult "to imagine circumstances more propitious to the[ir] rapid assimilation … in rural America."[3]

Other observed traits of English immigrants as a whole are confirmed and enhanced by our portrait of those from North Yorkshire: the proportions of those escaping sheer poverty were lower than other groups, a trait due in part to the more advanced state of the Britain's rapidly industrializing economy – and a long tradition of chain migration to both

Canada and the United States. So many of our stories show people who had substantial resources, sometimes very substantial, like the Russells, who were already wealthy when they moved from Castle Bolton to Nebraska. And though they were exceptional, many others were able to sell household and farming implements, livestock, even land to fund their move. It is not surprising that increasing English migration to America occurred during times of economic growth in England. And yet, many with resources were influenced by push factors that pointed to a bleak future in England. Some prosperous farmers left because they knew that their sons would never be able to own or even rent farms in Yorkshire. It must be stressed that many of the people featured in this portrait had poor backgrounds. Those who required government assistance to get to Nova Scotia and other parts of Canada struggled hard. The Gunnerside miners who were described to Parliament in 1818 were about as poor and desperate as people could get. Some were going hungry and could not even feed or clothe their children. But they did not leave – could not leave – until the economy recovered in the 1820s. By the time they left, they had scraped together enough resources. As we have seen, some of the miner-farmers who left the Yorkshire Dales for the Upper Mississippi were poor, but not desperately so. They had things to sell and people to help them, though their declining lead industry made the push very real.

Timing was crucial. When the lead boom ended in the early 1830s, the first large movement from the Dales to the Upper Mississippi began, and later movements correlated with swings in the lead industry. Push and pull forces worked together in a complex way: constant communication between the Dales and Upper Mississippi created a tantalizing information base and social network that prospective emigrants could rely on for long-term plans. The attraction was always there, and a downturn in Yorkshire's industry could signal the time to leave. Conversely – as happened with English farmers at mid-century – improving conditions and rising wages in Yorkshire gave some people the means to get to America. Paradoxically, leaving England during times of improvement could make sense – better to get to America and buy good cheap land before it was taken by others. In this way Yorkshire immigrants in North America were opportunistic, in the best sense of that word: they had a spirit of determination and adventure, tempered with a pragmatism that enabled them to take full advantage of their abilities and culture, and make better lives for themselves and their children. Their resourcefulness was remarkable, often astonishing, as was their resilience, as seen in their harrowing ocean journeys. Their skills, resources, hard work, and character – as well as their ambition and willingness to take risks – brought fresh strength to North America.

Overall, therefore, it appears that pull factors were most germane to the story of North Yorkshire migration to North America. Whether leaving lead mining in the Pennines or ironstone mining or farm labouring in the Moors, or any kind of work in the large varied area in between the western and eastern extremes of the region, the most common, powerful, and compelling force was the promise of North America, especially its land. Those with farming backgrounds might first enter a trade or even professional life and remain there. But many kept their agrarian spirit, became landowning farmers, and then perhaps entered business, a profession, politics, or some other position in their community. Lucille Campey concludes that for Canada "English immigration was driven primarily by a desire for economic self-betterment. Its motivation was *never* solely a flight from poverty."[4] As we have seen, some were escaping poverty. But even they probably had positive motives as well. Along with the attraction of economic and social improvement was "the freedom and benefits of a more egalitarian society."[5] This conclusion applies generally to North Yorkshire immigrants in all of North America.

The interconnectedness of North Yorkshire and North America is remarkable. In some ways, outmigration acted as a safety valve. North Yorkshire had an expanding population but shrinking employment opportunities; its population had grown faster than its employment requirements. Emigration to North America gave the farmers and others who stayed behind a chance to adjust to the changing economy; those leaving for the United States and Canada helped North Yorkshire's society and economy adjust to industrialization and modernization. Altogether, it appears that North Yorkshire and North America consisted of an "organic whole," with a symbiotic relationship operating through the people, capital, skills, ideas, and culture that left the former for the latter.[6]

In their act of leaving, North Yorkshire migrants also reflected the larger whole of English migration to America. The power of letters to encourage, inform, and create migration chains is a nearly universal feature of their story, and it affirms the conclusion of Dudley Baines that the decision to leave for America was based not so much on escaping local conditions but on networks of information that allowed careful calculations of what was to be gained and lost through migration.[7] Letters were the key. They provide a clearer understanding of how the system worked and help explain the high level of interest in specific villages of Yorkshire, their exact choice of destination, and means of adjustment. The epic drama of leaving a town or village, getting to the port, and then taking the incomprehensibly daunting, hard, and dangerous voyage – as described in such detail in so many letters – was experienced by others from England. So too was the often difficult journey into the American interior. Being willing and able to endure such a trek says a lot about the people who made it. It was the brave and strong, those willing to take risks and suffer great discomfort and possibly death itself – and sometimes the desperate – who were willing to undergo such a journey. It forever shaped their character and gave them an inner strength and resilience that helped them succeed and build new societies and economies.

In North America, North Yorkshire immigrants showed an ability to take up a new life, whether in agriculture, industry, or craft work. As with those from other parts of England, they came from a variety of backgrounds and experience that gave them options and high success rates. Many from the Dales to the Upper Mississippi had been miner-farmers in Yorkshire and did the same in Iowa, Wisconsin, or Illinois, usually long enough to get established and then set aside mining and smelting for larger scale farming, or perhaps for business and politics. And, like others from England, many Yorkshire immigrants had a craft or other skills to rely on if necessary or desirable. It was quite common for immigrants to take up farming in America with little or no immediate experience, a reminder of their complex and varied backgrounds – a reflection of England's more advanced state of industrialization, urbanization, and economic diversification.

Others were ill-prepared, some in ill-conceived English colonies, which soon withered because they did not fit the local farming requirements, and because the English did not necessarily need or want to live in such communities. The colonies' failures are more indications of the ability of the English to fit in with North American culture. This was especially so in Canada, where the immigrants followed each other and helped one another, while maintaining their identity in a culture that still had largely English traits.

The adjustments to North American life were not always easy, the work could be incredibly hard, and those who failed are probably under-reported because some returned to England without writing letters.

The environment in the United States and Canada could be shockingly different, in its scale, isolation, climate, and farming conditions. Native Americans were one example of the deep cultural differences. Rather few Yorkshire immigrants met Native peoples, but when they did, they expressed a mix of appreciation, even admiration, though also a sense of superiority based partly on their Christian religion. This was not surprising: religion was the foundation of the lives of the majority of North Yorkshire immigrants, as it was for English immigrants generally. It was the key to their identity. As we have seen throughout, religion was a basis for almost everything: decisions to leave, how to act and think, how to live. Churches were places not only of worship and fellowship, but of interaction with Americans and other English, and an essential institution for thriving in America. And the story of the Mormon Longstroth family is a reminder of how religion could also divide people, even families, while unifying and Americanizing people of that tradition.

Initially, North Yorkshire immigrants concentrated in Nova Scotia, Ontario, and the Upper Mississippi, but they did not limit themselves to those places. By the mid-century they had branched out into California as well as Iowa, Texas and other places new to settlement. Later they went farther west and filtered in the Prairies in both the United States and Canada. Their skills as miners, ambitions as farmers, and tradition of mobility – together with networks laid by previous Yorkshire immigrants – combined to expand their diaspora. In the United States rising tensions over reform, slavery, and catastrophic war posed new challenges, but generally this only bound them closer to their new country. The Civil War was a crucible that forged them into new Americans. Afterwards, even as transportation networks expanded and migration became easier, new difficulties arose. The farming economy was changing, leaving less room in the Midwest. So, they stretched out onto the Great Plains instead – some leaving comfortable situations in ancient English villages for sod huts out on the vast prairies of Nebraska, Kansas, Wyoming and other places. But their privations were usually temporary: some established estates scarcely imaginable back in England.

After the Civil War, people around Rosedale showed fresh interest in America as land agents like Thomas Wilson settled families who were frustrated or who saw a dim future there. But in Texas and the Great Plains, lands and farming were very different, as was life itself. It was partly for these reasons that people from North Yorkshire and England turned their attention to Canada, where more familiar kinds of land offered fresh farming opportunities, and they could remain British subjects among people much like themselves. Though some were ridiculed for their lack of skill and haughty character, these were a minority. Altogether, migration from North Yorkshire to North America – from colonial days through the long nineteenth century that spanned the American Revolution to the First World War – was impressive for its continuity and wealth of experience and contributions. Through these remarkable people we see features common to many English immigrants in general, and we also see features as distinctly North Yorkshire as the stone walls, ancient churches, and exquisite scenery they left behind.

Epilogue

If you think of coming back we think England is the best place yet.

WILLIAM ATKINSON

As we have seen, deciding to move to America and then actually doing it often brought doubts and regrets, at least for a while. After settling, especially among relatives and friends, most were satisfied. But this did not mean they had lost their love for Yorkshire. On the contrary, as Americans or Canadians, many thought about their old home frequently and intensely. Memories and emotions grew, even while they and their children assimilated.

Three decades after their migration the Willis family were still think-ing about their native Wensleydale so often that their relatives became concerned. As their niece remarked, "I should think by this time they will have grown quite American and almost forgot England." And when she reported that Wensleydale had "no snow of consequence" that winter and that "spring is early ... we are now busy with our lambing time," the Willis family likely thought about their old village fondly.[8] Others continued to dwell on the place they left behind, especially as they aged. In 1881 Richard Buxton, now sixty-eight and in the last year of his life, was often thinking about Yorkshire. Writing nearly thirty years after his move to Wisconsin, he was now a widower, and wrote from Benton back to his brother William, who had remained in Gunnerside, in early 1881: "I many times think about you and the family and the people at Gunnerside and how many have passed away to their long home since we left and it will be the way of us all soon the Lord Grant that we may be round ready and meet with those that have gone before. ... While I am writing I am alone and often feel desolate and forlorn ... And a tear occasionally will trickle down my cheek."[9]

Problems and setbacks only intensified memories of England. Two years after Richard wrote his letter, his brother John, who was living alone 40 kilometres away, reported that he had sold his farm but still lived in the house belonging to it. What he had done was "lend a man some money on note he was not secured ... And the man bust up and it was a dead loss. He could not recover anything." John was able to scrape together what he had left and bought 80 acres on which he lived and raised livestock.[10] But within a few years new problems arose: stock and grain prices were falling, and John felt the pinch. "Everything in farming ... seems to have a downward tendency in prices," he said, and the winters seemed to be getting harsher. His reflections on his children and grandchildren, and his faith in God, carried him through.[11] A year later he moved to Mineral Point, about 15 kilometres from his farm.[12]

Letters continued to provide links that often got more substantial as time went on. Toward the end of the century photos were commonly included, as were locks of hair, and it was still taken for granted that a letter from America would be passed around in the village where it was sent. In 1895 Thomas Walker ended a letter with a promise to send pictures "some time this week." He sent the letter that day, even though "it is very cold this morning 15 degrees below zero." And thinking about his old friends in Yorkshire, he continued, "give my kind love to all enquiring Friends and old chumes Metcalf Graham and Robert Mason and Richard Mason you can let aney one read my letter."[13]

As the immigrants grew older and watched their children marry and move away to raise their own families, they became more focused on their health and that of those still in Yorkshire. It was often a main feature and purpose of the letters to inquire about their friends and family who never joined them, and to see whether they were still "in the land of the living."[14] There was often a sadness, even a depression as people aged together but on opposite sides of the ocean, especially between parents and children who were separated.[15] When Samuel Fowler Smith died in 1879, after a highly successful career in industry in Indiana, his final thoughts were likely of his native Wetherby, where the church he attended as a boy still contains a brass lectern with the inscription, "In Memory of Samuel Fowler Smith."[16]

In 1895, forty-six years after leaving Wensleydale, the nearly seventy-year-old Thomas Walker again took up his pen to write his cousin back in Askrigg. He was just happy to be alive, never having fully recovered from the lung ailments he had contracted while serving in the Civil War, when his doctor told him some thirty years previously that he had not much longer to live. Thomas's brother Peter had left for Iowa, his sons for Nebraska, and one Tanner Walker homesteaded unsuccessfully in Colorado in 1887. But Thomas was still farming in Preston, Wisconsin, where bad weather and the Gilded Age culture were discouraging: "We had a long drought last summer the corn crop was allmost a failure all over the North West thare is a great deal of suffering in Nebraska and the decotas the rail road companies are shiping in to those parts donations … to the drought stricken sufferers."[17]

In March of 1900 Thomas Walker was seventy-five when from Preston, Wisconsin he wrote to his cousin's son about that cousin's death, also seventy-five. Looking back on a hard but rewarding life and perhaps growing nostalgic, he announced, "[I]t is 51 years the 25th of Febuarey, last since I left my naitive shore [.] It does not look very long to look at. I have seen a great maney ups and downs since that time but the best of all the Lord has been with me and he will be with me to the end if I trust him to the end." One of his recent "downs" was a bad fall on the ice, which he compared to a similar head injury he had sustained in Askrigg fifty-five years earlier – four years before he emigrated in 1849. Walker refers to John Dinsdale's daughter, who was in New York, indicating that the first generation of immigrants stayed in touch over the years and got to know each other's family members. That was certainly true of his relationship with the Dinsdales – Matthew had prepared the way for other Askrigg people, and John had accompanied Walker on the *Saxony* in 1849. Now, fifty-one years later, his nearest neighbour was a Mrs Richard Dinsdale. He was also following the latest news from South Africa about the Boer War, hoping for a quick end.[18]

Well into the twentieth century the Buxton clan in Swaledale kept in touch with those who had left for Wisconsin a half-century earlier. In 1906 George reported to his brother William that "Houses are very hard to sell in Gunnerside as there is a good few empty houses … I have little to tell you, as swaledale is very dull."[19] And the following year he said that he offered to sell his house for 55 pounds "and no less," but that he could still not sell it.[20] The annual Gunnerside Fair had become a mere shadow of its former self as "there were very few cattle and sheep shown" that year.[21] Three years later it was even worse – a "thin show as practically most of the sheep have been sold previously," though there was a concert to enjoy.[22]

As the immigrants reminisced about Yorkshire, their old homes and villages in Yorkshire continued to change. The lead districts continued their decline. Between 1801 and 1861 Swaledale and Upper Wensleydale lost over 90 per cent of their natural increase in population, due mostly to miners leaving their declining industry. Lower Wensleydale's loss of population was not as great – about half – because it was less dependent on mining. Swaledale, which was more dependent on mining, endured its greatest depopulation when mining activity fell. By 1891, when mining had all but ended, Swaledale lost nearly 40 per cent of its population as recorded in 1881.[23] The total number of Swaledale emigrants to America in the nineteenth century was about 2,000 persons, but about five times this number left for other places in England, such as Lancashire and the West Riding, to take up work in textiles or other industries.[24] For Swaledale and Wensleydale, as for England generally, emigration to America and internal migration within England apparently did not substitute for each other; rather they were complementary, and together lowered the population.[25]

But this depopulation struck the local economy hard. Crafts, industries, trade, and farm profits all suffered, as did traditional institutions. In the 1870s and 1880s the schools in Gunnerside and Reeth lost between a quarter and half of their students on the register. Likewise, the Methodist chapels lost critical masses of their members to emigration. As the local population dropped so did trade. One Reeth shopkeeper wrote in 1890: "Nothing but poverty; getting worse and worse and worse. Mines still poor, Trade horribly bad. I offer many things at below cost price."[26] Naturally, the decline could be seen in the deteriorating physical appearance of villages, especially the abandonment of houses and other buildings. Remarking on the effects of the vanishing lead industry, one observed that: "A melancholy array of deserted Hamlets in Swaledale, and to some extent in Wensleydale, are eloquent of it recent departure."[27] By 1891 one in ten houses in Wensleydale and one in four in Swaledale were uninhabited, some of them falling into states of dereliction.[28]

Thus, some North Yorkshire immigrants visiting their old village were shocked. And yet the hills and dales, walls and ancient villages, and churches remained. In May of 1900, Dixon and Elizabeth Cottingham left Dubuque with four other Yorkshire immigrant couples to see cousins in the old country. "Oh, what hills," Dixon could only exclaim, upon his return to Wensleydale. And Bolton Castle was as fine as ever. Cottingham also remarked: "Passed a lead mine, but no one working now." And travelling to Northallerton and then to York by train, they entered York Minster and gasped: "What a monster of a building – so fine inside. ... Oh, my, what sights we saw."[29]

When she was sixteen years old, in 1875, Matthew Dinsdale's daughter Annie and his wife Mary Ann left Matthew in Wisconsin and returned to Askrigg to see Mary's relatives and as much of England as possible. They reported the details back to Matthew, who was apparently not well enough to join them. "Askrigg looks clean and nice," Mary Ann observed. Annie, who had never been to England, was enchanted, as she soaked up the history and culture of her family's origin. Fountains Abbey enthralled her, as did the old local customs and traditions. "I Loved England," she gushed in her Memoirs, "and if it had not been that my dear father was on the other side of the ocean, I should have been loath to leave. English life appealed to me very strongly. I felt the dignity and culture and charm of the older civilization."[30]

Annie was the only child of Matthew and Mary Ann Dinsdale to survive their parents. Mary Ann died of a paralysis in 1896. Matthew died in 1898. Annie married Norwegian immigrant Magnus Swenson, who became president of the Norwegian-American Steamship Company. Annie graduated from the University of Wisconsin in 1880 and died in 1935, but not before establishing her family archive which tells us just part of the remarkable story of migration from North Yorkshire to North America.

Notes

Introduction

1 Richards, *Britannia's Children*, 4–6, 11, 119; Belich, *Replenishing the Earth*, 126, 152. I have calculated these percentage figures from the passenger data provided in N.H. Carrier and J.R. Jeffery, *External Migration: A Study of the Available Statistics, 1815–1950*, 95–6. These figures are for 1815–1929 and include the English and Welsh. Between 1815 and 1880 – before the migratory shift toward the Dominions – nearly 80 per cent chose the United States, and the remaining 20 per cent were roughly evenly divided between Canada and Australasia. (The numbers for South Africa and other places are too small to affect the percentage figures significantly.)

2 Campey, *Ignored but Not Forgotten*, 24.

3 Burk, *Old World, New World*, 380. Churchill had reported this quote of Bismarck in 1938 and agreed. See also Evans, "England's Migrant Crisis," 40–5.

4 John Bristed, *America and Her Resources*, quoted in Fischer, *Albion's Seed*, 831.

5 Tocqueville, *Democracy in America*, 429.

6 Emerson, *English Traits*, 42, quoted in Burk, *Old World, New World*, 306.

7 The 1790 census reveals that people of English origin or ancestry comprised about 60 per cent of the white population. And during this period "Anglicization" was growing as many Americans in search of their identity were standardizing their culture. Most white Americans, then, saw their heritage as largely English. See Spickard, *Almost All Aliens*, 60–2; Menard, "Migration."

8   Fischer, *Albion's Seed*; Van Vugt, *British Immigration*, vol.1, xi–xxiv. The
    Englishness of colonial American culture was "pronounced," especially
    in the South. See Gleeson, "England and the Antebellum South," in
    Gleeson, *English Ethnicity and Culture*, 139–54, especially page 140.

9   Oscar Handlin's *The Uprooted: The Epic Story of the Great Migrations that
    Made the American People* (Boston: Little, Brown and Company, 1973)
    does not even mention the English, while John Bodnar's rejoinder, *The
    Transplanted: A History of Immigrants in Urban America* (Bloomington:
    Indiana University Press, 1985) only mentions them in passing.
    The same is true for other surveys of immigration. See discussion in
    Spickard, *Almost All Aliens*, 4–7.

10 Campey, *Ignored but Not Forgotten*, 23.

11 Ibid., 22.

12 Conzen, et al., "The Invention of Ethnicity," 3–41.

13 See the essays in Gleeson, ed., *English Ethnicity and Culture* especially
    Donald M. MacRaild, "Ethnic Conflict and English Associational
    Culture in America," 37–63.

14 Bueltmann and MacRaild, *The English Diaspora*, 2–5, 9–12, 112, 287,
    310.

15 Berthoff, *British Immigrants in Industrial America*; Jeremy, *Transatlantic
    Industrial Revolution*; Van Vugt, *British Buckeyes*, ch. 5.

16 Tucker, *Samuel Slater*.

17 Milwaukee, for example, enumerated 36 per cent of its labour force in
    1850 as skilled, while 54 per cent of the city's British immigrants were
    skilled. The labour force of other cities exhibits this general pattern. See
    Erickson, "English," 330.

18 For a convenient collection of her early articles and essays and
    methodology, see Erickson, *Leaving England*.

19 Van Vugt, *Britain to America*, 77.

20 Baines, *Migration in a Mature Economy*. In this work Baines challenges
    some of the conclusions of Brinley Thomas in his works *Migration and
    Economic Growth* (1954), and *Migration and Urban Development* (1972).
    For details on Baines's method, see pp. 5–6 and chapter 4. Baines could
    not differentiate Yorkshire's three ridings.

21 Ibid., 282.

22 Many examples can be found in Van Vugt, *Britain to America*, and
    Van Vugt, *British Buckeyes*.

23 Campey, *Ignored but Not Forgotten*, 23. (The emphasis is mine.)

24 Ibid., 24.
25 On the general coherence of the "long nineteenth century" defined in this way, see Osterhammel, *The Transformation of the World*.
26 Baines, *Migration in a Mature Economy*, especially ch. 8.
27 See, for example, Rowe, *The Hard Rock Men*; Tweedale, *Sheffield Steel and America*; Todd, *The Cornish Miner in America*.
28 See, for example, Blewett, *Yankee Yorkshireman*.
29 Campey, *Ignored but Not Forgotten*, 24.
30 Hastings, *Essays in North Riding History*, 137; Deane and Cole, *British Economic Growth*, 108, table 25; 115, table 26.
31 Richards, "Malthus," 53.

Chapter One

1 Yorkshire was not officially split into the "ridings" of North, West, and East Yorkshire until 1889, and North Yorkshire was not created as a separate county until 1972, when the ridings were effectively abolished.
2 Hallas, *Rural Responses to Industrialization*.
3 Also known as the "North Yorkshire Moors." I will be using the more conventional name "North York Moors."
4 Hempton, *Methodism*.
5 Rudolph, *Francis Asbury*; Ludwig, *Francis Asbury: God's Circuit Rider*.
6 Hey, *History of Yorkshire*, 281, 384, 414. These distinctive cultural traits can also be seen in Yorkshire immigrants in New Zealand. See Watson, "Cooked in True Yorkshire Fashion," 169–84.
7 Robinson, "English Associational Culture," 131–52.
8 Hey, *A History of Yorkshire*, 384, 387.
9 Baines, *Migration in a Mature Economy*, ch. 8. Baines also concluded that internal migration and emigration did not act as substitutes; see p. 247.
10 See the database compiled by Charlotte Erickson (hereafter referred to the "Erickson Database") and explored by me, including an introduction, overview, its primary sources and methodology on in Van Vugt, "Relocating the English Diaspora," 8–36. Remarkably few in the database had been born in North Yorkshire but left from other counties: in addition to the five cases who left from the West Riding, there were only two who left from Lancashire, and one who left from Durham. The database does not allow reliable figures for internal migration within North Yorkshire before emigration overseas.

11 Raistrick, *Mines and Miners of Swaledale*, ch. 6; Fieldhouse and Jennings, *History of Richmond and Swaledale*, 198–9.
12 Hallas, *Rural Responses to Industrialization*, 193.
13 Ibid., 310.
14 Dales Countryside Museum display, Hawes, Yorkshire, 2014; Clough, *Lead Smelting Mills*, 108.
15 Raistrick, *Mines and Miners of Swaledale*, 85.
16 Cooper, *Muker*, 51–2.
17 Ibid.
18 Raistrick and Jennings, *History of Lead Mining*, 313.
19 Spensley, "Historical Development of Lead Mining,"190. For a thorough account of Wensleydale's mining industry, see Spensley, *Mines and Miners*.
20 Bagenal, *Miners & Farmers*, 8.
21 Hastings, "The Revolt of the Field in the North Riding of Yorkshire" in Hastings, *Essays in North Riding History*.

Chapter Two

W.H. Auden said that Keld was "one of my holy places." (See his "Streams")
1 Evans, *Emigrants*.
2 This source refers to Dods's home village as "Great Neck," an error as "Great Heck" is the only place in Yorkshire that is close to that name. It is possible that this "Land of Neck," later called "Great Neck," was a confusion of Dods's North Yorkshire village of Great Heck. See also Ransome, "Village Tensions," 365–81.
3 Ransome, "Wives for Virginia," 3–18.
4 Morris, *Dalesmen of the Mississippi*, 16.
5 "The Transportation of Felons to America 1717–1775," Quarter Sessions Records, North Yorkshire County Record Office (hereafter cited as NYCRO), Northallerton, North Yorkshire.
6 Morgan, *Slavery and Servitude*.
7 "Emigration to Canada: North Riding Pioneers," *Whitby Gazette*, 6 August 1948; Campey, *Ignored but Not Forgotten*, 39.
8 Dixon, "Aspects of Yorkshire Emigration," vol. 4, 1688.
9 Campey, *Ignored but Not Forgotten*, 41–2.
10 Bailyn, *Voyagers to the West*, 111, table 4.4. The numbers of English were 5,196, the number of Scots, 3,872, for a total of 9,068.

11 Ibid., 115, table 4.5.
12 Of course, some may also have left from Liverpool, though some from West Yorkshire likely chose to travel farther to eastern ports, just as some from North and South Yorkshire left from Liverpool, or some other port.
13 Based on Bailyn, *Voyagers to the West*, 216–17, table 6.4. Virtually none of those leaving London, for example were going to Nova Scotia. Put another way, 562 of the 622 English (90 per cent) who were going to Nova Scotia in the 1770s had left Yorkshire.
14 Ibid., 140, table 5.7.
15 Ibid., 146, table 5.10.
16 Campey, *Ignored but Not Forgotten*, 43.
17 Bailyn, *Voyagers to the West*, 163, table 5.14.
18 Ibid., 190–1, based on table 5.23. The corresponding figure of "positive" reasons for England as a whole is nearly 90 per cent. The broad "positive" category is Bailyn's.
19 East Riding Archives and Local Studies, DDX 1408 1/8.
20 Even those who arrived as individual servants were not necessarily destitute but found it wise to use that method of emigration in order to arrive with some savings. Van Vugt, "The British," in *A Nation of Peoples*, 78.
21 Campey, *Ignored but Not Forgotten*, 41.
22 Ibid., 43.
23 Ibid., 41.
24 Hastings, *Essays in North Riding History*, 137.
25 Campey, *Ignored but Not Forgotten*, 21.
26 Quoted in Campey, *Ignored but Not Forgotten*, 44.
27 Cashin, *King's Ranger*.
28 Campey, *Ignored but Not Forgotten*, 46. Eventually, up to 100,000 fled, half to Canada, and about 20,000 served in the British militia; see Wilson, "Loyalists in Canada."

Chapter Three

1 Hoock, *Scars of Independence*.
2 Van Vugt, "Did the Loss," 164–8.
3 Letter from John Adams, Minister to Britain, to John Jay, Secretary of State, reporting on his audience with the King, 2 June 1785, in National Archives, *Eyewitness*.
4 Gordon, *Empire of Wealth*, 94.

5   Taylor, *Civil War of 1812.*

6   A. Shaw, ed., *History of Dearborn County, Indiana: Her People, Industries and Institutions* (Indianapolis: B.F. Bowen, 1915); reprinted in Van Vugt, *British Immigration*, vol. 1, 110–11.

7   *Biographical and Genealogical History of Wayne, Fayette, Union and Franklin Counties, Indiana*, 2 vols (Chicago: Lewis Publishing Co., 1899); reprinted in Van Vugt, *British Immigration*, vol. 1, 114–15.

8   *History of Dearborn, Ohio, and Switzerland Counties, Indiana. From their Earliest Settlements, Containing a History of the Counties: Their Cities, Townships, Towns, Villages, Schools, and Churches; Reminiscences, Extracts, etc.; Local Statistics, Portraits of Early Settlers and Prominent Men; Biographies; Preliminary Chapters on the History of the North-West Territory, the State of Indiana, and the Indians* (Chicago: F.E. Weakley, Publishers, 1885); reprinted in Van Vugt, *British Immigration*, vol. 1, 122.

9   H.J. Eckley and W.T. Perry, eds., *History of Carroll and Harrison Counties, Ohio*, 2 vols (Chicago: Lewis, 1921); reprinted in Van Vugt, *British Immigration*, vol. 1, 123. A little farther south in Indiana, in Clark County on the Ohio River, Yorkshire immigrant James Howard was another pioneer who became the leading boat and ship builder of the region and helped boost the economy. He had originated from Oldham, in Lancashire but moved to West Yorkshire. See Van Vugt, *British Immigration*, vol. 1, 140–1.

10 Hallas, *Rural Responses to Industrialization*, 293.

11 Belich, *Replenishing the Earth*, 153–64.

12 *Hull Advertiser*, 20 April 1816, East Riding Archives, DDX 1408/1/6.

13 Albion, *Rise of New York Port*, 13, 15, 114.

14 Bueltmann and MacRaild, *The English Diaspora*, 34, table 1.3.

15 Campey, *Ignored but Not Forgotten*, 48.

16 Quoted in Campey, *Ignored but Not Forgotten*, 48.

17 Ibid., 71–3.

18 Ibid., 50, 73.

19 Elliott, "Regional Patterns," 63.

20 Campey, *Ignored but Not Forgotten*, 71. Bruce Elliott has explained the lack of records for immigrants to Canada, and has counted roughly 10,000 English immigrants arriving between 1815 and 1824. The English comprised between a fifth and a fourth of all arrivals there before 1820, and Yorkshire was the most common county of origin. Elliott counts roughly 300,000 English immigrants arriving in Canada before

Confederation in 1867. (See Elliott, "Regional Patterns," 53, 61.) The *Yorkshire Gazette* observed that in the first half of 1830 nearly 3,000 left from Hull, a figure triple that for all of 1829, and more than had left in the previous nine years. In the early 1830s emigration from North Yorkshire surged: nearly 6,000 sailed from Hull to Quebec between 1831 and 1834, and more than 6,000 left via Liverpool. In the same period more than a thousand sailed from Whitby and more than 500 from Stockton. North Riding emigration slackened between 1834 and the "Hungry Forties." See Hastings, *Essays in North Riding History*, 138, 141.

21   Elliott, "Regional Patterns," 65. Campey, *Ignored but Not Forgotten*, 71.

22   Campey, *Ignored but Not Forgotten*, 71.

23   Though the statistics for the origins of Canada's English immigrants are notoriously incomplete, Bruce Elliott has examined the English who provided their origin on their land registers during this period: nearly a third had come from Yorkshire, and an additional half from Yorkshire or nearby counties to the north. Elliott, "Regional Patterns," 57.

24   Campey, *Ignored but Not Forgotten*, 77.

25   Hastings, *Essays in North Riding History*, 140.

26   Hastings, "Chartism in the North Riding," 15.

27   Hastings, *Essays in North Riding History*, 139. Abstract of Census Returns 1831, 780, 783, 785, 787.

28   Parliamentary Papers 1833 V HC 612. Report of Select Committee on Agriculture. Evidence, 118, 120. Cited in Hastings, *Essays in North Riding History*, 140.

29   Campey, *Ignored but Not Forgotten*, 26.

30   Ibid., 95.

31   *Yorkshire Gazette*, 27 March 1830; 17 July 1830; 3 April 1830. Cited in Hastings, *Essays in North Riding History*, 138.

32   Hastings, *Essays in North Riding History*, 139.

33   *Yorkshire Gazette*, 19 April 1851, East Riding Archives and Local Studies, DDX 1408/1/6.

34   Campey, *Ignored but Not Forgotten*, 29.

35   Ibid., 31.

36   Ibid., 32.

37   In 1831 a third of the adult male immigrants to the United States were skilled craftsmen, whereas a quarter were farmers. But a little more than 10 per cent were labourers. Furthermore, workers in modernizing industries – especially those in textiles, metal production, and

engineering, who were more subject to technological unemployment
and recessions – altogether composed only about 16 per cent.
(Erickson, *Leaving England*, 237, table 6.4.). Because the writers of
some of the United States passenger lists, especially for those leaving
British ports, used dittos or even slashes in the occupational category,
often tagging all passengers as "labourers," Erickson and I have used
extensive, labour-intensive 1-in-10 sampling methods of the passenger
lists, backed by statistical tests of significance, to avoid the obviously
careless and misleading lists and focus on those that had occupations
carefully filled in, for more accuracy. Raymond Cohn has questioned
the significant extent of skilled workers among English immigrants.
But the United States statistics, on which Cohn partly relies, are
based on all lists, including those with "labourers" or "labourers and
farmers" applied to all passengers with slashes or ditto marks, and so
they exaggerate the unskilled workers among the English (and Scots
and Welsh). See Cohn, "Occupation of English Immigrants," 377–87.
It is not hard to find English immigrants who were carelessly listed as
"labourers," and counted as such in the official statistics, but who, as
other, more personal sources show, were clearly people with specific
skills. Some examples of skilled persons who were enumerated as
"labourers" on the passenger lists include several miners, a bootmaker,
a woollen operative, a gardener, and a law student. For specific names,
origins, destinations, occupations, and other details, see the Erickson
Database, ID cases 1215, 766, 977, 169, 936, 1294, 1296. In their
assessment of English migrants to North America, which focuses in
large part on those who needed assistance, Bueltmann and MacRaild
are prepared to "revise up" the proportions of unskilled labourers
published in Erickson's and my work, but not significantly enough to
challenge our conclusions. See Bueltmann and MacRaild, *The English
Diaspora*, 49–50.

38 Ibid., 142–3.

39 Campey, *Seeking a Better Future*, 127. Other examples are noted in
later chapters.

40 Bueltmann and MacRaild, *The English Diaspora*, 32.

41 Erickson Database. Of the sixty-nine North Yorkshire immigrants
in the database, forty-eight have something recorded about their
education, and only four of them had none. (Ones whose education is
not stated could still have had some education.) Of the sixty-one with

some form of known education, ten were apprenticed or had "learned a trade." Of the twenty remaining, little is known except that they had some education, as stated in sources like county histories and marriage certificates. One had attended a Diocesan college (generally for bishops), and an Anglican school.

42 Baines, *Migration in a Mature Economy*, ch. 7, especially pp. 205–12; ch. 8, pp. 220–7. Baines effectively challenges the Brinley Thomas thesis that the rising emigration was coming from rural areas and linked to swings in Britain's building cycle. See Thomas, *Migration and Economic Growth*.

43 Campey, *Seeking a Better Future*, 205.

44 Hastings, *Essays in North Riding History*, 145, citing *Yorkshire Gazette*, 30 July 1836.

45 Campey, *Ignored but Not Forgotten*, 27.

46 Ibid., 76.

47 Hastings, *Essays in North Riding History*, 139; Campey, *Ignored but Not Forgotten*, 27, 78.

48 Bruce S. Elliott, "Regional Patterns," 69.

49 Campey, *Seeking a Better Future*, 292.

50 Hastings, *Essays in North Riding History*, 138.

51 "Extracts from 'An Old Account Book for the Township of Brough commencing in the year of our Lord 1770'," display at St Michael's Church, Brough, Cumbria, July 2014.

52 Dixon, "Aspects of Yorkshire Emigration," 1466.

53 Dixon, "Aspects of Yorkshire Emigration," 1467; cites Raistrick and Jennings, 302.

54 *Sheffield Independent*, 6 February 1841.

55 Hastings, *Essays in North Riding History*, 143.

56 Ibid. The 1841 Census indicates that Leyburn's population had fallen by 174 people since 1831.

57 Cowan, *British Emigration*, 206.

58 Hastings, *Essays in North Riding History*, 141.

59 Ibid.

60 Campey, *Ignored but Not Forgotten*, 82.

61 Ibid., 30.

62 Baines, *Migration in a Mature Economy*, 71; Bueltmann and MacRaild, *The English Diaspora*, 36.

63 Hirota, *Expelling the Poor*.

Chapter Four

1   Clough, *Lead Smelting Mills*, 105.

2   Raistrick, *Mines and Miners of Swaledale*, 82.

3   Ibid.

4   Buxton Family Papers. Dales Countryside Museum, Hawes, Yorkshire.

5   Fieldhouse and Jennings, *History of Richmond and Swaledale*, 231; Barker, "Lead Miners of Swaledale," 4.

6   Barker, "The Lead Miners of Swaledale," 2–3. The 1851 census indicates that Reeth, the largest village in Swaledale, had only 7 per cent of its population enumerated as miners, while the figure for the area as a whole was 17 per cent.

7   Smelters averaged about £43 annually from 1851 to 1881. See Hallas, *Rural Responses to Industrialization*, 178, table 7.11.

8   Museum display, Dales Countryside Museum, Hawes.

9   Clough, *Lead Smelting Mills*, 27.

10   Bishop, "Women and Mining Communities," 30–31.

11   Quoted in Bishop, "Women and Mining Communities," 31.

12   Ibid.

13   Hallas, *Rural Responses to Industrialization*, 170–1.

14   Bishop, "Women and Mining Communities," 31.

15   Fieldhouse and Jennings, *History of Richmond and Swaledale*, 228–9; Clough, *Lead Smelting Mills*, 10, 18.

16   Bagenal, *Miners & Farmers*, 38, 40–1.

17   Raistrick, *Mines and Miners of Swaledale*, 47–9.

18   Fieldhouse and Jennings, *History of Richmond and Swaledale*, 212–15.

19   Fairbairn, *Lead Mine Waggons*, 8.

20   *The Morning Chronicle*, 14 March 1818, Buxton Family Papers, Dales Countryside Museum, Hawes, Yorkshire.

21   "The Travelling Preacher," *Methodist Magazine*, 19 February 1822, cited in Batty, *Gunnerside*, 15.

22   Fieldhouse and Jennings, *History of Richmond and Swaledale*, 216–17.

23   Ibid., 216–17.

24   Dixon, "Aspects of Yorkshire Emigration," vol. 4, 1449.

25   Diary of Edward Broderick, 16 October 1830, Richmondshire Museum, Richmond, North Yorkshire.

26   Fieldhouse and Jennings, *A History of Richmond and Swaledale*, 220–1.

27   Hallas, *Rural Responses to Industrialization*, 174–7.

28   Dixon, "Aspects of Yorkshire Emigration," vol. 4, 1433.
29   Raistrick, *Mines and Miners of Swaledale*, 19, 26.

Chapter Five

The chapter-opening quote from Samuel Fowler Smith comes from
Van Vugt, "An English Shoemaker in Indiana," 22.

1   Fender, *Sea Changes*; Gerber, *Authors of Their Lives*, 47.
2   Marjorie J. Harrison, ed., *My Dear Son: Letters to America 1852–1901*
     (York: Ainsty Books, 2005), 2–7.
3   Cited in Campey, *Seeking a Better Future*, 127.
4   Cited in Hallas, *Rural Responses to Industrialization*, 287.
5   Quoted in Malaney, "The Swaledale-Sharon Center Connection."
6   Letter to James Pratt, February 1849, Hunt Family Papers, Dales
     Countryside Museum, Hawes, Yorkshire. Published in Marriott, ed.,
     Those Who Left the Dales, 6–7. Notes to this letter claim that James
     Pratt "did not make the trip," but a James Pratt from Gunnerside did
     sail on the *Saxony* in 1849 (with his brother Metcalf). He is likely the
     same person, and is not to be confused with another James Pratt, from
     Gunnerside, who did emigrate with his wife, Hannah, in 1832. The
     earlier James Pratt left for Ohio because, he explained, "he wanted to be
     his own boss." See Morris, *Dalesmen of the Mississippi*, 112–13; Dixon,
     "Aspects of Emigration," 1462. See also chapter 11 for more on Pratt.
7   Letter dated 10 October 1844. Most of the extensive letters and journals
     of Matthew Dinsdale are located in the archives of the Wisconsin
     Historical Society Archives in Madison (Matthew Dinsdale papers,
     1836–1897, MAD 4 /47/F2) and portions are now available online:
     http://digicoll.library.wisc.edu/cgi-bin/WI/WI-idx?id=WI.Dinsdale1m.
     They were placed there by Dinsdale's daughter, Annie Dinsdale
     Swenson. Annie's daughter Edith and Edith's aunt Mary Swenson North
     preserved additional material that is not in the Wisconsin Historical
     Society Archives, but all was subsequently transcribed, compiled,
     and self-published by Abigail Curkeet – Matthew Dinsdale's great
     granddaughter – in 1980, as, *Ancestral Voices, Part I: The Circuit Rider*.
     Unless otherwise noted, the Dinsdale references here are from Curkeet,
     The Circuit Rider. For details see Marriott, *Those Who Left the Dales*, 74.
8   Edward Dinsdale to his brother Matthew Dinsdale, 26 March 1847, in
     Curkeet, *The Circuit Rider*, 152.

9   Ibid.

10 Willis Family Papers, Dales Countryside Museum, Hawes, Yorkshire.
    Fred J. Willis, "The Willis Family of Carperby," September 1986.
    Matthew was a self-styled "mountain Minstrel" who self-published a
    book of poems, "The Mountain Minstrel." He aspired to be "Yorkshire's
    answer to Scotland's Robert Burns." His poems and observations have
    been published in Edwards, *Pioneer Poetry*.

11 Elizabeth Dinsdale to her son Matthew Dinsdale, undated, in Curkeet,
    The Circuit Rider, 73.

12 Letter 1 dated 1 April 1849, Willis Family Papers, Dales Countryside
    Museum, Hawes, Yorkshire.

13 Ibid.

14 This was one of Baines's most important conclusions. *Migration in a
    Mature Economy*, 196–7.

15 Letter 1 dated 1 April 1849, Willis Family Papers, Dales Countryside
    Museum, Hawes, Yorkshire.

16 Matthew Dinsdale to his mother, from Pedlars Creek, 25 July 1845, in
    Curkeet, *The Circuit Rider*, 59.

17 Matthew Dinsdale to his mother, from Potosi, Wisconsin Territory,
    22 December 1845, in Curkeet, *The Circuit Rider*, 91.

18 Matthew Dinsdale to his mother, from Iowa County, Wisconsin,
    19 November 1847, in Curkeet, *The Circuit Rider*, 164. The emphasis is
    Dinsdale's.

19 Matthew Dinsdale to his mother, 25 July 1845, in Curkeet, *The Circuit
    Rider*, 58.

20 Ibid., 11 May 1847, 161.

21 Ibid.

22 Edward Dinsdale to his brother Matthew Dinsdale, from Askrigg,
    13 October 1845, in Curkeet, *The Circuit Rider*, 64–5.

23 Ibid.

24 See Van Vugt, "English Emigrant Guidebooks."

25 Matthew Dinsdale to his mother and siblings, from Pedlars Creek,
    14 February 1845, in Curkeet, *The Circuit Rider*, 52.

26 Campey, *Seeking a Better Future*, 187.

27 Letter dated 21 November 1856.

28 Dixon, "Aspects of Emigration," 1447.

29 Quoted in Malaney, "The Swaledale-Sharon Center Connection."
    Hallas, *Rural Responses to Industrialization*, 286.

30 The property was held by Elizabeth Dinsdale, Matthew's mother, who
    accompanied her son and new daughter-in-law to Wisconsin and died
    there in 1856. See the auction advertisement included in Curkeet, *The
    Circuit Rider*, 271. "Fog" was a valuable crop of new grass produced
    after the first hay cutting in a meadow. After an application of muck,
    another lush crop grows, called "fog," It could be used to graze dairy
    cows or be allowed to grow for another crop of hay, so it was precious
    and an important part of a farm's assets and surely to be mentioned
    in an auction. I am grateful to Marion Moverley for this insight. See
    Curkeet, *The Circuit Rider*, 275ff.

31 See the story of Thomas Lockey, who also emigrated after auctioning
    their property, in Dixon, "Aspects of Yorkshire Emigration," 1480.

32 Van Vugt, "An English Shoemaker in Indiana," 40. The emphasis
    is Smith's.

33 There seems to have been a tradition of emigrant preachers leaving after
    a farewell sermon amid great sadness. See the *The York Herald's* report
    that "Mr. Wm. Smothett (farmer) and family being about to emigrate
    to America, some friends presented him with a copy of Bagster's
    Comprehensive Bible; and on Wednesday evening, in the Wesleyan
    Reformers'-room, he preached a farewell sermon to a crowded auditory.
    He leaves the neighbourhood amid the regret of his friends, to whom his
    benevolent course of usefulness has commended itself." *The York Herald*,
    31 March, 1855, p. 6, col. 5.

34 Journal entry for 4 August 1844, in Curkeet, *The Circuit Rider*, 31.

35 Ibid., 5 August 1844.

36 Quoted in Malaney, "The Swaledale-Sharon Center Connection."

37 Hastings, *Essays in North Riding History*, 138; Campey, *Seeking a Better
    Future*, 125.

38 For a full explanation of the deficiency of British migration statistics,
    see Erickson, *Leaving England*, 170; Baines, *Migration in a Mature
    Economy*, 2–4.

39 *The York Herald*, Saturday, 24 April 1830.

40 Dixon, "Aspects of Yorkshire Emigration," 1505, 1514. In 1844 at least
    3 Swaledale families left together in the same way.

41 Eleazer Chapman to Barzillai, 13 February 1849, Grene House,
    Sheffield, in Curkeet, *The Circuit Rider*, 174.

42 Hull was dominated by emigrants who were leaving Yorkshire's East
    Riding and Lincolnshire. Liverpool was dominated by those leaving

Lancashire and the West Riding of Yorkshire, and emigrants from Gloucestershire and Somerset dominated Bristol. London was a port that catered more to Kent and Norfolk, as well as the city itself. Erickson, *Leaving England,* 159.

43   Morris, *Dalesmen of the Mississippi,* 17–19.

44   Ibid., 19–20.

45   Diary of Rev. Richard Allen, Vicar of Driffield, 23 March, 22 April 1830, East Riding Archives and Local Studies, DDX 1408/1/6.

46   *Yorkshire Gazette,* 19 April 1851, East Riding Archives and Local Studies, DDX 1408/1/6.

47   Diary of John Dinsdale on his trip from Askrigg, England to New Orleans, 1849, NYCRO.

Chapter Six

The chapter-opening quote from Samuel Johnson comes from James Boswell's, "The Table Talk of Dr. Johnson: Comprising Opinions and Anecdotes of Life and Literature, Men, Manners, and Morals," (London, 1825) quoted in AZ Quotes, http://www.azquotes.com/quote/817230.

1   The impact of the voyage on those who made it is analyzed in Berry, *A Path in the Mighty Waters.*

2   Journal entry for August 10 and 12, 1844, in Curkeet, *The Circuit Rider,* 31–2.

3   These Old Testament names and the frequent references to the scriptures probably led some to identify with the Israelites settling in Canaan and believe that God's purposes could be played out through migration. See Strong, *Victorian Christianity,* 83–4.

4   Letter dated 24 February 1849, Buxton Family Papers, Dales Countryside Museum, Hawes, Yorkshire. It appears that 107 boarded the *Saxony,* but it is hard to determine how many of these were from the two Dales because of misspelled names and vague entries on the passenger list.

5   New Orleans Passenger Lists, 1849, *Saxony* 30 April 30 1849. Originally transcribed by Daisy Grundy, accessed 26 July 2018, http://www.dalesgenealogy.com/saxony.htm.

6   Diary entry for 17 February 1849, Diary of John Dinsdale On His Trip from Askrigg, England to New Orleans, 1849, NYCRO.

7   Ibid.

8   Letter dated 24 February 1849, Buxton Family Papers, Dales
    Countryside Museum, Hawes, Yorkshire.
9   Ibid.
10 The role of religion in eighteenth-century voyages is explored in Berry,
    A Path in the Mighty Waters.
11 Whitby Lit. & Phil. Soc., "Journal of Mr. Dixon's voyage from Whitby
    to Quebec, April, 1832," cited in Stainsby, "More than an Ordinary
    Man," 9.
12 William Easton Diary and Letter, 18 May 1834, Whitby to Quebec,
    transcript by Roger G. Woodhouse, 1998. Whitby Museum.
13 Ibid.
14 The *St George's* passenger list shows seventy other English passengers.
    Except for a weaver, a smith, and a "gentleman," no occupations
    are recorded.
15 Matthew Dinsdale to his mother, from New York, 14 September 1844,
    in Curkeet, *The Circuit Rider,* 35. According to one historian, Dinsdale
    was so bored by the ocean voyage that he had "nothing to say about it,"
    but this was not so. Also, that "only a few writers could ... relate the
    ocean passage in detail and endow it with the feeling of drama." See
    Gerber, *Authors of Their Lives,* 164.
16 Journal entry for 23 August 1844, in Curkeet, *The Circuit Rider,* 32.
    The importance of appreciating nature during calm parts of the voyage
    is explored in Berry, *A Path in the Mighty Waters.*
17 Matthew Dinsdale to his mother, 14 September 1844, in Curkeet,
    The Circuit Rider, 35.
18 Ibid., 33–6.
19 Ibid., 33.
20 Ibid., 34.
21 Berry, *A Path in the Mighty Waters.*
22 Rozwadowski, *Fathoming the Ocean,* 6; cited in Berry, *A Path in the
    Mighty Waters.*
23 Matthew Dinsdale to his mother, 14 September 1844, in Curkeet,
    The Circuit Rider, 33–6.
24 Matthew to his mother, 14 February 1845, in Curkeet, *The Circuit
    Rider,* 52.
25 Diary of John Dinsdale On His Trip from Askrigg, England to New
    Orleans, 1849, NYCRO.
26 Ibid.

27 *Wensleydale Advertiser*, 25 May 1847, 44.

28 Letter from Hannah Buxton, New Orleans, to William and Richard Buxton, Gunnerside, 29 April 1849, Buxton Family Papers, Dales Countryside Museum, Hawes, Yorkshire. George Buxton may have helped with the letter as he signs it as well. See Marriot, *Those Who Left the Dales*, 64–5.

29 Van Vugt, "An English Shoemaker in Indiana," 41. For other examples see Berry, *A Path in the Mighty Waters*.

30 Note in Curkeet, *The Circuit Rider*, 122.

31 *York Herald*, Saturday, 21 September 1850. For a similar account see the *Darlington and Stockton Times*, 16 March 1850.

32 Letter dated 29 April 1849, Buxton Family Papers, Dales Countryside Museum, Hawes, Yorkshire.

33 Diary of John Dinsdale On His Trip from Askrigg, England to New Orleans, 4 April 1849, NYCRO.

34 William Smith, *An Emigrant's Narrative*.

35 *Hottinguer* passenger list, Willis Family Papers, Dales Countryside Museum, Hawes, Yorkshire.

36 Letter 1 dated 1 April 1849, Willis Family Papers, Dales Countryside Museum, Hawes, Yorkshire.

37 "History of the Eckles Family," East Riding Archives and Local Studies, DDX 270, 37.

38 "Log kept by Marmaduke Eckles covering the eight weeks voyage of the family from Hull, England to New York 1850," 16–24 May 1850, East Riding Archives and Local Studies, DDX 270.

39 Ibid., 29–31 May 1850.

40 Ibid., 10–11 June 1850.

41 Ibid., 16, 21 June 1850.

42 See the example in Van Vugt, *Britain to America*, 16.

43 Letter 1 dated 1 April 1849, Willis Family Papers, Dales Countryside Museum, Hawes, Yorkshire.

44 Richard Buxton writing to brother and sister, c. 1854, Buxton Family Papers, Dales Countryside Museum, Hawes, Yorkshire.

45 "Log kept by Marmaduke Eckles covering the eight weeks voyage of the family from Hull, England to New York 1850," Letter of July 1850, to nephew, East Riding Archives and Local Studies, DDX 270.

46 Hastings, *Essays in North Riding History*, 142; citing *Yorkshire Gazette*, 6 August 1831.

47 Hulme's story was recorded in Cobbett, *A Year's Residence*, 254–5.

48 Eva Ingham Barber, *The Woodward Genealogy – Genealogy of the descendants of William and Nancy Woodward* (Cleveland, privately published, dir. 1930), 6; cited in Malaney, "The Swaledale-Sharon Center Connection." Bell had married William Woodward's sister, Ann Woodward Bell.

49 "Notes re the Coates," NYCRO.

50 Matthew to his mother, 10 October 1844, in Curkeet, *The Circuit Rider*, 39. Dinsdale was a good judge of distance, as the length of the Erie Canal is just under 350 miles – about 560 kilometres.

51 Ibid.

52 Ibid.

53 Journal entry of 9 October 1844, in Curkeet, *The Circuit Rider*, 37; letter dated 14 September 1844, in Curkeet, *The Circuit Rider*, 33–6.

54 Van Vugt, *British Buckeyes*, 65–6.

55 Matthew Dinsdale, *Papers, 1836–1897*, Wisconsin Historical Society Archives, Madison, Wisconsin, WisMSS DL, folder 1 ([unpublished]), http://digital.library.wisc.edu/1711.dl/WI.Dinsdale1m.

56 Diary of John Dinsdale On His Trip from Askrigg, England to New Orleans, 1849, NYCRO.

57 Ibid.

58 Harstad, "Disease and Sickness," 203. Cholera first came to the United States, it appears, in 1832, via immigrants arriving at Montreal. The first epidemic hit Wisconsin in 1834, the second in 1849 and a third in 1850 which hit the lead region particularly hard. The observations of English immigrant Dr Steel is on Harstad, "Disease and Sickness," 215.

59 Bonson, *The Bonson Diaries*, 2. See also Morris, *Dalesmen of the Mississippi*, 50.

60 Rosenberg, *The Cholera Years*, 115.

61 Matthew Willis Letters, Willis Family Papers, Dales Countryside Museum, Hawes, Yorkshire.

62 Matthew Dinsdale to his family, 26 May 1849, in Curkeet, *The Circuit Rider*, 180–1.

63 Elizabeth Dinsdale to her son John, 1849, in Curkeet, *The Circuit Rider*, 176. From the misspellings, as the compiler noted, Elizabeth Dinsdale "wrote as she spoke." That is, she spelled phonetically.

64 Dixon, "Aspects of Yorkshire Emigration," 1531. Perhaps fifty people perished on the trip up the Mississippi in 1849; see Dixon, 1655.

Chapter Seven

The chapter-opening quote is from *Emigration* (London, 1849), reprinted in Van Vugt, *British Immigration*, vol. 3, 325.

1   Childs, *History of Dubuque County*, 458–60. See also Reuben Gold Thwaites, *How George Rogers Clark Won the Northwest* (Chicago: A.C. McClurg & Co., 1903), 324–32.

2   Thwaites, "Notes on Early Lead Mining," 276.

3   Ibid., 277.

4   Quoted by Thwaites, *How George Rogers Clark Won*, 313.

5   Ibid., 313–21.

6   Thwaites, "Notes on Early Lead Mining," 281.

7   Quoted in Thwaites, *How George Rogers Clark Won*, 315–16.

8   Thwaites, *How George Rogers Clark Won*, 318.

9   Ibid., 318, 324–7.

10   Ibid., 330. Thomas also estimated that in Missouri there were some 2,000 men employed in all related occupations, including teamsters, all labourers, farmers who also mined, and enslaved people.

11   Klein, *Dubuque*, 13.

12   Murphy, *A Gathering of Rivers*, 110.

13   Ibid., 101–02.

14   Ibid., 110.

15   Quoted in Murphy, *A Gathering of Rivers*, 114.

16   Erickson, *Invisible Immigrants*, 75, 130–1, 202, 251; Van Vugt, *Britain to America*, 141–4.

17   Erickson, *Invisible Immigrants*, 416.

18   Klein, *Dubuque*, 11–17.

19   By the time the Black Hawk War began, in 1832, Yorkshire immigrants were already established in the area and could not have avoided the tensions. Some miners fought in the war, though there are no known cases of English immigrants among them. After the war, which ended with the Battle of Bad Axe in August of 1832, the Native Americans were mostly gone from the Dubuque area and the miners returned to their former claims. See Klein, *Dubuque*, 14–15, 17.

20   Wright, *The Galena Lead District*, 103; Klein, *Dubuque*, 22–23.

21   Klein, *Dubuque*, 22.

22   Ibid., 23–4.

23   Ibid., 28.

24 Ibid., 24–7. The fact that Massey was a leading Methodist and most of
    the Yorkshire immigrants were also Methodists probably made this drama
    especially noteworthy.
25 Letter from Edmund Alderson, dated 28 January 1843, NYCRO 5/3/2.
26 Murphy, *A Gathering of Rivers*, 115. As quoted in Ollendorf et al., "Legacies of
    the Renards," 46.
27 Murphy, *A Gathering of Rivers*, 110–11.
28 Klein, *Dubuque*, 37.
29 Trowbridge and Shaw, *Geology and Geography of the Galena and Elizabeth
    Quadrangles*, 191; *History of Jo Daviess County*, 503, 547.
30 Quoted in Murphy, *A Gathering of Rivers*, 116.
31 For detailed accounts see *The Wensleydale Advertiser*, 15 August 1848, p. 66
    and *The Yorkshire Gazette*, 21 October 1848. For the court records see
    NYCRO, QSB 1848 4/6/26 – 27 Depositions Examinations. I am indebted to
    Dr Marion Moverley for bringing these documents to my attention.
32 Klein, *Dubuque*, 32.
33 Matthew Dinsdale to his mother and siblings, 14 February 1845, in Curkeet,
    The Circuit Rider, 48.
34 Matthew Dinsdale to his mother, 9 October 1845, in Curkeet, *The
    Circuit Rider*, 69.
35 Letter from Benton, undated but estimated "about 1855," Buxton Family
    Papers, Dales Countryside Museum, Hawes, Yorkshire. The piety of some
    Wensleydale immigrants is also evident in their choice of biblical names for their
    children: hence, Tirzah Dinsdale (Matthew's sister) marrying Barzillai Chapman.
36 Richard Buxton writing to his brother, 13 January 1881, Buxton Family
    Papers, Dales Countryside Museum, Hawes, Yorkshire.
37 Murphy, *A Gathering of Rivers*, 118.
38 Matthew Dinsdale to his brother Edward, 1 December 1845, in Curkeet,
    The Circuit Rider, 77.
39 Reprinted in Van Vugt, *British Immigration*, vol. 2, 155–6.
40 Matthew Dinsdale to family, from Potosi, Wisconsin Territory, 13 April 1846,
    in Curkeet, *The Circuit Rider*, 106.
41 Richard Buxton writing to brother and sister, undated, Buxton Family Papers,
    Dales Countryside Museum, Hawes, Yorkshire.
42 Journal entry of 26 October 1846, Matthew Dinsdale Papers, 1836–1897,
    Wisconsin Historical Society Archives, Madison, WI, WisMSS DL.
43 Matthew Dinsdale to his mother, 25 July 1845, in Curkeet, *The Circuit
    Rider*, 59.

44   Ibid.

45   Griffiths, *Two Years' Residence*, 34–5.

46   Ollendorf, "Legacies of the Renards," 48.

47   Ibid., 55.

48   Some of the very first emigrant miners from Yorkshire did not go to the United States but to South America, specifically, Santander, Colombia, where in 1825 John Harker arrived from Muker, in Swaledale. He was only twenty-one but had much experience in lead mining. In London he had probably used contacts with an English firm involved with the Colombia Mining Association, which was recruiting miners like Harker. Within a few years of his arrival there he married a Colombian, Mercedes Mutis, who was only fifteen, and together they had a son, Don Adolf. Harker was clearly a star in the company for it appointed him the director of the Zipaquirá mines, where he had introduced better methods that he had learned in Yorkshire. Then in 1829 he was made superintendent and signed a lucrative three-year contract at an impressive $2,500 per year. But Harker died in Colombia at age thirty-eight, apparently a victim of illness in a climate that did not suit him. The Harker family remains in Colombia to this day. Morris, *Dalesmen of the Mississippi*, 39–41.

49   Murphy, *A Gathering of Rivers*, 115; Dixon, "Aspects of Emigration," 1553, 1557, 1559–60.

50   Morris, *Dalesmen of the Mississippi*, 83.

51   Ibid., 91.

52   Within the following ten years Illinois had the greatest net gain of English immigrants – followed by New York, Michigan, Wisconsin, and Pennsylvania. Erickson, *Leaving England*, 39, table 1.2; p. 63, table 2.1; and p. 64, table 2.2. According to the 1846 territorial census there were 102,388 people in Iowa; the Federal census of 1850 recorded 192,214. Between 1850 and 1860 the number of foreign-born rose from 20,969 to 106,077. In 1850, there were 5,385 English, 2,571 Irish, and 585 Welsh in Wisconsin's lead counties (Grant, Iowa, Lafayette). In the whole state, 58,000 of the 305,000 were foreign-born. That is, the lead counties' foreign-born population was dominated by the English. See Schafer, *The Wisconsin Lead Region*, 45.

Chapter Eight

The chapter-opening quote is from a letter dated 22 January 1871, Thomas Lewis Walker Papers, Dales Countryside Museum, Hawes, Yorkshire.

1   Van Vugt, "An English Shoemaker in Indiana," 43.
2   Letter 1 dated 1 April 1849, Willis Family Papers, Dales Countryside Museum, Hawes, Yorkshire.
3   Journal entry of 3 November 1846, Matthew Dinsdale Papers, Wisconsin Historical Society Archives, Madison, Wisconsin, WisMSS DL.
4   Letter from Benton undated but estimated "about 1855," Buxton Family Papers, Dales Countryside Museum, Hawes, Yorkshire.
5   Matthew Dinsdale to his mother, 14 February 1845, in Curkeet, *The Circuit Rider*, 47. Letters sometimes showed the awareness of the difference in time zones. In 1871 John Flounders Dixon wrote from Iowa back to Yorkshire that "when we are getting up in the morning at 5 O'clock, you will be busy getting your dinners." Dixon, "Aspects of Yorkshire Emigration," 34–5.
6   Matthew Dinsdale to his mother, from Potosi, Wisconsin Territory, 22 December 1845, in Curkeet, *The Circuit Rider*, 87.
7   Undated letter December 1846, Matthew Dinsdale Papers, Wisconsin Historical Society Archives, WisMSS DL.
8   Journal entry of 24 October 1846, Matthew Dinsdale Papers, Wisconsin Historical Society Archives, WisMSS DL.
9   Matthew Dinsdale to his Mother, 11 May 1847, in Curkeet, *The Circuit Rider*, 160.
10 Ibid.
11 Wisconsin Historical Society, Platteville SC 59, reprinted in Van Vugt, *British Immigration*, vol. 3, 73–78.
12 Letter from William Atkinson, 28 October 1863, Letters from Farndale and Rosedale 1851–1878, Ryedale Folk Museum. 2009. 44. 38(2).
13 Matthew Dinsdale to his brother Edward, 1 December 1845, in Curkeet, *The Circuit Rider*, 78.
14 Matthew Dinsdale to his mother, 25 July 1845, in Curkeet, *The Circuit Rider*, 60.
15 Matthew Dinsdale to his mother, 25 July 1845, in Curkeet, *The Circuit Rider*, 54. This part of Yorkshire was famous for its rhubarb, and is still known as "the Rhubarb Triangle." "Forced" rhubarb was produced by

covering early shoots with straw, producing better taste. I thank Marion Moverley for this local insight.

16   Ibid.

17   Letter dated 28 January 1843, NYCRO ZSC 5/3/2.

18   Letter dated 3 June 1849. Wisconsin Historical Society, Platteville SC 59. Reprinted in Van Vugt, *British Immigration*, vol. 3, 73–78.

19   Letter 1 dated 1 April 1849, Willis Family Papers, Dales Countryside Museum, Hawes, Yorkshire.

20   John Russell Family Papers, Dales Countryside Museum, Hawes, Yorkshire.

21   Letter dated 18 January 1875 from Rama, Mifflin, Wisconsin, Willis Family Papers, Dales Countryside Museum, Hawes, Yorkshire.

22   Matthew Dinsdale to his mother, 11 October 1845, in Curkeet, *The Circuit Rider*, 70.

23   Horton, *Character of the Country*, 56.

24   Ernst, *Immigrant Life in New York*, 43–44; Bueltmann and MacRaild, *The English Diaspora*, 41.

25   Gerber, *Authors of Their Lives*, 20. If "dialect" is defined as a manner of speech that indicates one's origins, Yorkshire people certainly have a dialect.

26   From the Keld Resource Centre, Keld, Yorkshire.

27   Van Vugt, "An English Shoemaker in Indiana," 43.

28   John Strickland Diary, 31 July 1843, The Strickland Family Papers, Rosedale Abbey Reading Room, Ryedale, North Yorkshire.

29   Allen, *Great Britain and the United States*, 146.

30   "Emigration from the Hull Area," East Riding Archives and Local Studies, DDX 1408 1/7/.

31   Van Vugt, *British Buckeyes*, 200–1.

32   Van Vugt, "An English Shoemaker in Indiana," 48.

33   Ibid., 49.

34   Nash and Rogers, "The History, Architecture and Archaeology of the 'Lost' Town of Center Grove," 21. Dixon adds that "the basic identity of language and similarity of traditions allowed the rapid absorption of Yorkshiremen into the American social order;" see Dixon, "Aspects of Emigration," 1625.

35   Matthew Dinsdale to his mother, 10 October 1844, in Curkeet, *The Circuit Rider*, 38.

36   Ibid., 11 October 1845, 71.

37   Journal entry of 17 November 1846, Matthew Dinsdale Papers, Wisconsin Historical Society Archives, WisMSS DL.

38   Matthew Dinsdale to his mother, 11 May 1847, in Curkeet, *The Circuit Rider*, 162.

Chapter Nine

The chapter-opening quote was published in the *York Herald*, Saturday, 1 July 1854.

1   Berthoff, *British Immigrants in Industrial America*; Van Vugt, *Britain to America*, ch. 4; *British Buckeyes*, ch. 5.

2   Long, *Where the Sun Never Shines*, 57.

3   Van Vugt, *British Immigration*, vol. 3, xv.

4   Ollendorf, "Legacies of the Renards," 55.

5   Dixon, "Aspects of Yorkshire Emigration," 1562; Nash and Rogers, "History, Architecture and Archaeology of the 'Lost' Town of Center Grove," 17. The first English immigrants to the New Diggings area included John Redfearn, Thomas Peacock, the Calvert family, and Amos and Simon Harker. Morris, *Dalesmen of the Mississippi*, 86.

6   Morris, *Dalesmen of the Mississippi*, 74. When James Broderick visited Iowa in 1876–77, he saw "Dicky Waller," now eighty-one years old. He claimed that "there were several families in Swaledale who would have scorned the idea of marrying one of them and now he says, 'Ize wuth mar ta day ner them all put togither'.". [Translation: "I am worth more today than all of them put together."] Broderick, op. cit., 58. After the death of Mary, Robert Bonson returned to England and married Mahalah Kearton Clarkson, a widow. He then returned to the US to sell some of his holdings, and returned to England in June 1842 where they remained. He died in 1854. See Bonson, *The Bonson Diaries*, 1–11.

7   Childs, *History of Dubuque County*, 463; Letter dated 31 July 1864, Thomas Lewis Walker Papers, Dales Countryside Museum, Hawes, Yorkshire. Robert partnered with Waller to build and operate the first blast furnace. Peter Walker, who emigrated from Wensleydale with his brother Thomas refers to James Bonson in a letter back to Askrigg in 1864, saying that he was "a Swaledale man" who had remarried a young woman, "a widow with a fine little boy four years old."

8   Morris, *Dalesmen of the Mississippi*, 72.

9   Childs, *History of Dubuque County*, 463. Another Swaledale smelter at Center Grove, George Reynoldson, also went into tanning and a leather business in Dubuque. Morris, *Dalesmen of the Mississippi*, 74.

10   Childs, *History of Dubuque County*, 462–3.

11   Nash and Rogers, "History, Architecture and Archaeology of the 'Lost' Town of Center Grove," 22.

12   Mahoney, "Rise and Fall of the Booster Ethos," 376–7. According to the Langworthys, James arrived in the Galena area in 1824, and soon he "opened the mines of Hardscrabble" near Hazel Green, Wisconsin, and his brothers soon followed. See Shambaugh, *Iowa Journal of History and Politics*, 316–17.

13   Mahoney, "Rise and Fall of the Booster Ethos," 376–77.

14   Ibid., 379.

15   Ibid., 385.

16   Ibid., 394.

17   In addition to his expansive mining and smelting interests, Richard Bonson farmed, building his house on a hill north of Center Grove in 1853; meanwhile he purchased other farms and rented them out to tenants. Bonson grew wheat as a cash crop and traded and bartered various goods. By this time he was regularly making excursions to the smelters and mines that he had built or controlled, and became increasingly active in Center Grove Methodist Church and real estate in Dubuque. *Portrait and Biographical Record of Dubuque, Jones and Clayton Counties*, 261. Nash and Rogers, "The History, Architecture and Archaeology of the 'Lost' Town of Center Grove," 31.

18   Mahoney, "Rise and Fall of the Booster Ethos," 371–419.

19   Ibid., 378.

20   *George Washington*, arrived 5 June 1833.

21   *Portrait and Biographical Record of Dubuque, Jones and Clayton Counties*, 321. Shortly afterward he returned to England "to visit the scenes and associations of his youth."

22   Nash and Rogers, "The History, Architecture and Archaeology of the 'Lost' Town of Center Grove," 28–31.

23   Morris, *Dalesmen of the Mississippi*, 74.

24   Childs, *History of Dubuque County*, 473.

25   Pratt, *The Silent Ancestors*, 109–10; *The Telegraph Herald*, August 1983; Baines, *Migration in a Mature Economy*, 7, 251; Morris, *Dalesmen of the Mississippi*, 198; ref. by Hallas, *Rural Responses to Industrialization*, 289.

His migration was relatively rare among the people of Yorkshire because it was a rural-stage migration.

26 *The Dubuque Times*, 1 December 1869.

27 Morris, *Dalesmen of the Mississippi*, 74. Ann Watters, widow of Thomas, had several visits from Broderick in 76–7, south of Center Grove; she and her husband had first stopped in Rockdale and operated a mill, and later, a farm at Center Grove. Nash and Rogers, "The History, Architecture and Archaeology of the 'Lost' Town of Center Grove."

28 Marriott, *Those Who Left the Dales*, 178. Harker and Ruth Spensley were also on the *Saxony*, 1849, with their five children. They went to Dubuque then Shullsburgh to mine. Dixon, "Aspects of Yorkshire Emigration," 1533.

29 *Portrait and Biographical Album of Jo Daviess and Carroll Counties*, 659–60. Like most English immigrants in America, he voted Whig, then Republican.

30 Marriott, *Those Who Left the Dales*, 158, 178.

31 Nash and Rogers, "The History, Architecture and Archaeology of the 'Lost' Town of Center Grove," 27–8.

32 Morris, *Dalesmen of the Mississippi*, 83.

33 Morris, *Dalesmen of the Mississippi*, 113–4; Dixon, "Aspects of Yorkshire Emigration," 1582, 1634–6.

34 Schedule I, District No. 7, 1850 US Census. In 1860 James Pratt had a recorded $13,000 worth of property, and an English-born female servant and a twenty-two-year-old Welsh-born male were living with him as well.

35 Nash and Rogers, "History, Architecture and Archaeology of the 'Lost' Town of Center Grove," 21. There were coopers and harness makers from Pennsylvania and Kentucky, and a wheelwright from Virginia who lived with the Spensleys, probably as boarders.

36 Schafer, *The Wisconsin Lead Region*, 239–40.

37 Comments made by the editor after the letter dated 11 October 1845 in Curkeet, *The Circuit Rider*, 74. "English Hollow" was south of New Diggings; also Richmond on the banks of Fever River, Morris, *Dalesmen of the Mississippi*, 81.

38 Nash and Rogers, "The History, Architecture and Archaeology of the 'Lost' Town of Center Grove," 21, 26.

39 1860 US Census, Schedule 1, Julien Township, Dubuque County, Iowa, p. 338

40 Morris, *Dalesmen of the Mississippi*, 69–70.

41 *History of Jo Daviess County*, 839–42.

42 Morris, *Dalesmen of the Mississippi*, 71.

43 Schafer, *The Wisconsin Lead Region*, 101–04.

44 Matthew Dinsdale to his mother and siblings, 14 February 1845, in Curkeet, *The Circuit Rider*, 51.

45 Richard Buxton writing to brother and sister, undated, Buxton Family Papers, Dales Countryside Museum, Hawes, Yorkshire.

46 Childs, *History of Dubuque County*, 461.

47 Ibid., 467.

48 *History of Jo Daviess County*, 835, 837.

49 Childs, *History of Dubuque County*, 468.

50 Buxton Family Papers, Dales Countryside Museum, Hawes, Yorkshire.

51 Childs, *History of Dubuque County*, 470–1.

52 Richard Buxton writing to his brother and sister, undated, Buxton Family Papers, Dales Countryside Museum, Hawes, Yorkshire.

53 Letter from Benton undated but estimated "about 1855," Buxton Family Papers, Dales Countryside Museum, Hawes, Yorkshire.

54 Matthew Dinsdale to his mother, 25 July 1845, in Curkeet, *The Circuit Rider*, 58.

55 While the troubled lead miners of the Dales were heading for the lead mines of the Upper Mississippi, those from County Durham and Cumberland were heading for Upper Canada, especially north of Lake Ontario. They went there to farm, whereas those from the Dales went to the United States to mine, many to combine mining with farming, but ultimately to farm. The United States offered both options, whereas Upper Canada was more limited for miners. See Campey, *Seeking a Better Future*, 22.

56 Van Vugt, "Relocating the English Diaspora."

57 Thomas Lewis Walker Papers, Dales Countryside Museum, Hawes, Yorkshire; *Commemorative Biographical Record of Rock, Green, Grant, Iowa, and Lafayette Counties*, 290–1.

58 *Minneapolis Tribune*, 16 September 1979, p.5E.

Chapter Ten

The chapter-opening quote by John A. Macdonald was published in Waiser, "Macdonald's Appetite for Canadian Expansion, 343.

1 Campey, *Ignored but Not Forgotten*, 67.

2   Letter No. 1, 6 June 1830, John and Ann Knaggs Letters, Folk Museum. All misspellings are in the originals and have been kept.

3   Ibid.

4   Stainsby, *More Than an Ordinary Man*, 2. There were three Eastons who moved from Danby to Ontario: John, Thomas, and William – very likely brothers. William left Danby, not because of immediate poverty. Rather, he sensed his future in Danby was not bright, especially in rural communities dominated by subsistence farming. The letters to and from Danby and the emigrants in Ontario highlight the importance of the "chains" of family relationships and friendships, which channelled more and more people from one place to the other. See the Voyage and letter of William Easton, 1834, Whitby to Quebec, transcript by Roger G. Woodhouse, 1998, Whitby Museum, and the original manuscripts, also in the Whitby Museum, 5068.

5   Letter No. 7, 8 November 1834, John and Ann Knaggs Letters, Ryedale Folk Museum.

6   Ibid., Letter No. 2, 3 October 1830.

7   Ibid.

8   Ibid.

9   Stainsby, *More Than an Ordinary Man*, 18–20.

10   Letter No. 2, 3 October 1830, John and Ann Knaggs Letters, Ryedale Folk Museum.

11   Ibid.

12   Ibid., Letter No. 4, 25 October 1831

13   Ibid., Letter No. 5, 22 October 1832.

14   Ibid.

15   Letter No. 7, 8 November 1834, John and Ann Knaggs Letters, Ryedale Folk Museum.

16   Ibid., Letter No. 5, 22 October 1832.

17   Ibid., Letter No. 7, 8 November 1834.

18   Ibid., Letter No. 6, 17 November 1833.

19   Ibid.

20   Letter No. 7, 8 November 1834, John and Ann Knaggs Letters, Ryedale Folk Museum.

21   Clarence was the first town established in Erie County, in 1808. Two years later the town of Buffalo was separated out of Clarence and later became the city of Buffalo.

22   Letter No. 8, 16 September 1830, John and Hannah Hutchinson Letter, Ryedale Folk Museum.

23   Ibid.

24   Ibid.

25   Ibid.

26   Ibid.

27   Ibid.

28   Ibid.

29   Ibid.

30   Ibid.

31   "Excerpts from a book written by Joseph Ford (or Foord) … archive material relating to the Ford (Foord) family donated by Ian Ford," 145, Rosedale Abbey Reading Room, Ryedale, North Yorkshire.

32   Ibid., 146.

33   Stainsby, *More than an Ordinary Man*, 15.

34   "Excerpts from a book written by Joseph Ford (or Foord) … archive material relating to the Ford (Foord) family donated by Ian Ford," 144–6, Rosedale Abbey Reading Room.

35   Fewster Family History, Ryedale Folk Museum, 2008.13.1. Sundry box 6.

36   Ibid. The family surname appears to have changed from Feaster to Fewster, either their own choice or a clerical error. They may have been drawn to this part of Ontario by the Woodstockland promotion.

37   Fewster Family History, Ryedale Folk Museum. 2008.13.1. Sundry box 6.

38   Ibid.

39   Ibid.

40   Ibid.

41   John Strickland Diary, 5–27 April 1830, The Strickland Family Papers, Rosedale Abbey Reading Room.

42   Ibid., 28 April 1830.

43   Ibid., 1 May 1830.

44   Ibid., 12, 15, and 17 May 1830.

45   Ibid., 25 May 1830.

46   Ibid., 22 June 1830. Sam Patch was an American folk hero who became legendary by throwing himself into raging waterfalls. In 1829 he jumped twice into Niagara Falls and became a household name. See Johnson, *Sam Patch, the Famous Jumper*.

47 Ibid., 24 June 1830, The Strickland Family Papers, Rosedale Abbey Reading Room.

48 Ibid., 24–25 June 1830, The Strickland Family Papers, Rosedale Abbey Reading Room.

49 Ibid., 29 June 1830, The Strickland Family Papers, Rosedale Abbey Reading Room.

50 Ibid., 1 July 1830, The Strickland Family Papers, Rosedale Abbey Reading Room.

51 Ibid., July 1843, The Strickland Family Papers, Rosedale Abbey Reading Room.

52 Campey, *Seeking a Better Future*, 215.

53 John Strickland Diary, 22 July 1830, The Strickland Family Papers, Rosedale Abbey Reading Room.

54 Ibid., 2 December 1830.

55 Letter printed in the *Hull, Rockingham, and Yorkshire and Lincolnshire Gazette*, 2 April 1831.

56 Ibid.

57 John Strickland Diary, 7–10 July 1830, The Strickland Family Papers, Rosedale Abbey Reading Room. Kirkbymoorside is sometimes spelled "Kirbymoorside" and is midway between Helmsley and Pickering.

58 Ibid., 24 September 1830.

59 Ibid., 1–31 August 1830.

60 Ibid., 9 and 16 August 1830.

61 Ibid., 23 July 1830.

62 Ibid., 7–10 July 1830.

63 Ibid., 1 December 1830.

64 Ibid., 22 July 1830.

65 Ibid., 16–22 July 1843.

66 Obituary John Strickland, 1807–1895, *The Oshawa Vindicator*, c. 1895, The Strickland Family Papers, Rosedale Abbey Reading Room.

67 Letter No. 7, 8 November 1834, John and Ann Knaggs Letters, Ryedale Folk Museum.

68 Ibid.

69 Ibid.

70 Letter No. 5, 22 October 1832, John and Ann Knaggs Letters, Ryedale Folk Museum.

71 Ibid., Letter No. 7, 8 November 1834.

72 Ibid., Letter No. 8, 16 September 1830.

73 Ibid., Letter No. 2, 3 October 1830.
74 Ibid., Letter No. 3, 4 March 1831.
75 Ibid., Letter No. 4, 25 October 1831.
76 Cited in Campey, *Seeking a Better Future*, 127–8.
77 Campey, *Ignored but Not Forgotten*, 96.
78 Cited in Campey, *Seeking a Better Future*, 165.
79 Elliott, "Regional Patterns," 74.
80 Quoted in Elliott, "Regional Patterns," 74.
81 Ibid., 75.
82 "Hull as an Emigration Port, 1850–60," East Riding Archives and Local Studies, DDX 1408 1/8.
83 Stainsby, *More Than an Ordinary Man*, 16.
84 John Fell, Letter No. 10, Ryedale Folk Museum. This letter was published in *The Easingwold Chronical & Thirsk Times & Advertiser*. Cavan is a township 20 kilometres southwest of the city of Peterborough.
85 Ibid.
86 Ibid.

Chapter Eleven

The chapter-opening quote is from the Willis Family Papers, Dales Countryside Museum, Hawes, Yorkshire.

1 Van Vugt, *Britain to America*, ch. 3.
2 The "boom" is variously defined as the early 1850s, or even 1850–73, as in Roy Church's book, *The Great Victorian Boom, 1850–1873*. The boom is problematic. Even Church stressed that there is no true distinctive "historical unity" for these years, and yet with qualifications we can refer to a great "Victorian Boom" because prices and growth rose and average living standards improved significantly. As Martin Daunton has said, "By 1851, the bulk of the population was, for the first time, sharing in the benefits of economic growth with a sustained rise in income per head;" see Daunton, "Society and Economic Life," 51. Growth was most spectacular between 1853–56, 1863–65, 1871–73, though 1858 was a year of "profound depression." Generally, though the percentage of the labour force engaged in agriculture dropped from 22 per cent in 1851 to 14 per cent in 1871, it was a "golden age for British agriculture" with "'high farming' and high profits', with investment in new farm buildings,

drainage, and herds of animals to fertilize the soil." (Ibid., 53–4). But real wages rose significantly only from the mid-1860s onward (Ibid., 28, 74). Thus, the third quarter of the century, which is widely viewed as a period of economic growth in England and America, was especially propitious for both English farmers and farm labourers, but also those in rural crafts, to pursue farming in America.

3   Van Vugt, *Britain to America*, 22–4.

4   Van Vugt, *British Buckeyes*, ch. 4.

5   Historian David Hey concludes that during this period Yorkshire "was free from the serious social tension that afflicted the countryside in much of southern and eastern England," and that though "the burden of poverty was harsh enough for thousands of Yorkshire families in times of depression…it did not weigh as heavily as in many other parts of the land." *A History of Yorkshire*, 381.

6   *Yorkshire Gazette*, 9 June 1849, cited in "Hull as an Emigration Port, 1850–60," East Riding Archives and Local Studies, DDX 1408 1/8.

7   *Yorkshire Gazette*, 17 May 1850, cited in "Hull as an Emigration Port, 1850–60," East Riding Archives and Local Studies, DDX 1408 1/8.

8   *Yorkshire Gazette*, 5 April 1851, East Riding Archives and Local Studies, DDX 1408 1/6.

9   Van Vugt, *British Immigration*, vol. 3, xii–xiii.

10 This is discussed more fully in Van Vugt, *British Buckeyes*, 120–9.

11 Letter 1, dated 1 April 1849, Willis Family Papers, Dales Countryside Museum, Hawes, Yorkshire.

12 For examples, see Van Vugt, *British Buckeyes*, 123–4.

13 For example, George Davis, an 1845 Lincolnshire immigrant, was the largest stock dealer in Bath Township, Summit County, Ohio, and became well known for the cattle, sheep, and fine horses that he bred. Even poor English farmers made contributions. James Hammond arrived from Yorkshire in 1848 with a mere $26 in his pocket. He eventually became one of the most successful livestock breeders and dealers in Northeast Ohio and was duly elected president of the Summit County Agricultural Society. Also in Summit County, others specialized in breeding Norman horses and Merino sheep; see *Portrait and Biographical Record of Portage and Summit Counties*, 304–05, 446–47. See the case of William Baker of Leicestershire, in *History of Delaware County and Ohio*, 820.

14 Cutrer, *The English Texans*, 82.

15   Van Vugt, *British Buckeyes*, 127–8.
16   Van Vugt, *Britain to America*, ch. 3; idem., *British Buckeyes*, ch. 4. The English agriculturalists leaving for America appear to have been mostly farmers and their sons, rather than farmer labourers. However, the category is imprecise.
17   Erickson, *Leaving England*, 83–4.
18   Van Vugt, "Relocating the English Diaspora in America," 12–14.
19   Erickson, *Leaving England*, 81–2.
20   Dinsdale looked at land that resembled Bishopdale. Matthew Dinsdale to his mother, May 1846, in Curkeet, *The Circuit Rider*, 111.
21   Nash and Rogers, "The History, Architecture and Archaeology of the 'Lost' Town of Center Grove," 18; Allan Bogue, *From Prairie to Corn Belt: Farming on the Illinois Prairies in the Nineteenth Century* (Chicago: University of Chicago Press, 1963).
22   Nash and Rogers, "The History, Architecture and Archaeology of the 'Lost' Town of Center Grove," 18.
23   Ibid.
24   *History of Medina County and Ohio*, 629; Dixon, "Aspects of Yorkshire Emigration," 1462.
25   Van Vugt, "Relocating the English Diaspora in America"; *British Buckeyes*, 105–07; *Britain to America*, 50–52.
26   Van Vugt, *British Immigration*, vol. 2, 203–04.
27   Ibid., 197–8.
28   Van Vugt, "English Emigrant Guidebooks."
29   Obituary of Mrs. Ann George, 1877; Letter of Ann Swetnam George to her grandson Levi Moulthrop, 6 October 1864, Rockford, Illinois, signed Clarence S. George. These have been provided by Jacqueline Auclair. For another example of hunting game as a primary reason for moving to America see Van Vugt, *British Buckeyes*, 96–7.
30   Obituary of Mrs. Ann George, 1877, Letter of Ann Swetnam George to grandson Levi Moulthrop, 6 October 1864.
31   Thelma Gardner, *Illinois Sesquicentennial Edition of Christian County History*, 304. East Riding Archives and Local Studies DDX 422.
32   Ibid.
33   Ibid.
34   Ibid. There are other examples: when Matthew Dinsdale's brother-in-law Barzillai Chapman bought his own land in Wisconsin, he bought 140 acres of unimproved land of which 100 acres were prairie; see Matthew's letter of May 1846, in Curkeet, *The Circuit Rider*, 112.

35 "History of the Eckles Family," East Riding Archives and Local Studies, DDX 270.

36 Ibid.

37 Ibid.

38 Ibid.

39 Erickson, *Leaving England*, 67, n.10.

40 *Emigration* (London, 1849), excerpt, pp. 72–129, British Library of Political and Economic Science, OU1849/10B, reprinted in Van Vugt, *British Immigration*, vol. 3, 310, footnote.

41 Erickson, *Leaving England*, 75, 77.

42 Biography reprinted in Van Vugt, *British Immigration*, vol. 3, 214–15.

43 Matthew Dinsdale to his mother, 14 February 1845, in Curkeet, *The Circuit Rider*, 49.

44 Ibid., 25 July 1845, 61.

45 Ibid., 11 October 1845, 67.

46 *Wensleydale Advertiser*, 23 June 1846, 50. This letter is also included in Fred J. Willis, "The Willis Family of Carperby," September 1986, Willis Family Papers, Dales Countryside Museum, Hawes, Yorkshire.

47 Matthew Willis Jr. to his uncle Matthew Willis, 21 August 1846, in Curkeet, *The Circuit Rider*, 95; Matthew Dinsdale to family members in Askrigg, 13 April 1846, in Curkeet, *The Circuit Rider*, 107.

48 Thomas Longm[a]ire to his son-in-law Matthew Willis, from Bleathgill, Stainmore, 23 February 1847, in Curkeet, *The Circuit Rider*, 145.

49 Ibid., 146. Willis emigrated in 1845.

50 Comments made by editor after the letter of dated 11 October 1845, in Curkeet, *The Circuit Rider*, 74; Fred J. Willis, "The Willis Family of Carperby," September 1986, Willis Family Papers, Dales Countryside Museum, Hawes, Yorkshire.

51 3 June 1849, Wisconsin Historical Society, Platteville SC 59, repr. in Van Vugt, *British Immigration*, vol. 3, 73–8.

52 Letter 1, dated 1 April 1849, Willis Family Papers, Dales Countryside Museum, Hawes, Yorkshire.

53 Ibid.

54 Wisconsin Historical Society, Platteville SC 59, repr. in Van Vugt, *British Immigration*, vol. 3, 73–8.

55 Ibid.

56 Ibid.

57 Ibid., 73–8.

58 *The Hull Packet and East Riding Times*, 15 June 1849.

59   Letter dated 31 July 1864, Thomas Lewis Walker Papers, Dales Countryside Museum, Hawes, Yorkshire.

60   Ibid.

61   Letter dated 5 December 1859 from Carperby, Wensleydale, Willis Family Papers, Dales Countryside Museum, Hawes, Yorkshire.

Chapter Twelve

The chapter-opening quote is from *Emigration* (London, 1849), repr. in Van Vugt, *British Immigration*, vol. 3, 325.

1   Van Der Zee, "British Emigrants in Iowa."

2   Parker, *Iowa: Pioneer Foundations*, 23.

3   Quoted in Birch, "The Editor and the English," 629. See also Van Der Zee, *The British in Iowa*. The guide "Emigration" (1849) reported that "Mr. George Shepherd, the editor of the *Eastern Counties Herald*, who spent several years in both States, and subjected himself to personal experience of their manner of life, by roughing it like the natives, supplies intelligent, and we have no reason to believe, other than trustworthy details on the subject, of their actual condition, advantages, and drawbacks;" *Emigration*, repr. in Van Vugt, *British Immigration*, vol. 3, 327.

4   *Hull Advertiser*, 17 May 1850, East Riding Archives and Local Studies, DDX 1408 1/7.

5   "Emigration from the Hull Area," East Riding Archives and Local Studies, DDX 1408 1/7/.

6   Quoted in Birch, "The Editor and the English," 634.

7   Ibid., 622.

8   *History of Clinton County, Iowa: Containing a history of the County, Its Cities, Towns &c.* (Chicago: Western Historical Company, 1879), 58.

9   *Hull Advertiser*, 9 June 1850, p. 5, from East Riding Archives and Local Studies, DDX 1408 1/7.

10   *History of Clinton County, Iowa*, 642.

11   Ibid.

12   "Emigration from the Hull Area," East Riding Archives and Local Studies, DDX 1408 1/7/.

13   Birch, "The Editor and the English," 635.

14   *Herald*, 26 September 1850, 6, quoted in Birch, "The Editor and the English," 637.

15 *Herald,* 23 January 1851, 6, quoted in Birch, "The Editor and the English," 638.

16 "Emigration from the Hull Area," East Riding Archives and Local Studies, DDX 1408 1/7/.

17 Birch, "The Editor and the English," 642–3.

18 Van Der Zee, *British in Iowa,* part I, ch. III, http://www.iagenweb.org/sioux/books/british/british_1_3.htm. On how the English blended in and had diffuse settlement in Iowa compared to other immigrants in the state, see Rosenberg, Morton M. "The People of Iowa on the Eve of the Civil War." *The Annals of Iowa* 39 (1967), 105–133, esp. p. 124.

19 *History of Clinton County, Iowa,* 642.

20 "Emigration from the Hull Area," East Riding Archives and Local Studies, DDX 1408 1/7/.

21 This history was recorded by J. Berry Ware, grandson of John Ware, Sr, one of the most prominent members of the colony, who had left from Rosedale. See Ware, "English Colony." Newhall died of cholera in Missouri in 1849.

22 William Bateman, Jr, (the son of the colony's leader, who arrived as a child) refers to the ship as the *George Washington,* in "Old English Colony History," typescript in Ryedale Folk Museum. Ware, "English Colony," 4, 15.

23 Ware, "English Colony," 5–6.

24 Ibid., 8,11, 28–9.

25 Sloat, "The Noble Experiment Eventually Failed."

26 *Portrait and Biographical Album of Lee County, Iowa,* 202; Ware, "English Colony," 36–7.

27 Ware, "English Colony," 35–6.

28 Ibid., 6.

29 Ibid., 35–6.

30 *Portrait and Biographical Album of Lee County, Iowa,* 203. Ann Wilson Ware died in 1869; Ware, "English Colony," 37.

31 *Portrait and Biographical Album of Lee County, Iowa,* 203.

32 Ware, "English Colony," 38.

33 Letter of 30 June 1851, Letters from Farndale and Rosedale 1851–1878, Ryedale Folk Museum, 2009, 44. 38(2).

34 *Hull Advertiser,* cited in Dixon, "Aspects of Emigration," vol. 2, 458. The *Harlequin* sailed from Hull to New York in 1853 with sixty-six passengers, ten of whom were farmers.

35 Dixon, "Aspects of Emigration," vol. 2, 453. For more *Hull Advertiser* articles with details about selling goods, homesickness, the lack of beggars in Iowa, see "Emigration from the Hull Area," East Riding Archives and Local Studies, DDX 1408 1/7.

36 In 1862, William Atkinson – apparently the father-in-law of Charlotte Ware – wrote from Ingleby Greenhow (a village about 5 kilometres south of Great Ayton, on the northwest edge of the North York Moors) to Charlotte and other local people who had settled in Lee County.

37 This was immigrant Daniel Stephenson, observing the difficulties of his brother Samuel, who was "not doing very well at farming." Cited in Erickson, *Invisible Immigrants*, 238, see also p. 302.

38 A full account of the Le Mars Colony is provided by Harnack, *Gentlemen on the Prairie*. See also Pagnamenta, *Prairie Fever*.

Chapter Thirteen

The chapter-opening quote by Captain John Smith is from National Park Service, "Indians and Smith."

1 Hinderaker, *Elusive Empires*.

2 The common understanding that Native Americans would have had better lives without the American Revolution has recently been challenged by Dowd, "Indigenous Peoples without the Republic," 19–41.

3 White, *The Middle Ground*. See also Colley, *Captives: Britain, Empire, and the World*.

4 Kirk, *The Memoirs and Adventures of Robert Kirk*. See also the example of Nicholas Cresswell, in MacVeagh, *The Journal of Nicholas Cresswell*. See also the example of the captive Thomas Ridout, in Van Vugt, *British Buckeyes*, 18–20.

5 Matthew Dinsdale to his mother, from English Prairie, 10 October 1844, in Curkeet, *The Circuit Rider*, 41.

6 Chief Oshkosh (1795–1858) was the Chief of the Menominee and led the negotiations to protect their lands from incoming New York Indians and white pioneers. During the War of 1812 he fought on the British side but he supported the Americans during the Black Hawk War of 1832. Dinsdale was observing the Menominee people right before the 1848 Treaty of Lake Poygan, in which Oshkosh sold their remaining Wisconsin lands to the United States, in exchange for

about 600,000 acres in Minnesota. Oshkosh later claimed that they were pressured to sign the 1848 treaty, and in 1852 the Menominee were allowed to remain on a temporary reservation in northeastern Wisconsin. Oshkosh was killed in a drunken fight in Kenosha in 1858. See Ourada, *The Menominee Indians*.

7   Journal entry for 27 November 1844, in Curkeet, *The Circuit Rider*, 46.

8   Matthew Dinsdale to his mother and siblings, 14 February 1845, in Curkeet, *The Circuit Rider*, 49.

9   Journal entry of 19 October 1846, Matthew Dinsdale Papers, WisMss DL.

10   Linklater, *Measuring America*, 5, 43–4, 208, 210.

11   Journal entry of 17 November 1846, Matthew Dinsdale Papers, WisMss DL.

12   Ibid.

13   Ibid.

14   Ibid.

15   Ibid.

16   Ibid.

17   Ibid.

18   Ibid.

19   Matthew Dinsdale to his mother, from Lake Winnebago, 23 September 1846, in Curkeet, *The Circuit Rider*, 123.

20   Ibid., 124.

21   Ibid.

22   Matthew Dinsdale in Upper California to Brother Dyer, a fellow minister, printed in a Mineral Point newspaper, 2 July 1850, in Curkeet, *The Circuit Rider*, 230.

23   California Diary, 22 July 1850, in Curkeet, *The Circuit Rider*, 239. For a horrifying account of a British immigrant on his way West during this time and witnessing Native Americans flay a person alive, see Van Vugt, *British Buckeyes*, 159.

24   *Album of Genealogy and Biography of Cook County, Illinois*, 212. For other information on Heslington, see Erickson Database, ID 344.

Chapter Fourteen

The chapter-opening quote by Francis Asbury is quoted in http://www.asburymethodist.org/welcome/.

1   Hempton, *Methodism*, 11–18.
2   Other English institutions hid the English Diaspora in America, the
    English-modelled colleges and Masonic lodges among them. They also
    served as conduits for more English immigrants. American political
    institutions also retained much of their English political traditions,
    so that English immigrants were the quickest to become governors,
    congressmen, or judges. The essential commonality is more striking than
    the differences. As Gordon Wood sums it up, "The most important fact
    about the [American] Founders may not have been the creativity of their
    imaginations but their Englishness." See Wood on Bernard Bailyn, in
    Wood, "Creating the Revolution," 53.
3   Strong, *Victorian Christianity*, 278.
4   Van Vugt, *British Buckeyes*, 180–3, 189.
5   Journal entry for 17 November 1844, in Curkeet, *The Circuit Rider*, 46.
    "Love Feasts" originated as substitutes for Holy Communion services in
    parishes that excluded Methodists because they were not ordained. The
    tradition continues in some parts of Yorkshire, with special recipes for
    Love Feast Cakes.
6   Van Vugt, *Britain to America*, 133, table 6. In the Erickson Database
    there are sixty-nine from North Yorkshire, and of these we know the
    religion of forty-two; twenty-one were described as Methodist, two as
    Primitive Methodists, and three as Wesleyans (some of those described
    as Methodist were possibly Primitive Methodists). Nine were Anglican
    or Episcopal, only one was a Catholic, and a few others were described
    as Congregational or "Christian Church."
7   Van Vugt, *British Buckeyes*, ch. 6; Carwardine, *Transatlantic
    Revivalism*, 32.
8   Gerber, *Authors of Their Lives*, 23.
9   Carwardine, *Transatlantic Revivalism*, 135. The Yorkshire immigrants
    were essential in transferring their Methodism to the New Diggings
    area. See Dixon, "Aspects of Emigration," 1661ff.
10 Wisconsin Historical Society, Platteville SC 83, repr. in Van Vugt, *British
    Immigration*, vol. 3, 152.
11 Carwardine, *Transatlantic Revivalism*, 104–07.
12 Van Vugt, *British Immigration*, vol.1, xlii.
13 Watson, "National Identity and Primitive Methodism," 32–52. See also
    the early book by Tyrrell, *Steeples on the Prairies*.

14 *Primitive Methodist Magazine*, 3rd series, 6 (1848), 631, repr. in Van Vugt, *British Immigration*, vol. 3, 292.

15 Acornley, *A History of the Primitive Methodist Church*, 54.

16 "Progress of the Work of God at Mineral Point, Wisconsin," *Primitive Methodist Magazine*, 3rd series, 8 (1850), 247, repr. in Van Vugt, *British Immigration*, vol. 3, 292–4.

17 Ibid., 292–4.

18 Ibid., 293.

19 Ibid., 292–4.

20 *Teesdale Mercury*, 5 November 1930.

21 "Wisconsin," *Evangelist* 2:10 (October 1851), 151, repr. in Van Vugt, *British Immigration*, vol. 3, 294–5.

22 Ibid., 292–4. On the history of Leekley, who had organized the Primitive Methodists in Galena, but eventually withdrew from the ministry because of a "sense of his unfitness for the work," see Acornley, *A History of the Primitive Methodist Church*, 376. The *Primitive Methodist Magazine* reported from the same conference that "we learn there were then, in this distant branch of our church, 7 travelling-preachers, 43 local-preachers, 41 class-leaders, 6 chapels, 37 other preaching-places, and 681 members; being an increase of 220 for the year;" 3rd series, 9 (1851), 181–2, repr. in Van Vugt, British Immigration, vol. 3, 295.

23 "Wisconsin," *Evangelist* 2:10 (October 1851), 151, repr. in Van Vugt, *British Immigration*, vol. 3, 296.

24 *Primitive Methodist Magazine*, 3rd series, 9 (1851), 379–80, repr. in Van Vugt, British Immigration, vol. 3, 296–7. Kirk Carrion is in the valley of the river Lune, so it is between Lune and Middleton, not Lime, as recorded in the document.

25 *Primitive Methodist Magazine*, 3rd series, 10 (1852), 368–71, repr. in Van Vugt, *British Immigration*, vol. 3, 296–7.

26 Ibid., 297.

27 Ibid., 298.

28 Ibid.

29 He recorded in his journal entry of 17 November 1844, that "A Lovefeast was held this morning at nine o'clock which was a good time. Methodism and Religion are the same in character and power and value in America as in England." Less than a year after he reported his "good time" at the "Lovefeast," in October 1845, Dinsdale wrote to his mother

to report that "I have again removed" from Pedlars Creek to Potosi,
where he was "received on probation by the Rock River Conference of
the Methodist Episcopal Church." His emotions were mixed as he was
"again amongst strangers. But I look to Heaven as my ultimate and
eternal resting place and home." In Curkeet, *The Circuit Rider*, 46.

30   Matthew Dinsdale Papers, 1836–1897, WISMSS DL, folder 1, p.1.

31   Matthew Dinsdale to his mother, 11 October 1845, in Curkeet, *The
     Circuit Rider*, 35.

32   Matthew Dinsdale to his mother, from Potosi, Wisconsin Territory, 22
     December 1845, in Curkeet, *The Circuit Rider*, 87–8.

33   Matthew Dinsdale to family, from Potosi, Wisconsin Territory, 13 April
     1846, in Curkeet, *The Circuit Rider*, 107. In a few years he would find
     some relief and a change of life in the California Gold Rush. Then,
     after returning to England in 1853 to marry Mary Ann Mann, of York,
     he returned to preach and in 1858 he entered the West Wisconsin
     Conference. In the 1870s he preached in Madison. After retiring, he
     died in 1898. Matthew Dinsdale Papers, 1836–1897, WISMSS DL,
     folder 1, p.2.

34   Matthew Dinsdale to his mother, from Linden, Wisconsin Territory,
     21 January 1848, in Curkeet, *The Circuit Rider*, 165.

35   Strong, *Victorian Christianity*, 65.

36   In 1840, the first English converts arrived in Nauvoo, and moved on
     to Utah in 1848. Soon more than 5,000 other English converts arrived,
     and between 1853 and 1856 about 16,000 more followed.

37   Cannon, "Migration of English Mormons to America," 436–55.

38   And in 1880 Salt Lake County, Utah recorded 22 per cent of its 31,977
     people as English-born – a legacy of the earlier huge influx of English
     Mormon converts. Van Vugt, *Britain to America*, ch. 9; Van Vugt,
     British Buckeyes, ch. 6. The second highest was Wisconsin in 1850, with
     6.2 per cent.

39   Not to be confused with the John Knaggs who left the Rosedale area for
     Ontario in the 1830s.

40   "Letter From a Hull Mormon in America," *Hull Packet and East Riding
     Times*, 2 December 1853.

41   *York Herald*, Saturday, 23 August 1856.

42   "Longstroth Family and their journey across the plains of America,"
     Stephen Longstroth Family Papers, Dales Countryside Museum,
     Hawes, Yorkshire.

43 Details are illegible – apparently blotted out later.

44 Letters dated 12 and 13 December 1841, Stephen Longstroth Family Papers, Dales Countryside Museum, Hawes, Yorkshire.

45 Van Vugt, *British Immigration*, vol. 2, 155–6.

46 Though Longstroth had prospered spiritually in Clitheroe he suffered in other ways: he continued to live in poverty, probably labouring in the textile mills, and by 1841 two of his eight children had died. "Longstroth Family and their journey across the plains of America," Stephen Longstroth Family Papers, Dales Countryside Museum, Hawes, Yorkshire.

47 Letter dated 1 January 1844, Stephen Longstroth Family Papers, Dales Countryside Museum, Hawes, Yorkshire.

48 Ibid.

49 Ibid.

50 Letter dated May 1844, Stephen Longstroth Family Papers, Dales Countryside Museum, Hawes, Yorkshire.

51 Ibid.

52 Ibid.

53 Ibid. Longstroth's use of the American term of "fall" instead of "autumn" could be a sign of his assimilation.

54 Ibid.

55 Letter dated 6 July 1845, Stephen Longstroth Family Papers, Dales Countryside Museum, Hawes, Yorkshire.

56 Matthew Dinsdale to his mother, 11 October 1845, in Curkeet, *The Circuit Rider*, 71.

57 Letter dated 6 July 1845, Stephen Longstroth Family Papers, Dales Countryside Museum, Hawes, Yorkshire.

58 Ibid.

59 Ibid. Stephen now signed his name "Stephen Longstroth, Carpenter, Nauvoo."

60 Letter dated 19 March 1848, Stephen Longstroth Family Papers, Dales Countryside Museum, Hawes, Yorkshire.

61 Ibid., Letter dated 28 July 1850, Stephen Longstroth Family Papers, Dales Countryside Museum, Hawes, Yorkshire.

62 Ibid., Letter dated 19 March 1848, Stephen Longstroth Family Papers, Dales Countryside Museum, Hawes, Yorkshire.

63 Ibid., Letter dated 28 July 1850, Stephen Longstroth Family Papers, Dales Countryside Museum, Hawes, Yorkshire.

64 Ibid.
65 Ibid.
66 Ibid.
67 Ibid., Letter dated 1 May 1854, Stephen Longstroth Family Papers, Dales Countryside Museum, Hawes, Yorkshire.
68 Ibid.
69 Ibid.
70 Ibid.
71 Ibid.

Chapter Fifteen

The chapter-opening quote is by Matthew Dinsdale to his brother Edward, from North Yuba, California, 28 October 1850, in Curkeet, *The Circuit Rider*, 243.

1   *Wensleydale Advertiser*, 16 January 1849, p. 2.
2   *Yorkshire Gazette*, Saturday, 27 January 1849.
3   Eleazer Chapman to his brother Barzillai, 13 February 1849, Grene House, Sheffield, in Curkeet, *The Circuit Rider*, 174.
4   Van Vugt, *Britain to America*, 89–91; Wright, *The Galena Lead District*, 102. On the length of time to cross from Dubuque to the gold fields, see *Encyclopedia Dubuque*, "Dubuque in the California Gold Rush."
5   *Primitive Methodist Magazine*, 3rd series, 10 (1852), 368–71, repr. in Van Vugt, *British Immigration*, vol. 3, p. 298.
6   *Yorkshire Gazette*, Saturday, 27 January 1849.
7   Ibid., 20 January 1849.
8   Erickson, *Leaving England*, 39, table 1.2.
9   Some who left Dubuque for San Francisco via the longer water route took about the same time as those who crossed over land – about six months. See *Encyclopedia Dubuque*, "Dubuque in the California Gold Rush."
10 Matthew Dinsdale to his mother, from New York, 17 November 1849, in Curkeet, *The Circuit Rider*, 191.
11 Ibid., 29 November 1849, in Curkeet, *The Circuit Rider*, 192. See Reade, *J.B. Gough: A sketch of his life*.
12 Matthew Dinsdale to his mother, from New York, 29 November 1849, in Curkeet, *The Circuit Rider*, 192. Apparently, this is a continuation of his 29 November New York letter.

13 Matthew Dinsdale to his sister Elizabeth, from Panama, 21 December 1849, in Curkeet, *The Circuit Rider*, 195.

14 Matthew Dinsdale, California Diary, 12–13 December 1850, in Curkeet, *The Circuit Rider*, 201.

15 Ibid., 18–21 January 1850, in Curkeet, *The Circuit Rider*, 202.

16 Ibid., 22 January 1850, in Curkeet, *The Circuit Rider*, 203.

17 Ibid., 11 April 1850, in Curkeet, *The Circuit Rider*, 224.

18 Letter from Matthew Dinsdale in Upper California, to Brother Dyer, a fellow minister, printed in a Mineral Point newspaper, 2 July 1850, in Curkeet, *The Circuit Rider*, 230.

19 Matthew Dinsdale, California Diary, 18 February – 13 March 1850, in Curkeet, *The Circuit Rider*, 203–5.

20 Ibid., 17 and 19 March 1850, in Curkeet, *The Circuit Rider*, 205–6.

21 Ibid., 8 April 1850, in Curkeet, *The Circuit Rider*, 223.

22 Ibid., 27 April 1850, in Curkeet, *The Circuit Rider*, 228.

23 Ibid., 5 July 1850, in Curkeet, *The Circuit Rider*, 252.

24 Letter from Matthew Dinsdale in Upper California, to Brother Dyer, a fellow minister, printed in a Mineral Point newspaper, 2 July 1850, in Curkeet, *The Circuit Rider*, 233.

25 Matthew Dinsdale, California Diary, 1–3 April 1850, in Curkeet, *The Circuit Rider*, 207.

26 Matthew Dinsdale to his brother John, from Upper California, 7 April 1850, in Curkeet, *The Circuit Rider*, 220–21.

27 Letter from Matthew Dinsdale in Upper California, to Brother Dyer, a fellow minister, printed in a Mineral Point newspaper, 2 July 1850, in Curkeet, *The Circuit Rider* 232.

28 Matthew Dinsdale to his brother Edward, 28 October 1850, in Curkeet, *The Circuit Rider*, 241.

29 Letter from Matthew Dinsdale in Upper California, to Brother Dyer, a fellow minister, printed in a Mineral Point newspaper, 2 July 1850, in Curkeet, *The Circuit Rider*, 232. For another case of a Wensleydale immigrant successfully gold mining in California, see the case of John Russell, in chapter 20. It was news of the California Gold Rush that lured Russell to America. Once on her shores he traveled six weeks around Cape Horn and up the Pacific coast, and was one of the relatively few Forty-Niners who made "a very substantial amount of money."

30 Matthew Dinsdale Papers 1836–1897, WisMSS DL, folder 1, 3–4.

31 Matthew Dinsdale to his brother Edward, from Philadelphia, 9 June 1852, in Curkeet, *The Circuit Rider*, 258. Also, in one day having to walk 40 kilometres "thru mud from the ankle to the knee, with torrents of rain falling most of the day and for two nights" and sleepless nights." Ibid., 257.

32 Matthew Dinsdale to Mary Ann Mann, February 1853, in Curkeet, *The Circuit Rider*, 275–6. The emphasis is Dinsdale's.

33 Marriage certificate, Askrigg, April 1853, 427/149. St Catherine's House, London. See also obituary for Mrs. M.A. Dinsdale in Curkeet, *The Circuit Rider*, 460–1.

34 Mary Ann Mann had some doubts: though committing to marrying Dinsdale, she feared that the migration from the magnificent city of York to the primitive Wisconsin frontier could never be reversed. See letter from Matthew to Mary Ann, 28 March 1853, in Curkeet, *The Circuit Rider*, 285; also Mary Ann's obituary in Curkeet, 460–1.

35 Note from Curkeet, *The Circuit Rider*, 331.

Chapter Sixteen

The chapter-opening quote is by Matthew Willis Jr to his uncle Matthew Willis, from Rama, 21 August 1846, in Curkeet, *The Circuit Rider*, 97.

1 Blewett, *Constant Turmoil*.
2 Briggs, *Victorian People*, 171.
3 For examples see Van Vugt, *British Buckeyes*, 30–2, 140, 155, 169–70, 173, 215–19; also the examples in the county histories, published in Van Vugt, *British Immigration*, vols. 1–4.
4 Kleppner, *The Third Electoral System*, 61, 64, 147–8, 163–5; Van Vugt, *British Buckeyes*, 219.
5 Flanders, *Nauvoo*; Reeve and Parshall, *Mormonism: A Historical Encyclopedia*.
6 Letter dated 6 July 1845, Stephen Longstroth Family Papers, Dales Countryside Museum, Hawes, Yorkshire.
7 Gerber, *Authors of Their Lives*, 19.
8 Richard Buxton writing to brother and sister letter dated "about 1855," Buxton Family Papers, Dales Countryside Museum, Hawes, Yorkshire.
9 Carwardine, *Transatlantic Revivalism*, 90.
10 Allen, *Great Britain and the United States*, 121.

11 Van Vugt, *Britain to America*, 56–7, 137. Average annual consumption of alcohol among Americans aged fifteen and above fell from seven gallons in 1825 to less than two in the late 1840s. See Rorabaugh, *The Alcoholic Republic*.

12 Davis, *Inhuman Bondage*. Philadelphia saw the first abolitionist society, in 1775, and Benjamin Franklin became its president in 1787, though it remained very limited.

13 Davis, *Inhuman Bondage*, 234.

14 Quoted in Gleeson, "England and the Antebellum South," 151.

15 Blackett, *Divided Hearts*; Harwood, "British Evangelical Abolitionism," 288, 290–1.

16 Jeffrey, *The Great Silent Army of Abolitionism*, 24–5, 110–12, 122–3.

17 Van Vugt, *British Buckeyes*, 195, 210.

18 Allen, *Great Britain and the United States*, 123.

19 Reprinted in Van Vugt, *British Immigration*, vol. 4,

20 Van Vugt, *British Buckeyes*, 195–6.

21 "George Metcalfe," *Legacies of British Slave-ownership database*.

22 Matthew Dinsdale to his mother, 11 October 1845, in Curkeet, *The Circuit Rider*, 67.

23 Gleeson, "England and the Antebellum South," 144–49.

24 After the war an arbitration tribunal in Geneva ruled that building the *Alabama* prolonged the war, and this eventually resulted in huge legal penalties against Britain.

25 Blackett, *Divided Hearts*; Lillibridge, *Beacon of Freedom*, 46; Foreman, *A World on Fire*.

26 Quoted in Briggs, *Victorian People*, 202.

27 Lillibridge, *Beacon of Freedom*, 46; Foreman, *A World on Fire*; Blackett, *Divided Hearts*.

28 Gleeson, "England and the Antebellum South," 150–1.

29 Foreman, *A World on Fire*, *passim*.

30 Van Vugt, *Britain to America*, 147–8.

31 Compiler's note in Curkeet, *The Circuit Rider*, 359.

32 Letter dated 31 July 1864, Thomas Lewis Walker Papers, Dales Countryside Museum, Hawes, Yorkshire.

33 Ibid.

34 Ibid.

35 Ibid. Mary Ann lost her brother at Petersburg – Thomas was there too, in the same regiment. John Harker, born in Askrigg in 1823, came

to Wisconsin in 1854, married Yorkshire immigrant Eden Robinson
in 1857, but died in a Tennessee Hospital in 1863 from his battle
wounds. Dixon, "Aspects of Emigration," 1538. Other North Yorkshire
immigrants who fought in the war as members of Company C, 21st
Iowa Volunteer Infantry, were Thomas Locke and Richard J. Raw, both
killed at Vicksburg. James Brunskill survived and fought in Mississippi
and Alabama as well. And N.F. Simpson was wounded at the Battle
of Beaver Dam Creek and then took part in the siege of Vicksburg.
Dixon, 1582. Some lead miners in New Diggings joined the Knights of
the Golden Circle, which was established to resist the draft. But James
Harker was appointed as the local deputy sheriff to help enlist men.
Many Yorkshire immigrants and their sons can be seen on the muster
roll of the Lafayette Guard. As John Dixon puts it, "The roll-call of
privates in the Lafayette Guard could easily be mistaken for members of
the Loyal Dales Volunteers, formed as Home Guard in Yorkshire…to
combat the menace of Napoleonic invasion." Dixon, 1659, citing
F.J. Carter, *New Diggings in an Old Diggings*, 59–60.

36 Letter dated 31 July 1864, Thomas Lewis Walker Papers, Dales
Countryside Museum, Hawes, Yorkshire.

37 "History of the Eckles Family," East Riding Archives and Local Studies,
DDX 270, 28–9, 48.

38 Letter from Rama, Wisconsin, dated February 1865, Willis Family
Papers, Dales Countryside Museum, Hawes, Yorkshire.

39 Ibid.

40 Letters from Farndale and Rosedale 1851–78, letter from William
Atkinson, May 1863, Ryedale Folk Museum, 2009. 44. 38(2). The letter is
incomplete and marked "probably from Cousin Henry Wilson Farndale."

41 Letter from Rama, Wisconsin, dated February 1865, Willis Family
Papers, Dales Countryside Museum, Hawes, Yorkshire.

42 Letter dated 31 July 1864, Thomas Lewis Walker Papers, Dales
Countryside Museum, Hawes, Yorkshire.

43 Ibid.

44 Letter from Rama, Wisconsin, dated February 1865, Willis Family
Papers, Dales Countryside Museum, Hawes, Yorkshire.

45 Ibid.

46 Buxton Family Papers, Dales Countryside Museum, Hawes, Yorkshire.

47 Thomas Lewis Walker Papers, Dales Countryside Museum,
Hawes, Yorkshire.

48   Letter dated 22 January 1871, Thomas Lewis Walker Papers, Dales
      Countryside Museum, Hawes, Yorkshire.

49   Even the celebrations at the war's end could be tragic. James Thorpe,
      who had emigrated from Yorkshire in 1848 and served as a railroad
      machinist, was put in charge of a cannon to celebrate the victory; but
      it exploded prematurely and tore off his right arm in front of horrified
      spectators. The accident "checked the festivities." See Van Vugt, *British
      Buckeyes*, 205.

Chapter Seventeen

The chapter-opening quote is by Townsend Harris, quoted in AZ
Quotes, http://www.azquotes.com/author/45049-Townsend_Harris.

1   Hallas, *Rural Responses to Industrialization*, 232–4; Dales Countryside
      Museum, Hawes, Yorkshire, display, 2014.

2   Baines, *Migration in a Mature Economy*, 140; Woods, *Population of
      Britain in the Nineteenth Century*, 35. Some estimate that the figure is
      closer to 50 per cent. See Richards, *Britannia's Children*, 169.

3   Letter from Rama, Mifflin, Wisconsin, 18 January 1875, Willis Family
      Papers, Dales Countryside Museum, Hawes, Yorkshire.

4   Horton, *Character of the Country*, 24.

5   Letter from Woodhall Cottage, Wensleydale, 13 August 1868, Willis
      Family Papers, Dales Countryside Museum, Hawes, Yorkshire. Richard
      Bonson made return visits in 1862 and 1869. See Bonson papers,
      Swaledale Museum for some details.

6   Letter from Mifflin, Wisconsin, 23 May 1869, Willis Family Papers,
      Dales Countryside Museum, Hawes, Yorkshire.

7   Dixon, "An Emigrant's Letter from Iowa, 1871," 5–41.

8   Ibid., 9.

9   Ibid., 11.

10   Ibid., 13.

11   Ibid., 14.

12   Ibid.

13   Ibid., 16.

14   Ibid., 15–16.

15   Ibid., 20–1.

16   Ibid., 21–2. "Fond" in the Yorkshire dialect means "stupid" or "useless."

17   Ibid., 19.

18 Ibid., 6,7; 40, n. 20.
19 Ibid., 24. The emphases are Dixon's. "Houted" is an example of Dixon's spelling indicating his Yorkshire accent, when he meant "outed."
20 Ibid., 8.
21 Ibid., 20. The emphases are Dixon's.
22 Ibid., 22.

Chapter Eighteen

The chapter-opening quote is from Mark Twain, *A Connecticut Yankee in King Arthur's Court* (1889).

1 For a good summary on Britain's economy in the late nineteenth century, see Black and MacRaild, *Nineteenth-Century Britain*, ch. 3.
2 Daunton, "Society and Economic Life," 53–4.
3 Wilson, *The Victorians*, 427–8.
4 Fletcher, "The Great Depression of English Agriculture," 30–55.
5 Belich, *Replenishing the Earth*, 180.
6 Allen, *British Industries and their Organization*, 92; Belich, *Replenishing the Earth*, 119.
7 Sewell, "All the English-Speaking Race is in Mourning," 674.
8 *Reports on the Census of England and Wales; Census of Scotland* (1851). These figures are also presented and analyzed in Black and MacRaild, *Nineteenth-Century Britain*, Table 5.1, 56–61. *Historical Census Statistics on Population Decennial Summary* Series B 1–12.
9 Though most of the transfer of industrial technology had already occurred, British immigrants continued to bring new methods and machinery, including worsteds, silk, and tinplating. Van Vugt, *British Buckeyes*, ch. 5.
10 Allen, *Great Britain and the United States*, 84. Both Britain and the United States also saw industrial depression from 1873 to the 1880s.
11 Richards, *Britannia's Children*, 193.
12 Spickard, *Almost All Aliens*, 97, table 3.2.
13 Richards, *Britannia's Children*, 193.
14 Erickson, *Leaving England*, ch. 3; Baines *Migration in a Mature Economy*, 165–6.
15 Ibid.; Ibid., ch. 7.
16 Erickson, "English," 328.
17 Fieldhouse and Jennings, *History of Richmond and Swaledale*, 224.

18   Quoted in Spensley, *Mines and Miners of Wensleydale*, 41.
19   Spensley, *Mines and Miners of Wensleydale*, 106.
20   Fieldhouse and Jennings, *History of Richmond and Swaledale*, 226–7; Dixon, "Aspects of Yorkshire Emigration," 1663.
21   Hallas, *Rural Responses to Industrialization*, 273–75.
22   Letter from Benton undated but estimated "about 1855," Buxton Family Papers, Dales Countryside Museum, Hawes, Yorkshire.
23   Morris, *Dalesmen of the Mississippi*, 101.
24   Horton, *Character of the Country*, 41; Dixon, "Aspects of Yorkshire Emigration," 1676.
25   Dixon, "Aspects of Emigration from Yorkshire," 1595–6, 1642.
26   Stainsby, *More than an Ordinary Man*, 16.
27   Letter from William Atkinson, 22 March 1866, Letters from Farndale and Rosedale 1851–1878, Ryedale Folk Museum, 2009. 44. 38(2).
28   Hastings, "Emigration," in *Essays in North Riding History, 1780–1850*. NYCRO Publication No. 28. (1981). See also Hastings, "The Revolt of the Field in the North Riding of Yorkshire," typescript in the Whitby Museum.
29   Soon a new generation of iron works was being built on Teesside. These used Bessemer converters to turn the iron into steel, which was increasingly in demand. By 1883, therefore, production of Cleveland iron ore peaked at 6 ¾ million tons. GB Historical GIS / University of Portsmouth, History of Teesside, in Middlesbrough and North Riding, Map and description, *A Vision of Britain through Time*.
30   Letter from William Atkinson, 10 December 1862, Letters from Farndale and Rosedale 1851–1878, Ryedale Folk Museum. 2009. 44. 38(2).
31   Ibid., May 1863.
32   Letter from Elizabeth Wilson, 12 March 1869, Letters from Farndale and Rosedale 1851–1878, Ryedale Folk Museum. 2009. 44. 38(2).
33   Letter from "WA" [William Atkinson], 5 February 1871, Letters from Farndale and Rosedale 1851–1878, Ryedale Folk Museum. 2009. 44. 38(2); William Atkinson, 1872, writing from "Tees Iron Works, Middlesbro on Tees," Letters from Farndale and Rosedale 1851–1878, Ryedale Folk Museum, 2009. 44. 38(2).
34   Letter from Elizabeth Wilson, 12 March 1869, Letters from Farndale and Rosedale 1851–1878, Ryedale Folk Museum, 2009. 44. 38(2).
35   Letter from "WA," 1 April 1869, Letters from Farndale and Rosedale 1851–1878, Ryedale Folk Museum, 2009. 44. 38(2).

36 Letter from Elizabeth Wilson, 12 March 1869, Letters from Farndale and Rosedale 1851–1878, Ryedale Folk Museum, 2009. 44. 38(2).

37 Quoted in Spensley, *Mines and Miners of Wensleydale*, 38.

38 *Yorkshire Gazette*, 1 January 1870, cited in Hastings, "The Revolt of the Field in the North Riding of Yorkshire."

39 Ibid., 7 November 1874.

40 Letter from "WA," 5 February 1871, Letters from Farndale and Rosedale 1851–1878, Ryedale Folk Museum, 2009. 44. 38(2). A letter of 7 July 1873 states: "everything is dear now."

41 *Yorkshire Gazette*, 20 April 1872, cited in Hastings, "The Revolt of the Field in the North Riding of Yorkshire."

42 Ibid., 2 November 1872; 22 February 1873; 11 April 1874; 2 May 1874.

43 Ibid., 20 June 1874; 18 July 1847; 25 September 1875.

44 Letter from Elizabeth Wilson, 12 March 1869, Letters from Farndale and Rosedale 1851–1878, Ryedale Folk Museum, 2009. 44. 38(2).

45 Ibid.

46 Ibid., Letter from "WA," 2 March 1870.

47 William Atkinson wrote in January 1878, from Martin House, Stokesley, Ryedale Folk Museum. 2009. 44. 38(2).

48 See case ID 77 in the database explored by Van Vugt "Relocating the English Diaspora in America," 8–36.

49 "The Wilson Family of Primrose Villas & Texas," in the Wilson Family Papers, Rosedale Abbey Reading Room, Ryedale, North Yorkshire, 2014.

50 Wilson, "Advocate for Texas."

Chapter Nineteen

1 Gates, *The Illinois Central*; Bogue, *From Prairie to Corn Belt*.

2 Barney, *Passage of the Republic*.

3 Letter from Rama, Wisconsin, dated 24 March 1867, Willis Family Papers, Dales Countryside Museum, Hawes, Yorkshire.

4 The new income taxes that Lincoln and Congress imposed during the war were not repealed until 1872; see American Civil War Story, "Income Tax History."

5 Matthew Dinsdale to his daughter Annie Dinsdale, 11 August 1875, in Curkeet, *The Circuit Rider*, 391.

6   Letter from Rama, Wisconsin, dated 24 March 1867, Willis Family Papers, Dales Countryside Museum, Hawes, Yorkshire.
7   Ibid., Letter from Rama, Wisconsin, undated but soon after the Civil War.
8   Ibid.
9   Ibid.
10 Letter from Rama, Wisconsin, dated 24 March 1867, Willis Family Papers, Dales Countryside Museum, Hawes, Yorkshire.
11 Ibid.
12 Fred J. Willis, "The Willis Family of Carperby," September 1986, Willis Family Papers, Dales Countryside Museum, Hawes, Yorkshire.
13 Letter from Rama, Wisconsin, dated 24 March 1867, Willis Family Papers, Dales Countryside Museum, Hawes, Yorkshire.
14 Ibid.
15 Ibid.
16 Ibid.
17 The diary has been published in Horton, *Character of the Country*.
18 Horton, *Character of the Country*, 96–7.
19 Hallas, *Rural Responses to Industrialization*, 287–8.
20 Horton, *Character of the Country*, 48–50.
21 Ibid., 11.
22 Surviving records indicate a relatively high rate of intermarriage between British immigrants and Americans. In 1920 the British had the highest rate of all immigrants. See Van Vugt, "British," in Barkan, *Nation of Peoples*, 75–95. In contrast, the Dales immigrants in the Upper Mississippi seem to have married fellow immigrants more frequently.
23 Horton, *Character of the Country*, 42–3.
24 Ibid., 13.
25 Letter from Rama, Mifflin, Wisconsin, dated 2 March 1870, Willis Family Papers, Dales Countryside Museum, Hawes, Yorkshire.
26 See many such cases in Van Vugt, *Britain to America*, and Van Vugt, *British Buckeyes*.

Chapter Twenty

1   Winther, "Promoting the American West," 506–13; Winther, "English Migration to the American West," 115–25.
2   The first such settlement was established in Fairmont, Martin County, Minnesota, in 1856. Others were established after the war in Decorah

and Le Mars, Iowa, and in Kansas. See Van Vugt, *Britain to America*, 118–21; Pagnamenta, *Prairie Fever*.

3   Quoted in Hallas, *Rural Responses to Industrialization*, 289. By 1870, G.M. Binks was appointed Pastor, but the Wights continued to live here. O.S. died on 7 August 1912 at his home near Pilot Rock. He was buried next to his wife in Pilot Rock Cemetery. G.M. Binks organized the first quarterly meeting of the Methodist Church held in the McLean Hotel. See Leckband, "Celebrating 150 Years."

4   *Ripon Gazette*, 27 June 1874, quoted in Tring, "Nineteenth Century Immigration from England," 360–5.

5   Tring, "Nineteenth Century Immigration from England," 364.

6   Dixon, "An Emigrant's Letter from Iowa, 1871," 24.

7   Ibid., 27.

8   Ibid., 29.

9   Ibid.

10   Ibid., 30. George Standing bought 80 acres, "so accidentally cheap at 5 dollars per acre," 31.

11   Ibid., 30–1. Speculators were not necessarily bad. On the Iowa frontier they helped people obtain land at reasonable prices, introduced credit, and created jobs. See Robert P. Swierenga, *Pioneers and Profits: Land Speculation on the Iowa Frontier*. Ames: Iowa State University Press, 1968.

12   Ibid., 31.

13   Ibid., 32, 35.

14   Ibid., 24–5. Like other English immigrants farming in America, Dixon reported enthusiastically about Indian corn, p. 25.

15   Ibid., 23.

16   Letter from Rama, Wisconsin, dated 24 March 1867, Willis Family Papers, Dales Countryside Museum, Hawes, Yorkshire.

17   Dixon, "An Emigrant's Letter from Iowa, 1871," 26.

18   Ibid., 28.

19   Ibid., 27.

20   Ibid.

21   Ibid.

22   Ibid., 25.

23   Ibid., 33.

24   Ibid., 32.

25   Ibid., 26.

26   Ibid., 28.

27 Marriott, *Those Who Left the Dales*, 20; "Reminiscences of Early Days of Alice (Wilkinson) Hansen, of Custer County, Nebraska Homestead Days," Wilkinson Family Papers, Dales Countryside Museum, Hawes, Yorkshire; *Progressive Men of the State of Wyoming*, 258–60. For John Wilkinson, see ibid., 274–5. John and Anthony's sister Alice married John Sidgwick, who was the innkeeper at the Blue Bell Inn in Kettlewell, which thrives to this day. They followed in 1889 and came to Cheyenne, Wyoming.

28 "Reminiscences of Early Days of Alice (Wilkinson) Hansen, of Custer County, Nebraska Homestead Days," Wilkinson Family Papers, Dales Countryside Museum, Hawes, Yorkshire.

29 Ibid.

30 Ibid.

31 John Russell Family Papers, Dales Countryside Museum, Hawes, Yorkshire.

32 Ibid.

33 Burt, "Freemasonry and Business Networking," 657–88.

34 "William, Robert and Elizabeth Pratt Carter from Arkengarthdale to North America," Swaledale Museum in Reeth. See also Marriott, *Those Who Left the Dales*, 172–3.

35 Van Vugt, *British Immigration*, vol. 4, 121.

36 Ibid., 162–6. A surprising number of English immigrants from all counties became fruit growers. See Van Vugt, "Relocating the English Diaspora," 17. The Erickson Database records an impressive twenty cases of English immigrants (from all counties) who became California fruit farmers. See the following case ID numbers: 16, 983, 996, 1004, 1008, 1023, 1034, 1043, 1045, 1048, 1049, 1052, 1059, 1066, 1071, 1079, 1122, 1140, 1155, 1156.

Chapter Twenty-One

The chapter-opening quote by Davy Crockett was published in Texas Bob, Texas Quotes, http://texasbob.com/txdoc/txquotes.html, accessed 30 March 2020.

1 This was done because of starvation on their ship, and this account was recorded by Richard Hakluyt in his *The Principall Navigations, Voiages and Discoveries of the English Nation* (1589). Hakluyt was not completely convinced of its accuracy though others were. See *Handbook*

of Texas Online, John L. Davis and Phillip L. Fry, "English," uploaded
  12 June 2010, https://tshaonline.org/handbook/online/articles/pie02.

2 Davis and Fry, "English." In the 1830s, attempts at colonization began
   on a much larger scale, though again with limited success.

3 Roeckell, "Bonds Over Bondage," 257–78.

4 Cutrer, *The English Texans*, 14.

5 Merk, *Slavery and Annexation*, 42–3.

6 Quoted in Bernstein, "Special Relationship and Appeasement," 725–50.
   Palmerston's views hardened over the McLeod affair of 1837, in which the
   Canadian militia intercepted the American ship *Caroline* and destroyed
   it for carrying weapons to anti-British rebels. The Americans demanded
   reparations, but Palmerston refused. When the Americans arrested a
   British citizen named McLeod for murdering an American woman on the
   Caroline, Palmerston declared that executing McLeod would lead to war.
   Though McLeod was acquitted the dispute over the Maine boundary kept
   tensions high. See ibid., 727–8. For an account of the Irish in Texas that
   covers some of these themes and events, see Davis, *Land!*.

7 Rister, "Beales's Rio Grande Colony."

8 Roeckell, "Bonds over Bondage," 257–78; Shepperson, *British
   Emigration to North America*, 29–31; Davis and Fry, "English."

9 *Leeds Times*, Saturday, 7 September 1839, quoting the *Bolton Free Press*.

10 Kennedy, *Texas*, vol. 2; Cutrer, *The English Texans*, 31.

11 Belcher represented the company and about a hundred settlers on
   27,000 acres on the Brazos. The famous Native American artist George
   Catlin was involved in the company for a while. Yancy, "Belcher,
   Edward."

12 Ribb, "Colony of Kent" Cutrer, *The English Texans*; Renick, "The City of
   Kent," 51–65.

13 *Emigration* (London, 1849), excerpt, 72–129, British Library of Political
   and Economic Science, OU1849/10B, reprinted in Van Vugt, *British
   Immigration*, vol. 3, 362.

14 Ibid., 363.

15 The excerpt concludes by saying "Texas is hopelessly bad, New Mexico,
   if possible, worse, and California worst." If Texas was not as bad as
   California, it must have been quite good after all. Ibid., 363.

16 "Hunting in Western Texas," *The Field*, 6 December 1879, in
   Wilson, "Advocate for Texas," Appendix F-1; "The Wilson Family of
   Primrose Villas & Texas," Rosedale Abbey Reading Room, Ryedale,
   North Yorkshire.

17 Diary of Thomas Wilson, in Wilson, "Advocate for Texas," appendix B-2–3; "The Wilson Family of Primrose Villas & Texas," Rosedale Abbey Reading Room, Ryedale, North Yorkshire.

18 "The Wilson Family of Primrose Villas & Texas," Rosedale Abbey Reading Room, Ryedale, North Yorkshire.

19 Ibid.

20 Wilson, "Advocate for Texas."

21 "The Wilson Family of Primrose Villas & Texas," Rosedale Abbey Reading Room, Ryedale, North Yorkshire, 2014.

22 The agent in London was William Kingsbury, a dentist from Caldwell County, Texas, who was recruited by the GH&AR Company and stationed in London to promote their lands to prospective English emigrants. See Wilson, "Advocate for Texas."

23 Wilson, "Advocate for Texas."

24 "The Wilson Family of Primrose Villas & Texas," Rosedale Abbey Reading Room, Ryedale, North Yorkshire, 2014, letter of 12 March 2014. He donated the communion wafer box as well.

25 "The Wilson Family of Primrose Villas & Texas," Rosedale Abbey Reading Room, Ryedale, North Yorkshire.

26 Ibid.

27 Henry Thirlway to Matthew Dinsdale, from Blackpool, England, 4 September 1883, in Curkeet, *The Circuit Rider*, 408–09. The Bird's Eye Primrose, which grows low to the ground, was apparently a different variety than the one Wilson brought to Texas, which grows taller and can intertwine with hedgerows.

28 "The Wilson Family of Primrose Villas & Texas," Rosedale Abbey Reading Room, Ryedale, North Yorkshire.

29 Ibid.

30 The girls were clearly valued for their work, because they received presents from the families. Inexplicably, Mary Ellen "found a gold mine in their garden containing 235 dollars in gold." See "A Rosedale Man in Texas" and "The Wilson Family of Primrose Villas & Texas," Rosedale Abbey Reading Room, Ryedale, North Yorkshire.

31 Schmitz, "Diplomatic Relations of the Republic of Texas."

32 Ibid.; Pagnamenta, *Prairie Fever*, ch. 9. On American resentment of extensive English ownership of Texas lands, see Crapol, *America for Americans*.

33 Notes for Thomas Wilson Sr., "The Wilson Family of Primrose Villas & Texas," Rosedale Abbey Reading Room, Ryedale, North Yorkshire 2014.

34 "The Wilson Family of Primrose Villas & Texas," Rosedale Abbey Reading Room, Ryedale, North Yorkshire, 2014.

35 Ibid.

36 Wilson, "Advocate for Texas." Some of the names of the immigrants that Wilson settled include Carter, Moore, Taylor, Ireland, Yolland, Ervine, Batey, Eiband, Glithero, Wallace, Fisher, and Lowther. "Nearly all" of them brought along "large families who were a real asset to the social and cultural life." From "Do You Remember? Early Days in Luling, Texas," in "The Wilson Family of Primrose Villas & Texas," Rosedale Abbey Reading Room, Ryedale, North Yorkshire, 2014.

37 Shmitz, "Diplomatic Relations of the Republic of Texas."

38 Wilson, "Advocate for Texas."

39 Ibid.

40 Quoted in Cutrer, *The English Texans*, 82.

Chapter Twenty-Two

The chapter-opening quote is a phrase used in section 91 of the *British North America* Act, 1867 (now called the *Constitution Act, 1867*).

1 Spickard, *Almost All Aliens*, 97, table 3.2.

2 Campey, *Seeking a Better Future*, 293.

3 Quoted in Dennis, "Foreigners Who Live in Toronto," 52.

4 Quoted in Elliott, "Regional Patterns," 51.

5 Campey, *Ignored but Not Forgotten*, 266.

6 Bueltmann and MacRaild, *The English Diaspora*.

7 Address to the St George's Society, in Campey, *Seeking a Better Future*, 288.

8 Campey, *Seeking a Better Future*, 288, 297. This was also true of English immigrants in New Zealand at the same time. However, Yorkshire Societies did flourish for a while in New Zealand, while a Yorkshire society in Canada was established but did not thrive. See Watson, "Cooked in True Yorkshire Fashion," 169–84.

9 Campey, *Ignored but Not Forgotten*, 218. Their speedy assimilation is discussed on p. 289.

10 Ibid., 218.

11 Ibid., 226.

12 Ibid., 264.

13 Lloyd, "The Englishmen Here Are Much Disliked," 135–49.

14   Campey, *Ignored but Not Forgotten*, 220, 229.
15   Campey, *Seeking a Better Future*, 225.
16   Ibid., 231–2.
17   Ibid., 229.
18   The Strickland Family Papers, Rosedale Abbey Reading Room, Ryedale, North Yorkshire.
19   Norman Creaser collection, East Riding Archives and Local Studies, LBEA DDX 1408/1/15.
20   Ford Family Documents, Rosedale Abbey Reading Room, Ryedale, North Yorkshire.
21   2 May 1894, John Cherry Letters, NYCRO CRONT 2456 (2).
22   4 May 1894, John Cherry Letters, NYCRO CRONT 2456 (2).
23   Ibid., 9 May 1894.
24   Ibid., 10 May 1894, John Cherry Letters, NYCRO CRONT 2456 (2)
25   Ibid., 11 and 12 May 1894.
26   29 May 1894, John Cherry Letters, NYCRO ZLB 11/27/4.
27   10 June 1894, John Cherry Letters, NYCRO ZLB 11/27/5.
28   Ibid.
29   Ibid.
30   Ibid.
31   Ibid.
32   Ibid.
33   The Hardraw Brass Band Competition is still popular today, and until very recently the Green Dragon held a prestigious folk music festival. The waterfall is also called "Hardraw Force," and is England's highest single-drop waterfall. Today Hardraw Scaur is also spelled "Scar."
34   8 July 1894, John Cherry Letters, NYCRO ZLB 11/27/5.
35   Ibid.
36   9 September 1894, John Cherry Letters, NYCRO ZLB 11/27/8.
37   Ibid.
38   8 July 1894, John Cherry Letters, NYCRO ZLB 11/27/5.
39   Ibid.
40   Lloyd, "The Englishmen Here are Much Disliked," 142–3.
41   8 July 1894, John Cherry Letters, NYCRO ZLB 11/27/5.
42   The census shows that between 1881 and 1891 quite a number of Swaledale lead miners moved to the Liverpool area – West Derby in Lancashire – to take that option in order to adjust to an industry on the verge of extinction. They included George and Ann Alderson,

Ralph Harker (a lead miner born in 1861) Thomas and Dinah Lowis, and James March, a lead miner and farmer. *The Dalesman*, May and June 1978. See also the John Cherry Papers Collection, p. 29. Simon Cherry (1874–1924) was the younger brother of John Cherry (1837–1901) and Mary (Alderson) Cherry (1845–1924) his sister. Simon was a patient at the Royal Infirmary in Liverpool. Beginning in March 1894, he eventually recovered and returned to Reeth to work as a joiner and builder. See p. 42 in the John Cherry Papers Collection.

43   9 September 1894, John Cherry Letters, NYCRO ZLB 11/27/8.
44   19 November 1894, John Cherry Letters, NYCRO ZLB 11/27/9.
45   9 September 1894, John Cherry Letters, NYCRO ZLB 11/27/8.
46   19 November 1894, John Cherry Letters, NYCRO ZLB 11/27/9.
47   Ibid.
48   27 November 1894, John Cherry Letters, NYCRO ZLB 11/27/10.
49   Ibid.
50   Ibid.
51   Ibid.
52   Campey, *Ignored but Not Forgotten*, 160–61.
53   Gagnon, "Settling the West."
54   For a personal account of a Norfolk immigrant in Manitoba, originally published in 1883, see Wells, ed., *Letters from a young emigrant in Manitoba*.
55   Campey, *Ignored but Not Forgotten*, 111–13.
56   Ibid. 140–9.
57   Van Vugt, "English Emigrant Guidebooks."
58   Campey, *Ignored but Not Forgotten*, 138.
59   *Beverley Guardian*, 26 April 1882, quoted in Campey, *Ignored but Not Forgotten*, 173.
60   Campey, *Ignored but Not Forgotten*, 119.
61   Ibid., 173.
62   Ibid., 108.
63   Ibid., 114–15. For an example of a Newcastle coal miner becoming a homesteader, see p. 136.
64   Ibid., 205. Barnardo's ran an industrial farm in Manitoba; see p. 211.
65   Ibid., 130.
66   Ibid., 135.
67   Bueltmann, "Mutual, Ethnic, and Diasporic," 64–87.

68 Campey, *Ignored but Not Forgotten*, 171.
69 Ibid., 149.
70 Ibid., 123.
71 Ibid., 163.
72 Ibid., 187–8.
73 Ibid., 188.
74 Ibid.
75 Carrier and Jeffery, *External Migration*; Spickard, *Almost All Aliens*, 97, table 3.2. The statistics do not separate the English from the Welsh.
76 Hutchinson, *Immigrants and Their Children*; Lines, *British and Canadian Immigration*.
77 Spickard, *Almost All Aliens*, 97, table 3.2. The figure for the 1920s is 341,552, though this includes the Scots and Irish after 1926.
78 The 1920 Census reveals that the English, Scots, and Welsh generally had the highest rates of intermarriage with Americans and were thus distinct for their rapid assimilation with the native-born. See Hutchinson, *Immigrants and their Children*.
79 Elliott, "Regional Patterns," 53.
80 Letter to Frank Raw, dated 3 June 1913, from Nutana, Saskatoon, Letter no. 11, Watson Archive, Rosedale Abbey Reading Room, Ryedale, North Yorkshire.
81 Letter dated 18 August 1913, Letter no. 12, Watson Archive, Rosedale Abbey Reading Room, Ryedale, North Yorkshire.
82 Stainsby, *More Than an Ordinary Man*, 20.
83 Van Vugt, "The British: English, Scots, Welsh, Scots Irish, 1870–1940," 235–44.; Van Vugt, "The British: English, Scots, Welsh, Scots Irish, 1940–2010," 785–92.

Conclusion and Epilogue

The chapter-opening quote is by Matthew Dinsdale to his brother Edward, from Lake Winnebago, 16 March 1847, in Curkeet, *The Circuit Rider*, 152.

The epilogue-opening quote is from a letter by William Atkinson, 10 December 1862, Letters from Farndale and Rosedale 1851–1878, Ryedale Folk Museum, 2009. 44. 38(2).

1 Fischer, *Albion's Seed*.

2   Swierenga, "Dutch Immigration Patterns"; Semmingsen, *Norway to America*; Semmingsen, "Norwegian Emigration in the Nineteenth Century"; Ostergren, *A Community Transplanted*.

3   Erickson, "English," 332.

4   Campey, *Ignored but Not Forgotten*, 23. (The emphasis is mine.)

5   Ibid., 24.

6   Hallas, *Rural Responses to Industrialization*, 294; Richards, "Malthus," 54. See also Belich, *Replenishing the Earth*.

7   Baines, *Migration in a Mature Economy*, ch.7.

8   Letter to Matthew and Jane Willis, from Wensleydale, undated, Willis Family Papers, Dales Countryside Museum, Hawes, Yorkshire.

9   Letter of Richard Buxton writing to his brother, dated 13 January 1881, Buxton Family Papers, Dales Countryside Museum, Hawes, Yorkshire.

10   Ibid.

11   John Buxton writing to his brother, 22 June 1883, Buxton Family Papers, Dales Countryside Museum, Hawes, Yorkshire.

12   John Buxton writing to his nephew, 3 June 1884, Buxton Family Papers, Dales Countryside Museum, Hawes, Yorkshire. In another letter to his nephew dated 16 January 1898, John Buxton mentions that he had not seen his brother Richard "since I came back to America," suggesting a return visit to Gunnerside.

13   Letter dated 22 January 1871, Thomas Lewis Walker Papers, Dales Countryside Museum, Hawes, Yorkshire.

14   For example, see letter from Rama, Wisconsin, dated 24 March 1867, Willis Family Papers, Dales Countryside Museum, Hawes, Yorkshire.

15   Letter from Rama, Wisconsin, dated 24 March 1867, Willis Family Papers, Dales Countryside Museum, Hawes, Yorkshire.

16   Van Vugt, "An English Shoemaker in Indiana," 56.

17   Letter dated 20 January 1895, Thomas Lewis Walker Papers, Dales Countryside Museum, Hawes, Yorkshire.

18   Ibid., Letter dated 11 March 1900.

19   Letter from Gunnerside dated 21 June 1906, Buxton Family Papers, Dales Countryside Museum, Hawes, Yorkshire.

20   Ibid., Letter from Gunnerside, dated 21 May 1907.

21   Ibid., dated 6 November 1907.

22   Ibid., dated 22 October 1910.

23   Hallas, *Rural Responses to Industrialization*, 273–5.

24 Between 1821 and 1901 Swaledale had a net loss of about 10,000 because of emigration; Hallas, *Rural Responses to Industrialization*, 292–3.

25 This is consistent with the work of Baines, who also found that emigration and internal migration generally did not substitute for each other for England as a whole. Baines, *Migration in a Mature Economy*, 247. Sell also Hallas, *Rural Responses to Industrialization*, 292–3.

26 Letter of J. Raisbeck, 23 December 1890, quoted in Hallas, *Rural Responses to Industrialization*, 290.

27 J. Morris, *The North Riding of Yorkshire* (1906), 17, quoted in Hallas, *Rural Responses to Industrialization*, 291.

28 Hallas, *Rural Responses to Industrialization*, 291.

29 Dixon Cottingham Diary, Swaledale Museum, Reeth, Yorkshire.

30 Letter from Askrigg to Matthew Dinsdale, 17 September 1875, and excerpts from Annie's Memoirs, in Curkeet, *The Circuit Rider*, 393–5.

Bibliography

Archives, Museums, and the Like

Dales Countryside Museum, Hawes, Yorkshire.
- Buxton Family Papers, Dales Countryside Museum, Hawes, Yorkshire.
- Stephen Longstroth Family Papers, Dales Countryside Museum, Hawes, Yorkshire.
- Thomas Lewis Walker Papers, Dales Countryside Museum, Hawes, Yorkshire.
- Willis Family Papers, Dales Countryside Museum, Hawes, Yorkshire.
- Wilkinson Family Papers, Dales Countryside Museum, Hawes, Yorkshire.
East Riding Archives and Local Studies, Beverley, East Yorkshire.
Keld Resource Centre, Keld, Yorkshire.
Matthew Dinsdale Papers, 1836–1897, Wisconsin Historical Society Archives, Madison, Wisconsin, MAD 4/47/F2. Portions are also available online at http://digicoll.library.wisc.edu/cgi-bin/WI/WI-idx?id=WI.Dinsdale1m
- Additional material related to Matthew Dinsdale was also transcribed and compiled by his great-granddaughter Abigail Curkeet as *Ancestral Voices, Part I: The Circuit Rider*. Mount Hoteb [i.e. Horeb], Wisconsin: published by the author, 1980.
North Yorkshire County Record Office (NYCRO). Northallerton, North Yorkshire.
Richmondshire Museum, Richmond, North Yorkshire.
Ryedale Folk Museum, Ryedale, North Yorkshire.
- Fewster Family Letters, Ryedale Folk Museum.
- John and Ann Knaggs Letters, Ryedale Folk Museum.

- Letters from Farndale and Rosedale 1851–1878, Ryedale Folk Museum, 2009.

Rosedale Abbey Reading Room, Ryedale, North Yorkshire.
- Ford Family Documents, Rosedale Abbey Reading Room, Ryedale, North Yorkshire.
- Strickland Family Papers, Rosedale Abbey Reading Room. Ryedale, North Yorkshire.
- Watson Archive, Rosedale Abbey Reading Room, Ryedale, North Yorkshire.
- "The Wilson Family of Primrose Villas & Texas," Rosedale Abbey Reading Room, Ryedale, North Yorkshire.

Swaledale Museum, Reeth, Yorkshire.

Books and Articles

Acornley, Rev. John H. *A History of the Primitive Methodist Church in the United States of America from its origin and the landing of the first missionaries in 1829 to the present time.* Fall River, MA: B.R. Acornley, 1909.

Albion, Robert G. *The Rise of New York Port.* New York: Charles Scribner's Sons, 1939.

Album of Genealogy and Biography of Cook County, Illinois. Chicago: La Salle Book Company, 1900.

Allen, G.C. *British Industries and Their Organization.* 3rd ed. New York: Green, 1956.

Allen, H.C. *Great Britain and the United States: A History of Anglo-American Relations, 1783–1952.* London: Odhams Press, 1954.

American Civil War Story. "Income Tax History." Article published 14 March 2018. Accessed 30 March 2020. http://www.americancivilwarstory.com/income-tax-history.html.

Bagenal, Timothy. *Miners & Farmers.* British Mining no. 62. Exeter, UK: Northern Mine Research Society, 1999.

Bailyn, Bernard. *Voyagers to the West: A Passage in the Peopling of America on the Eve of the Revolution.* New York: Knopf, 1986.

Baines, Dudley. *Migration in a Mature Economy: Emigration and Internal Migration in England and Wales 1861–1900.* Cambridge: Cambridge University Press, 2009.

Barker, L. "The Lead Miners of Swaledale and Arkengarthdale in 1851." Unpublished paper.

Barney, William L. *The Passage of the Republic*. Lexington: D.C. Heath, 1987.

Batty, Margaret. *Gunnerside Chapel and Gunnerside Folk*. Teessdale: Teessdale Mercury Press, 1967.

Belich, James. *Replenishing the Earth: The Settler Revolution and the Rise of the Angloworld, 1783–1939*. New York: Oxford University Press, 2009.

Bernstein, George L. "Special Relationship and Appeasement: Liberal Policy Towards America in the Age of Palmerston." *The Historical Journal* 41, no. 3 (1998): 725–50.

Berry, Stephen R. *A Path in the Mighty Waters: Shipboard Life & Atlantic Crossings to the New World*. New Haven: Yale University Press, 2015.

Berthoff, Rowland T. *British Immigrants in Industrial America, 1790–1950*. 1953. Reprinted, New York: Russell and Russell, 1968.

Birch, Brian P. "The Editor and the English: George Sheppard and English Immigration to Clinton County." *The Annals of Iowa* 47 (1985): 622–42.

Bishop, Janet. "Women and Mining Communities in the Dales." In *Memoirs 2011*, 30–2. British Mining no. 92. Exeter, UK: Northern Mine Research Society, 2011.

Black, Jeremy, and Donald M. MacRaild. *Nineteenth-Century Britain*. London: Palgrave Macmillan, 2003.

Blackett, Richard J.M. *Divided Hearts: Britain and the American Civil War*. Baton Rouge: Louisiana State University Press, 2001.

Blewett, Mary. *Constant Turmoil: The Politics of Industrial Life in Nineteen-Century New England*. Amherst: University of Massachusetts Press, 2000.

– *The Yankee Yorkshireman: Migration Lived and Imagined*. Baton Rouge: Louisiana State University Press, 2001.

Bogue, Allan. *From Prairie to Corn Belt: Farming on the Illinois Prairies in the Nineteenth Century*. Chicago: University of Chicago Press, 1963.

Bonson, Robert E. *The Bonson Diaries, 1840–1904*. Self-published, 2008.

Briggs, Asa. *Victorian People: A Reassessment of Persons and Themes, 1851–1867*. Chicago: University of Chicago Press, 1975.

Bueltmann, Tanja. "Mutual, Ethnic, and Diasporic: The Sons of England in Canada, c. 1880 to 1910." In *England, the English, and English Culture in North America*, edited by David T. Gleeson, 64–87. Columbia: University of South Carolina Press, 2017.

Bueltmann, Tanja, and Donald MacRaild. *The English Diaspora in North America: Migration, Ethnicity and Association, 1730s–1950s*. Manchester: Manchester University Press, 2017.

Burk, Kathleen. *Old World, New World: Great Britain and America from the Beginning*. New York: Atlantic Monthly Press, 2007.

Burt, Roger. "Freemasonry and Business Networking During the Victorian Period." *Economic History Review* 56 (November 2003): 657–88.

Campey, Lucille H. *Ignored but Not Forgotten: Canada's English Immigrants*. Toronto: Dundurn, 2014.

– *Seeking a Better Future: The English Pioneers of Ontario and Quebec*. Toronto: Dundurn, 2012.

Cannon, M. Hamlin. "Migration of English Mormons to America." *American Historical Review* 52, no. 3 (April 1947): 436–55.

N.H. Carrier and J.R. Jeffery, *External Migration: A Study of the Available Statistics, 1815–1950*, General Register Office, Studies on Medical and Population Subjects, no. 6. London: HMSO, 1953, 95–6.

Carwardine, Richard. *Transatlantic Revivalism: Popular Evangelicalism in Britain and America, 1790–1865*. Westport, CT: Greenwood Publishing Group, 1978.

Cashin, Edward J. *The King's Ranger: Thomas Brown and the American Revolution on the Southern Frontier*. New York: Fordham University Press, 1999.

Childs, C. *The History of Dubuque County, Iowa*. Chicago: Western Historical Company, 1880.

Church, Roy A. *The Great Victorian Boom, 1850–1873*. London: Macmillan, 1975.

Clough, Robert T. *The Lead Smelting Mills of the Yorkshire Dales and Northern Pennines*. 2nd ed. Keighley, Yorkshire: published by the author, 1980.

Cobbett, William. *A Year's Residence in the United States of America*. 1819. Reprinted, New York: Centaur Press Ltd, 1964.

Cohn, Raymond L. "The Occupation of English Immigrants to the United States, 1836–1853." *Journal of Economic History* 52, vol. 2 (1992): 377–87.

Colley, Linda. *Captives: Britain, Empire and the World, 1600–1850*. London: Pimlico, 2003.

Commemorative Biographical Record of Rock, Green, Grant, Iowa, and Lafayette Counties, Wisconsin. Chicago: J.H. Beers & Co., 1901.

Conzen, Kathleen Neils, David A. Gerber, Ewa Morawska, George E. Pozzetta, and Rudolph J. Vecoli. "The Invention of Ethnicity: The View from the USA." *Journal of American Ethnic History* 12 (Fall, 1992): 3–41.

Cooper, Edmund. *Muker: The Story of a Yorkshire Parish*. Clapham, Yorkshire: The Dalesman Publishing Co., 1948.

Cowan, Helen. *British Emigration to British North America: The First Hundred Years*. 1928. Revised and enlarged. Toronto: University of Toronto Press, 1961.

Crapol, Edward P. *America for Americans: Economic Nationalism and Anglophobia in the Late Nineteenth Century*. Westport, CT: Greenwood Press, 1973.

Curkeet, Abigail. *Ancestral Voices, Part I: The Circuit Rider*. Mount Hoteb [i.e. Horeb], Wisconsin: published by the author, 1980.

Cutrer, Thomas W. *The English Texans*. San Antonio: The University of Texas Institute of Texan Cultures, 1985.

Daunton, Martin. "Society and Economic Life." In *The Nineteenth Century: The British Isles 1815–1901*, edited by Colin Matthew, 41–84. Oxford: Oxford University Press, 2000.

Davis, David Brion. *Inhuman Bondage: The Rise and Fall of Slavery in the New World*. Oxford: Oxford University Press, 2006.

Davis, Graham. *Land!: Irish Pioneers in Mexican and Revolutionary Texas*. College Station: Texas A&M University Press, 2002.

Davis, John L., and Phillip L. Fry. "English." In *The Handbook of Texas Online*. Texas State Historical Association. Uploaded 12 June 2010; last modified 18 September 2019. https://tshaonline.org/handbook/online/articles/pie02.

Deane, Phyllis, and W.A. Cole, *British Economic Growth 1688–1959*. 2nd ed. Cambridge: Cambridge University Press, 1967.

Dennis, Richard. "'Foreigners Who Live in Toronto': Attitudes toward Immigrants in a Canadian City, 1890–1918." In *Canadian Migration Patterns from Britain and North America*, edited by Barbara J. Messamore, 183–200. Ottawa: University of Ottawa Press, 2004.

Dixon, John Flounders. "An Emigrant's Letter from Iowa, 1871." Edited and introduced by Charlotte Erickson. *Bulletin of the British Association for American Studies* 12 (1966): 5–41.

Dixon, John Thornton. "Aspects of Yorkshire Emigration to North America, 1760–1880." PhD thesis, University of Leeds, 1981.

Dowd, Gregory Evans. "Indigenous Peoples without the Republic." *Journal of American History* 104, no. 1 (June 2017): 19–41.

Edwards, Phyllis Ruth, ed. *Pioneer Poetry: A Quaker Reflects on the Civil War Era in the United States: Matthew Willis, Iowa County, Wisconsin, 1799–1883*. Pacific Grove, CA: Park Place Publications, 2015.

Elliott, Bruce S. "Regional Patterns of English Immigration and Settlement in Upper Canada." In *Canadian Migration Patterns from Britain and North America*, edited by Barbara J. Messamore, 51–90. Ottawa: University of Ottawa Press, 2004.

Encyclopedia Dubuque. "Dubuque in the California Gold Rush." Last
  modified 28 February 2015. http://www.encyclopediadubuque.org/index.
  php?title=DUBUQUE_IN_THE_CALIFORNIA_GOLD_RUSH.
Erickson, Charlotte. "English." In *Harvard Encyclopedia of American Ethnic
  Groups,* edited by Stephen Thernstrom. Cambridge: Harvard University
  Press, Belknap Press, 1980.
– *Invisible Immigrants: The Adaptation of English and Scottish Immigrants in
  19th Century America.* Coral Gables, Fla: University of Miami Press, 1972.
– *Leaving England: Essays on British Emigration in the Nineteenth Century*
  Ithaca, NY: Cornell University Press, 1994.
Ernst, Robert. *Immigrant Life in New York, 1825–63.* 1949. Reprint, Syracuse,
  NY: Syracuse University Press, 1994.
Evans, James. *Emigrants: Why the English Sailed to the New World.* London:
  Orion, 2017.
– "England's Migrant Crisis." *History Magazine* (July 2017): 40–5.
Fairbairn, R.A. *Lead Mine Waggons.* British Mining no. 54. Exeter, U.K.:
  Northern Mine Research Society, 1995.
Fender, Stephen. *Sea Changes: British Emigration and American Literature.*
  Cambridge: Cambridge University Press, 1992.
Fieldhouse, R., and B. Jennings. *A History of Richmond and Swaledale.*
  London: Phillimore & Co Ltd, 1978.
Fischer, David Hackett. *Albion's Seed: Four British Folkways in America.*
  Oxford: Oxford University Press, 1989.
Flanders, Robert B. *Nauvoo: Kingdom on the Mississippi.* Urbana, IL: Illinois
  University Press, 1965.
Fletcher, T.W. "The Great Depression of English Agriculture 1873–1896."
  In *British Agriculture 1875–1914,* edited by P.J. Perry, 30–55. London:
  Methuen, 1973.
Foreman, Amanda. *A World on Fire: Britain's Crucial Role in the American Civil
  War.* New York: Random House, 2010.
Gagnon, Erica. "Settling the West: Immigration to the Prairies from 1867
  to 1914." In *Immigration History.* Canadian Museum of Immigration at
  Pier 21. Accessed 30 March 2020. https://pier21.ca/research/immigration-
  history/settling-the-west-immigration-to-the-prairies-from-1867-to-1914.
Gardner, Thelma. *Illinois Sesquicentennial Edition of Christian County History,*
  Book I, 1880. Edited by Dorothy D. Drennan and Helen B. Broverman.
  1880. Reprinted Jacksonville, Illinois: Production Press, 1968.
Gates, Paul W. *The Illinois Central and Its Colonization Work.* Cambridge:
  Harvard University Press, 1934.

"George Metcalfe." In *Legacies of British Slave-ownership database*. UCL Department of History. Accessed 25 March 2020. https://www.ucl.ac.uk/lbs/person/view/1289142589.

Gerber, David. *Authors of Their Lives: The Personal Correspondence of British Immigrants to North America in the Nineteenth Century*. New York: New York University Press, 2006.

Gleeson, David T. "England and the Antebellum South." In *English Ethnicity and Culture in North America*, edited by David T. Gleeson, 139–54. Columbia: University of South Carolina Press, 2017.

Gordon, John Steele. *Empire of Wealth: The Epic History of America's Economic Power*. New York: HarperCollins, 2004.

Griffiths Jr, D. *Two Years' Residence in the New Settlements of Ohio, North America: With Directions to Emigrants*. London: Westley and Davis, 1835. Reprint, Ann Arbor, MI: University Microfilms, Inc., 1966.

Hallas, Christine. *Rural Responses to Industrialization: The North Yorkshire Pennines, 1790–1914*. Bern: Peter Lang Publishers, 1999.

Harnack, Curtis. *Gentlemen on the Prairie*. Ames, Iowa: Iowa State University Press, 1985.

Harstad, Peter T. "Disease and Sickness on the Wisconsin Frontier: Cholera." *The Wisconsin Magazine of History* 43, no. 3 (Spring, 1960): 203–20.

Harwood, Thomas F. "British Evangelical Abolitionism and American Churches in the 1830s." *The Journal of Southern History* 28, no. 3 (August 1962): 287–306.

Hastings, R.P. "Chartism in the North Riding of Yorkshire and South Durham, 1838–1848." *Borthwick Paper* 105. Edited by Philippa Hoskin and Edward Royle. York: University of York Press, 2004.

– *Essays in North Riding History, 1780–1850*. NYCRO. No. 28, 1981.

Hempton, David. *Methodism: Empire of the Spirit*. New Haven: Yale University Press, 2005.

Hey, David. *A History of Yorkshire: 'County of the Broad Acres.'* Lancaster: Carnegie Publishing, 2011.

Hinderaker, Eric. *Elusive Empires: Constructing Colonialism in the Ohio Valley, 1673–1800*. New York: Cambridge University Press, 1999.

Hirota, Hidetaka. *Expelling the Poor: Atlantic Seaboard States and the Nineteenth-Century Origins of American Immigration Policy*. New York: Oxford University Press, 2017.

History of Clinton County, Iowa: Containing a history of the County, Its Cities, Towns &c. Chicago: Western Historical Company, 1879.

History of Delaware County and Ohio. Chicago: O.L. Baskin & Co., Historical
    Publishers, 1880.
*History of Jo Daviess County, Illinois: Containing a History of the County, Its
    Cities, Towns Etc.* Chicago: H.F. Kett & Co., 1878.
History of Medina County and Ohio. Chicago: Baskin and Battery, 1881.
Hoock, Holger. *Scars of Independence: America's Violent Birth.* New York:
    Broadway Books, 2017.
Horton, Loren N., ed., *The Character of the Country: the Iowa Diary of James
    L. Broderick, 1876–1877.* Iowa City: Iowa State Historical Department,
    Division of the State Historical Society, 1976.
Hutchinson, E.P. *Immigrants and Their Children, 1850–1950.* New York: John
    Wiley & Sons, 1956.
Jeffrey, Julie Roy. *The Great Silent Army of Abolitionism: Ordinary Women in the
    Antislavery Movement.* Chapel Hill: University of North Carolina Press, 1998.
Jeremy, David. *Transatlantic Industrial Revolution: The Diffusion of Textile
    Technologies Between Britain and America, 1790–1830s.* Oxford: Blackwell,
    1981.
Johnson, Paul E. *Sam Patch, the Famous Jumper.* New York: Hill and Wang, 2003.
Kennedy, William. *Texas: The Rise, Progress, and Prospects of the Republic of
    Texas in Two Volumes.* Vol. 2. London: R. Hastings, 1841.
Kirk, Robert. *The Memoirs and Adventures of Robert Kirk, Late of the Royal
    Highland Regiment, Written by Himself...* Limerick, Ireland: J. Ferrar, 1770.
Klein, Robert F., ed. *Dubuque: Frontier River City, Thirty-five Historical
    Sketches.* By Chandler C. Childs. Dubuque: Research for Dubuque Area
    History, Loras College Press, 1984.
Kleppner, Paul. *The Third Electoral System, 1853–1892: Parties, Voters, and
    Political Culture.* Chapel Hill: University of North Carolina Press, 1979.
Leckband, Mike. "Celebrating 150 Years." *Chronicle Times,* 19 August 2008.
    https://www.chronicletimes.com/story/1454014.html.
Lillibridge, George D. *Beacon of Freedom: The Impact of American Democracy
    upon Great Britain, 1830–1870.* 1955. Revised, New York: A.S. Barnes, 1961.
Lines, Kenneth. *British and Canadian Immigration to the United States since
    1920.* San Francisco: R&E Research Associates, 1978.
Linklater, Andro. *Measuring America: How an Untamed Wilderness Shaped the
    United States and Fulfilled the Promise of Democracy.* New York: Walker &
    Company, 2002.
Lloyd, Amy J. "'The Englishmen Here Are Much Disliked': Hostility towards
    English Immigrants in Early Twentieth-century Toronto." In *Locating the
    English Diaspora, 1500–2010,* edited by Tanja Bueltmann, David T. Gleeson,

and Donald M. MacRaild, 125–49. Liverpool: Liverpool University
Press, 2012.

Long, Priscilla. *Where the Sun Never Shines: A History of America's Bloody Coal
Industry.* New York: Paragon House, 1991.

Ludwig, Charles. *Francis Asbury: God's Circuit Rider.* Milford, Michigan: Mott
Media, 1984.

MacVeagh, Lincoln, ed. *The Journal of Nicholas Cresswell: 1774–1777.* New
York: The Dial Press, 1924.

Mahoney, Timothy R. "The Rise and Fall of the Booster Ethos in Dubuque,
1850–1861." *The Annals of Iowa* 61 (2002): 371–419.

Malaney, Frank N. "The Swaledale-Sharon Center Connection." Privately
published, 1998.

Marriott, Glenys, ed. *Those Who Left the Dales.* Upper Dales Family History
Group, York Publishing Services, 2010.

Menard, Russell R. "Migration, Ethnicity, and the Rise of an Atlantic
Economy: The Re-Peopling of British America, 1600–1790." In *A Century
of European Migrations, 1830–1930,* edited by Rudolph J. Vecoli and
Suzanne M. Sinke, 58–77. Urbana: University of Illinois Press, 1991.

Merk, Frederick. *Slavery and Annexation.* New York: Knopf, 1972.

Morgan, Kenneth. *Slavery and Servitude in Colonial North America: A Short
History.* New York: New York University Press, 2001.

Morris, David. *The Dalesmen of the Mississippi River.* York: William Sessions,
Ltd, 1989.

Murphy, Lucy Eldersveld. *A Gathering of Rivers: Indians, Metis, and Mining
in the Western Great Lakes, 1737–1832.* Lincoln, Nebraska: University of
Nebraska Press, 2000.

Nash, Jan Olive, and Leah D. Rogers. "The History, Architecture and
Archaeology of the 'Lost' Town of Center Grove." *Journal of the Iowa
Archeological Society* 51 (2004): 17–31.

National Archives. "John Adams – Audience with King George III, 1785."
In *Eyewitness: American Originals from the National Archives.* Accessed
16 March 2020. https://www.archives.gov/exhibits/eyewitness/html.
php?section=19.

National Park Service. "Indians and Smith." In *Captain John Smith
Chesapeake.* Last updated 31 December 2015. https://www.nps.gov/cajo/
learn/historyculture/indians-and-smith.htm.

Ollendorf, Amy L. "Legacies of the Renards, Mina De Plomo, and
'Swaledalers' in the Upper Mississippi River Valley." *Journal of the Iowa
Archeological Society* 51 (2004): 43–59.

Ostergren, Robert C. *A Community Transplanted: The Trans-Atlantic Experience of a Swedish Immigrant Settlement in the Upper Midwest, 1835–1915.* Madison: University of Wisconsin Press, 1988.

Osterhammel, Jurgen. *The Transformation of the World: A Global History of the Nineteenth Century.* Translated by Patrick Camiller. Princeton: Princeton University Press, 2014.

Ourada, Patricia K. *The Menominee Indians: A History.* Norman, OK: University of Oklahoma Press, 1979.

Pagnamenta, Peter. *Prairie Fever: British Aristocrats in the American West 1830–1890.* New York: W.W. Norton & Company, 2012.

Parker, George F. *Iowa: Pioneer Foundations.* Volume 2. Iowa City: The State Historical Society of Iowa, 1940.

Portrait and Bibliographical Record of Portage and Summit Counties, Ohio. Logansport, IN: A.W. Bowen & Co., 1898.

Portrait and Biographical Album of Jo Daviess and Carroll Counties, Illinois. Chicago: Chapman Brothers, 1889.

Portrait and Biographical Album of Lee County, Iowa. Chicago: Chapman Brothers, 1887.

Portrait and Biographical Record of Dubuque, Jones and Clayton Counties, Iowa. Chicago: Geoffrey Chapman Publishers, 1894.

Pratt, Mildred Claire. *The Silent Ancestors: The Forebears of E.J. Pratt.* Toronto: McClelland and Stewart, Ltd., 1971.

Progressive Men of the State of Wyoming. Chicago: A.W. Bowen & Co., 1903.

Raistrick, A. *Mines and Miners of Swaledale.* Clapham, Yorkshire: Dalesman Publishing Company, 1955.

Raistrick, Arthur, and Bernard Jennings. *A History of Lead Mining in the Pennines.* London: Longman, Green and Company, 1965.

Ransome, David R. "Village Tensions In Early Virginia: Sex, Land, and Status At the Neck Of Land In The 1620s." *The Historical Journal* 43, no. 2 (June 2000): 365–81.

– "Wives for Virginia, 1621." *William & Mary College Quarterly* 48 (January 1991): 3–18.

Reade, A. Arthur. *J.B. Gough: a sketch of his life, work and orations, in America and Great Britain, with portrait & personal description.* Pamphlet. London, 1878. Reprinted in "Sketch of John Gough's Life." In *Teach US History.* Accessed 25 March 2020. http://www.teachushistory.org/second-great-awakening-age-reform/resources/sketch-john-goughs-life.

Reeve, W. Paul, and Ardis E. Parshall, eds. *Mormonism: A Historical Encyclopedia.* Santa Barbara, CA.: ABC-CLIO, 2010.

Renick, Dorothy Waties. "The City of Kent." *Southwestern Historical Quarterly* 29 (July 1925): 51–65.

Ribb, Richard H. "Colony of Kent." In *The Handbook of Texas Online*. Texas State Historical Association. Uploaded 12 June 2010. https://tshaonline. org/handbook/online/articles/uecvj.

Richards, Eric. *Britannia's Children: Emigration from England, Scotland, Wales and Ireland since 1600*. London: Bloomsbury Academic, 2004.

– "Malthus and the Uses of British Emigration." In *Empire, Migration and Identity in the British World*, edited by Kent Fedorowich and Andrew S. Thompson, 42–59. Manchester: University of Manchester Press, 2013), 53.

Rister, Carl Coke. "Beale's Rio Grande Colony." In *The Handbook of Texas Online*. Texas State Historical Association. Uploaded 12 June 2010. https://tshaonline.org/handbook/online/articles/uebo1.

Robinson, Lesley. "English Associational Culture in Lancashire and Yorkshire, 1890s–c.1930s." *Northern History* 51, no. 1 (2014): 131–52.

Roeckell, Lilia M. "Bonds Over Bondage: British Opposition to the Annexation of Texas." *Journal of the Early Republic* 2 (Summer, 1999): 257–78.

Rorabaugh, W.J. *The Alcoholic Republic: An American Tradition*. New York: Oxford University Press, 1979.

Rosenberg, Charles E. *The Cholera Years: The United States in 1832, 1849, and 1866*. Chicago: University of Chicago Press, 1987.

Rowe, John. *The Hard Rock Men: Cornish Immigrants and the North American Mining Frontier*. New York: Barnes & Noble Books, 1974.

Rudolph, L.C. *Francis Asbury*. Nashville: Abingdon Press, 1966.

Schafer, Joseph. *The Wisconsin Lead Region*. Madison: State Historical Society of Wisconsin, 1932.

Schmitz, Joseph W. "Diplomatic Relations of the Republic of Texas." In *The Handbook of Texas Online*. Texas State Historical Association. Uploaded 12 June 2010; modified 12 July 2019. https://www.tshaonline.org/handbook/entries/diplomatic-relations-of-the-republic-of-texas.

Semmingsen, Ingrid. *Norway to America: A History of the Migration*. Translated by Einar Haugen. Minneapolis: University of Minnesota Press, 1978.

– "Norwegian Emigration in the Nineteenth Century." *Scandinavian Economic History Review* 8, no. 2 (1960): 150–60.

Sewell, Mike. "'All the English-Speaking Race is in Mourning': The Assassination of President Garfield and Anglo-American Relations." *The Historical Journal* 34, no. 3 (September 1991): 665–86.

Shambaugh, Benjamin F., ed. *The Iowa Journal of History and Politics*. Iowa City: The State Historical Society of Iowa, 1910.

Shepperson, W.S. *British Emigration to North America: Projects and Opinions in the Early Victorian Period.* Minneapolis: University of Minnesota Press, 1957.

Sloat, Jerry. "The Noble Experiment Eventually Failed." *Fort Madison Daily Democrat*, October 19, 2010. http://www.mississippivalleypublishing.com/daily_democrat/opinion/the-noble-experiment-eventually-failed/article_a64a9c4b-8e75-5ae0-8ea5-941d3196e6fb.html.

Smith, William. *An Emigrant's Narrative, or a Voice from the Steerage: a brief account of the sufferings of the emigrants in the ship, "India,"….* New York: published by the author, 1850.

Spensley, Ian M. *Mines and Miners of Wensleydale.* UK Book Publishing, 2014.

– "The Historical Development of Lead Mining in the Wensleydale Area to 1830." In *50 Years of Mining History*, 172–93. British Mining no 90. Exeter, U.K.: Northern Mine Research Society, 2010.

Spickard, Paul. *Almost All Aliens: Immigration, Race, and Colonialism in American History and Identity.* New York: Routledge, 2007.

Stainsby, Michael. *More Than an Ordinary Man: Life and Society in the Upper Esk Valley, 1830–1910.* Helmsley: North York Moors National Park Authority, 2006.

Strong, Rowan. *Victorian Christianity and Emigrant Voyages to British Colonies c.1840–c.1914.* Oxford: Oxford University Press, 2017.

Swierenga, Robert P. *Pioneers and Profits: Land Speculation on the Iowa Frontier.* Ames: Iowa State University Press, 1968.

– "Dutch Immigration Patterns in the Nineteenth and Twentieth Centuries." In *The Dutch in America: Immigration, Settlement, and Cultural Change*, edited by Robert P. Swierenga, 15–42. New Brunswick, NJ: Rutgers University Press, 1985.

Taylor, Alan. *The Civil War of 1812.* New York: Knopf, 2010.

Thomas, Brinley. *Migration and Economic Growth.* Cambridge: Cambridge University Press, 1954.

– *Migration and Urban Development: A Reappraisal of British and American Long Cycles.* London: Methuen and Co., 1972.

Thwaites, Reuben Gold. *How George Rogers Clark Won the Northwest.* Chicago: A.C. McClury & Co., 1903.

–, ed. "Notes on Early Lead Mining in the Fever (or Galena) River Region." In *Collections of the State Historical Society of Wisconsin*, Vol. 13. Madison: Democrat Printing Company, 1895.

Tocqueville, Alexis de. *Democracy in America*. Vol. II. (1835) Translated and edited by Harvey C. Mansfield and Delba Winthrop. Chicago: University of Chicago Press, 2000.

Todd, Arthur Cecil. *The Cornish Miner in America: The Contribution to the Mining History of the United States by Emigrant Cornish Miners – the Men Called Cousin Jacks*. Cornwall: Barton, Clark, 1967.

Tring, Frederick Charles. "Nineteenth Century Immigration from England to Dakota Territory: The Example of Wensleydale." *North Dakota History* 38 (1971): 360–5.

Trowbridge, Arthur C., and Eugene Wesley Shaw. *Geology and Geography of the Galena and Elizabeth Quadrangles*. State of Illinois State Geological Survey, Bulletin No. 26.

Tucker, Barbara M. *Samuel Slater and the Origins of the American Textile Industry, 1790–1860*. Ithaca: Cornell University Press, 1984.

Tweedale, Geoffrey. *Sheffield Steel and America: A Century of Commercial and Technological Interdependence, 1830–1930*. Cambridge: Cambridge University Press, 1987.

Tyrell, Charles W. *Steeples on the Prairies: A Pen Sketch of Midwestern Primitive Methodism*. [n.p.]: Primitive Methodist Church in the United States of America, 1987.

Van Der Zee, Jacob. "Part I: British Emigrants in Iowa, Chapter III: British Elements in the Population of Iowa." In *The British in Iowa*. Iowa City: The State Historical Society of Iowa, 1922. Iowa Online Genealogy Books. Published online 2003. http://www.iagenweb.org/sioux/books/british/british_1_3.htm.

Van Vugt, William E. "An English Shoemaker in Indiana: The Story of Samuel Fowler Smith." *Indiana Magazine of History* XCI, no. 1 (March 1995): 16–56.

– *Britain to America: Mid-Nineteenth-Century Immigrants to the United States*. Champaign: University of Illinois Press, 1999.

– "British (English, Welsh, Scots, Scotch-Irish)." In *A Nation of Peoples: A Sourcebook on America's Multicultural Heritage*, edited by Elliott Barkan, 75–95. Westport, CT: Greenwood Press, 1999.

– *British Buckeyes: The English, Scots, and Welsh in Ohio, 1700–1900*. Kent: Kent State University Press, 2005.

– *British Immigration to the United States, 1776–1914*. London: Routledge, 2009.

– "Did the Loss of the Thirteen Colonies Have a Significant Impact on the British Empire?" In *History in Dispute: The American Revolution, 1763–1789*, vol. 12, edited by Keith Krawczynski, 164–8. Detroit: Thomson Gale, 2003.

– "English Emigrant Guidebooks and Pamphlets 1860–1899: The Image of America." Unpublished MA thesis, Kent State University, 1981.

– "Relocating the English Diaspora in America." In *English Culture and Ethnicity in North America*, edited by David T. Gleeson, 8–36. Columbia: University of South Carolina Press, 2017.

– "The British: English, Scots, Welsh, Scots Irish, 1870–1940." In *Immigrants in American History: Arrival, Adaptation, and Integration*, vol. 2, edited by Elliott Barkan, 235–44. Santa Barbara, Cal.: ABC-CLIO Books, 2013.

– "The British: English, Scots, Welsh, Scots Irish, 1940–2010." In *Immigrants in American History: Arrival Adaptation, and Integration*, vol. 3, edited by Elliott Barkan, 785–92. Santa Barbara, Cal.: ABC-CLIO Books, 2013.

Waiser, Bill. "Macdonald's Appetite for Canadian Expansion: Main Course or Leftover." In *Macdonald at 200: New Reflections and Legacies*, edited by Patrice Dutil and Roger Hall. Toronto: Dundurn, 2014.

Ware, J. Berry. "English Colony: The British Emigrant Mutual Aid Society's Colony in Lee County Iowa." Bonaparte, Iowa: self-published, 1918.

Watkins, John. *The Emigrants: A Tale of the Times*. Whitby: Horne and Richardson, 1835.

Watson, James. "'Cooked in True Yorkshire Fashion': Regional Identity and English Associational Life in New Zealand before the First World War." In *Locating the English Diaspora, 1500–2010*, edited by Tanja Bueltmann, David T. Gleeson, and Donald M. MacRaild, 169–84. Liverpool: Liverpool University Press, 2012.

Watson, Kevin. "National Identity and Primitive Methodism in the United States: A Transatlantic Perspective." *American Nineteenth Century History* 4, no. 2 (June 2003): 32–52.

Wells, Ronald A., ed. *Letters from a Young Emigrant in Manitoba: A Record of Emigrant Life in the Canadian West*. Winnipeg: University of Manitoba Press, 1981.

White, Richard. *The Middle Ground: Indians, Empires, and Republics in the Great Lakes Region, 1650–1815*. Cambridge: Cambridge University Press, 1991.

Wilson, A.N. *The Victorians*. New York: W.W. Norton & Company, 2003.

Wilson, Bruce G. "Loyalists in Canada." In *The Canadian Encyclopedia*. Article published 2 April 2009; last edited 4 December 2019, http://www.thecanadianencyclopedia.ca/en/article/loyalists/.

Wilson, Francis W. "Advocate for Texas: Thomas Wilson." Luling, TX: self-published, 1987. In Wilson Family Papers, Rosedale Abbey Reading Room, Ryedale, North Yorkshire.

Winther, Oscar. "English Migration to the American West, 1865–1900." In *In the Trek of the Immigrants*, edited by Oscar F. Ander, 115–25. Rock Island, IL.: Augustana College Library, 1964.

– "Promoting the American West in England, 1865–1890," *Journal of Economic History* 16 (December 1956): 506–13.

Wood, Gordon. "Creating the Revolution." *The New York Review of Books*, 13 February 2003. https://www.nybooks.com/articles/2003/02/13/creating-the-revolution/.

Woods, Robert. *The Population of Britain in the Nineteenth Century.* Basingstoke: Macmillan, 1992.

Wright, James E. *The Galena Lead District: Federal Policy and Practice, 1824–1847*. Madison, University of Wisconsin, 1966.

Yancy, Karen. "Belcher, Edward." In *The Handbook of Texas Online.* Texas State Historical Association. Uploaded 12 June 2010. https://tshaonline.org/handbook/online/articles/fbe29.

Index

Alberta, 285–7
Alderson, Edmund, 93, 105–6
Alderson, George and Thomas,
   45–7, 50
Allen Brown, 78–9, 155
America: British economy and,
   231–3; climate, 77, 104–7, 134,
   160–2, 255–8; Emergency Quota
   Act, 288; emigrant expectations
   of, 59–61, 160; equality, 144,
   212, 216–17, 252–3, 293; farming
   practices, 150–1, 157, 231–3, 243,
   246, 253–5, 256–7; greenback
   paper money, 222, 245; immigrant
   descriptions of, 55–6, 58–60,
   76–7, 80–2, 96–9, 134–6, 194–5;
   Industrial Revolution, 112–13,
   212, 232–4; political freedom, 61,
   212; urbanization, 233–4. *See also*
   individual states
American culture, 141–2, 212,
   256–7, 291; Anglo-American, 4–5,
   164–5, 167, 301n7, 302n8; English
   characteristics, 4–5, 141, 164–5
American Revolution, 10, 28, 30, 108,
   173–4, 336n2; Loyalist refugees,
   28, 130
Arkengarthdale, 43–4, 46, 49, 51, 69,
   93, 105, 235, 262
Asbury, Francis, 17, 181
Askrigg, 55, 57, 60, 62–3, 67, 69, 71,
   83, 94, 102, 188, 218–19, 300
assisted emigration, 37–40, 136,
   276–7, 279, 287–8, 292
Atkinson, William, 104, 170, 220,
   238–9, 241–2, 296, 336n36
Australia, 34–5, 288

Baines, Dudley, 8, 9, 18, 36, 293,
   309n42, 361n25
Bateman, William, 168–9, 170
Beevers, Benjamin and Mary, 152–3
Bell, Metcalf, 54–5, 152
Benton, WI, 79, 88, 95–6, 100, 127,
   128, 236
Binks, G.M., 251–2, 352n3
Bismarck, Otto von, 4
Bohemian immigrants, 122, 168, 248
Bolton Castle, 97–8, 251, 260–1, 288,
   292, 300

Bonson, Richard, 113, 115–18, 152,
249–50, 324n17, 347n5
Bonson, Robert and Mary, 85, 113–15,
120, 323n6
Boyes, Captain Henry Ernest, 263
Bravender, Isaac, 144–5
British Columbia, 285–7
British Emigrant Mutual Aid Society,
168–9, 170
Britain; British. *See* England; English
Broderick, Edward, 51, 54–5, 62,
63–4, 248
Broderick, James, 107, 225, 236,
248–9, 323n6
Brunskill, Joseph and Elizabeth,
114–15, 116, 118–9, 121, 152
Bueltmann, Tanja, 6, 36
Buffalo, NY, 81–2, 133–6, 143, 153, 174,
327n21, 328n21
Bugg, Joseph and Susanna, 154–5
Buxton, George, 94, 223, 298, 316n28
Buxton, John and Mary, 69–70, 74,
75–6, 79, 297
Buxton, Richard and Isabella, 95, 96,
102, 127, 214, 236, 296–7
Buxton, Thomas, 47–9

California, 262–3; Gold Rush, 13,
187, 200, 204–10, 260; Native
Americans, 179–80; San Francisco,
207–8, 263, 342n9
Campey, Lucille, 5, 8, 293
Canada, 13, 77–8, 278, 283; assisted
emigration, 37–40, 136, 276–7, 279,
287–8, 292; culture, 12, 34–5, 146,
275–7; English immigrants, 3–4,
213, 234, 275–7, 287–9, 293, 306n20,
307n23; immigrant descriptions of,

130–2, 135–6; Irish, 3–4, 37, 40, 146,
276; North York Moor immigrants,
129–33, 134–9, 143–6, 278–9; North
Yorkshire migrants, 9, 24–7, 32–5,
278–82, 289, 291, 306–7n20; Scots,
3–4, 276; Sons of England, 287;
timber trade, 32–3; Upper, 12, 25,
131; urban laborers, 234, 277, 285–6,
287, 291; Western, 285–8; Yorkshire
Dales immigrants, 279–82. *See also
individual provinces and cities*
Carter, Robert, 262
Castle Bolton. *See* Bolton Castle
Cather, Willa, 243, 251
Catholics, Roman, 24, 94, 139, 182,
207, 287, 338n6
census data, 121–2, 145–6, 148, 250,
262, 287, 301n7
Center Grove, IA, 112–13, 115–16, 117,
119, 121–2, 152, 324n17
chain migration, 12, 18, 82–3, 270,
287, 290; families, 120–1, 132–3,
152–3, 155, 210–11, 226, 259–60,
327n4; letters and, 53–8, 76–8;
work associates, 122–3, 280–1
Chapman, Barzillai, and Jane 60,
68–9, 204, 332n34
Cherry, John, 279–4
Chicago, 81, 120, 153, 155, 157, 229
Chinese immigrants, 280, 281
cholera, 76, 85–6, 143, 187, 317n58
Civil War, 13, 36, 109, 128,
232–3, 243, 347n49; Confederacy,
English support, 216–17, 221–2;
Emancipation Proclamation, 217,
221; Union, English immigrants,
216–18, 346–7n35; Union, English
support, 216–17

clearing land, 27, 119, 130–1, 134–5, 144, 155–6, 171, 254–5, 257

Clitheroe, 192–3

coal mining, 47, 112, 120, 169–70, 285

colonies, English ethnic, 12, 83, 164–70, 171–2, 214, 266–8, 286–7, 294

Colorado, 234, 235, 262, 298

Cornish miners, 123, 205, 248, 248

Corn Laws, 147–8, 149, 231

craft workers, 33–6, 308n7; farming and, 151, 156–7, 166–7, 169; textile workers, 7, 20, 33–4, 192–3, 217

Crockett, Davy, 264

Cumberland, 37, 111, 285, 326n55

culture: Anglo-American culture, 4–5, 164–5, 167, 301n7, 302n8; Canadian, 12, 34–5, 146, 275–7; mining, 18–20, 92–6, 99–100, 128, 158, 208–9; North Yorkshire, 17–18, 99–100, 107–8, 109, 113, 122, 138–9, 164, 249–50, 291. *See also* American culture

Dakota, 251–2, 298

Danby, 17, 38, 130, 136–7, 141, 145, 289, 327n4

democracy, 212, 217

Democrats, 212–13

depressions: of 1840, 7, 38, 147–8; Great Agricultural Depression, mid-1870s, 231–2, 240, 277; Great Depression, 1930s, 288, 289

diaspora, definition, 6

Dinsdale, John, 70, 73–4, 75–6, 86, 298

Dinsdale, Matthew, 55–6, 59–63, 110–11, 198, 247, 290, 298, 300;

California Gold Rush, 204, 206–11, 340n33, 344n31; Civil War, 216, 218; farming, 157–9, 271; journey, 68–9, 71–3, 81–4, 315n15; Methodism, 59, 102–3, 159, 180, 188–90, 339–40n29; mining, 124, 127, 189; letters and journals, 102–3, 104–5, 311n7; Native Americans, 174–80; Wisconsin, 94–5, 97–8, 107, 210–11, 250, 344n34

diseases, sicknesses, 107, 154, 205–6, 246; ague, 107, 141, 143, 154–5; cholera, 76, 785–6, 143, 187, 317n58; sea sickness, 71–2, 207, 210, 224–5, 227–8, 279–80

Dixon, John Flounders, 225–30, 252–5, 256–8

Dods, John, 22–3, 304n2

Douglass, Frederick, 215

Dubuque, IA, 300, 318n19; lead mining, 85, 92–4, 99, 107, 113–18, 124–5, 164, 236–7

Dubuque, Julien, 88–90

Dutch immigrants, 168, 229, 248, 290

Earlham, IA, 226, 229–30, 252–3, 256

Eastern Counties Herald, 165–7

Easton, John and Ann, 144, 327n4

Easton, Thomas and Hannah, 129–30, 327n4

Easton, William, 71, 327n4

East Riding, 15–16, 17, 24, 66, 78, 141, 154, 286, 313n42

Eckles, Marmaduke and Hannah, 78–9, 80, 155, 219

economic growth, migration and, 7–8

Emancipation Proclamation, 217, 221

Emerson, Ralph Waldo, 4
emigrants, 13, 63–4, 292–4; assisted,
    37–40, 136, 276–7, 279, 287–8,
    292; craft workers, 33–6, 308n7;
    felons, 23; guidebooks, 60–1, 70,
    153, 156, 165, 268; indentured
    servants, 23, 305n20; journey,
    64–7, 68–75, 139–41, 294; poor,
    27, 34, 36, 37–40, 136–7, 148–9,
    165, 192, 292, 293; reverse, repeat,
    27–8, 162–3, 167, 224, 230, 278–9,
    288, 294–5, 323n6; skilled labour,
    7–8, 26–7, 35–6, 302n17, 307–8n37;
    wealthy, 171–2, 251, 286; well off,
    affluent, 26, 34, 36–7, 62, 78,
    134–5, 139, 145, 148–9, 226, 261,
    270, 291–2. See also craft workers;
    farmers; miners; motivations for
    emigration; recruiting emigrants
England: America, relations with,
    182–3, 264–5; British Empire
    Settlement Act, 1922, 288–9;
    Civil War, American, 215, 216–17,
    221–2, 223; Corn Laws, 147–8,
    149, 231; depression 1840, 7, 38,
    147–8; empire, 31, 173–4; Great
    Agricultural Depression, mid-
    1870s, 231–2, 240, 277; Mormons,
    190–1, 213, 234, 295; Poor Laws,
    37–40, 48–9; Texas and, 264–5,
    272–3; Victorian boom, 148, 330–
    1n2; working classes, slavery and,
    216–17, 221–2. See also individual
    areas and cities
English, 5–6, 181–2; anti-English
    hostilities, 108–9, 165, 277; ethnic
    colonies, 12, 83, 164–70, 171–2,
    214, 266–8, 286–7, 294; farming

practices, 149–50, 160, 169; Native
    Americans and, 173–4, 176–7, 295
English Prairie, IL, 82–3
Erickson, Charlotte, 5, 7, 291,
    303n10, 308n37
Erie Canal, 80–2, 108–9, 136, 141,
    148, 165, 174, 317n50
equality, in America, 144, 212, 216–17,
    252–3, 293
Ewbank, John, 30–1

farmers, 30–1, 34, 277–8; North
    York Moor, 129–36, 137–42, 143–6;
    North Yorkshire, 148–9, 159–60,
    170–1, 237–8, 240–2; recruiting, 24,
    57, 165–6, 251–2, 273, 277, 285–6;
    Yorkshire immigrants, 151–3, 234,
    292–3, 295–6
farming, 8, 12; American practices,
    150–1, 157, 231–3, 243, 246, 253–5,
    256–7; chinch bugs, 162, 244; craft
    workers and, 151, 156–7, 166–7,
    169; dairy, 280–1, 282–4, 313n30;
    English practices, 149–50, 160, 169;
    livestock, 44–5, 99, 138, 150–2, 157,
    172, 237, 256–7, 331n13; mining
    and, 20–1, 44–5, 69, 91, 119–20,
    151–2, 218, 241, 294, 324n17,
    326n55; prairie, 154–7, 159, 169,
    180, 231–2, 252–5; speculation,
    118, 253–4, 352n11; working bees,
    130–1, 138
Farndale, 170–1, 220, 238–9
Fell, John, 146
Fewster, Robert, 137–9, 328n36
fire, 159, 240, 255
First World War, 6, 289
food, 60, 107, 130, 144, 195, 258

France, 24, 88–90, 221, 247; Franco-
Prussian War, 239; Napoleonic,
29–30, 31, 33
Fremington, 279, 281, 282–3

Galena, IL, 88, 90–1, 93–4, 120, 124,
183–6, 220
Garrison, William Lloyd, 214–15
George, King, 29
George, Samson, 153–4
German immigrants, 122, 168, 182,
229, 248, 250, 262
Gilded Age, 13, 233, 298
gold mining, 209–10, 285; California
Gold Rush, 13, 187, 200, 204–11,
260
Grant, Ulysses S., 220
Great Agricultural Depression, mid-
1870s, 231–2, 240, 277
Great Ayton, 34, 104, 226, 228–30,
252–3, 256, 279–80
Great Depression, 1930s, 288, 289
Great Lakes, 81, 174
guidebooks, 60–1, 70, 153, 156, 165,
268
Gunnerside, 47–9, 69, 96, 102,
112–19, 292, 296–7, 298–9

Hall, Frederick, 45–7
homesickness, 59–60, 78, 101–3,
110–11, 132, 155, 160, 167, 207–8,
281–2
Hull, 24–5, 27, 33, 34, 64, 66, 77–8,
145, 154, 171, 307n20, 313n42
Hull Advertiser, 32, 165–6, 171
*The Hull Packet and East Riding
Times*, 61, 161, 191–2
Hulme, Thomas, 80

Humphrey, John, 57, 101–2, 106, 150,
160–1
Hutchinson, John and Hannah,
133–7, 143, 153

Illinois, 153–4, 155, 157, 180, 320n52.
See also individual cities
immigrants, 13, 27–8, 107–8, 110–11,
247–8; assimilation, integration,
121–3, 134–5, 181, 217–18; return
visits, 31, 53–4, 62, 72, 79, 109,
138–9, 210–11, 225, 273, 299–300;
women, single, 143, 145–6. *See
also individual places of origin,
destinations, occupations*; letters,
immigrant
indentured servants, 23, 305n20
Indiana, 30–1, 133, 154–5, 306n9
industrial capitalism, 212, 243
Industrial Revolution, 6–8, 31, 35–6,
231, 289, 291–2; American, 112–13,
212, 232–4; mining and smelting,
45–7; North Yorkshire, 31, 237–8,
291–2, 293–4
industrialization, 14, 21, 61, 234, 278,
289, 293, 294
Iowa, 12, 88, 166, 250, 320n52,
323n6; Clinton County, 164–8;
farming, 166–7, 169–71, 226,
229–30, 252–5; immigrant
descriptions, 165–6, 256; Lee
County, 168–70, 171, 336n36; Le
Mars, 171–2; Methodists, 93, 94,
113, 121–2; prairie, 252–5. *See also
Center Grove, IA; Dubuque, IA;
Earlham, IA*
Ireland, 80, 159, 182, 217, 250, 356n36
Irish immigrants, 73, 80, 182, 187,

228, 248, 250, 288; to Canada, 3–4,
37, 40, 146, 276
ironstone mining, 238–42, 269

Jamestown settlement, 22–3, 173
Johnson, Samuel, 68, 314
journals, 11, 63–4, 107, 249; Dinsdale,
Matthew, 73, 97, 102–3
journeys, 68–75, 139–41, 294; to
Liverpool, 64–7, 136, 139, 210,
227, 279–80. See also transatlantic
voyages
Joyce, James, 3

Keld, 14, 22, 41, 65, 108, 304
Kirk, Robert, 174, 177
Knaggs, John and Ann, 25, 129–33,
134, 137, 143–4, 190–1

Langrick, George Francis, 262–3
land, 153–4, 222–3; clearing, 27, 119,
130–1, 134–5, 144, 155–6, 171, 254–5,
257; motive for emigration, 130–1,
135–7, 146, 147–8, 149, 194, 251–2,
293; owning, 159–60, 167, 170–1,
175–6, 229–30, 241; prairie, 154–7,
159, 169, 180, 231–2, 252–5, 285–6,
395; ranches, 258–9, 272–3, 286
language, assimilation and, 17, 107–9,
122, 138, 167–8, 192, 230, 249–50,
291, 322n34; Swaledale accent,
107–8, 122
Langworthys, 116–18, 324n12
lead mining, 18–21, 41–4, 88–92,
123–6, 128; American, 235–7;
Dubuque, IA, 85, 92–4, 99, 107,
113–18, 124–5, 164, 236–7; Native
Americans, 88–92; Old Gang

Mine, 45–7, 49, 50, 235; Pennines,
21, 47, 123, 127, 293; Swaledale,
42–4, 45–6, 49–50, 67, 94, 99,
113–14, 118, 120–2, 249, 299;
Upper Mississippi rush, 90–5,
112–13, 123–6; Wisconsin, 88–9,
93, 121–2, 123–6, 128, 186–7, 237;
Yorkshire Dales, 18–21, 38, 41–7,
49–50, 62, 235–6, 292, 299–300
Leekley, John, 185–7, 339n22
letters, immigrant, 8, 11, 70, 102–5,
131–2, 153, 286, 293–4, 297–8;
America, descriptions of, 55–6,
58–60, 76–7, 80–2, 96–9, 134–6,
194–5; bias, 53–4, 144, 194; climate,
77, 104–7, 134, 160–2, 255–8;
food, 60, 107, 130, 144, 195, 258;
packages, 104–5, 132
Lincoln, Abraham, 221
Lincoln, Zeborah, 136
Liverpool, 24–5, 32, 73, 214, 283,
307n20, 313–14n42; journey to,
64–7, 136, 139, 210, 227, 279–80;
Mormons, 190, 193; runners,
thieves, 69–70, 80, 227
livestock farming, 44–5, 99, 138,
150–2, 157, 172, 237, 256–7, 331n13;
dairy, 280–1, 282–4, 313n30;
ranches, 258–9, 272–3, 286
Locke, John, 175–6
log cabins, 97, 120, 138, 154, 156–7,
208
London, 24–5, 26, 170, 305n13,
314n42
Longmire, John, 159, 219
Longstroth, Stephen and Ann,
192–202, 213, 295, 341n46
Lower, Arthur R. M., 276

MacRaild, Donald, 6, 36
Manifest Destiny, 175–6
Menominee, 174–7, 336–7n6
Metcalf, George, 76, 124
Metcalf, Thomas, 75
Metcalfe, Christopher, 47–8
Metcalfe, George, 216, 345n21
Methodism, Methodists, 12, 94–5,
  139, 319n24, 338n5; abolitionism,
  214, 216; American-British
  relations, 182–3; Dinsdale,
  Matthew, 59, 102–3, 159, 180,
  188–90, 339–40n29; English, 17,
  30; Episcopal, 83, 172, 178–7, 185,
  189; Iowa, 93, 94, 113, 121–2; Native
  Americans, 178–9; Primitive, 183–8,
  189, 247, 269, 338n6, 339n22;
  religious freedom, 24, 181–2;
  temperance, 213–14; Wisconsin,
  83–4, 94–5, 122, 184–7, 188–90;
  Yorkshire Dales, 49, 113, 188–90,
  213–14, 299
Mexico, 264–5
Michigan, 141–2, 152–3, 156–7, 174–5
Milwaukee, WI, 302n17
Mineral Point, WI, 86, 91, 94, 124,
  127, 157–8, 184–5, 222, 246, 297
miners, 112–13, 205–6; Cornish, 123,
  205, 248, 248; farming and, 20–1,
  44–5, 69, 91, 119–20, 151–2, 218,
  241, 294, 324n17, 326n55; North
  Yorkshire, 18–21, 41–4, 88–92, 123–
  6, 128, 292; recruiting, 113–14, 285,
  320n48; South America, 320n48;
  Swaledale, 42–4, 45–6, 49–50, 67,
  94, 99, 113–14, 118, 120–2, 249,
  357–8n42; wages, 47–52; women

and children, 43–4; Yorkshire
  Dales, 8, 45, 89, 99, 113–18, 121–3,
  123–6, 183–6, 247–8
mining, 8; camps, 42, 126–7;
  coal, 47, 112, 120, 169–70, 285;
  culture, 18–20, 92–6, 99–100, 128,
  158, 208–9; farming and, 20–1,
  44–5, 69, 91, 119–20, 151–2, 218,
  241, 294, 324n17, 326n55; gold,
  209–10, 285; ironstone, 238–42,
  269; ore dressing, 43–4; silver,
  234, 262; smelting, 43, 45–7,
  90–1, 113–17, 123; zinc, 236–7. See
  also California Gold Rush; lead
  mining
Mississippi River, Upper Region, 8,
  11–12, 291; architecture, 97–100,
  126, 156; climate, 77, 104–7; lead
  rush, 90–5, 112–13, 123–6; women,
  95–6; Yorkshire Dales immigrants,
  97–9, 123–6, 151, 292. See also
  Illinois; Iowa; Wisconsin
Missouri, 91, 194, 318n10
modernization, 8, 121, 293
Montreal, 80, 317n58
Mormonism, Mormons, 12–13,
  176–7, 192–202, 340n36; English,
  190–1, 213, 234, 295
motivations to emigrate, 7–8, 10,
  21; economic advancement, 24–5,
  26–7, 34, 36–7, 55–7, 78, 120,
  273–4, 293; economic recession,
  32, 38, 47–9, 51–2, 66; land, 130–1,
  135–7, 146, 147–8, 149, 194, 251–2,
  293; political freedom, 61, 80,
  212–13; religious freedom, 24, 56,
  181–3, 194

Native Americans, 12, 22, 93, 95,
142, 195, 200; California, 179–80,
263; English and, 173–4, 176–7,
295; Iowa, 164, 172, 318n19; lead
mining, 88–92; Menominee,
174–7, 336–7n6; Methodist,
178–9; Oshkosh, Chief, 175, 176–8,
336–7n6; Pawnee, Nebraska,
261–2; Wisconsin, 174–9, 187, 188,
336–7n6
Nauvoo, IN, 190–1, 195–200, 202
Nebraska, 258–60, 260–2, 298
Nevada, 235, 262
New Brunswick, 27, 32–3, 64
New Diggings, WI, 93, 105, 128,
185–6, 323n5, 338n9, 346n35
New Orleans, 80, 85–7, 169, 193
New York, 30, 32, 37, 80, 228–9;
farming immigrants, 133–6
New Zealand, 34, 269, 288, 303n6,
356n8
Niagara Falls, 82, 140, 328n46
North Riding, 17, 23, 24, 240,
307n20
North York Moors, 15, 21, 34, 38–9,
64, 137, 170–1, 235, 237–9, 241–2.
See also individual cities
North Yorkshire, 9–10, 15–16, 331n5;
California Gold Rush, 204–6;
Civil War, American, 218–21, 238,
295; coast, 15–16; culture, 17–18,
99–100, 107–8, 109, 113, 122,
138–9, 164, 249–50, 291; farmers,
farming, 148–9, 159–60, 170–1,
237–8, 240–2; industrialization, 31,
237–8, 291–2, 293–4; language, 17,
107–9, 122, 138, 167–8, 192, 230,
249–50, 291, 322n34; railroads,

224, 237, 238–9; religion, 16–17,
49, 113, 188–90, 213–14, 299,
338n6; Texas and, 265–6, 269–70,
273–4; Vale of Mowbray, 14–15;
Vale of York, 14–15, 21, 54, 240.
See also individual areas and cities;
lead mining
Nova Scotia, 10, 24, 26–8, 32–3, 292,
305n13
Norwegian immigrants, 106, 122,
248, 300

Ohio, 31, 80–1, 99, 108–9, 114, 152,
156, 174, 306n9; abolitionists,
215–16; Akron, 118–19
Old Gang Mine, 45–7, 49, 50, 235
Old Northwest, United States, 148,
150–1, 174, 234, 250, 278
Ontario, 28, 33, 37, 130; English
farm workers, 277–8; St. George
Societies, 6, 18, 276, 287;
immigrant descriptions of, 130–2,
135–6, 140–1, 142, 143–6. See also
individual cities
Oregon, 265
Oshkosh, chef, 175, 176–8, 336–7n6
Ottawa, 280–4

Palmerston, Lord, 215, 265, 354n6
Panama, 207
Panic of 1893, 283
Panic and Crash of 1857, 118
passenger lists, 22, 25, 69, 74, 76;
kinds of workers, 35–6, 119, 145,
148, 307–8n37, 308–9n41; reasons
for leaving, 7, 26–7
Pennines, 14, 47, 123, 127, 293; lead
mining, 21, 47, 123, 127, 293

Pennsylvania, 55
Philadelphia, 29, 55, 210, 226, 345n12
Peters, William S., 265–6
Pickering, 15, 34, 38, 134, 141, 144,
    149, 171, 240
pioneering, 83, 195–7, 248–50;
    log cabins, 97, 120, 138, 154,
    156–7, 208; prairie, 256–60, 261–2;
    wilderness, 28, 80, 101, 111, 138, 142,
    154, 200, 259–60
Platteville, WI, 100, 113–14, 128, 183,
    205
poor emigrants, poverty, 27, 34, 36,
    37–40, 136–7, 148–9, 165, 192, 292,
    293
prairie, 285–6, 395; farming,
    154–7, 159, 169, 180, 231–2, 252–5;
    pioneering, 256–60, 261–2
Pratt, James and Hannah, 119–20,
    131, 152, 311n6, 325n34
preachers, 16, 83, 95, 184–5, 187, 189,
    269, 313n33, 339n22
Primitive Methodists, 183–8, 189,
    247, 338n6, 339n22
Prince Edward Island, 32
Protestants, 17, 24, 181–2, 287

Quakers, 16, 56, 95, 159, 214, 219–20,
    226, 229–30
Quebec, 33, 36, 57–8, 64, 129, 133,
    145, 280, 307n20

railroads, 66, 118, 167, 224, 232,
    239–40, 272; American, 226–9,
    232, 261, 268–9, 273; Canadian,
    285–6; train travel, 70, 136, 155,
    261, 280
Ramsden, Henrietta, 215–16

ranches, 258–9, 272–3, 286
recruiting emigrants, 190, 277, 355n22;
    farmers, 24, 57, 165–6, 251–2, 273,
    277, 285–6; miners, 113–14, 285,
    320n48; Texas, 265–8, 269–70
religion, 69–70, 181–2, 295, 298,
    319n35; Catholics, 24, 94, 139, 182,
    207, 287, 338n6; lead mining towns,
    93–4; pilgrimage, 69–70, 314n3;
    preachers, 16, 83, 95, 184–5, 187, 189,
    269, 313n33, 339n22; Protestants,
    17, 24, 181–2, 287; Quakers, 16, 56,
    95, 159, 214, 219–20, 226, 229–30;
    North Yorkshire, 16–17, 49, 113,
    188–90, 213–14, 299, 338n6; See
    also Methodism, Methodists;
    Mormonism, Mormons
Republicans, Whigs, 212–13, 264
return, repeat migration, 27–8,
    162–3, 167, 224, 230, 278–9, 288,
    294–5, 323n6
return visits, immigrant, 31, 53–4, 62,
    72, 79, 109, 138–9, 210–11, 225, 273,
    299–300
Richards, Willard, 192, 197, 201–3
Rockdale Mills, 119–20
Rockport, 193–5
Roman Catholics, 24, 94, 139, 182,
    207, 287, 338n6
Rosedale, 139, 140–2, 168–9, 238–9,
    241–2, 269–70, 273–4, 278–9
runners (port thieves), 69–70, 73, 80,
    227–9
Russell, John and Hannah, 260–2,
    292, 343n29

sailing, 70–5, 129–30, 139–40, 206–7,
    210

Salt Lake City, 200, 201, 234

San Francisco, 207–8, 263, 342n9

Saxony, 69–70, 73–6, 85–6, 128, 311n6, 314n4, 325n28

Scarborough, 24–5, 149, 171

Scots, 3–4, 177, 215, 248, 265, 276, 288

seasickness, 71–2, 207, 210, 224–5, 227–8, 279–80

Sedgwick, Richard, 30–1

settlement patterns, 4–5

Sharpe, John, 184–5

Sheppard, George, 165–7, 334n3

shipwrecks, 74–5

silver mining, 234, 262

Simpson, John, 139–41

skilled labour, 7–8, 26–7, 35–6, 302n17, 307–8n37

slavery, 91, 211; abolition of, 183, 194, 207, 214–16, 217; English working classes and, 216–17, 221–2; Texas and, 264–5; Yorkshire immigrants, 215–16

smelting, 43, 45–47, 90–1, 113–17, 123

Smith, Captain John, 22, 173, 336

Smith, Joseph, 13, 190, 195, 197–8, 199, 213

Smith, Samuel Fowler, 63, 74–5, 101, 108–9, 297–8

Spain, 235

Spanish, 49, 50, 88

speculation, farms, 118, 253–4, 352n11

Spencer, John, 192–3

Spensley, James and Alice, 120–1

Spensley, James/John and Margaret, 121–2

steamships, 13, 224–3, 232, 279–80

Stowe, Harriet Beecher, 215

Strickland, John and Hannah, 139–42

Swaledale, 14, 20, 235–6, 281–2, 298–9, 310n6; emigration from, 10, 23, 54, 63–4, 65–6, 69, 77, 81, 85, 235–6, 249, 279–84, 299; Iowa, 118, 120, 250; farmers, 21, 119, 152, 248, 283–4; language, accent, 107–8, 122; lead miners, mining, 42–4, 45–6, 49–50, 67, 94, 99, 113–14, 118, 120–2, 249, 357–8n42; Old Gang Mine, 45–7, 49, 50, 235; religion, 16–17, 74; *Saxony*, 69–70, 73–6, 85–6, 128, 311n6, 314n4, 325n28; Wisconsin, 110, 112–13

Syracuse, 133–4

Taylor, Zachary, 91–2

Teesside, 237, 349n29

temperance movement, 186, 207, 213–14, 227, 229–30, 279

Texas, 13, 267, 150, 242, 268–9; Galveston, 266, 270; Kent, 266–8; Luling, 269–72; Revolution, 264–5; San Antonio Railroad Company, 269–70; settlement projects, 265–8; textile workers, 7, 20, 33–4, 192–3, 217

Thirsk, 14, 148

Tomkins, W., 187–8, 205

Tocqueville, Alexis de, 4

Toronto, 30, 54, 130, 141–2, 154, 276–7, 279, 287, 291

transatlantic voyages, 22, 32–3; sailing ships, 70–5, 129–30, 139–40, 206–7, 210; sea sickness, 71–2, 207, 210, 224–5, 227–8, 279–80; steamships, 13, 224–3, 232, 279–80

Twain, Mark, 231, 233

United States. *See* America

Upper Mississippi River Region. *See* Mississippi River, Upper River Region

urban labourers, 234, 277, 285–6, 287, 291

Utah, 190–1, 192, 193, 194, 199–201, 206, 234, 286, 340n36, 340n38

Vickers, Thomas, 215–16

Victorian boom, 148, 330–1n2

Victoria, Queen, 213, 215, 216, 217

Walker, Peter, 162, 218–19, 221–2, 323n7

Walker, Thomas Lewis, 101, 128, 218, 223, 297–8

Waller, Richard and Ann, 113

War of 1812, 30, 31, 108, 336n6

Ware, James and Ann, 168–71

Watters, John and Ann, 120, 121, 325n27

wealthy emigrants, 171–2, 251, 286; Le Mars, 171–2

Welsh, 35, 36, 248, 288

Wensleydale, 14, 97–8, 147, 162–3, 224; emigration from, 66–7, 69, 74, 252, 258–9; immigrant letters to, 55–7, 60–1, 81, 94–5, 104–5, 111, 157–9, 195–201, 221–2, 225, 244–6, 296–7; immigrants from, 246–7, 259–60, 319n35, 323n7; lead mining, miners, 20–1, 44, 49, 235–6, 299–300; farming, 20–1. *See also individual cities*; Willis, Matthew and Jane

Wensleydale Advertiser, 158, 204

Wesley, John and Charles, 17

West Riding, 9, 238, 299, 303n10, 314n42

West Yorkshire, 18, 21, 33–4, 111, 171, 237–8, 305n12

Wetherby, 53, 63, 101, 109, 148, 297–8

Whitby, 23, 64–5, 71, 307n20

wilderness, 28, 80, 101, 111, 138, 142, 154, 200, 259–60

Wilkinson, Anthony, 258–9

Wilkinson, John, 259–60

Willis, Matthew and Jane, 56–9, 60, 86, 212, 296, 312n10; Civil War, 219–20, 222–3; family, 219–20; Rama farm, 76–7, 101–2, 150, 157–62, 244–7, 248–9; Wisconsin, 79, 86, 104–5, 106–7, 157–63, 247–8, 255

Willis, Richard, 107

Willis, Thomas, 225, 245–6

Wilson, Elizabeth, 239, 241

Wilson, Henry, 220, 238–9

Wilson, Thomas and Mary, 242, 267, 269–74

Wisconsin, 12, 55, 57–8, 100, 122, 214; farming, 76–7, 101–2, 150, 157–62, 218, 244–7, 248–9; government, 247–8; immigrant descriptions of, 96–100, 159, 186–7, 244–6; lead mines, 88–9, 93, 121–2, 123–6, 128, 186–7, 237; Methodists, 83–4, 94–5, 122, 184–7, 188–90; Native Americans, 174–9, 187, 188, 336–7n6; winters, 105–7, 160–2, 255, 297. *See also individual cities*; Willis, Matthew and Jane

Wyoming, 258–9

York, city of, 14, 54, 153, 191, 300

York Herald, 65, 75, 112

Yorkshire Dales, 14, 19; farming, 20–1; lead mining, 18–21, 38, 41–7, 49–50, 62, 235–6, 292, 299–300; Methodists, 188–90, 213–14; miners, 89, 113–18, 121–3, 124–6; Old Gang Mine, 45–7, 49, 50, 235; Upper Mississippi River region and, 8, 11–12, 84, 89, 97–100

Yorkshire Dales immigrants, 5, 10, 38, 101, 110–11; assisted emigration, 37–40, 136, 276–7, 279, 287–8, 292; California Gold Rush, 205–11; to Canada, 279–82; chain migration, 55, 83, 210–11; farmers, 151–3, 158, 244–7, 248–50, 286; groups, 51–2, 69–70, 73–4, 75–6, 85–6, 122, 128, 210–11; Methodists, 49, 113, 188–90, 213–14, 299; miners, 8, 45, 89, 99, 113–18, 121–3, 123–6, 183–6, 247–8; Mormons, 192–202; Upper Mississippi region, 97–9, 123–6, 151, 292; Wisconsin, 151–3, 158. *See also* Dinsdale, Matthew; Willis, Matthew and Jane

Young, Brigham, 190, 192

zinc mining, 236–7